Library of Shakespearean Biography and Criticism

I. PRIMARY REFERENCE WORKS ON SHAKESPEARE

II. CRITICISM AND INTERPRETATION

    A. Textual Treatises, Commentaries
    B. Treatment of Specal Subjects
    C. Dramatic and Literary Art in Shakespeare

III. SHAKESPEARE AND HIS TIME

    A. General Treatises. Biography
    B. The Age of Shakespeare
    C. Authorship

Series III, Part A

To Meet
Will Shakespeare

Library of Shakespearean Biography and Criticism

To Meet
Will Shakespeare

BY

FRANK ERNEST HILL

Illustrated by Addison Burbank

BOOKS FOR LIBRARIES PRESS
FREEPORT, NEW YORK

TO RUTH

FOREWORD

THIS book was written for readers, regardless of age, who want to know Shakespeare—person, player, man of affairs, writer. It is not a book for specialists, although I hope that many of these will find it not without interest. Rather it is a volume for the intelligent reader who is not expert in Elizabethan or Jacobean literature, and it seeks to tell the Shakespeare story in a direct and human fashion.

In order to do this, To MEET WILL SHAKESPEARE employs a certain amount of fictionalization. This device was adopted to quicken the pace of the story and create a sharper sense of reality. It has been helpful to me as the writer; I hope it will help and please readers.

I have tried to fictionalize around our knowledge of Shakespeare rather than around our ignorance of him. I have not attempted to solve the mysteries of his marriage, or of the Friend or the Dark Lady of his *Sonnets*. On the other hand, I have built up dozens of scenes and conversations on material supplied us by lawsuits, town records, letters, events, and, in some cases, legends and reasoned conjectures. If these fictional passages carry out the intention behind them, they will bring more vitality and color into the story without distorting its essential character as this can be determined by research.

In most cases the fictional character of episodes is clearly indicated in the text. In particular, the reader can be sure that whenever Shakespeare himself speaks (except in a single case toward the end of the volume) an imaginary element has been added.

The book presents no new discoveries about Shakespeare. However, every effort has been made to use the rich historical, biographical, personal, and literary materials which enable us to know the playwright's age with exceptional fullness, and to enrich our sense of his own activities. Shakespeare's Stratford, his London, his playhouses, his family, his business transactions, his residences, his writing habits —all are set forth as notable parts in a complex of information related to the world's greatest writer.

If the book has any originality of approach, this lies in an effort to inter-relate the many phases of Shakespeare's life. For understandable reasons we have a number of works which deal mainly with the man, subordinating his literary and professional activity. Others concern themselves chiefly with his writings, still others with his profession. It has long seemed to me that the person, the writer, and the player were so much one that any general account of Shakespeare should give just place to all of them, and to the effect of one upon the other. This I have tried to do.

If I have been especially concerned with any single question, it is the question of why William Shakespeare is generally acknowledged to be the greatest writer known to mankind. If we study his life and do not find an answer or answers, much of our interest and thought have been in vain. Accordingly, without losing sight of Shakespeare the person or man of affairs, I have tried to follow most closely his creative accomplishments. I have traced what seem to me to be the chief successive advances in originality and power, and have attempted to indicate something of their total effect and meaning.

I have tried also to draw comparisons between Shakespeare's age and our own. The two touch at many points, and offer sharp contrasts at others. Shoreditch and the Bankside were often startlingly like Broadway, Radio City, and Hollywood; the social structure of England was amazingly unlike ours, as were its hygienic and religious practices. For Shakespeare and his associates, their age was a today. I have made every effort to bring readers into a sense of its aliveness and immediacy. As they can catch the spirit and look of that era, their sense of Shakespeare will deepen.

In a postscript, The Impostors, I have considered the claims made for some dozen other persons as possible authors of some or all of

Shakespeare's plays and poems. I believe that the average reader needs a clear digest of the "evidence" that has been presented, and a clear sense of who has the chief responsibility to present proof.

In quoting from plays, poems, and prose writings of Shakespeare's time I have modernized the spelling and in cases altered the punctuation of "standard" texts. In the case of the poet's own works, these texts are of course quite different in such respects from the quartos published during the author's life, or the First Folio of 1623. These older publications in turn reflected the practices of printers, copyists, and "editors" of the day perhaps more than they did Shakespeare's own preferences. I have therefore seen no profit in preserving a few contractions, spellings, and other survivals from the orthography and punctuation of these not wholly Shakespearean originals. I have made quotations as modern as I could without interfering with the sense of the original. In a few cases where spelling and punctuation are part of evidence to be weighed, I have naturally kept the original form.

I wish to thank my wife, Ruth Nickel Hill, for her continuous encouragement and help with research, the planning of the book, and the preparation of the manuscript to the press. Acting for Dodd, Mead & Co., Miss Dorothy Bryan suggested my writing To MEET WILL SHAKESPEARE, and I must thank her for having invited me to so enjoyable a task. Both she and Mr. Edward Dodd, Jr., have been helpful with advice and constructive criticism. I am also grateful to Margaret Nickel, Catherine and Russell Hill, and Allan Nevins for aid while the book was still in manuscript form.

FRANK ERNEST HILL

New York City, January, 1949.

CONTENTS

To Meet
Will Shakespeare

I: THE PLAYERS COME TO STRATFORD

AT a little past eleven on a summer morning in the year 1573 Master John Shakespeare, alderman of Stratford-upon-Avon, stood in his shop talking to a visitor.

The sunlight streamed in through the small-paned windows, falling on the beam-and-plaster walls of the large room. It touched the workbenches with their soft piles of dressed leather, their array of delicate tools, their skins stretching on frames. A pair of gloves on which the tradesman had been working lay with his glover's knife on a counter, for he had just started cutting them out.

"You do me honor to remember me, Master Ranleigh," he was saying. "It is four years since you were last here, if I mistake not, and that is long to keep a name in memory."

The visitor smiled. He was dressed richly in gold and blue, and carried himself with confidence. The colors were those of the Earl of Leicester. Ranleigh was a member of the troupe of actors who worked under the protection of that nobleman.

"Nay, Master Shakespeare," he said, "a player does well to bear the name of a bailiff in mind. The more so one like you, who showed a liking for our labors in the way we value most. For, to be plain, we of the stage find that proof we have pleased is still best when paid out to us in hard silver."

The other chuckled. "Aye, I warrant you."

"I trust," Ranleigh continued, "that my having left the Queen's Men to join My Lord of Leicester's will give me and my fellows no less favor in your eyes."

"Nay, nay," Shakespeare assured him. "You could not serve a better! But, sir," he went on regretfully, "as to the performance you would give tomorrow—there I cannot help you. You must wait upon the present bailiff, Master Plymley, or on my good friend Adrian Quyney, the high alderman—"

He stopped as the heavy door to his right, leading from the shop to his living quarters, which were under the same roof, swung open suddenly. A boy of nine stood in the doorway, pausing at the sight of a stranger.

"Come in, Will, come in," said the glover.

The boy entered and closed the door behind him. He was slight but well knit, with auburn hair and clear hazel eyes. These glowed for an instant as they fell upon the stranger.

"This is my lad Will," John Shakespeare told Ranleigh. "And you, sirrah," he said to his son, "could perhaps give a shrewd answer if I asked you who stands here beside me."

"By his colors, sir, and since the procession came this morning—"

"What do you know of a procession?" his father cut in with a bantering severity. "Were you not busy in school with your books this morning long?"

Will Shakespeare gave his father a half smile.

"The sound of a trumpet and fife will not stop at an open window, sir, be it even that of a schoolroom."

Ranleigh laughed.

"Nor keep any lad bent over his desk if he can look out of that same window, Master Shakespeare," he said. "Indeed, it is our purpose so to enter a town that men and wives, as well as boys, will leave their tasks to look at us!"

"Well, you guess shrewdly enough, Will," said his father. "This is Master Ranleigh of My Lord of Leicester's Players. He was of the Queen's Men that played here four years ago, when I was bailiff."

The boy made his bow to the stranger.

"And will you give a play here, sir?" he asked eagerly.

The actor smiled.

"So I came hither to inquire, myself, but it seems I must ask elsewhere."

Will turned to the glover.

"Shall I see it, Father?"

"You?" asked John Shakespeare in mock astonishment. "What will you make with vanities that drive good Latin from your mind?"

"Nay, Father, the Latin will sit there well enough."

"Will it?" demanded his parent. "What did you study this morning?"

"The dialogues of Corderius," answered the boy. He hesitated an instant, then, with a gleam in his eye, recited glibly: *"Adfuistine concione sacrae hodie? Adfui. Quis habuit concionem? Dominus Dyos."*

"I make nothing of that save the name of our vicar, Master Dyos," John Shakespeare grumbled. "And I take no joy in it, for I doubt if he holds sound doctrine. Humph! Had I at your age the fortune to get some good schooling, I'd have learned my letters in no such magpie fashion."

"Nay, they are well learned," protested Ranleigh, "and deserve better from you, Master Shakespeare."

"He means, Father," said Will quickly, "that you should lessen the lesson."

The two men chuckled, and John Shakespeare roughed his son's hair good-humoredly.

"Well, Will, I will bait you no more. If there is a play tomorrow, you shall see it. And I promise you it will be given, since the players are the servants of our own Lord Robert. A man of the true reformed faith," he added, "that many Englishmen would have climb higher."

It was a reference to the fading hope that the Earl might still marry his unwed queen.

"Well said," murmured Ranleigh.

"They do say Her Majesty will marry no subject, as being less than she," said Will impulsively.

"You hear too much of such talk," his father broke in with a frown. He paused a moment, then asked: "You came to bid me to dinner?"

"Yes, Father."

"Then we will go eat it, and Master Ranleigh with us, if he will."

"No, no," said the actor hastily. "I must seek out your bailiff and get my answer from him before I dine."

He asked directions for finding Plymley or Quyney, and made his good-bys.

As the door of the shop closed after him, Will turned to his father, his eyes dark with excitement.

"What will they play, Father? Something from the Court, do you think? Master Hunt told us of a play done there from a story written by the Greeks."

"We'll have nothing pagan here." The alderman shook his head vehemently. "It will be something godly and moral."

"Like the Coventry plays!" cried the boy. "Will one have a bludgeon, as the Devil did there, and lay about him?"

"Nay, these are gentleman players," said his father. "They'll swing no cudgels stuffed with wool."

"But perhaps one will rant, like Herod!" persisted Will. He struck a posture and declaimed:

"Another way? Out, out, out!
Have these false traitors done me this deed?
I stamp, I stare, I glare about!
Might I them take, I should burn them at a glede!" [1]

The alderman laughed again.

"Well remembered, lad! No, you'll hear better rhymes than those, and better rendered. These players are no tailors or smiths or drapers. It is a craft with them, the playing of plays, and I should give my Lord Robert less than his due did I not rate them the best in England. But come," he broke off, "your mother will wonder if you have lost your way crossing a threshold."

The two turned toward the living quarters, the tradesman looming high and burly above the slight figure of his son. As he opened the door, he took up again what he had been saying:

"You shall see them yourself, lad. Aye, you shall see them tomorrow, and judge if I speak not truth. These players are different."

Everything was different, the boy told himself the following afternoon, as he watched in the Guild Hall, sitting beside his father. The stage was different. It was no mere wagon, garishly decked out, like those he had seen in Coventry as stages for the miracle plays; with the people noisily crowding about them. No, the stage here was a broad, raised platform, more spacious, with curtains at the rear through which the players came and went. To be sure, it jutted out into the audience, but it was firm and seemed to exist as a small, separate world.

The costumes were richer, too; and the boy recognized an authentic art about them that was sharply in contrast with the showy garments of the crafts players. Stage properties had the same character. There was nothing so elaborate as the Mouth of Hell on the Smiths' wagon, with jaws that opened and spat fire. But each article fitted into the

---

[1] Fire.

mimic world of which it was a part, and caught a kind of glamour from its rightness.

Yet chiefly the difference between this play and the cruder ones he had watched was that here the players controlled each scene like so many lords. They made the words they spoke seem like music. Each intonation was right, each gesture easy and perfect. When the idle crew who tempted Mankind danced around the simple hero, Will wanted to dance himself. He seemed to be in the heart of revelry. When the rascals tricked their victim, cutting his long coat down to a jacket, and persuading him it was a finer thing, the boy laughed with the crowd at the absurdity of it. When Mercy scattered the rascals and quietly led the repentant hero back to right ways, Will felt the justness of the reproof and the hope of a better existence as if he himself had been in error. It was all as true as life and yet it shone with a kind of radiant clarity that was somehow above life.

As the actors bowed backward through the curtains, crowding impulses filled and disturbed him. It seemed as if he had come upon some great discovery, something he could not utter or understand, yet felt to be miraculously alive.

The townfolk clapped noisily and the players reappeared, bending low as they saluted the audience. Will himself clapped, but to him it was far more than an hour of miming.

He stared at the stage and vague hopes jostled in his mind. Perhaps one day he might stand bowing on such a platform. He might even learn the magic of making rhymed words, of devising those happenings, so like life yet brighter and more astounding, which had held him spellbound. He did not know how it could be, but for a moment it seemed a promise that was sure of fulfillment. His heart swelled with pride as he stood there clapping with the others, and the costumed actors bowed low, as if in assent.

II: THE BOY AND THE TOWN

THE boy who watched My Lord of Leicester's Players that night
in Stratford-upon-Avon had been born in the town. Partly it was
the town that made him what he was and what he would become.

7

What was this town of Stratford? What kind of life had it poured into him?

Later, men of the shire of Warwick, in which Stratford lay, were proudly to call their region the heart of England, and there was none which could better claim that title. It was a fruitful district,

> With shadowy forests and with champaigns riched,
> With plenteous rivers and wide-skirted meads,

as the boy himself would one day write. And it lay just a little to the west, or the left, of the center of the land, as the heart lies a little to the left of the center of the body.

Heart of England it was also because within its bounds there had lived and mingled all the chief peoples who had played a part in making the one people called English.

There had been the ancient Britons first. The Welsh, their descendants, still dwelt in the mountains to the southwest, and there were Stratford townfolk who still spoke English with a Welsh accent, and even talked in that strange but melodious tongue.

There had been the Romans. Will Shakespeare may have found an encrusted copper disk near the bank of the Avon River that showed the wreathed head of an emperor.

Saxons, Danes, Normans—these had come later, and men still told legends about their heroes.

Probably few in Stratford during Will's boyhood knew that the town had come into being as a cluster of huts about a monastery built by the Saxon Bishop of Worcester. "Strat-ford"—it was the ford in the old Roman road, or "street," as the early English called such highways. But all in the town were familiar with an institution which had appeared in the fourteenth century, when Stratford had grown into a thriving market town. Even in early childhood Will Shakespeare had wondered about its name.

"Mother, why do they say 'the Guild Chapel' and 'the Guild Hall'? Is it a guild like the tanners' or drapers'?"

"No, child, nothing like. It was a company religious, that all folk joined for the good of their souls. But it is no more now, since King Harry the Eighth broke up the monasteries."

"But have not *we* souls that need help?"

"Aye, boy; but we help them otherwise."

Soon Will Shakespeare knew more about the Guild, a fraternity that had offered two great benefits: help for the souls of its members after death and, somewhat less important, a certain amount of aid while they were still on earth.

If a man lacked the money to pay for these benefits, he could pay in services. Thousands paid in both ways. And every member knew that in illness prayers would be said for him, and that after his death the great candle and eight smaller ones would be borne before him to his grave, while all his fellow members would follow the chanting priests with prayers for his soul.

The Guild grew strong and rich in Stratford. Great buildings of stone—the Hall, the Chapel, the College where dwelt special priests of the order—rose to accommodate its activities. Finally a school was built, the very one which Will Shakespeare began to attend one hundred and fifty years after its founding.

And gradually the Guild took over the government of the town. Its members brought their disputes before their own officers, rather than before the steward of the Bishop of Worcester, once more or less the ruler of the place. These officers became in reality the police and judges of the community.

Will Shakespeare knew this story. He knew how certain members of the Guild had become great ones in the land. Two of its priests, Robert of Stratford and John of Stratford, had become chancellors of England. Then there was Sir Hugh Clopton, another member who had gone forth from Stratford to become a wealthy merchant.

"Aye, Will, Lord Mayor of London he was," John Shakespeare or another would have told him. "But he came back here to dwell later, and built New Place yonder, on Chapel Lane. And mark, lad, before Sir Hugh's time no bridge here was safe from the river, poor things of timber that they were. Folk dared not come to Stratford when the river was up, or did so in peril of life."

"He built the bridge of stone?"

"Aye, with the fourteen arches and the causeways of stone on either side. Well may this town remember Sir Hugh."

2

Such men, and the memory of the Guild, and the structures that spoke of both, gave the boy a pride in his birthplace. Yet not far from Stratford lay castles and walled towns and sites of memorable happenings with power to send the imagination soaring even higher.

Only eight miles to the north and east lay the town and castle of Warwick. The castle rose up sheer from the Avon, set upon "a high rock of stone." It was associated with tales of great heroes. Guy of Warwick was one—a warrior in the time of Saxon King Athelstan. Richard Neville was another—"Warwick the Kingmaker" men called him. In the great Wars of the Roses, which had torn England for a generation, that earl had lifted the white rose of York into power. Later he died fighting for the red rose of Lancaster. In his time of prosperity he had fed thirty thousand people a day in his various mansions, armies had sprung up at his lifted hand, and kings had listened when he spoke.

An Earl of Warwick sat in the castle in Will Shakespeare's day, but he was a lesser man than his brother Robert Dudley, the Earl of Leicester, whose "servants" the boy had seen perform in the Guild Hall at Stratford. And Kenilworth Castle, Leicester's seat, was a more pretentious pile than Warwick. Queen Elizabeth had made a gift of it to the Earl, and he had spent £60,000 to restore and enlarge it—more than three million dollars in the value of money today.

Northeast from Warwick lay Coventry, the third largest city in the land. High walls studded with turrets still encircled it. Coventry was ancient in English life and legend. Here, in Saxon times, Lady Godiva had ridden through the streets on a white charger, with no covering save her own long hair. Here great religious orders had thrived, and here in more recent years the trade guilds had taken over the presentation of the miracle plays, of which more than forty were commonly given.

They had, wrote Master Robert Dugdale in Shakespeare's own day, "theaters for several scenes, very large and high, placed upon wheels, and drawn to all the eminent parts of the city for the better advantage of spectators."

On these wagon-stages, in appearance much like "floats" in modern parades, the worthy craftsmen set many ingenious devices. The drapers, playing The Last Judgment, used a great barrel to make "earthquakes," and a torch "to set the world afire." The smiths fashioned an artificial head for the actor playing Herod, and another more horrible one for the Devil. They spent eight pence, or almost three dollars of our money, for "dressing" this mask, and half again as much to build the "Mouth of Hell."

Trappings for the Devil and other unsavory characters seem to have been more expensive than those for worthy or holy ones. "A pair of gloves for God" cost only tuppence!

3

The churches, castles, and walled towns; the legend and history that clung about them; the lusty pageantry of the guilds—all these belonged to the world of the Middle Ages, to the age of chivalry.

All were part of a way of living—a way based upon Authority. There was the authority of the King over his greater nobles and his free towns; there was the authority of the earls over lesser nobles and the gentlemen-farmers. There was the authority of these farmers over their farm tenants and laborers, some of whom were little better than serfs. And in a similar fashion the authority of the Church covered the world of the spirit. Here, too, there were layers of power, with the Pope supreme, and archbishops, bishops, abbots and priests administering in turn their lessening domains.

Yet the breath of a newer world was sweeping this older one away. Great forces of various kinds had already twisted and broken its patterns by the time Will Shakespeare was a boy.

Chief among these was the Renaissance, that surging revival of interest in old arts and in new types of creative activity which had begun in Italy, and boiled over into France, Germany, the Low Countries, and finally England. The printing press, invented by German craftsmen of the fourteen-hundreds, had given it wings. Even amid the turmoil of the Wars of the Roses, Caxton had launched printing in England. And now everywhere books, once copied painfully by hand, were being stamped out by the presses. They scattered ideas about in what seemed a miracle of profusion. Textbooks for boys like Will Shakespeare, volumes of poetry, romances, sermons, Bibles—all leapt forth like so many champions fighting to quicken the imagination of men.

Bibles—they were associated with the work of the German friar, Martin Luther, who had denounced certain practices of the Church and begun the Reformation. Luther and the "Protestants" who followed him encouraged a wide reading of the Scriptures. The movement he had launched was still a living, even a violent, force in Will Shakespeare's England, for Henry VIII, after waiting impatiently for the Pope to grant him an annulment of his marriage to his first queen, Catherine of Aragon, had broken away from Rome. He had set up a separate church in England with himself as its head. The officials of this new English Church had quickly granted him the freedom he demanded, and he had married a young Englishwoman of noble family, Anne Boleyn. She soon became the mother of a daughter, Elizabeth.

But with his own church Henry not only got a new queen, but great wealth and powers he had never enjoyed before. At a stroke he took over full control of all religious organizations, including their monasteries and schools, their extensive lands, and their plate and moneys. What he did with these rich resources rocked all England, and perhaps no place more than the little town of Stratford-upon-Avon.

Meanwhile, as Europe and England had changed with the new learning and the new religion, the world beyond them also was changing. In fact, this world had grown in size, suddenly and immensely.

It had grown eastward, where merchants like Marco Polo built up an overland commerce with Persia, India, and China.

It had grown to the south. Portuguese explorers pushed down the western coast of Africa, rounded the Cape of Good Hope, and crossed the seas to the Indies, as the Far East was known.

Finally, Columbus had pointed his three small ships into the unknown westward sea and discovered America.

The English had been quick to take up the exploration of new lands which now followed. The Venetian navigator, John Cabot, had sailed west on behalf of Henry VII, finding what are now Newfoundland and the eastern and northeastern Canadian coasts. Later, English captains sailed north and east, hunting a new passage to the Indies. They failed to locate that, but from the White Sea they went by land to Moscow and the Czar of the Russians. They set up a trading post on the site of what later became the port of Archangel.

As Will Shakespeare grew toward manhood, the excitement of all this new geography was pushing in upon England with a thousand reports, strange products, and prodigious fables. In the fifteen-seventies, more than a hundred English vessels were seining cod each year off the banks of Newfoundland. English ships were soon bringing back timber, vegetables, and plants from a new coast across the ocean which Sir Walter Raleigh named Virginia for his unmarried queen. Among these products was the tobacco leaf, a "weed" that young noblemen smoked in pipes of clay, silver, or ivory. All this time young Englishmen talked enviously of the gold of Mexico and Peru. Sir John Hawkins and other seamen had already traded with the Spanish settlements in the Americas, and later they would begin to attack the galleons bearing treasure to Spain from the mines of the new lands.

4

On a day in the year 1535, the Commissioners of His Majesty King Henry VIII, charged with reporting on the religious institutions of the realm, rode into the town of Stratford.

They stepped briskly about and found the Warden of the Guild, five priests, and four choristers comfortably feeding at the College. Sniffing suspiciously, they took an inventory of the Guild's possessions, for the King had now decided to break up all churchly institutions. "Tut, tut," they buzzed. "What an amount of silver, lands, buildings, and money this rather feeble fraternity has acquired!" (For the Guild had now lost much of its vitality, partly to the trade guilds which had grown under its encouragement.)

Their worships the commissioners appropriated 260 ounces of silver and gold plate, and made a report on the Stratford Guild to the King.

That was just a beginning. Soon, as all monasteries, chantries, and free chapels in England were suppressed by royal order, the Guild was dissolved. Its holdings passed to the royal name or into the royal treasury. One of Henry's favorites got the College as a private residence. What was more important, with the Guild, Stratford lost its government!

Thus the town collided with the new age. But in the end the collision was not unpleasant for most of its citizens. To acquire a government, Stratford became an incorporated town. The King (now young Edward VI) accepted a plan by which a council of aldermen and burgesses, chosen from the community, would administer its affairs. The Guild School and Guild Hall became town properties. The councilmen appointed such town officials and made such rules for trade and order as they felt to be necessary.

With this reorganization, Stratford shook off the semimonastic control of the Guild. The great nobles in the vicinity, Warwick and Leicester, favored the reformed Puritan faith. So did the citizens, mostly tradesmen, who now governed the town. These reformers, although often severe in matters of morals and doctrine, were brisk and enterprising in practical affairs.

It was in these days that John Shakespeare appeared in Stratford. Perhaps the changing nature of the times helped to bring him there. In a more settled period he might have stayed with his father, tilling a farm nearby. Richard Shakespeare rented his acres from a gentleman-farmer by the name of Arden. One of Richard's sons, Harry, followed the father's way of life.

But John Shakespeare broke with it. Probably he served a term as apprentice to a Stratford merchant. He was living in the town as early as 1552. Four years later, now a glover and "whittawer," or whitener of skins, he became the purchaser of two houses. One was a building on Henley Street which he used as a shop.

John Shakespeare was a vigorous fellow with plenty of ambition. Soon he was elected town ale-taster—that is, he tested the ale sold to the townfolk, most of whom used it as a drink rather than water.

That same year—1557—John Shakespeare married the daughter of his father's landlord. This was a step up in the world for him.

His own family had been a humble one. Scholars think the name was originally Norman—perhaps "Sakespee," from *saquer,* meaning to draw vigorously, and *epee,* a sword. "Shakespeare" (earlier spelled "Sakesper," "Saxberd," "Saxper," and in other ways) was the English version of the French original, and kept the military meaning of the name, although it changed the weapon from a sword to a spear. But in any case, in the fifteen-hundreds the Shakespeares were hard-working tillers of the soil who were quite *un*military. Richard Shakespeare hadn't done badly. He owned tools and animals and furniture worth several thousand dollars in our money. But he was a poor man compared with Robert Arden, who not only owned the land that Richard worked, but other farms as well.

Also, the Ardens were "gentlefolk." They had a coat of arms. One branch of the family, the Ardens of Park Hall, claimed among its ancestors Guy of Warwick, King Athelstan, and Alfred the Great. Robert Arden died in 1556, leaving his eight daughters well provided for. His favorite seems to have been Mary, the youngest. She received a tidy sum of money, some household goods, and a fifty-acre farm called the Asbies. It was Mary Arden whom John Shakespeare married in the spring or summer of 1557.

So the young tradesman acquired a wife of "gentle" family, with perhaps a dash of royal Saxon blood. He may have been ignorant of, or indifferent to, the blood. To his wife's money and property he could scarcely have been indifferent.

John Shakespeare rose quickly to a place of importance among the less than two thousand folk of Stratford. Soon he was elected town constable, then filled other offices. In 1565 he was chosen alderman.

He now had considerable powers and responsibilities, and the title of "Master." In 1568 he was elected high bailiff, or mayor.

Meanwhile two daughters had been born to him and his wife Mary, but both had died. Then, on April 26, 1564, a son, William Shakespeare, was baptized in the Stratford church. "Gulielmus filius Joannes Shakspere," reads the entry in the church register. It seems certain that the boy was born on the 22nd or 23rd day of April—scholars have argued much about the exact day. For all practical purposes the 23rd has won.

5

So the boy became a part of the town. If we wish to understand him, we must remember both the past of Stratford and the new life that had changed and still was changing it as he grew through boyhood to manhood.

The past, the age of chivalry, was very close to the village. Its churches and castles still stood. Its battles and its older religion were as well known to Will Shakespeare as the War Between the States or the trek of covered wagons are known to American youth today. Chivalric customs and attitudes of mind still lived on in the middle fifteen-hundreds. The medieval world helped to mold the boy's imagination, his feeling for daily conduct, his ideas of right and wrong.

But he was also part of the newer world. The flood of printed books, the growing interest in art and poetry, the concern with fact and the actual nature of things which would soon become modern science, the changes in religion, the discoveries of far lands and peoples—these forces too would play upon Will Shakespeare. They would help give wings and fire to his mind and pen.

That he was born between these two conflicting worlds is perhaps as important a thing as we can remember about him. When a boy grows to manhood between an old world and a new one, the clash of the two is bound to affect him. Sometimes it is like a meeting of chemical elements, which produces startling effects and even, by interaction, a substance never before known.

III: "THE ROD IS THE SWORD"

ON July 11, 1564, the Reverend John Bretchgirdle, Vicar of Stratford, noted in his register the death of Oliver Gunn, an apprentice, and wrote after the entry, *Hic incipit pestis.*

"Here begins the plague!" It was a sinister entry. "The plague" in Europe of that day was an epidemic taking several forms, some like the bubonic plague which parts of the modern world have known in recent years. There was no knowledge then of how to prevent, check, or cure it. The disease swept through villages and cities alike, while people vainly burned incense, took huge drafts of ill-tasting "plague water," hung juniper and rosemary branches in their chambers, or sprayed them with vinegar or rose water.

The plague at Stratford in 1564 slew one-seventh of all the inhabitants of the town. The story of Will Shakespeare, born a few months earlier, might well have ended then and there.

But the boy escaped. Probably his mother fled with him to the country—to the farm of Harry Shakespeare, her husband's brother, or to that of her sister, Margaret Webb, both at Snitterfield, three miles to the north.

Nevertheless, the shadow of the plague fell upon the child with a kind of prophetic grimness. All his life the pestilence was to have its part in his affairs, sometimes happy, sometimes disastrous.

As Will Shakespeare grew older, one of the women who helped his mother with her household and children would have told him tales of that "plague year" of his birth. And one tale in particular held him wide-eyed with fearful wonder.

"Aye," he heard, "even Clopton House was not safe. The pestilence went there, and none had remedy for it. There was Mistress Charlotte, with her blue eyes and her golden hair like an angel's, and a heart as near an angel's as any of human kind. Ah, that was a sad thing."

"She was taken of the plague?"

"Yes, child, and seemed to die of it. Aye, they laid her out for burial, poor thing, and bore her to the church. They set her upon her bier in the vault where all the Cloptons have lain since Sir Hugh himself. And then—"

The woman paused and shook her head.

"Yes, nurse—and what then?"

"Why, in less than a week another in that house was taken. And died, and was carried to the vault like her. And when they opened it, Mistress Charlotte lay not upon the bier."

Her voice sank almost to a whisper, and woman and child stared at each other.

"She had broken from the vault!"

"Nay, boy, through stone walls she could not go. But it seems that the plague had not brought death to her, but rather a kind of swooning very like it. And she had come to her senses again, and risen from the bier. They found her standing against the wall, where she had perished for want of food and air."

The girl set living in the tomb—escaping Death only to fall again into his horrid arms! That was an image to stamp itself upon a child's imagination. Years later he would put on the lips of young and fearful Juliet the horror he felt as he listened fascinated to the story.

Yet it was only one of many dark incidents that grew from the kind of place that Stratford was in that age. Let us consider the little town as it appeared in the fifteen-sixties, as young Will Shakespeare saw it.

He looked at a natural setting of great loveliness. There was the clear river, flowing gently through meadows and forests; there was in summer a profusion of flowers and singing birds. These were noted even by men of that time, to whom birds and flowers were common.

The boy walked the streets of a town that was picturesque. The taller buildings of brick and stone gave it dignity, even distinction. The Church of the Holy Trinity was older than the Conquest, and the Guild College, Hall, and Chapel had been built well. New Place, the stone bridge that spanned the Avon—both were structures to catch the eye of a sensitive youth. But even the common houses had charm and color. They were the Tudor beam-and-plaster dwellings, with thatched roofs, and Will must have liked the bold crisscross of the painted timbers against the light plaster, the little porches at the doors, the gables and carved railings. In the yards behind he saw shade trees and fruit trees nodding above clay walls.

The streets he walked were rude ones—mere alleys of rutted mud in winter; in rainless summer, broken and dusty. There was paving only near the town pump, where stood also the stocks and pillory for the punishment of evildoers. Along the streets Will sometimes picked his way among heaps of filth. Pigs and chickens scampered from under his feet as he went. There were odors of many kinds. Stratford looked better to the eye than it smelled to the nose.

When the boy entered his own house on Henley Street he stepped onto a floor almost level with the street—a floor of tamped clay, strewn with rushes. Probably these were changed in the Shakespeare home

every two weeks or once a month. This was not so in many houses.
"I warrant you Mistress Rudge has not swept her floors this half
year," he heard his mother say as she came in from a visit to a neigh-
bor. "The smell of the rushes is sour, and I do think they are lousy.
The smoke is all about the rooms, too, for the house has no chimney."

The foul floor covering of rushes and the lack of chimneys—these
were two conditions against which many citizens of Stratford spoke
out in that day. As to the lack of chimneys—many houses had hearths
which were merely raised platforms of brick called "reredoses." The
only outlet for the smoke was a hole in the wall above. Naturally much
of it did not get out, but drifted about the rooms, darkening the walls
and sometimes half-stifling the inmates. The Shakespeare house had
a chimney and a spacious fireplace.

In Will's home the furnishings were simple, if not crude. He sat
before the fire on a wooden stool; he ate at a heavy wooden table from
dishes of wood and pewter. Upstairs in his room was a sturdy wooden
bed with a crisscrossing of rope or leather thongs, on which rested
a pallet, or "tick," stuffed with straw. On this he slept, probably with
his brother Gilbert. (The bed his mother and father used was carved
and perhaps canopied; it may have cost as much as all the other furniture in the house together.)

Will had a wooden chest for his clothing, a bench on which stood a
pewter pitcher and a basin. He washed in the basin, using homemade
soap, and dried his hands and face on a "napkin"—about the size of
a large guest towel in our homes today. He used a napkin at the table,
too, and often, because he had only a knife and spoon, and handled
much of his food with his fingers. Forks were just being imported
from Italy by those ready to try out novelties.

The toilet was an outhouse in the yard back of the dwelling. In
this yard there may also have been a well; if not, Will was sometimes
bidden to help lug pails of water from the town pump, which supplied
many Stratford homes. Since it had to be brought into the house by
hand in any case, he and his family were careful about using water.

In the winter, neither he nor many others in Stratford bathed frequently.

At night Will would sometimes hear the rumble of cart wheels, and the voices of the carters shouting to their horses. He knew that the butchers were taking the waste from their trade out beyond the borders of the town. Often the smell of the half-spoiled offal drifted in with the sounds he heard.

At other times, on rainy nights in spring or early summer, he would sit wide-eyed as his father stamped in, laid his wet cloak and dripping hat on the table before the fireplace, and spoke to his wife.

"The river has risen a good yard since four o'clock."

"Is there danger, John?"

"Danger enough. There are few timbers riding the flood now. But come a foot or two more water and we may have beams from half the barns in the shire knocking against the arches."

"Do you think they'll hold?"

"They may. Hah! There's water enough about town already. 'Twill be a wet world hereabouts after the river goes down."

A wet world, and an unpleasant one! For days after such floods there were sinks of mud about Stratford, littered sometimes with broken timbers and the bodies of drowned cattle.

The rude toilet facilities, the foul rushes, the heaps of refuse, the floods—all these made easy the work of the plague. They attracted rodents, and these passed the disease on to men through fleas and lice. A new architecture, a new type of water supply and sewage disposal must come before Stratford or any town in England could shake off the enemy who might strike any summer—the plague season—as if from the blue skies and flowers.

And if the town as Will Shakespeare knew it was an easy mark for pestilence, it was also a rather grim place in other ways. In winter, with no heat save that of open fires, most of the townfolk shivered about, twitching with chilblains. At night the village was hedged in by the dark. And it was a prey to sudden fires, especially likely to start in houses without chimneys, where sparks from the open hearths flew out freely through the holes in the walls and set the thatched roofs ablaze.

Of course John Shakespeare would have stared in surprise at anyone who might have suggested that his town was a rude and dangerous place.

"What now?" he would have exclaimed. "Are the streets not better kept than ever a man here can remember? Myself as alderman have helped make ordinances that bid men clear away the filth before their dwellings. And must not all now build chimneys by our command, to lessen the peril of fires? Do I not eat from pewter and even from glass, where my grandsire had dishes only of treen? [That is, from the tree, of wood.] Do I not worship in a church free of Rome? And cannot my sons learn Latin like clerks at the Free School and thereby lift themselves to the place and port of gentlefolk?"

No, to John Shakespeare, and to his son Will, Stratford was looking toward a brighter future and was already a town that could challenge comparison with any of its size in England.

2

It was a little before six o'clock of a winter morning and the boy came up reluctantly from sleep, shaken by the brisk hand of his father. He climbed half-dazed out of his bed, shivering, and dressed himself by the light of a tallow candle. He splashed icy water on his hands and face, staggered downstairs to a bowl of porridge, and went out into the dark—

> the whining school-boy, with his satchel
> And shining morning face, creeping like snail
> Unwillingly to school.[1]

Glumly he squashed his way along the muddy streets to the Free School, where he would join in prayer and a hymn at seven o'clock

[1] *As You Like It*, II. vii. 145–147.

precisely, and then begin his daily wrestling bout with Latin.

This brusque beginning of the school day set the tone for what would follow. School was not supposed to be a pleasant place, but rather one for work. Few youngsters then had the privilege of getting educated, and they were expected to use their good fortune well. The school day was long, with a break of two hours at noon, but scant time out for other recesses until its end at five in the evening.

The teachers were men, and most of them ruled with a hard hand. One of the great schoolmasters of the age, Roger Ascham, tells how at Sir William Cecil's luncheon table at Windsor one day a dispute arose about discipline in the schools. Cecil, later Lord Burghley, was then Secretary of the Queen's Council. He deplored severe punishment as a supposed aid to teaching.

"Scholars who might else do well are driven to hate learning before they know what it means," he declared.

"Master Secretary," spoke up his friend Sir William Peter, "the rod is the sword that must keep the school in obedience. I marvel that you put it in question."

Sir Thomas Wotton, another guest, protested:

"Nay, nay, the schoolhouse should be the house of pleasure, not of fear and bondage. So, as I remember, Plato makes Socrates say in a certain place."

Haddon, the Master of Requests, lined up with Peter, and went further.

"I tell you plainly," he announced, "that the best schoolmaster of our time is the greatest beater."

He named the man.

Ascham himself now spoke up.

"As to that," he said indignantly, "it was indeed the good fortune of that teacher to send from his school one of the best scholars of our time. Yet wise men do think that this came to pass because of the great talent of the boy rather than because of the great beating of the master. To my mind young children are sooner allured by love than driven by beating to attain good learning."

That is all we have of the conversation, but it reflects the conditions and opinions of the day. Severe discipline had been the rule. Now those of liberal mind were questioning it.

In the Stratford school Will Shakespeare probably found his masters strict. The standard there was high. But the teachers seem to have been men of more than usual education and background. The first head of the Free School as Will knew it was Walter Roche, a graduate of Oxford University. Next came Simon Hunt, who was also an Oxford Bachelor of Arts. He came of a "gentle" family. Apparently he lost his place because he was suspected of Roman Catholic tendencies, and the suspicion later proved to be justified. Thomas Jenkins took over in 1577. Shakespeare may have used him as a model for the Welsh schoolmaster in *The Merry Wives of Windsor*.

The King's Free School of Stratford occupied the overhall, or upper story, of the Guild of the Holy Cross—a single large room or hall in which the oak beams that supported the roof were clearly exposed.

There Will sat on one of the benches, sharing with other boys a plain, heavy table, on which they read and wrote. Windows at one side of the hall gave him good light on sunny days. He had a candle which he himself furnished for the early hours in winter, or on dark days.

Having learned his letters, a little reading, and the catechism before he had entered the Free School at the age of seven, Will plunged at once into the study of Latin. He learned this from a textbook— Lily's *Latin Grammar;* in fact he had to learn the entire volume by heart. He then passed on to *Aesop's Fables* and the *Dialogues* of Corderius, perhaps with Bible reading in English and some mathematics to study at the same time. Then came Mantuan, Caesar, Livy, Virgil, Horace, Seneca, Plautus and Ovid. Rhetoric and logic also may have been studied.

A great deal of the work was memorizing and translating. But in the course of reading his Latin authors and turning them into English,

Will learned grammar, something of history, and not a little about classical literature. He became familiar with three really great poets—Virgil, Horace, and Ovid.

While he jested later about the drudgery of the school, the boy must have been fired by the wit, the beauty and the sheer music that he found in such authors. Michael Drayton, born in Warwickshire one year earlier than Will Shakespeare, tells how he was stirred by his first contact with poetry as a child.

Studying his Latin, he came upon the word "poet." He had only a vague understanding of what it meant, but was greatly excited about it. He came to his tutor as the latter was reading.

"Master," he said, twining himself about the young man's knee, "can't you make me a poet? Do it, and you'll see that I'll soon become a man!"

The tutor smiled at him.

"Well, boy," he promised, "if you will play no idle tricks, and I see that you are diligent in your learning, I'll shortly read some poets to you."

Drayton was delighted. He studied hard. And when his teacher read poetry to him—Mantuan first and then Virgil—it was as marvelous as he had imagined it! In fact, it seemed to be sheer magic. "I thought," he wrote describing his feelings later, "that I was mounted on Pegasus himself!"

This episode shows that not all masters of that day were "beaters," that in fact eager students could speak with them as they could with friends and older brothers, and get kind words and help. The boy Shakespeare, like the boy Drayton, probably had his sympathetic teachers who helped him to find an exciting new world in his books.

3

School filled a big part of Will's life in these years, but by no means all of it. There were games encouraged by the school itself on Thursday and Saturday half-holidays. In such hours Will would have learned to pull the long bow, to wrestle and leap. And outside the school lay the town and the green countryside.

In the town there was his father's shop. The clean smell of leather hung about it. Here Will saw various skins being "tawed" and stretched for the making of gloves. He learned how leather was cut, sewn, dyed, embroidered, furred. As he grew older, he doubtless helped with such work. For a time he was the only child old enough to assist his father. Gilbert was two and a half years younger than he. His two sisters and two other brothers were younger still.[2]

Outside the shop, the town in general had its exciting events. As the trading center for the countryside, Stratford held market day every Thursday, and fairs at various times from early spring to September. For these occasions, and for the fairs particularly, the country folk would flock in. The paved market place rang with the hoofs of their cattle, sheep and goats, and with the heavy wheels of their crude wagons bearing farm produce. At the merchants' booths Will would follow the seesaw of barter as the farmers bought their lumber, cement, cloth, lime, gloves and shoes.

Then there were Maypoles, morris dances, bear-baitings, and sports on the bowling green, where the staid merchants vied with each other on the broad, smooth turf.

The boys of Stratford had their own special games. With the Wedgwoods and Badgers and Hornsbys—neighbors on Henley Street—or with Richard Quyney or Richard Field, Will "whipped" tops, played hide-and-seek, leapfrog, or nine-men's morris (much like fox and geese of today). He kicked a football about, tossed quoits, or trundled hoops. On spring days he hunted birds' eggs in the woods or chased the hare on foot.

Sometimes he roamed his uncle Harry's farm, or his aunt Margaret's. He saw the dark soil curl outward from the plowshare, saw the

[2] The brothers and sisters were born as follows: Gilbert, 1566; Joan, 1569; Anne, 1571; Richard, 1574; and Edmund, 1580. Anne died in 1579.

green shafts of sprouting grain, or watched the pruning and grafting of fruit trees.

From the time he was old enough to wander cross-country with other boys, he had seen the huntsmen and their dogs from Charlecote or Clopton manor houses ranging across meadow and forest land. The dogs fascinated him—dogs bred for hunting,

> With ears that sweep away the morning dew,
> Crook-kneed, and dew-lapped like Thessalian bulls;
> Slow in pursuit, but matched in mouth like bells,
> Each under each.[3]

He saw the fowlers riding past, with falcons on their wrists. He wondered at the sharp, eager eyes of these little trained hawks, and their swift flight after dove or grouse, and how they returned when their keepers called them. An old falconer explained this to him.

"Look you, boy, the bird has had no meat today. She is sharp and passing empty."

"Then when she kills the bird, why does she not eat it?"

"Because she is used to eat from *my* hand, sirrah, and she knows that I have meat for her. That is what we call the lure. She'll fetch the bird to me and get her payment—when she is safe on the wrist again."

Will may have seen an owl attack and kill a falcon.[4] He saw the crafty fox in flight. He saw the hungry eagle

> Shaking her wings, devouring all in haste,
> Till either gorge be stuffed, or prey be gone.[5]

He sometimes surprised the egg-sucking weasel that stole by night and shrieked and jabbered angrily when disturbed by day.

Perhaps in his later teens he himself stayed for a time at some nearby hall, dressed in livery and helping with the "gentler" tasks. Well-spoken young men from farms and towns often served the people of

[3] *A Midsummer Night's Dream*, IV. i. 125–128.
[4] *Macbeth*, II. iv. 12–13.
[5] *Venus and Adonis*, 57–58.

the Warwickshire estates. If he did so, he could have ridden with the falconers, or with the huntsmen after the deer, seeing not a few lordly stags

> Turn on the bloody hounds with heads of steel
> And make the cowards stand aloof at bay.[6]

Thus in school, in the town, in the countryside, Will was finding the thousand fragments of what men were thinking, writing, and doing with which each child in any age or place builds up that understanding of life which is called an education. He absorbed and remembered much from these years. And as they passed he was capturing the smooth turns of speech of the vicar or master or the lord of the hall and the homelier strength of the speech that hostlers and tradesmen used. In a similar fashion he was feeling the force and beauty of poetry as the Latin poets made it. Perhaps he already saw that nothing like this had as yet been done in English, and was wondering if it could be.

[6] *I Henry VI*, IV. ii. 51–52.

IV: A QUEEN, AN ALDERMAN

AT three o'clock on Monday, August 11, 1572, some fifty citizens of Warwick waited on Ford Mill Hill, several miles southwest of their town.

They were dressed bravely. The attendants and assistants of the bailiff wore coats of a color between russet and black, trimmed richly with lace. The gowns of the burgesses or councilors of the town were of the same hue, lined with satin and damask. The bailiff himself, bearing the mace that was the sign of his office, stood proudly in a robe of scarlet.

Suddenly the sound of hoofs and carriage wheels came to the group, faintly at first, then louder; and a ripple of talk and laughter was borne to them on a gust of wind.

"Her Majesty approaches!" rang out a voice.

The citizens dropped to their knees. They were waiting to receive their queen, Elizabeth, at "the uttermost confines of their liberty—" or, in plainer words, at the outer edge of the territory of the "free" town of Warwick.

A cavalcade of heralds in dazzling coats, of gentlemen-ushers wearing their finest, of plumed nobles with gemmed and embroidered cloaks trotted toward the group. They were escorting the open carriage in which the Queen herself sat with the comely Countess of Warwick.

The carriage drew up near the foremost of the kneeling citizens. Elizabeth the Queen sat smiling pleasantly. She was a woman of almost forty years of age. Under her red hair the face was milk-white, with well-chiseled features, and keen, deep-set hazel eyes. A jeweled cap glittered upon her head. There were ropes of pearls across her bodice, and rings flashed light from her fingers.

Edward Anglionby, the town recorder of Warwick, rose and made an address of welcome. Then the bailiff in his scarlet gown came forward, knelt and offered his sovereign a purse "very fair wrought," containing twenty pounds in sovereigns of gold.

Finally a Master Griffin, a preacher, advanced and offered an address written in Latin verse. The Queen took the manuscript, bowed, smiled and handed it to the Countess of Warwick. The heralds and ushers then lined up the dignitaries and their followers for the march into town.

The procession went down the road and across the River Avon on the Great Bridge that led to the town and the castle. As it entered the streets the townfolk were massed on either side, in their best apparel. The houses were new-painted and decked with garlands and flowers. Great cheers surged up and caps and kerchiefs fairly filled the air. Thus Elizabeth rode into Warwick, nodding and smiling.

In the crowd that lined the streets an eight-year-old boy from the nearby town of Stratford may have stared at the procession and the Queen. It was only eight miles from his home to Warwick and he had kinfolk there.

He may have stood near the castle the Sunday following, watching the discharge of cannon and a display of fireworks in the Queen's honor. There were dozens of cannon, and there was a dragon that flew gallantly through the air, "casting out huge flames and squibs."

The flares and fire-pieces lit up the sky for miles around, and the salvos of the cannon were heard for twenty miles. If Will Shakespeare was not on the spot, marveling, he soon heard full details of that noisy and flaming celebration.

2

It was something like a personal introduction to the Queen who would color the next thirty years of Will's life. She was remarkable among all women and rulers, past and present. She could sparkle with a charm and vivacity mostly inherited from her unhappy mother, Anne Boleyn; she could speak and act with a force as great as her lusty father's. She read Greek and conversed in many languages. And always, behind smiles and gracious speech or storming anger, behind indecisions and changes of mind that drove her statesmen frantic, she was a shrewd judge of men and events and iron-willed to carry out her final decision.

Partly Elizabeth had been taught by ill fortune. Under her sister Mary she had been suspected of a share in Protestant plots and had been imprisoned. In later years she had been reminded often that the Roman Catholic rulers of Europe looked upon her mother's marriage as irregular and therefore considered her no true queen. Even many of her own subjects regarded Elizabeth's younger cousin, the lovely Mary Queen of Scots, as their sovereign. Mary had fled to England from rebellious subjects in 1568, begging Elizabeth for hospitality. The latter had her in prison now. But the daughter of Anne Boleyn never forgot that her throne was secure only while she was alert, resourceful and strong.

Perhaps that very knowledge helped to give her a kind of shining vitality which aroused a devotion almost religious among her nobles, her poets and the masses of the people. But she was loved and esteemed for other qualities, too—for her wit, her learning, for the sheer physical energy that made her a graceful dancer, a huntress, a Diana who could lean to the longbow. Her subjects loved her also because she symbolized an English church; and, finally, because, as she herself said, she was the most English sovereign the land had known since Harold Godwinsson. Had not her mother been entirely English, and her father far more so than earlier rulers with their Norman heritage and their French, Flemish and Spanish wives?

The visit of 1572 was not the first the Queen had made to Warwickshire. She had come there when Will Shakespeare was a child of two. She came again in 1575, during his twelfth year. On this occasion she was in the shire for almost three weeks, chiefly at Kenilworth, where the Earl of Leicester and his retainers outdid themselves to provide novel and gorgeous entertainments for her.

Kenilworth lay three miles farther from Stratford than Warwick. Yet Will Shakespeare was older now, and better able to manage a pilgrimage from his home. And others were faring forth to see the Queen. They came by thousands from Warwick and farther points to catch a glimpse of their sovereign and to enjoy the festivities which her chief favorite had prepared for her. perhaps in a final bid for her hand and the kingship.

3

"At the first gate of the castle," said the merchant with a self-important preciseness, "there appeared a sibyl, which, as you may know, is a kind of priestess. She was clad all in white silk."

The listeners looked at him fixedly as he paused. They had come to the inn to hear exactly what had happened at Kenilworth on the Queen's arrival, and they knew their fellow townsman would tell them in full. He had been permitted to ride in the Earl's retinue from Long Ichington the night before, when Leicester brought Elizabeth from dinner there to the castle. Will Shakespeare hung with the rest on the tradesman's words, savoring every syllable.

"This sibyl," the privileged one continued, "welcomed Her Majesty with smooth rhymed verse. She spoke clearly. And the verse, they say, was penned by one of the best poets of London.

"Then at the second gate," he continued, "came forth a burly porter, who pretended great astonishment. But soon, recognizing Her Majesty, he approached and tendered her his club and the keys to the castle. And at his command came forth many trumpeters—men of great height, with trumpets nigh a yard in length, and they led her onward through the tiltyard to the inner gate, and on to the shores of the lake which lies by the castle. And then there appeared a movable island, all bright with blazing torches, and on it stood the Lady of the Lake, who told in sweet verse all the story of the lake and the castle even from King Arthur's day."

So the news of the Queen's arrival came to the townfolk of Stratford, and to the eleven-year-old boy who stood among them. Each detail of the fabulous reception glowed jewel-like in his mind. He himself must see something of this splendor which he knew would be prolonged through the coming days.

And indeed, it was not only prolonged, but surpassed. In the twilight of a day that followed soon, the Lady of the Lake came up from the shore to the Queen, leading no less a person than Triton, the God of Waters. They announced the coming of Arion, renowned musician of Greek fable. And soon he came toward the Queen across the water, mounted upon a dolphin. It was a huge fish, some twenty-four feet in length, cunningly painted, and stroking its way with fins under whose glittering scales were oars. Arion sang to the music of instruments concealed in the belly of the fish.

One Robert Laneham, a learned fellow who was of the company, wrote to a friend in London about this episode.

"The song," he reported, "by a skillful artist into his parts so sweetly sorted, each part in his instrument so clean and sharply touched . . . and this in the evening of the day, resounding from the calm waters, where the presence of Her Majesty and the longing to listen had utterly damped all noise and din; the whole harmony conveyed in time, tune, and temper thus incomparably melodious—with what pleasure . . . this might pierce into the hearers' hearts, I pray ye imagine yourself; for, so God judge me, I cannot express it, I promise you."

Did Will Shakespeare himself stand there bewitched in a similar fashion? Later he put on the lips of the Fairy King, Oberon, in his play, *A Midsummer Night's Dream,* what seems like a picture of the very scene—

> My gentle Puck, come hither: thou remember'st
> Since once I sat upon a promontory,
> And heard a mermaid on a dolphin's back
> Uttering such dulcet and harmonious breath
> That the rude sea grew civil at her song,
> And certain stars shot madly from their spheres
> To hear the sea-maid's music.[1]

These lines were probably spoken before the Queen herself, and were intended to bring back to her that moment by the lake, although Arion had turned into a sea-lady, and the ocean had taken the place of the quiet water beside Kenilworth Castle.

4

The coming of the Queen was an exciting event for any boy in Warwickshire. Doubtless Will talked of it much with his father and mother, his brother Gilbert, his companions at school. And later, when Will Shakespeare the man looked back on the pageants at Warwick

[1] II. i. 148–154.

and Kenilworth, they probably shone the brighter in his memory because they came at a time when his father was prosperous and honored in Stratford.

John Shakespeare has been described by some writers as an uncouth and ignorant fellow who could not possibly have had a son who became a great writer. Such commentators have also called Stratford a provincial village where a boy would seldom hear the speech of educated men, and would lack especially any knowledge of the feelings and formalities known to the wellborn and wellbred.

The second assumption is clearly a false one. Stratford was indeed small; but, as we have seen, it harbored men of learning and was close to many families of quality. In the Earls of Warwick and Leicester it knew two of the greatest nobles of the realm, men of the Court who had the Queen's love and favor. Aside from London itself, there was scarcely a better spot in England for a boy to learn the ways of those who had knowledge and power.

In the same fashion, the picture of John Shakespeare as a crude provincial nobody is untrue. We lack direct evidence that he could read and write. He never signed his name, but made his "mark," usually a neat representation of the glover's compasses he used in his daily work. His wife also "marked." But these facts prove neither of them illiterate. The documents in question were prepared by clerks and often all signatures were written in the same handwriting and then "marked." Adrian Quyney, John Shakespeare's fellow alderman, sometimes used a mark, although we know that he wrote easily in Latin or English.

Indeed, the presumption is that Will Shakespeare's father had some "learning." He occupied many town offices, including the highest ones of bailiff and chief alderman. He acted as town chamberlain, or treasurer; sat as judge; rode to London at least twice to negotiate business for the town; conferred with vicars and schoolmasters; and helped to frame town ordinances. There can be no doubt of his high *intelligence;* a stupid man would not have been given such duties, and could not have performed them. It seems certain that he could read sufficiently to verify with his own eyes the many documents he helped to prepare and was called upon to approve.

Certainly he commanded the respect of his fellow townsmen. He was "Master Shakespeare." For twenty-one years his name stood on the records of the town council. He wore a furred gown in public. When he went from his house to the Guild Hall he walked behind an escort of sergeants bearing their maces of office. He and his family sat at church in a front pew, and when plays were given in the Guild Hall the Shakespeare family occupied seats of honor.

John Shakespeare in these years was also a man of considerable property. The dowry his wife had brought him, as we have seen, greatly added to the holdings he himself had already acquired. In 1573 he had inherited a part of his father's goods. Two years later he bought the entire block on which his house and shop stood, and thus owned in town four buildings, two "orchards," and the gardens adjoining the houses. He had tools and materials in his shop, and the livestock and implements for operating several farms. With five growing children and a position which frequently demanded contributions for the public good, he could use these resources, but they meant comfort bordering on wealth.

One of John Shakespeare's acts during this period of prosperity proves clearly that his position was in all ways a good one. In the year 1576 he applied for a coat of arms, the badge of a "gentleman."

This was a distinction not lightly to be granted. Will Shakespeare's father must be able to prove, before attaining it, that he could live without "manual labor," and that he could "bear the port, countenance and charge of a man of substance." His wife must dress well and keep servants.

John Shakespeare was able to satisfy such requirements. The offices he had held as bailiff and chief alderman automatically gave him the "port and countenance" of distinction that was required. His property was sufficient to meet the other stipulations.

The formula for his coat of arms was recorded. It called for a shield of gold with a black band running from the upper left-hand corner to the lower right. On the band was to appear a spear of gold with a point of silver. Above the shield a falcon of silver, with outspread wings, would grasp a spear of gold with a point of steel. (The bird shaking the spear was, of course, a play upon the alderman's name.) Above the falcon was to run a motto in French: *Non sanz Droit*—"Not Without Right."

The preliminary grant for the coat of arms was approved. The honor which John Shakespeare clearly desired was now to become his for the making of a final payment.

But at this point evidently a change in his position occurred, for he dropped the proceedings which would have brought him the distinction he sought.

Moreover, in the following years there are evidences of increasing financial difficulties for him. Suddenly he ceased to attend meetings of the Stratford Council—for the first time in years. On November 14, 1578, he mortgaged for £40 his greatest possession, the estate in Wilmecote, called the Asbies, inherited by his wife from her father. A year later he sold an interest in some property at Snitterfield, near the farm his father had tilled. He failed to pay the fines levied upon him for nonattendance at the council. (With singular patience his fellow officials excused him from such payments for ten years.)

What was the cause of this dramatic fall in his fortunes? It has been said that trade fell off in Stratford, and there is evidence to show that the wool trade did. Yet if John Shakespeare suffered, why more than others of his fellow aldermen? What became of the moneys he had received in 1578 and 1579 from the sale and mortgage of lands—a sum worth some thousands of dollars in the value of our money today? Why did he refuse to pay the trifling levies for his absences from the council?

A reason other than the falling off of trade has been offered for what happened. It is this: that John Shakespeare was a "recusant," or one who failed to attend church and support the established religion.

To understand such a possibility, we must remember the extremely unsettled state of religion in England at this time. A considerable group of the English people were still Roman Catholics, and longed for the return of the old religion. Perhaps a comparable number were Puritans. A third group, the largest, was well satisfied with an English church independent of Rome, the creed and ceremonies of which differed relatively little from the Roman Catholic.

Elizabeth belonged to this latter group. She was automatically in opposition to Roman Catholicism, but she liked Puritanism no better. She felt that its emphasis on the personal responsibility of worshipers tended to promote differences of religious opinion and practice. She wanted one church, free of disputing factions.

The time had now come when the Queen believed she could work for a uniformity of religion, and through carefully chosen church officers she began to insist on a standard Anglican practice.

This policy made difficulties for both Puritans and Roman Catholics. There were no churches except those controlled by the Queen (and a relatively few private chapels in the castles of nobles or the homes of the wealthy). If a Puritan congregation found itself with a non-Puritan vicar, and a type of service suddenly altered, its members must accept what was given them or stay away from the place of worship. So with Roman Catholics. Many of both convictions did stay away.

Possibly John Shakespeare was one of the Puritans who refused to attend church services of which he could not approve. The Queen's new policy began to be enforced sternly in the late fifteen-seventies. John Shakespeare clearly belonged to the Puritan faction. As a town official he had aided in removing images and in whitewashing the paintings in the Stratford church. He and his associates disposed of church vestments, and apparently engaged vicars with Puritan tendencies. Those acts followed the popular trend in and about Stratford. Mary Shakespeare's family in the main had been Catholic, but she would have respected, and in the end would probably have accepted, her husband's attitude.

However, staying away from church was not a simple matter. Those who did not attend could be severely punished. So the "recusants" resorted to various devices to escape the penalties they might otherwise have had imposed upon them. One such device was to pretend to be in financial difficulties. The recusant might even mortgage his properties to friends or relatives, and refuse to pay assessments. He could then stay away from church on the ground that he feared to be arrested for debt. His friends and relatives, sympathetic with him, although not so stanch in belief themselves, were expected to restore his properties when church officials were changed or grew more tolerant.

Was this the course that John Shakespeare followed? It would explain a number of his actions. And it is borne out by a fine of £40 that was levied upon him by the Queen's Bench at Westminster in the year 1580. This was one of a number of fines imposed upon citizens, chiefly Puritans, who failed to appear in court at this time, apparently because they chose to risk being fined rather than meet an even worse penalty such as imprisonment.

What happened in the case of the mortgage on the Asbies, held by John Shakespeare's brother-in-law, might also fit into this explanation. From court records we know that the mortgage was in the form of a sales agreement, but that if the Shakespeares "did pay unto the said Edmund Lambert the sum of forty pounds upon the feast day of St. Michael the Archangel in the year one thousand five hundred and eighty, at the dwelling house of the said Edmund Lambert in Barton-on-the-Heath, that then the said grant, bargain, and sale should cease and be void."

On the appointed day John Shakespeare, according to testimony which he gave some sixteen years later, rode over to Lambert's house, fifteen miles from Stratford, and offered the money. But to his astonishment Lambert refused to accept it. We can imagine the scene—the amazed alderman, ready with his money, staring at his kinsman.

"Not receive the money?"

"No, I'll have none of it. Nor give you the deeds to the property."

"But, kinsman, it reads in the bond that you must."

"You owe me other moneys."

"A paltry five pounds, which has nothing to do with the agreement as to the Asbies."

"I'll not return the deeds."

"Then are you open to a suit in court, for I have witness that I rode forth this day to pay you the money, and you yourself under oath dare not deny it."

"I think I shall not need to. For a recusant to bring suit has its great dangers."

"Now, by my troth and faith—"

"Softly, brother John. I am in no mind to have this property put in hazard because of your Puritan scruples. Wait until your danger is past, and then if you tender the money, I will fulfill the agreement. Do you think I would serve my wife's sister an ill turn?"

"You do already. But if you will not deal honestly with me, I must wait for a better day. When it comes, see that you keep your promise."

So John Shakespeare rode back to Stratford without the title to the Asbies. Through misplaced trust he had lost, temporarily at least, his richest possession. It was to be years before the persecution of recusants passed and he could attempt to recover it.

V: RHYMING AND MIMING

WILL let the book lie before him, and looked out through the open casement window into the garden.

His little room in the rear upper story of the house faced northeast,

41

but although the sun was low, it slanted over the thatched roof and
shone with its late afternoon light on the apple and pear trees, and
beyond on a bank of marigolds. The leaves of the trees, underlined
with shadow that itself seemed touched with light, stood out separate
and polished. The unripe fruit, brushed here and there with a rusty
red, hung carved in the stillness. Somehow it was like the poem he
had been reading—

> Summer is come, for every spray now springs:
> The hart hath hung his old head on the pale;
> The buck in brake his winter coat he flings;
> The fishes float with new repairèd scale.

But it was not any clear likeness between this sonnet of the Earl of
Surrey and the quiet summer world outside that made Will pause in
his reading. On this Sunday afternoon he had long been savoring the
book the new schoolmaster had lent him, and he was at a point to
stop and brood upon it.

It held a different kind of poetry from any in the other books of
English verse that he had borrowed. He had read at Chaucer and
Gower, but the older language they used made a certain amount of
difficulty for him. He had chuckled in spots over the satires in Barclay's *Ship of Fools,* but on the whole they were long and heavy.
Skelton wasn't heavy, and there was a dancing beat in some of his
lines—

> Merry Margaret
> As midsummer flower
> Gentil as falcon
> Or hawk of the tower.

But those older poets were clumsy and crabbed in comparison with
these "Songs and Sonnets" gathered together by Master Tottel. The
new poems had an air about them, like the noblemen Will had seen
riding through the town in gemmed cloaks and plumed hats, sitting
easy in carved leather saddles on their clean-limbed horses. The poems
in this book had been written by such men; indeed, the master had
brought it from London, and the very printing spoke of courts and

cities. And these newer poets wrote of their loves and meditations with a smooth authority. That proud one, for instance—

> Give place, ye lovers, here before
> That spent your boasts and brags in vain—

Sure and arrogant, the poet proclaimed his own mistress as much above comparison with others as sunlight was to candlelight. And the ending —Will liked that especially. What was it now? He turned the pages and read it again—

> Sith Nature thus gave her the praise
> To be the chiefest work she wrought,
> In faith, methink, some better ways
> On your behalf might well be sought
> Than to compare, as ye have done,
> To match the candle with the sun!

"To match the candle with the sun!" The bold line, finishing the poem like a sword stroke, tingled down his spine. He had got thrills like that from his Latin—Virgil and Horace, and especially Ovid. In these hours of reading he had forgotten that he was finished with the elegance and drudgery of school, where he had spoken only in Latin throughout the final year, and was now busy with deerskin and kidskin in his father's shop.

He closed the book with a sigh. He didn't like the shop. Gilbert, although more than two years younger than he, did better work, and was content to be doing it. Will remembered how he himself had come home one day about a year ago with school behind him for good and had tried to talk to his mother about what lay ahead. He spoke of two Stratford youths who had gone to London.

"There are good tidings of Dick Field in the city," he said. "He likes the printing trade well, and his master the Frenchman. Roger Locke also does well there."

His mother smiled in her quiet way. She caught his meaning well enough.

"Your mind turns to London, Will?" she asked.

"Better fortune may lie there than here for one who is schooled," he said somewhat stubbornly.

"In what will it lie for you, my son?"

"Nay, I know not," he said.

Desperately he wished that he could tell her of the urgent feeling he had that he must strike out from Stratford. Years later he was to put it into clear words, as he pictured another youth leaving his home.

> Cease to persuade, my loving Proteus,
> Home-keeping youth have ever homely wits.
> Were't not affection chains thy tender days
> To the sweet glances of thy honored love,
> I rather would entreat thy company
> To see the wonders of the world abroad,
> Than, living dully sluggardized at home,
> Wear out thy youth with shapeless idleness.[1]

But at fifteen Will had been far from being able to phrase the vague uneasiness and yearning that were in him. Even now, a year later, he could not have come much closer to doing so. But the ferment was working in him again as he sat by the open window.

It had come with a rush as he laid the book aside, sending his mind to fumble at the door of the future through the remembered past. He had been no scholar to delight the stiff master, Thomas Jenkins, who had succeeded the more courtly Simon Hunt. But Jenkins had praised his rendering of Ovid into English.

"You have prought some of the music ofer," he would say, stumbling a little on his *b*'s and *v*'s, like the Welshman he was. "That is a fery gracious rendering. If you would work with as good a will on the grammar, poy, you would earn much praise."

But Will could not care, as Jenkins did, for perfection in grammar. He turned Ovid into colorful English because the stories stirred him, and he felt the vividness of the scenes the poet painted in his sonorous Latin. Icarus soaring dangerously toward the sun on his wings of wax

[1] *The Two Gentlemen of Verona,* I. i. 1–8.

and feathers; Atalanta stooping in her footrace with Hippomenes to snatch at the golden apples; Medea making her prayers to the night and the stars and the many gods of earth, air and water, as she prepared a magic brew that would renew an old man's youth—these acts challenged him to bring something of their color and excitement into his own language.

Ovid had stirred the creator in him, set him to dreaming of poems. But what could he do with any such dream? His father was battling stubbornly to preserve shop and home, and knew only one way to fight—to work at his trade. He meant to have Will's help.

Yet just as he had been moved as a child on seeing his first play, so at sixteen Will had been moved today by the poetry he had been reading. He was drawn toward the magic of it. "You have a part in this," it seemed to say. But how could he have one? Jenkins had said that if he worked at it he could serve well enough as a clerk.

The thought brought him out of his dream with a bump. Perhaps Jenkins had pointed the way for him. At least clerking would take him away from the shop. He sighed and sat staring out into the garden where the fading light pricked out the shapes of the leaves and the globes of the unripened fruit.

2

Hours like this one the youth must have known in those years. There is no record of exactly when he left school. Some say that it was as early as 1576 or 1577, with his course there unfinished. The reason given is the sudden fall in his father's fortunes. But John Shakespeare was feeling only the first pinch of difficulty at that time. Moreover, the school was free, and in this period Will's younger brothers seem to have attended it. Later Gilbert signed his name with the clear, assured script of a well-educated man—"Gilbart Shakespere." Edmund became a player, a craft which would require him to read easily. If John Shakespeare could keep his younger and less gifted sons in school, he could keep Will there, too, until his course was completed, probably in 1579.

It was logical that Will should then be trained as an apprentice in some trade or calling. John Aubrey, who wrote the first brief account of Shakespeare in the late sixteen-hundreds, says that the youth worked for his father and that John Shakespeare was a butcher. We know that the last statement is untrue—the father is always referred to in the town records as a glover or whittawer, and could not have had two trades. Aubrey, coming to Stratford eighty years after Will Shakespeare had died, picked up gossip that was truth, half-truth and fable jumbled together. His "life" is a mere essay, only a few pages long.

Probably Will worked in his father's shop for a time. Later, in his writing he showed knowledge enough of skins and their uses. That writing also suggests that he was reading widely in these years. It shows that he knew such collections of poetry as Tottel's, for he quotes a line from one of the poems in his play *King Henry IV, Part II*. It is from a short lyric beginning

> O Death, O Death, rock me asleep,
> Bring me to quiet rest—

and the rogue Pistol bellows it out in mock-heroic fashion—

> Then, Death, rock me asleep, abridge my doleful days!

Of course, Will Shakespeare might have read the poem as a man in London, but the casual way in which he uses it suggests long familiarity.

Where did he get the books he read? With the reduced family income, he could have bought few, if any. But others had books. We have a complete list of the volumes belonging to Master Cox of nearby Coventry, a tradesman. He owned the poems of Skelton and Barclay, many ballads, Malory's *Morte d'Arthur*, Rabelais's *Gargantua*, and a great number of romances in verse and prose, to some of which Shakespeare later referred.

Will would have got such books from similar libraries in Stratford.

Learning was new, and many men who had it loved to encourage the thirst for knowledge in a promising youth. Books would have come to Will as they came more than two hundred years later to boys in the American towns and frontier country—boys like Patrick Henry and Abraham Lincoln, who walked miles to borrow books, and read them eagerly by candlelight or firelight. From books Will Shakespeare learned, as he learned from field and forest and sport, countless names and details that were to make him seem marvelously familiar with every scene or activity he wrote of, and to give him the greatest armory of words that any writer ever used.

Such reading brought him into the stream of English poetry that was growing ever broader and stronger in those days. We have seen that two great influences had played upon him through the town of Stratford—one from the medieval world that was passing away, another from the surging modern world of new learning, exploration and growing freedom for the individual. These two influences were at work in the poetry he read.

The old ballads, for instance, were purely medieval. So was Malory.

But in poets like Wyatt, Surrey, Gascoigne and John Heywood, the modern spirit could be heard and felt. These writers knew the classics, and they had read French and Italian poetry and prose. The medieval accent had given way in them to a clear directness like a freshening wind. They had launched a new movement in English writing, with new poetic forms, a new personal quality, and a spirit that reflected the richer and more active world about them. Will must have caught the fire in them; he could not have missed it, having the genius to write as he did in years to come.

3

Did Will Shakespeare abandon his father's shop soon, perhaps to work as an assistant to the town clerk, or as a helper at the Stratford school, or as an attendant at some nearby manor house? We can only wonder.

But one other thing seems sure about this little-known time in his life. It is this: just as he was seeing and feeling the surging change in the poetry of his land, so also he was seeing and feeling a change in its drama. For year by year in these days English playwrights and actors were making a new kind of theater. And what they were doing was spread clearly before Will's eyes, for almost every summer in this period of his life troupes of London actors were coming to Stratford.

The Earl of Leicester's Men had come in 1575; the following year brought the Earl of Worcester's Players. Leicester's and Worcester's were both at Stratford in 1577. Lord Strange's Men came in 1579 and again in 1580. In that year the Countess of Essex's troupe played in the town, too, and the Earl of Derby's.

Each arrival was an event for Stratford. The troupes came in with all the gaiety and assurance of the circus that paraded into American towns three hundred years later. There was music of fife and trumpet, there were the players themselves, dressed proudly in the liveries of their patrons. Some on horseback bore banners; their wagons, hauling their costumes and properties, were brightly painted and perhaps decked with garlands.

Will doubtless leapt from behind his father's counter or from the town clerk's office to see any such procession. And when the players had waited upon the bailiff, shown their patent and won permission to give performances, Will would be on hand—either at the mayor's play, given free (but rewarded by a fee from the town funds), or at a showing in the courtyard of one of the inns; or at both!

Often he hung about as the crowd broke up, watching the handymen of the company knock down the stout planks laid on barrels that had served as a stage and pack the curtains and costumes. One company had played a tragedy called *Cambyses,* the story of the Persian king who seized a bow and shot the son of a courtier to prove that wine did not affect him, and who executed his own brother and later his own wife. After the play, Will stood near the actor who had taken the role of the king. Still in his costume, the player directed the packing and cast a friendly look at the serious-faced youth who watched him.

"Well, lad," he said after a time, "how did you like the play? Had we pleased you better with an old morality, with more clowning?"

"Not me," Will answered. "He who made the play could well have spent less time than he did on the clowning, and more on making a better story. So, I think, will play-makers do in time to come, be their plays comic or tragic."

The player started a little at the rather mature and discerning reply.

"Why, I think they will," he nodded. Then he added thoughtfully: "You have more than an idle interest in this business of plays, it seems to me."

"We are all eager enough for plays hereabouts," said Will. "I myself have played in them in school, and seen what I could—"

"Aye, aye," the other agreed. Then on an impulse he added, "Come sit with me at the inn and we will speak of these things, if you like."

A little later the two were together at a deal table, sipping from the pewter tankards a serving boy had set before them. And the player, in an expansive mood, was holding forth on the great changes that were taking place in the theater.

"It is a new thing these last ten years," he asserted. "Look at the companies of actors that go about like ours. In my father's time you could not have named one of them truly commissioned by a lord and working year in and out; yet now they multiply like flies. And still the people flock to the inns and town halls and already in London are two houses built especially for the playing of plays."

"Houses for plays? What manner of places are they?"

"Why, buildings with spacious stages and seats for the better quality, and rooms for our dressing and for the storing of habits and devices used in the plays," the other replied. "They stand outside the city itself," he added, "in the Liberty of Holywell. There the city authorities cannot forbid us to play, for the place was once a church property and answers not to city law, but only to the Queen."

"The City Council would forbid the giving of plays?" Will asked, startled.

The other laughed grimly. "Forbid? Why, if they dared, they'd clap the last player in London into a dungeon and make a bonfire of our playhouses." He glowered a moment and resumed bitterly, "For the sake of order, they say, mark you. Yes, they are a sour-faced lot of Puritans, these city fathers. They'd have folk always at prayer and meditation." He laughed. "But the Queen and the nobles like to see plays, and encourage them; and even at city inns they are given often enough, despite the spoil-sports. Nay, lad, the plays sweep all before them. They are at the very beginning of a new life that will bring in comedies and tragedies worthy of the ancients themselves."

"Sir," asked Will, his eyes fixed earnestly upon the player's, "what do you think has brought this about? Was it not but a few years since there were only the miracles and moralities?"

"Aye." The player nodded, while he thought the matter over. "Well," he said at last, "these same miracle and morality plays served a purpose. Men say that the priests began them, and, like enough, you have heard they were once played in the churches. Then they were performed in the town streets and squares, as being too lively for the altar, and the tradesmen took them over. But to my mind the change began when the kings and nobles gave plays for *their* pleasure. They had the gold to pay for a kind of splendor in playmaking. Aye, I have seen castles and trees at the court pageants, wondrous like the reality, and boys appareled like goddesses, and music to ravish the ear—"

"As My Lord of Leicester did at Kenilworth for Her Majesty's pleasure," put in Will.

"Why, so he did. I myself had a part in those festivities. And who wrote the words for them?" he went on with new excitement. "Why, the best poets in the realm! Mark you, lad, it is like the printing of books, that has come suddenly and widened all knowledge. These writers have gone beyond the clowning and ranting of the tradesmen. They are making dramas that are better ordered and better written. And we who act them have learned our craft as none knew it in our fathers' time."

He broke off and watched his companion shrewdly.

"You would have a part in this for a little persuasion?" he asked.

"Yes, if I could," the other replied with a directness that left the player somewhat at a loss.

"Well," he temporized, "many a lad has done it. There are no bars to this trade. Gentlemen come to it and the sons of tradesmen as freely. And it is a good calling. Some make fortunes in it, and all are merry enough. Have you skill in acting?"

"So some have said." Will hesitated, flushed, and then said stanchly, "And—with writing, too, somewhat."

"So?" The player looked at him as if uncertain whether that confession were a happy one or not. "Well," he said at last, "keep watch and try your fortune when the time comes. You are green yet—too old to try women's parts and not yet ripe for men's. But a year or two from now, if I come here again—"

Will did not see him again. Perhaps his company never returned to Stratford, or perhaps he stayed in London when they came. Perhaps he was a victim of one of the plagues that still swept the city in the summer. But he had brought Will a sense of the growing world of the theater, with its newer and bolder dramas. The boy soon saw some of these—*Ralph Roister-Doister,* perhaps, or romantic pieces like *The History of the Solitary Knight, Delight* and *Preder and Lucia.*

Yet despite its increasingly modern accent, the world of the theater still had a medieval quality. The stage was more like the stage of the morality plays than like that of the ancients or our theater of today (as we shall see later). The very companies existed by grace of an important medieval custom. Each "served" a nobleman or the Queen. Thus they had a precise place in society—a thing that was the very blood and bone of medieval practice, for of all persons who were looked on with abhorrence in that day, none were more distrusted and avoided than "masterless men."

But the players were using their medieval status in a modern fashion. They had really become merchants, trading their talents and positions for sound money.

"For a penny or two we will give you the very entertainment that has pleased the Queen and the nobles and the wealthy folk of London," they promised in effect to the people of towns like Stratford. And who would not pay at such a promise?

Indeed, the actors used their standing as the "servants" of great ones to put some tactful pressure upon town authorities. With an air almost of challenge they presented their commission and stood watching the honest burghers expectantly. And could a mayor or a council refuse to let the Queen's or the Earl of Oxford's or the Earl of Worcester's Men perform in their town? A denial might offend the great patron. Hmm—perhaps bad business for the community, that. So even when the authorities didn't want any plays, they usually opened the town purse.

"Here," they said in effect, "we want to show our respect for your lord, and our good will. Take these ten shillings and move along, please!"

This was agreeable to the players. It was pay without work.

But usually the troupes were welcomed and invited cordially to perform. Indeed, with the newer kind of plays they were showing, and the growing excellence of their acting, they eventually won an almost fabulous popularity. Don't forget the acting. The stage, set up in an inn courtyard or a hall, was better than a wagon top, but it was still a rude affair. So the actors had to depend much upon their own power to create an illusion. And they had become marvelously skilled at doing this. Beginning early, each actor served his apprenticeship, laboring at the art of speaking, gesturing and often singing and dancing. Soon English players would travel in Denmark and Germany, appearing before townfolk and princes, and crowds broke down stout wooden walls to see and hear them.

In fact, like so many wizards, they had transformed the theater, making it a new thing. They were driving out the crude miracles and moralities, and people were paying them for doing it. The play! Here was cunning, trained art and new writing flashing into mature life with as great an effect as the motion picture more than three hundred years later.

Will Shakespeare was hovering at the door of this house of magic, with its curtains, costumes, gestures and resounding verse. Was there a place for him in the new palace of pleasure, where master mimers stilled their listeners with grief or awe, or lifted them with excitement, or rocked them with laughter?

Already old hopes that had stirred often in him, but vaguely, were taking on the form and boldness of something that could be put into action.

VI: THE MYSTERIOUS MARRIAGE

BUT that action did not come soon. A boy of seventeen *might* have skipped off to London in the year 1581, but Will Shakespeare did not. He waited, and before long there were happenings which kept him in Stratford.

Probably before his seventeenth birthday came, he had left his father's shop. As already suggested, he may have served for a while at a manor house. He may have found a place where he could use his schooling, perhaps with the town clerk, Henry Rogers.

There is no direct proof of this. Indeed, we have little proof as to much that Will Shakespeare did for some years to come. Yet clerical work of some kind was what a young man of keen mind and a good education might seek as soon as he could, and the way in which

Shakespeare wrote in later years strongly suggests that he sought it. For much of his writing shows an unusual acquaintance with law terms.

An emphasis should be put on "unusual." Most Elizabethans were fascinated with law, and many of them, including John Shakespeare, brought suits with what seems to us a remarkable zest and energy. Many poets and dramatists besides Shakespeare used law terms and made similes and metaphors of a legal sort. However, in the writings of William Shakespeare law terms and legal ways of thinking burst out in such surprising and even inappropriate places that they seem the result of a personal experience. It is as if the law and its language and methods had become a habit—as if he were saturated with them and they spilled out as he wrote, in spite of him.

For instance, Will Shakespeare later composed 154 sonnets, most of them love poems. But in these sonnets he falls time and again into legal phraseology. In one, sonnet 146, talking with his own soul, he demands of it—

> Why so large *cost,* having so short a *lease,*
> Dost thou upon thy fading mansion spend?
> Shall worms, *inheritors* of this *excess,*
> Eat up thy *charge?* Is this thy body's end?

He talks of arrests, bail, suits, pleas, denials, terms and dozens of other legal matters. Whole sonnets picture the love relationship in legal terms of bonds, patents and conveyances. Yet what he does in the sonnets is not so surprising as what he does in his plays, where kings, generals, court ladies, and girls in love all babble like so many law clerks. There is young Juliet, for instance, only fourteen, an heiress who could scarcely have been educated in law, and was madly in love. Yet in a moment of deep emotion she exclaims—

> O, I have bought the *mansion* of a love,
> But not *possessed* it, and, though I am *sold,*
> Not yet *enjoyed.*[1]

[1] *Romeo and Juliet,* III. ii. 26–28.

This is only one of many occasions on which Juliet, the very symbol of young romance, speaks out a passionate feeling in correct law language. Of course she would not have known enough to do it, and would not have done it anyway. Not even a lady lawyer would talk about her love as if pleading a case. She would talk about it like a woman in love. But Juliet is only one of a number of law-minded ladies whom Shakespeare presents, including Rosalind, Venus (in *Venus and Adonis*), Paulina, Silvia, and Miranda.[2]

Work in a town clerk's office would have given Will Shakespeare a familiarity with the special language of the law. It would have made law images and procedures a habit. And it would have acquainted young Will with a number of nice legal points affecting people.

For instance, on February 11, 1580, Henry Rogers, as coroner, approved the verdict of a Stratford jury in the case of the death of Katherine Hamlet.

The jury found, to translate the Latin into which they put their opinion, that Katherine, "going with a milk-pail to draw water from the River Avon, standing on the bank of the same, suddenly and by accident slipped and fell into the river, and was drowned, and met her death in no other wise or fashion."

This decision was a happy one for the relatives of the poor woman, for had the jury found that she had purposely drowned herself, she would not have been given proper burial. Years later, in his play *Hamlet,* Shakespeare told of the drowning of Ophelia, and referred to the penalty for suicide, which was held to violate the commandment "Thou shalt not kill." Had Ophelia intended to destroy herself, the priest explains in the drama,

> She should in ground unsanctified have lodged
> Till the last trumpet; for charitable prayers,
> Shards, flints and pebbles should be thrown on her.[3]

[2] E. I. Fripp, in his *Shakespeare, Man and Artist,* pp. 138–145, quotes item after item to show Shakespeare's resolute use of law terms.

[3] *Hamlet,* V. i. 252–254.

Will Shakespeare, pushing a pen for Henry Rogers, may well have had the episode of Katherine Hamlet's death fixed in his memory, to be used thus later in one of his greatest tragedies.

2

But compiling law records by day, and reading poetry and romances by night, and seeing the plays that were still coming to Stratford—these activities did not fill all Will's time. He found hours for outdoor sport. He was strumming a lute and singing (for later he showed a precise knowledge of the way that musical instruments should be played, and of all kinds of singing—catches, trolls, dumps, carols, anthems, chants, prick songs and others). Elizabethans loved music, and sheets for playing and singing were to be found in most houses, even in many whose owners had no books. Will was also listening in these years to talk of war, politics, and religion—and talking of them himself. Religious wars were being fought in France and the Low Countries, and England was buzzing with fear of Spain and the imprisoned Mary Queen of Scots (soon to lose her head on the block). And finally, Will's thoughts, like most young men's, would have turned to the girls of the town and nearby countryside.

At Shottery, a village not far from Snitterfield, where his father had been reared, lived Richard Hathaway, a tenant farmer.

Richard was a friend of John Shakespeare, who had stood surety for him in 1556 (that is, made himself responsible for Hathaway's fulfilling some obligation). John Hathaway, Richard's father, had held town offices in Stratford. The family was hard-working and respectable.

Richard Hathaway had been married twice. By his second wife, Joan, he had a flock of five young children, and there were three older ones from his first marriage. In the spring of 1581, Anne, the oldest, was twenty-five; Bartholomew, a son, was a year or two younger; and Catherine was seventeen.

Will Shakespeare might well have had an interest in Catherine, only half a year his senior, or even in Joan Hathaway, the oldest of her half sisters, who was then fifteen. But it was Anne, eight years older than he, who attracted him. This was strange, for she was well past the usual age for marrying. Anne, herself, may have twitted him about his preference.

"You should keep company with maids less than your years, Will."

"Nay, they are too green. They know nothing, and babble of it. I crave a riper understanding."

"To match your book learning, or some woman you've found there?"

"Why, book learning, they say, is only what men have set down about living. And of that a woman knows more than a girl."

Like many gifted youths, Will may thus have turned to those older than himself, men or women. Years later, one of his characters, Duke Orsino, set forth the opposite view—

> Let still the woman take
> An elder than herself, so wears she to him.[4]

However, Shakespeare pictured Orsino as a romantic fellow, and a bit of a fool!

But Anne Hathaway did not too greatly discourage the youth who came to court her. Perhaps she saw in Will a final opportunity for marriage. At any rate, on November 27, 1582, when the young man was in his nineteenth year, he went to Worcester, the seat of the bishop of the diocese, to get a special license to marry Anne Hathaway after a single publication of the banns. And about six months later he became the father of a little daughter.

Many scholars have sighed over these events and called them very sad ones for Shakespeare.

"Here is a young man of more imagination than sober common sense," they remark. "He rashly hurries or is tricked into a relationship with a shrewd older woman. He finds himself in a position where he is forced to marry her. Imagine!—a genius tied to a much older mate

[4] *Twelfth Night,* II. iv. 30–31.

of limited understanding, with children soon coming along further
to complicate his unhappy situation!"

But the more idealistic scholars have leaped up to shout their protests.

"This is a needless insult to Shakespeare and Anne Hathaway!" they
cry. "We haven't a shred of proof that the marriage was not the purest
love match, and one that brought happiness. Why not at least give the
two the benefit of all reasonable doubts?"

And they set forth evidence for doing so.

For one thing, they call attention to the nature of a betrothal in those
days. Betrothal was in most ways like an "engagement" today, but
it was formally announced before witnesses and was far more binding.
No legal record was made of it, but it was really a kind of preliminary marriage. Once betrothed, there was no breaking the pact except
for very unusual cause, and young people often lived together as if
married. If and when it became clear that a child would be born, the
wedding ceremony was performed. Stratford records of Will Shakespeare's time show that such was often the course that was followed.
There are known cases where even members of the nobility followed
it. This, argue the idealists, is what Shakespeare and Anne did.

They also explain very convincingly why a special license was taken
out. From December 2 until January 12 was the season of Advent.
During this period no marriage could be celebrated without special
permission purchased at great expense. From January 27 to April 7
came a similar period. Thus there would be no time between the two
for the banns to be published on three successive Sundays—the usual
requirement. Therefore unless Will and Anne were married *before*
December 2, a wedding would be delayed for four months, or would
be tremendously costly. But a special license taken out *before* December 2 would make a regular ceremony possible after only *one* reading
of the banns. To secure such a license was troublesome, but cost little.
A bond of £40 had to be posted, and the consent of Will's father was
necessary, for the youth was not yet of age. (Anne's father had only
recently died—in August, 1582.) As a recusant, John Shakespeare

would not have dared to post the bond. Two friends of Anne did that
But he must have given his consent, so that the marriage was in no
sense a hasty elopement.

The license was granted and the marriage undoubtedly took place
although no record of it exists. It is supposed to have been made in
the little town of Temple Grafton, near Stratford, where the registers
for this period are missing. The license still exists and is granted to
Will Shakespeare and "Anne Whateley," and some people have found
further mystery in that. But doubtless it was a clerk's error. The records of Stratford and other nearby towns show many similar mistakes

A reader today can make his own choice as to what Shakespeare
and Anne may have felt about their marriage. Those who want to
believe that it was wholly natural and happy have proof that it *could*
have been. At the same time, this proof can be accepted, and still, for
all we know, the marriage may have been a somewhat unwelcome
necessity for the young man who was the bridegroom and not long
afterwards became a father.

3

Richard Hathaway's will left his daughter Anne £6, 13s, 4d, "to
be paid unto her at the day of her marriage." The words suggest that
the wedding of the two may have been planned as early as August. The
money was worth about $500 in our values today. It was a considerable
help to the young couple.

Probably Will and Anne moved in with John and Mary Shakespeare
on Henley Street, using a part of the house there. Here their first child,
Susanna Shakespeare, seems to have been born, for we know she was
baptized at Stratford on May 26, 1583. In Stratford, too, Shakespeare
and Anne's twin children, Hamnet and Judith, were christened on
February 2, 1585.

Will Shakespeare now had increasing responsibilities—a wife, a
child, then a wife and three children. For the moment the dream of
going off to London with a troupe of players must have dimmed and
perhaps wholly faded. He needed money to support his family, and

needed it at once. Perhaps his work with Henry Rogers, if he was clerking then, supplied enough. But perhaps, too, he may have found a better position as a schoolmaster in some school near Stratford.

There is evidence to support this possibility.

When Aubrey gathered his material in the late sixteen-hundreds for the first life of Shakespeare, he not only went to Stratford, but talked with actors and writers in London who might know something about the dramatist. One such actor was William Beeston, the son of Christopher Beeston. Christopher had played for at least ten years in the same company as Shakespeare (from 1592 or earlier until 1602). William Beeston, when Aubrey visited him, told the latter a number of things which he had learned from his father. He spoke, for instance, of Shakespeare's learning. Ben Jonson, a playwright and poet of Queen Elizabeth's time who was renowned for his knowledge of the classics, had written that Shakespeare had "small Latin and less Greek." Beeston mentioned this and added that he (Shakespeare) "understood Latin pretty well, for he had been in his younger years a schoolmaster in the country."

This is a small bit of evidence, but it is definite, and it fits in with what we know about Shakespeare. And it fits in with his situation at the time of or just after his marriage.

What were his feelings then? First of all, naturally, there was the obligation to his new family. But his father's position must have been in his mind, too. John Shakespeare had begun life as the son of a tenant farmer. He had established a business, prospered, won honor as mayor of the town, chief alderman. He had come to the very verge of winning a coat of arms, the badge of a "gentle" family. Will must have shared the keen disappointment of his father when this honor had suddenly faded, just as John Shakespeare was prepared to grasp it. He must have felt concern and anger over Edmund Lambert's failure to return the title to the Asbies, his father's most valuable possession. And he must have recognized his own obligation to serve not only himself, but his family.

The post of schoolmaster would have seemed a first step toward accomplishment on his part. It was a position of dignity. Probably it paid better than clerking. And for him personally it offered a chance to associate with well-schooled men, some of them with university degrees. It meant books, and the urge to read more books. It meant learning more, growing in knowledge and in the skill of writing. Perhaps it might even lead toward London and the theater. Schoolmasters had already written plays. There was Nicholas Udall, who had done *Ralph Roister-Doister,* and Richard Edwards with his *Damon and Pythias.*

These must have been the thoughts of a gifted young man about to become a "schoolmaster in the country." And being Will Shakespeare, with a natural talent for observing, learning and doing, the actual work of teaching must greatly have developed his abilities. He became more familiar with the great Latin poets. Probably at this time he read the *Menaechmi* of Plautus, a comedy which he saw could be recast as an English play. He could have read it only in Latin, for no English translation was published until 1595. And he *did* read it, for his play, *The Comedy of Errors,* which we know was performed in 1594 and was probably played at least two years earlier, was built up from the old Latin play.

Will may even have made a rough draft of this comedy while teaching. At his school Will Shakespeare directed Latin plays given by the students (most schools gave them). He may have written an English play for the school. In *The Two Gentlemen of Verona,* which he penned a few years later, there is a scene which suggests this. The youth Sebastian tells the lady Silvia that he knows another young woman, Julia, about whom Silvia is curious, "almost as well as I do myself." This is quite true, for Sebastian is Julia masquerading in boy's clothes. But for us the point is that the youth describes what happened once in his town at Pentecost. In some "pageants of delight" he took the part of a woman. Julia lent him a gown of hers, and it fitted

As if the garment had been made for me.

Sebastian then tells what happened further:

And at that time I made her weep agood,
For I did play a lamentable part.
Madam, 'twas Ariadne passioning
For Theseus' perjury and unjust flight.[5]

Was it some such "pageant" that young Will Shakespeare wrote, based on a story from Ovid like that of Theseus and Ariadne? By now he must have been writing—poems or plays—sharpening his pen for the work he would do.

4

For we know that soon Will left Stratford to seek a fortune in London.

There is a legend about that—one which millions of readers have enjoyed and have liked to believe.

The legend first appeared in the year 1708, when a clergyman, the Reverend Richard Davies, was editing some notes about English poets left after his death by a fellow minister. Davies wrote of Shakespeare—

Much given to all unluckiness in stealing venison and rabbits, particularly from Sir . . . Lucy, who had him oft whipt, and sometimes imprisoned, and at last made him fly his native country, to his great advancement; but his revenge was so great that he is his Justice Clodpate, and calls him a great man, and that, in allusion to his name, bore three lowses rampant for his arms.

The pronouns get rather jumbled in this paragraph. Davies means that Shakespeare took revenge upon Lucy by picturing the latter as Justice Shallow in *The Merry Wives of Windsor*.

This was a delicious morsel for anyone writing about Shakespeare. The playwright had been a daring fellow. He had defied a local nobleman, perhaps had been jailed for it, and had been forced to try his luck in London, thereby winning his fortune.

The legend grew. Sir Thomas Lucy was given a deer park, a keep-

[5] *The Two Gentlemen of Verona*, IV. iv. 168–173.

er's lodge and a keeper. Shakespeare was made not only to satirize the nobleman in a play some ten or twelve years later, but he was also said to have written a ballad against Sir Thomas. Finally, in the middle seventeen-hundreds, an old man was found near Stratford who claimed to know this very ballad. Here is a stanza.

> A parliamente member, a justice of peace,
> At home a poor scare-crowe, at London an asse,
> If *lowsie* is Lucy, as some volke miscall it,
> Then Lucy is *lowsie,* whatever befall it.
> He thinks himself greate, yet an asse in his state
> We allowe by his ears but with asses to mate!
> If *Lucy* is *lowsie,* as some volke miscall it,
> Sing lowsie Lucy, whatever befall it.

The ballad, all scholars agree, is so bad that even a young and prank-playing Shakespeare should have done better. Of course Sir Thomas Lucy *was* a member of Parliament, and *did* have three luces (a kind of fish) on his coat of arms.

But, on the other hand, a great many facts have been discovered which throw doubt on the whole episode.

For one thing, why did no one in Stratford tell Aubrey about it? He went there in the sixteen-hundreds, and makes no mention of it. It turns up for the first time 120 years or more after Shakespeare left Stratford for London.

Again, Sir Thomas Lucy had no deer park, no keeper, no lodge.

Still, again, he was a rather stout man, while Justice Shallow in *The Merry Wives of Windsor* is as thin as a rake. Moreover, Shallow is wholly in the right in his dispute with Falstaff and his companions, who unlawfully shot a deer and beat and robbed poor Shallow. If Shakespeare had meant Shallow to be Lucy, and wanted to ridicule him, would he not have made Shallow at least somewhat in the wrong?

Further, Shakespeare pictures Sir William Lucy, Sir Thomas's grandfather, in his historical drama *Henry VI, Part I,* and makes him a most admirable gentleman. Apparently he had no feeling against the Lucy family.

Finally, Mr. Leslie Hotson, a great digger in Elizabethan documents, has recently shown that Shakespeare was more likely holding up to ridicule in Shallow a very mean-spirited magistrate near London named William Gardiner, who had three luces on *his* coat of arms, and had brought suit against Shakespeare and others not long before *The Merry Wives of Windsor* was first produced.

All this doesn't mean that Shakespeare never shot a deer, or even that he never wrote the ballad in question, which after knocking about for 175 years might have been changed considerably for the worse. But it does show that the legend is full of errors and is not a satisfactory explanation of why Shakespeare left Stratford. If he once killed a deer, he probably did it when in his teens, and not after he was married, and a schoolmaster, and the father of three children.

There is a more natural and logical reason than deer slaying for Shakespeare to have left his native town. This takes us back to the players.

These had continued their visits to Stratford. Worcester's Men came in 1581, also Lord Berkeley's; the two troupes visited the town again in the following year. In 1583 came Berkeley's Players and Lord Chandos's; in 1584 the Earl of Oxford's, Worcester's and the Earl of Essex's; in 1586 some company whose name is not given; and in the following year the Queen's Players, Essex's, the Earl of Leicester's, the Earl of Stafford's and an unnamed company.

Thus more companies than ever were playing in the town. Will would have seen that the number of troupes was increasing, and he would have heard more and more of their life and work in London.

Aubrey says that "being inclined naturally to poetry and acting," Will "came to London, I guess, about eighteen." We can throw out the guess; for the records show that Shakespeare was in Stratford until he was twenty-one, and probably until he was twenty-three; the fact of his going and the reasons remain.

For years Will had been seeing the troupes trumpet their way into

Stratford. For years he had sat or stood to watch them perform in the Guild Hall or in one of the inn courtyards; perhaps, as we have seen, he had talked with actors. For years he had read the new poetry that men were writing in England; he had heard the players declaim such lines in ringing tones. He had listened eagerly but soberly to rumors of their London successes; he himself had tried his hand at writing, and felt the call of it and the conviction that he could pit his growing skill against others' to some purpose.

Little lay before him in Stratford. If he were ever to strike for a larger and richer life, it must be soon.

We can imagine such thoughts stirring and prodding him, we can imagine him talking with Anne about what he felt.

"Men do great things in London now with the plays. They win fortunes. One waits for a man who can act and write. I could do both."

"Leave Stratford, Will? Leave us?"

"Not without the prospect of a place that will bring silver—perhaps more than I get here. But I tell you I can find one, and do better than most when I have my hand in."

"It is leaving a sure place for an unsure."

"Sure? What's sure here but that I shall rise no higher? If I seek a better place I must pit myself against university men; for teaching they have the name and the preference. With players I need no degree. Skill and wit count only."

And we can see him watching the companies as they came and went, making opportunities to speak with the players. The Earl of Worcester's Company, with young Edward Alleyn—tall, full-voiced, commanding—an actor who would soon fire all London, might have beckoned to him. But there was the Earl of Leicester's troupe, with its clowning leader, Will Kemp. Kemp had been to Denmark and Germany, and had left most of his companions there in the fall of 1586, coming back to England with his "boy," or apprentice, Daniel Jones. He got up a new company for the summer of 1587.

At this time Kemp was already second only to the great Dick Tarleton as a comedian. He was a small but well-knit fellow, a master jigger, a genius at embellishing his parts with absurd grimaces and impromptu jests. His fame was already spreading throughout Europe, and would grow greater after Tarleton's death the following year.

He came to Stratford with his new troupe that summer, and Shakespeare must have marveled at his impudent buffoonery. Perhaps he heard that the company was short-handed. Now was the moment he had waited for. So Kemp, changing his clown's costume after the play, may have looked shrewdly at a "handsome, well-shaped man, very good company, of a very ready and pleasant smooth wit" (Aubrey's words) who waited on him with a quiet confidence.

"A schoolmaster, eh? And you would leave your books for the boards? Hah! These fellows who watch us want no instruction, Master Shakespeare, but jests and jigs!"

"What better instruction to a merry life, as you yourself show, Master Kemp?"

"Hmm. Not ill-turned. But to be plain, sir, this business of miming is strange to you, I take it."

"In the act, true—though I have done enough in such plays as we give here. But in my thought it is not strange."

"Aye, and so it is with dozens that come asking to join us. Why, they think skill in our craft as easy to come by as a mug of ale, or the boldness to bawl a ballad in a tavern."

"I think to find nothing easy. But I have considered this matter long. I have written lines for pastorals, and made bold to shape a play."

"Hmm—shape a play—and of *what* shape, marry?"

"One that I hope will please you. If so, I'll call it a good one."

Kemp stared at the trim, smiling, persistent young teacher.

"Eh," he said. "You've a certainty I like, lad. Can you make a rhyme? Turn a jest?"

"So some have said. But you may look at my scribbling yourself, and judge what promise it has, if any."

"You'd be only a hired man with us."

"No matter how I begin."

The comedian scratched his shaggy head.

"Well, we could use another hand. And one who could put a patch on some of these old interludes, to give them a new face, or a new kind of doublet at least. I'll sample your wares, Master Shakespeare. And if you shake a pen as well as a spear, we may strike a compact."

In some such fashion Will may have knocked at the door of the theater and found admission. And early one morning he would have left Stratford behind him, riding among new companions on the road that led to London.

VII: THE CITY AND THE THEATER

WILL looked past the cottages, through the almost naked limbs of the tall oaks etched against the sharp air, to the line of turrets and steeples beyond. He and his companions were at the edge of the city. For a moment the weariness of the long journey on horseback over muddy December highways fell away from him. Already the road was thickening with people. Farmers clattered by in empty carts, returning home. A few sober merchants cantered toward them, bound for their night's lodging at some inn. Suddenly, as if shot from a cannon or a catapult, a group of richly caparisoned horsemen thundered by them toward the city, sending up a shower of mud as they passed with arrogant indifference.

The troupe had been on the road since summer. In the last month, however, the players had been working toward London, performing at Norwich in mid-November and then later at Oxford. So they came in from the northwest. But instead of making for the spires and walls that lay to the south, they veered eastward through scattered houses, orchards and gardens. Soon they approached a broad open space which was apparently a kind of playground. In one part of the area a dozen youths were kicking a football about, charging, shouting, laughing. Farther off, Will could see a group of targets, and robust apprentices leaning to their longbows as they launched their feathered shafts.

"It is Finsbury Field," said Daniel Jones at Will's elbow. "And see," he pointed, "yonder are the playhouses. Just beyond, in Shoreditch, lie our lodgings. Eh! It will be no displeasure to get one's boots off, and wash, and sit down to a joint for dinner!"

Will's eyes followed Daniel's arm. Across the fields he saw the shapes of two huge structures—seemingly round, perhaps 40 feet in height and fully twice as broad.

His heart gave a leap. This was what he had come for! He would have liked to spur his tired nag toward these playhouses of which he had heard—symbols of his new craft, bulking high and solid in the late day. But he knew that the image of the warm tavern and its noisy tankards and steaming victuals filled the minds of all his companions. To them, as seasoned players, the Theatre and the Curtain were an old story. Well, he thought, with an inward grin, he himself was a player of sorts now.

"Aye," he said to Daniel. "A warm room and water and a trencher of mutton will be good."

2

So Will came to the city, or into its outskirts. To him the moment was a great one. Although he could not know that at the time, it was a great moment also for the theater, and for England.

Why it was great for the theater, the story of Will Shakespeare himself will tell. Its greatness for England was somewhat sensed by all the folk of the land, Will included.

For as the year 1587 moved toward its end, there were few in the realm whose thoughts were not turning to the threat of invasion. The tension between England and Spain had long been growing. Philip II in Madrid was busy planning a master stroke against England.

He had been prince-consort to Mary, Elizabeth's elder sister. When Mary died and the daughter of Anne Boleyn took the throne, he had dreams of courting and marrying her, and of bringing England back to the Roman faith! But the new Queen wanted neither Philip nor his religion. And in time her armies were helping the Dutch against Spanish troops, while her privateers looted Spanish settlements in the New World and seized royal treasure ships returning from them. Philip was at last preparing his answer to these affronts—a gigantic armada. With its more than a hundred ships he meant to sweep English vessels from their own Channel, or sink them in their harbors. Then he would pour his soldiers into England, subdue it, and restore the true faith there.

The English looked fearfully toward the south, listened for news of the enemy. Never since the Conquest had they faced so great a danger. The fate of their Queen hung upon the outcome, hers and that of the church which most of them supported. If the Spaniards won, the days of "Bloody Mary" might be with them again, and they shuddered at the thought. Even Roman Catholics roused to the Spanish threat and reached for weapons with which to defend their land and ruler. As for the Puritans, to them the invasion was a work of Satan. They would resist it to the last drop of their blood.

Thus, as Will Shakespeare rode into London, England was at bay, and working slowly toward the fever pitch. And the impending clash would make a new and different England. London would be the center of its growing pride and activity.

While the newcomer finds his lodgings in Shoreditch and sleeps away the fatigue of his journey, let us look briefly at this city of London. Let us get a feeling for its shape and color, and see a little of the place it had in the life of its land.

It was not a big city as we know cities. Its hundred thousand people

—with perhaps as many more in nearby towns and villages—made it in our sense of size more like Utica, New York, or Duluth, Minnesota, than London or New York of our own day. Except for a small area at its center, it was also a city of fields, trees, orchards, gardens. These broke its blocks of houses and gave it a clean and almost country air. There was of course no smoky industry or iron-wheeled traffic. The modern "London fog," a mixture of coal dust and mist, was as yet unknown. The Thames River, flowing through the town, was still a clean stream well stocked with fish, where swans floated among the boats and barges. If most of the streets were unpaved, or badly paved lanes, as dirty in their fashion as Stratford's, that was natural to the folk of Elizabeth's London.

The heart of the city was enclosed by the old wall which had once made the place a fortress. The rampart was still in good repair. It made a great half circle, arching north from the banks of the river. The stream bordered the southern side of the town. Here walls, quays and stout castles made a line that could have been well defended. The water lapped against the buildings, and men stepped from the streets or their stone houses into barges or boats.

The wall had seven gates—eight, counting the gate by the great Tower of London that completed the enclosed town at the south-eastern end. Aldgate, Bishopsgate, Margate, Cripplegate, Aldersgate, Newgate, Ludgate—these are still names in London. But they were actual breaks in the stone barrier then, with arches and heavy doors of wood and iron. At night these great doors were shut; and walled London, half the city in population, was locked up against strangers and the dark.

But in area more than half the city lay outside the wall. It sprawled northward in villages and buildings and churches. (Shoreditch was one of such settlements.) To the west lay similar areas. The Inns of Court were just outside the wall (the chambers where law students studied). Farther westward, along the river, after a cluster of prisons, stood lordly mansions, castles and royal palaces, ending more than a mile upstream with the imposing buildings, gardens, orchards and courts of the Queen's Westminster Palace.

All this was to the north of the Thames. Across it on the southern shore lay more of London, and one could go there by boat or by the great London Bridge, of which we shall soon hear more. Part of this London beyond the river was a very unsavory district at the stream's edge, appropriately called the Bankside. Here were taverns where thieves and cutthroats loitered. Here, too, were several rude enclosures called bear gardens where bears and bulls were attacked by dogs or by men with whips, to the yells of the bloodthirsty crowds. Sometimes plays were given in these "gardens." A new theater, the Rose, had just been built in the Bankside. In years to come, Will Shakespeare would know the area well.

That is the general sweep of London as it lay in the year 1587. It was an old city. The wall, the Tower, many of the palaces along the river were evidence of this. So was the great cathedral of St. Paul's, its tower rising high above the houses toward the western side of the walled area. (The St. Paul's with its huge dome that modern visitors have stared at was built later, after the cathedral of Shakespeare's time was destroyed by fire in 1666.) So were many of the 150 other churches in and beyond the heart of the town. So were many of the old inns, shops and houses that stood everywhere.

And it was a proud city. It was the seat of English government, the great center of trade where ships from Holland, Germany, Sweden, Italy, Russia and Portugal brought their merchandise. It was the center of religion in England, too, even though Canterbury housed the chief archbishop of the land; for the Queen ruled the church and churchmen came to wait upon her. Further, London was a religious center for the Puritan element that wished to simplify the forms of public worship. Rich Puritan merchants controlled the town government.

London was also the center of social life and of fashion, for the Court was always in or near it, with nobles and ladies ready to spend freely. Many of the greater families had houses along the Thames, or elsewhere in or about the city. Shops were at hand to serve them. Some sold costly cloaks and gowns; others hats; still others ruffs and the finest linens. There were shops for rapiers and firearms, for gold and silver ornaments, for jewels, for wigs and the dressing of hair.

Finally, London was the home of the arts. Writers and learned men lived in the city or came there on visits. Musicians and painters made it their home. And London, of course, was the headquarters of the player companies, and the site of their theaters.

So if it was small as we know size in cities, it was mighty in industry, faith, fashion, trade and art.

> The sight of London to my exiled eyes
> Is as Elysium to a new come soul,

wrote, a few years later, a playmaker of whom we shall shortly know more.[1] It was a magic city to many Englishmen, and it was to be such a city to Will Shakespeare.

3

When Will had found a room in Shoreditch and unpacked his few clothes and well-worn books—Ovid among them, probably, and the Geneva Bible, and perhaps Holinshed's *Chronicles* and a book or two of English verse—he was ready to go into the city. The next morning after a breakfast of bread and ale and cold mutton, he passed through Bishopsgate or Margate, eyed casually by the liveried city constable on guard under the four-storied stone arch with its windows and carvings.

Although the hour of nine had not yet struck, the city was in full tide of activity. Will's eyes bulged at its jostling busyness. Through the ill-paved streets the noisy crowd bubbled like a plunging river. Porters went by with great burdens, stately housewives strolled along followed by maids with baskets, merchants passed in furred robes, servants in livery swerved adroitly between apprentices bearing wares for customers and venders crying their services or products. The voices of the latter rang our clearly—

> "Sweep, chimney sweep, mistress, with a hey derry sweep
> From the bottom to the top! Sweep, chimney sweep!"

[1] Christopher Marlowe, *Edward II*, 10–11.

"Fine Seville oranges, fine lemons!"

"Quick periwinkles, quick, quick, quick!"

"Salt, salt, white Worcestershire salt!"

Most of the cries were sung, and the up and down of their chants made a crude music for the traffic.

Through the hurrying people on foot lumbered carts and occasionally one of the coaches that were now becoming common. Painted and gilded, with its austere, liveried coachman and retainers, and a footman running before it to clear the way, such a vehicle was still a wonder in the town. As Will went on, working his way toward St. Paul's, he passed shops where some of the apprentices cried their wares. He saw a fresh-cheeked girl calling to a gallant and his lady,

"Mistress, would you have fair linen cloth? I will show you the best in London-town, and if you like it not, you may leave it! Yours only the pleasure to look at it, ours the care to show you!"

As Will stared, he was bumped aside with an almost contemptuous "By your leave," and saw a plumed hat and a white ruff above an embroidered cloak disappear in the crowd, leaving only a strong whiff of perfume behind.

Will continued on his way southward through a street that, like many in London, was a mere lane, with heaps of garbage here and there. The upper stories of the beam-and-plaster houses jutted out above his head, making a kind of cavern. He passed, staring, through the market at Cheapside and went on toward St. Paul's. Finally he entered a shop not far from the cathedral, and asked of a bright-eyed boy who came forward if Master Field was about. Soon he was grasping the hand of an old Stratford schoolmate, whose apron and smudged face showed that he had been busy with a press.

"Will!" the Londoner exclaimed. "You in London? What, with My Lord of Leicester's Men? This is a happy thing, indeed!"

The two stood talking excitedly, for Richard Field and Will Shakespeare had grown up together, and it was eight years since Dick had left for London to serve as apprentice to Thomas Vautrollier, one of the best printers of the time. Finally Shakespeare asked about the Master.

"Why," Field replied, "had you not heard? You know he was two years in Scotland, for printing the writings of Giordano Bruno—and splendid they are, though pronounced heretical. You shall see a copy one day," he added in a low voice. Then he continued, "Only a short time after his return—it was last summer—he died."

"Ill news, ill news," murmured Shakespeare. "And you?"

"Why, I had been working with Madame, his wife, during his time away," answered Field, "and this February last became a freeman to the Stationers. And—well, as I am complete now in my craft, and I know the shop and its custom, and we have worked long together, Jacqueline and I—"

"Why," his friend broke in, "you and she will be married, and you shall become benedict and master printer in a day!"

"It is so," the other smiled. "And," he continued, a bit sheepishly, "stepfather to four fine boys! But you must greet my lady and the lads. Jacqueline!" he called, "Simeon, Thomas, James, Manasses! Come hither! Here stands a friend from Stratford that you must know—and love well for my sake!"

It was an hour later when Will left the shop amid the protestations of the comely Madame Vautrollier, and with a promise to return and sup with the family. Field went with him, for he wished to take some books to John Harrison, whose book shop, the White Greyhound, was one of many near the Cathedral. Will clutched in one hand a copy of *Plutarch's Lives* translated from the Greek by Sir Thomas North, and printed ten years since by Vautrollier. Little did he guess how much of his future life lay in that volume, waiting to be unrolled. Field explained the location of the bookshops as the two went along.

"All the better of them are at St. Paul's," he said, "and there you will see every new thing printed in English. And why? Because, even now every man in London who would meet his friends and get the latest news will be walking in and about the church and will thereby become a customer, perchance. And, each by his pillar in the aisle of the church, you'll see the lawyers talking with their clients. And as for your gallants who would show their Italian doublets and Spanish boots and silver spurs and lace-spangled cloaks—why, you shall count a hundred, if one!"

"One, I think, elbowed me into the wall not far back and nigh choked me with his scent," Will smiled.

"Aye, they are a plaguey sort," said Field, "spending a year's living on a satin suit or their silken hose. But we are coming to the stalls," he pointed out. "Here are whole libraries set out on these trestles."

They were indeed in the book world, which was part the journalist's world, too, for here were pamphlets and ballads (though the latter were mostly sold by venders). The pamphlets, indeed, were the magazine articles and editorial pages of the Elizabethans, for newspapers were a good century from being born. The ballads carried spicier items; they were the nearest thing in their day to a modern tabloid scandal sheet. Murderers, courtesans, sea captains, traitors and heroes of the wars all re-enacted their adventures in the rude stanzas of these popular songs.

"See a new book, buy a book, sir!" called one of the boys to Will as he stared, and another chanted, "A new play, sir, printed as writ by Master John Lyly and played before Her Majesty!"

Field grinned at his companion.

"Now if I have any knowledge of you, Friend Will, you will stay here the better part of an hour," he gibed, "and go away with a lighter purse and more books on your arm."

"No, Dick," said Will, "the purse is already too light to put a heavier load on the arm. But I'll look about, by your leave, and find my way back here some other day."

It was some time after Field parted with him that he left the stalls and made his way toward the river. Titles of romances like Montemayor's *Diana* (from the French), of poems like Byrd's *Psalms, Sonnets and Songs,* or tracts like Sidney's *Defense of Poesie,* and of romances like Greene's *Pandosto* still danced before his eyes. Never had he stared at so many books, and never had he so yearned to buy and possess them. But such pleasures, he knew, must wait for a more prosperous day. If this play he was refashioning of nights proved usable—

He went on to the river, and thrilled to its clear waters, its busy wharves, its boatmen shouting, "Eastward ho!" "Westward ho!" "Southward ho!" He saw a gilded barge making its way upstream with several gallants and ladies wrapped richly against the sharp but pleasant air. Then the bridge caught his eye. It towered above the water on its stone arches like a little city, for at its ends were fortresses, and water mills for grinding grain, and on the span itself were houses. As Will drew nearer, he noticed a line of some thirty heads stuck high on pikes above the bridge walls and the jostling traffic. Then he heard a voice at his side.

"Aye, there they bleach and whiten, and so may all enemies of the Queen and the Faith."

Will turned to see a soberly dressed citizen with the stern features and intense expression that often went with the extreme Puritan.

"See you the third?" continued the stranger. "It is one who crept into London whispering foreign counsels—bidding honest Englishmen forsake their faith but hide their apostasy until the moment when the mask should be thrown off and swords be lifted for Rome. Well, the wicked has his reward. And they shall all perish," he cried, his voice rising, "though they come on great ships from Spain with the legions of the murderous Parma! For the Lord will protect His own and smite His enemies!"

Will stared at the fanatic, and edged away with a muttered assent. He had no love for bigots, Puritan or papist. His old master, Simon Hunt, had been a gentle and learned man, and if his conscience took him toward Rome, was that wickedness or the affair of his conscience? Men would be better if they dwelt less on differences of dogma and more on the simple truths of religion.

He went on toward the Tower. He would see that. In Holinshed's *Chronicles* he had read of princes who had lain there—yes, and kings too. Richard II, Clarence, the two princes slain at Richard Crookback's word, Anne Boleyn, Lady Jane Grey, yea, the Queen herself on a time—

Well, he must see it, and then find an inn and some victuals, and so back to Shoreditch. There was some business that Kemp had afoot and wanted to discuss with him.

4

It was one-thirty o'clock and the crowds in Shoreditch were making their way toward the Theatre. The performance would start soon—the flag at the top of the playhouse promised it; and although the December day was mild and sunny, there would barely be light to see the performance through if it began by two. In this respect the theater of those times was like an American football stadium more than three hundred years later. It depended on the sun.

Will walked with Daniel Jones toward the great structure. As they approached it, he saw that it was not really round, as he had thought on the afternoon of his arrival in the city. Rather it was eight-sided; and, he thought to himself, that was natural. Under the outer facing of plaster the frame was wood. It would be cheaper—and just as pleasing to the eye—to have a shape that would not require the beams to be bent.

The entrance lay on the northern side, and Will and Daniel came in with a jostling crowd—apprentices, tradesmen, sailors, stoutly dressed in wool or leather against the coolness of the year. There was a smell of unwashed bodies, and Daniel, after paying the penny due for general admission, urged Will up a few steps toward a door where another money-taker stood.

"We'll go into the tuppenny gallery," he said, "away from the stench of the groundlings. There we can sit, instead of shifting from foot to foot in the pit for two hours. And I will pay," he added firmly, "for this is your first London play, and I know you have those in Stratford that leave you a light purse."

Will smiled.

"As you will, then," he answered. "If I mend this old play to Kemp's liking, my purse will gather weight, and then you shall be guest to me."

They passed through the door to the gallery and stood within the playhouse. They had entered the lower of three balconies that followed the octagonal shape of the building. Each was about 12 feet deep, with benches on ascending levels. The top gallery was roofed. The rest of the theater was ground-level space—the pit—and was open to the sky, except for the stage.

That lay directly opposite to where Will and Daniel stood, and Will looked at it with keen interest. To call it the stage was hardly accurate. It was much more. Will saw the main platform at its base jutting out into the pit. It was between 4 and 5 feet in height, some 24 in width, and almost 30 feet deep. At its rear the wall rose upward for three stories. The fourth story hung over the stage, from which two stout pillars rose to support it. Will realized that this superstructure would protect the players below from rain, and from the glare of light on sunny days.

Daniel tugged at his elbow.

"We are early enough to have some choice of seats," he whispered. "Let us get nearer to the stage."

Will nodded, and the two moved to the right and out of the section which, being opposite the stage, was farthest from it, and into the next one. Finally Daniel stopped, and they took their seats on one of the benches near the gallery rail.

Both looked about the playhouse. Above and below it was filling with people. It had a little the effect of an amphitheater, Will thought, remembering an illustration he had seen in some half-forgotten book. The galleries bent in octagonal shape about the stage-unit, as the Greek or Roman tiers of seats had bent about the playing platform of the ancients. The pit was now filled, and there was some shoving and jostling for the better places. The galleries were rapidly darkening with people.

"Why," Will murmured, "the place must hold above a thousand."

"Nay, double that, I warrant you," Daniel assured him. "It makes the largest innyard but the merest closet space. Yet there's not a man here but sees the stage well, and can hear easily what is spoken."

"Yes," Will agreed. "It must be scarce fifteen paces from mid-platform to the farthest man that sits here. Or stands—for the groundlings have as good a view as any."

Daniel nodded, and the two watched the crowd. It was a motley of costumes. In the pit were apprentices in their garbs of varying colors. There too were rough countrymen, soldiers fresh from the wars in the Low Countries, sailors just off their ships. Girls were elbowing their way about with baskets of apples and oranges, nuts, fresh sugar buns. They were crying their wares, and finding customers. So were others in the galleries, where sat the better-dressed folk— merchants, students from the Inns of Court, gentlemen, and a few masked women (no honest matron would show her countenance at a playhouse). Near the stage, in boxes, lounged the wealthier spectators, splendid in fresh-laundered ruffs and cloaks crusted with lace. Light flashed from their jeweled fingers and sword hilts. Several were puffing at ornate pipes of silver or ivory, and a gust of wind brought Will the faint scent of the new "weed," tobacco. It made this arena of make-believe at once more real and more fantastic. The smell was reality. But all compounded of fantasy were the visions it conjured up of immense, far seas; of strange shores and savage men; of curious fragrant vegetation.

Daniel was talking of the stage.

"Master Kemp bade me tell you of it," he said. "The main platform below is like to what you have known; and there they play the most, being closest to the audience."

Will nodded.

"And it may be," he suggested, "that those curtains at the rear hide what I have heard called the inner stage or study."

"True enough," agreed Daniel, eagerly. "Even now they may have set a scene there—such as the room of a palace. At a whisk of these same curtains, it will be revealed; and perhaps will take you in imagination to some far country."

"Well devised," Will murmured.

"Aye, but in the new playhouses like this there are more stages than two," Daniel continued. "Do you see that recess on the second level? 'Tis called the gallery. There I have seen players stand and speak to others below—perhaps as if on the upper floor of a house, or on the walls of a city."

"I have seen the same thing in the galleries of the inns, above the courtyard," said Shakespeare.

"It may have been built with such uses in mind," conceded Daniel, "but here all is better arranged. For look—not only may they use the space as a battlement—it may also at will become a small chamber. There you may see a lady talk with her maid, or watch two lovers in pretty conference. And on either side, the windows that you see can be put to good use."

"It multiplies the powers of a play," mused Shakespeare.

"Nor is that all," Daniel continued. "You yourself have heard how gods descend in these new theaters from the sky. Well, look at the ceiling above the stage. There is a trap door in it, and in a room above are men and certain machines. When the trap door is lifted, the workmen can lower through the opening a goddess on a throne."

"Most cunning, most cunning."

"That device they may not use today. I think it belongs not to this tragedy. But the talk goes that for color and glitter and shouting there was never such a play. Master Edward Alleyn surpasses himself in it. Aye, the whole town is agog about the piece. See, every space for sitting or standing is filled now." He grasped Will by the arm. "And look, the trumpeter appears."

On a small platform near one of the huts which topped the stage roof a richly garbed figure had appeared. He lifted his trumpet, sounded a blast. The noise of talk and laughter died, for this was the first signal that the performance was soon to begin. Twice more he blew, and the audience waited breathless.

Then from between the curtains of the study at the rear of the main stage an actor stepped forth. He wore the traditional Prologue's long black velvet cloak, and on his forehead rested a thick wreath of bay. He walked toward the forward part of the platform, halted and faced the crowd. Then he spoke in a casual yet ringing tone, his first words edged with scorn.

> From jigging veins of riming mother wits,
> And such conceits as clownage keeps in pay—

he paused an instant to let the gibe at rough comedians like Kemp go home, then swelled and hammered—

> We'll lead you to the stately tent of War,
> Where you shall hear the Scythian Tamburlaine
> Threatening the world with high astounding terms
> And scourging kingdoms with his conquering sword.

Again a moment's pause, then, in a lowered voice, came the concluding lines—

> View but his picture in this tragic glass,
> And then applaud his fortunes as you please.

He bowed, and a kind of sigh that grew to a roar and the clapping of hands greeted him as he turned and walked back and disappeared between the draperies which masked the study.

A trumpet sounded, and the applause died suddenly. The curtains of the inner stage swept back, revealing a king seated upon his throne, with richly garbed nobles on either side.

As the monarch speaks, the audience discovers that he is the weak ruler of Persia, Mycetes, the butt of his more manly brother Cosroe's wit. Mycetes sends his captain, Theridamas, with a thousand horse to wipe out the Scythian shepherd, Tamburlaine, a robber who has been preying upon merchant trains bound for Damascus and Bagdad.

> I long to see thee back return from thence,
> That I may view these milk-white steeds of mine
> All loden with the heads of killéd men!

Theridamas goes out. The king and his retainers follow. Only Cosroe, the brother, and a friend are left. They talk of a plot to make Cosroe king, and soon his captains enter and proclaim him. The trumpets sound, the soldier-actors march toward the rear, their coats of mail agleam and their colored cloaks flaring. The curtains of the inner stage close after them, and the scene is ended.

Will turned to Daniel excitedly, as the applause swelled.

"By the mask of tragedy itself," he whispered, "this is a play to lift a man from his seat. Who wrote it, did you say?"

"They call him Marlowe—a university wit."

"He makes a fine spectacle, and forges lines that ring," muttered Shakespeare. "I thought to do something like it myself—"

"Sh-h," said Jones. "You've seen little, I warrant. Look!"

Both stage doors open. From one side enters a man of great stature, clad in a sheepskin coat and shaggy boots, with a naked sword in his hand. By the other he drags a reluctant young woman, richly dressed; behind him come his captains, costumed like him. From the other door soldiers in even ruder dress pour forth, bearing chests and bales, which they deposit in the middle of the stage. As the giant comes forward, the playhouse bursts into applause, for this is Edward Alleyn enacting the part of Tamburlaine.

From his words it soon becomes clear that Tamburlaine has captured Zenocrate, daughter of the Soldan of Egypt, with her followers and her treasure. And he announces a purpose—

> But, lady, this fair face and heavenly hue
> Must grace his bed that conquers Asia,
> And means to be a terror to the world.

With a contemptuous word he casts aside his coat of sheepskin, dons armor, seizes a heavy curtail-ax, and stands transformed. He tells Zenocrate of the wonders she shall have as his empress:

> A hundred Tartars shall attend on thee,
> Mounted on steeds swifter than Pegasus.
> Thy garments shall be made of Median silk,

> Enchased with precious jewels of mine own,
> More rich and valurous than Zenocrate's.

As the deep-voiced Alleyn intones the full-voweled verse, standing where most of his audience can see each changing expression of his face, he seems indeed one to shake the world. No wonder that when Theridamas appears with his thousand horse, he is charmed and awed into forsaking his feeble king and joining Tamburlaine. As the chieftain leaves the stage with Zenocrate, who with her lords had hoped that the Persians would free her, the audience knows that this is only a prelude to further surprises.

And they come quickly. Cosroe seeks and receives Tamburlaine's help in overthrowing Mycetes. After the victory, he marches off, while one of his captains promises that he will soon "ride in triumph through Persepolis."

Tamburlaine, with his captains about him, stands looking after the monarch he has made. Then he repeats the words of the captain·

> "And ride in triumph through Persepolis?"
> Is it not brave to be a king, Techelles?
> Usumcasane and Theridamas,
> Is it not passing brave to be a king
> And ride in triumph through Persepolis?

The others eagerly assent.

> O my good lord, 'tis sweet and full of pomp!

> To be a king is half to be a god!

Theridamas is intoxicated by the thought. He exclaims:

> A god is not so glorious as a king! . . .
> To wear a crown enchased with pearl and gold,
> Whose virtues carry with it life and death,
> To ask, and have—command, and be obeyed;
> When looks breed love, with looks to gain the prize—
> Such power attractive shines in princes' eyes!

Tamburlaine looks at him thoughtfully and asks—

> Why, say, Theridamas, wilt thou *be* a king?

His captain is a bit alarmed. Perhaps Tamburlaine suspects his loyalty. He hedges deftly.

> Nay, though I praise it, I can live without it.

But this is not the answer his master seeks. He turns to the others.

> What says my other friends, will *you* be kings?

They sense his drift. Yes, yes, they would! Their leader nods.

> Why, then, Casane, shall we wish for aught
> The world affords in greatest novelty
> And rest attemptless, faint and destitute?

He answers his own question, slowly, impressively.

> Methinks we should not. I am strongly moved
> That if I should desire the Persian crown—

he eyes them, and seems to swell with terrific power—

> *I could attain it with a wondrous ease!*

He bids them send after Cosroe, and challenge him. They "only made him king to make us sport." He, Tamburlaine, shall have Persia. They shall be kings of Parthia, Scythia, Media.

And so the pageant marches its incredible way. Zenocrate is overwhelmed with admiration for this demigod who soon masters Cosroe as he promised, and moves on to further triumphs. She all but worships him when he subdues the mighty Bajazeth, Emperor of the Turks, puts him in a cage, and then brings him out onto the stage to use as a footstool while the groundlings roar. And finally, when Tamburlaine captures her own father, the Soldan of Egypt, even that becomes a joy. For her lover dries her tears, heaps new wealth upon the the captive Egyptian, and gives orders to prepare for the marriage that will unite him with the lovely daughter.

5

Will left the theater with Daniel, dazzled with magnificence. The trumpets, the gorgeous costumes, the clashing swords, the magnificent words, seemed to lift him above the earth. How this fellow Marlowe fashioned lines! Now they floated in beauty, now they crashed like thunderbolts. Now they seemed to leap across the world—

> Until the Persian fleet and men of war,
> Sailing along the Oriental sea,
> Have fetched about the Indian continent
> Even from Persepolis to Mexico,
> And thence unto the straits of Jubalter,
> Keeping in awe the Bay of Portingale,
> And all the ocean by the British shore—
> And by this means I'll win the world at last!

Why, confound the man, he *had* made a world conqueror. The form of Tamburlaine towered like a Cyclop. No wonder all London was talking of the play. Here, it seemed to Will, was a drama as great as Rome or Greece had known, and he himself was a part of the theater that was producing it. Could he, Will Shakespeare, match that beauty and power? Later he was to see the limitations of Marlowe's work, but for the moment it seemed perfect to him. Yet even now it did not appear as a cause for discouragement, as something wholly beyond his reach. It was rather a challenge, even an invitation. He had come to the city and the theater, and found a magnificence worthy of his most soaring dreams. *Tamburlaine* seemed to beckon him toward its splendor, as to something he could learn to understand and share.

VIII: TWO MEN OF LONDON

MY LORD of Leicester's Players did not linger long in the city. There seemed a better prospect in travel, and by mid-January they were off to the towns of the south coast, with their sun and sea winds. In February they played in Dover, and Will Shakespeare had his first glimpse of the ocean and of the chalky cliffs that the Romans had seen from their war galleys. From those white headlands came the old name for the land—Albion.

Here Will found watchers on the shore, waiting for a first sight of the Spanish fleet. When the troupe arrived at Plymouth in May the townsfolk were in a fever of impatience. The English ships lay in the Sound, ready to pounce upon the unwieldy galleons of the Spaniard. Howard and Drake, captains of the defending forces, had no fear of an enemy they had boarded and plundered in many oceans, and the folk of Devon had caught their spirit. Anxiety had given way to eagerness for the clash.

" 'Tis a great fleet the Spaniard has sharked up, lad," said a burly sailor to Will. "Yea, none greater ever made sail. But the Lord is stronger than many kings, and—" here his eyes twinkled— "he hath put that in English wit and will and pointed steel which the Spaniard cannot abide. Fear not, but pray that they come quickly."

But the Armada still waited for favoring winds and Will's troupe went off to Exeter and Bath, then with summer turned northward to Gloucester, Coventry and York. The shadow of expected invasion hung everywhere. Companies levied by the towns were at drill—marching and doubling, lifting or trailing pikes. Gunners were unlimbering their pieces. Horsemen from the manors hung about smithies, seeing to the repair or fashioning of equipment. When the players broke off their labors in mid-July, Will went to Stratford, but there too he found warlike preparations. Then suddenly one night the church bells began to ring wildly. From the street came excited voices.

"The Spaniards have come. There are bonfires down Banbury way!"

"To arms! To arms! All meet in Market Square!"

The bells clanged on, and men lighted a great bonfire in the gravel pits to the east of town. That very night horse and foot moved clanking out of Stratford, and indeed from all the towns of central England, to join the Queen and her generals (Leicester, Essex and others) at Tilbury.

It was a gallant but needless muster. Even then the English ships were harrying the heavy Spaniards like fierce greyhounds. Along the Channel they drove them, broke them at Gravelines. The mighty Armada fled into the North Sea. While its ships maneuvered there, a tempest struck and scattered them. Finally they sailed north around Scotland and Ireland, bound for home. But a new storm dashed many of them on the rocks of the Irish coast. In October, one Englishman counted eleven hundred Spanish corpses there. To the English it was the hand of the Lord, with fearful blows completing the attack that their ships and fighting seamen had begun.

By this time Will and his fellow players were on the way back to London. Before they got there they heard news that cooled their jubilation over the national triumph. Their patron, the Earl of Leicester, had died on his way to Bath, to seek a "perfect cure" for an illness that had troubled him. It was a hard stroke for the Queen. Though she had rejected Leicester as a husband, she loved him as a kinsman and friend, valued him as a counselor. He had written her only a week before he died, and his message still survives, endorsed in Elizabeth's hand, "His last letter."

In a practical way, the death of the great Earl was a harder blow to Kemp and his fellows than to the Queen.

"We've lost a master," said the great comedian to the others when the news of Leicester's death reached them. "And since our lord had no heir, there's none to fill his place."

"And until we find someone who will, we are masterless men," said Pope.

"Which we cannot be," Kemp added sharply, picking up the talk. "Sirs, we must get on quickly to the city, and seek a new patron, or find a place with others who already have one."

There could be no question about it. They pushed on to London. Kemp with Bryan and Pope (the other chief actors of the troupe) joined Lord Strange's Men. Probably Shakespeare did, too. As yet he held no position which would get him listed as a chief player in any records of the time, as more important actors were. But when his name first appeared five years later, he was in the same company as Kemp, Bryan and Pope.

His real life in the London playhouses began with this second arrival in the city. His first had been only a visit. Now he had come to stay.

2

The Armada had been completely scattered. With it went for generations all fear in England of a foreign invasion. The nation arose from the shadow of a great threat into the sunshine of power and growing wealth. Soon English merchant companies were building greater fleets, planting colonies in America. English industries throve. The nation took a prouder place among her European neighbors. And with peace and the sense of power came the will to write and sing. As the Armada and its menace was swept out, a golden time for English authors swept in.

So far as drama was concerned, this meant the stronger upsurge of a progress already begun. Will Shakespeare himself had seen a part of that progress as he sat in the Theatre watching and listening to the color and clash of *Tamburlaine*. What were the forces that had brought such a play to birth?

We have seen already how all through the years of Elizabeth's reign the player-companies had been growing in skill and accomplishment. We have seen how this was apparent to Will Shakespeare in Stratford. But he had caught only fragmentary glimpses of what had occurred.

For instance, he heard only rumors of the Court theater and its boy players. These boys were attached to choirs—that of St. Paul's for instance, and from an early age they were trained with amazing skill and thoroughness in singing, dancing and speaking. The Queen paid for a considerable part of their training, and they performed before her.

They and the royal theater with its lavish appointments were under the direction of the Master of the Revels. The Master also supervised all affairs dramatic. With years, his powers would increase, and he would become a kind of censor for plays, who collected tidy sums from all the companies.

The Master regularly invited the chief adult companies to play before the Queen. They were well paid for this. And when the players performed at Court they used the theater the Master provided. It had resources to make the eyes of any actor bulge. Forests and castles were set up on the stage. Movable clouds and thrones appeared as they were needed. Little scenes were set behind curtains while other scenes were in progress, and at the desired moment were revealed with a whisk of the draperies. Marvelous and ingenious costumes dazzled the eyes of the professionals. One lot, which they did not wear themselves, was fashioned for Venus and six of her nymphs, who seem to have been ancestors of the American Follies girls.

Besides the experiments it made with scenery and costumes, the Court theater helped to raise the level of playwriting. The Master of the Revels got some plays free (perhaps by poets eager to please, perhaps by gifted noblemen like the Earl of Oxford). For others he paid good silver or gold. This forced the professional players to think about paying writers for their plays. They too played for the Queen and for great nobles at their town or country houses. The dramas presented on such occasion must meet the highest standard. We shall see later how one writer employed by the Queen had an influence on the public theaters, and on Will Shakespeare himself.

In a similar fashion, the players had to meet the standards of production and acting which the boy companies and their skillful directors set. It would have been embarrassing had a patron said: "Methinks it would be some profit for you gentlemen to mark the antics of these children. By my faith, they outdo you, and could give you some instruction in your quality" (that is to say, their profession). Probably hints to this effect were actually dropped more than once, and kept the professionals on their toes.

Thus the influence of the Court performances was joining with the growing interest of the public to lift the standards of the player-companies. We can get some idea of what these forces had brought about up to the time of Will Shakespeare's arrival in London by considering two men. One had to do with play producing and acting, the other with play writing.

3

James Burbage was the first man. Early in life he had been a carpenter. He left this trade for acting, and appears in the records of the early fifteen-seventies as the head of Leicester's Players. Then, about 1575, he had an idea.

It was both new and practical. Burbage calculated that it would serve two purposes. First, it would help to solve an exasperating and expensive difficulty which the players in London had been facing. Second, it would make money for James Burbage.

Let us first look at the difficulty. At that time the companies gave their public performances in the inns of London. The chief ones were the Bell Savage, the Cross Keys, the Bell, the Bull, the Boar's Head. All these inns were built about central courtyards, with one or more balconies looking out upon them. The arrangement suited the players. They set up a stage at one end of the yard, collected their penny from the people who wished to stand on the ground level, got a better price from those who sat or stood in the balconies. The innkeepers were glad to have the players. A play attracted people to the inn, and the host could expect a neat profit from the sale of ale and food.

The performing of plays thus went merrily until it began to trouble the city authorities. Many of the people who came to see the shows were rough fellows, full of blood and ready for adventure. Often, following the play, some of them got to brawling, and made work for the city constables. Rival groups of high-spirited apprentices actually came to the inns by agreement, with staves, ready to have a set-to afterwards. London gangs met there and went on to stage riots, or to break into a jail and deliver some of their unlucky cronies. At the inns many of the gallants picked up loose women and some were said to use the plays to entice silly but honest girls into evil ways. Then there was the danger that the "throng and press" of people would spread the plague.

"The politic state and government of this city," declared one harassed Lord Mayor of London, "by no one thing is so greatly annoyed and disquieted as by players and plays and the disorders which follow thereupon."

The Puritans and their preachers especially were outraged by such goings-on. Plays were performed on Sundays if weather permitted, and drew people from the churches.

"Many can tarry at a vague play two or three hours," wrote one angry minister, "when they will not abide scarce one hour at a sermon."

Then, too, the Puritans were keenly aware of the loose and vicious character of much of the acting and clowning devised to please rough crowds.

"What is there," demanded one, "which is not abused thereby? Our hearts with idle cogitations; our eyes with vain aspects, gestures and toys; our ears with filthy speech, unhonest mirth and ribaldry; our whole bodies to uncleanness; our bodies and minds to the service of the Devil!"

Many of these plays of the inn courtyards were, indeed, no moralities with sober lessons. They were written for the rough city crowds. The Puritans set out to scourge the abominations from the city. They even blamed the plague on the plays.

"The cause of the plagues is sin and the cause of sin are plays," shouted one Reverend Thomas White in an indignant sermon. *"Therefore the cause of plagues are plays!"*

For a time the city authorities were less interested in these moral objections than they were in the menace to health and order which they saw in theatrical performances. They tried to cut down the giving of plays on such grounds. But the players had their patrons—high nobles who often sat on the Queen's Privy Council. The Queen herself wanted the players to prosper, for if they were driven out of business they could scarcely play before her. When the city fathers began a drive on plays the Privy Council therefore interfered, although it did permit plays to be banned at times when the plague raged.

But in 1573 the Puritans elected a Lord Mayor in London and found themselves with majorities on the Board of Aldermen and the Common Council. Then the players ran into such trouble as they had never known. For several years they had to summon all the influence they could muster in order to play at all. The City Council drew up ordinances that would have fettered and all but choked them, and promptly rushed in to prohibit all performances whenever the deaths by plague began to rise.

Now let us get back to Burbage and his plan. From the very start he had in mind a great improvement in playhouse facilities. After all, the inns had not been built for the presenting of plays, and were far from ideal places for that activity. The stages had to be set up, and were rude affairs. There was no space for storing costumes and properties. There were no proper dressing rooms. The seating capacity was limited. Why not a building planned for players—built to set off their acting to better advantage, to give them a stage with several extensions, to provide the best ways of getting onto and off it? Why not a playhouse with three, five, or ten times the capacity of an innyard? That would mean money!

It would if these devastating bans on acting by city authorities could be checked. And Burbage had a plan to check them. It was this—*to build the new playhouse in the city, but in a place where the authorities would have no power over it.*

How could that be done?

Surprisingly, there was a way. Before the time of King Henry VIII there had been various parts of London on which church schools or monasteries stood. These were governed directly by the King. No city constable could enter them, and no city law applied there. When Henry took over all the church properties and abolished all "colleges" and monasteries, he kept his legal control over the lands they had occupied. Such areas, called "liberties" (because free from city rule), were scattered throughout London. Burbage proposed to put up a playhouse on one of these.

In the year 1576 he did. There were "liberties" within the London walls, but either land and buildings there were expensive, or no site was available at the time. But in Shoreditch, only a short walk from the wall, there was some empty land in the Liberty of Holywell. Burbage leased a plot of it from one Giles Alleyn for twenty-one years, with the privilege, if he met certain conditions, of using it for ten years longer. Now he needed nothing but the money to build his playhouse.

He had some resources of his own, and he got the rest of what he needed from a brother-in-law, John Braynes. Braynes was a grocer, and a prosperous one. He seems to have gone a little mad about this first of playhouses. It cost far more than Burbage had expected (£700, all told, or about $50,000 in money values of today). Braynes kept digging into his savings, and finally sold his business to help pay for the theater. Not long afterwards he died. There was to be a lively sequel to this pathetic story. For that matter, an exciting situation would also develop as a result of the lease Burbage had signed with wily Giles Alleyn. Will Shakespeare, as will be seen in time, was to find himself in the middle of that. But for the present we can concern ourselves with the building that Burbage finally completed, and opened in the fall of 1576.

It was a great event in the story of the English drama. Never before had a playhouse been erected solely for the giving of public plays. In a sense, no real playhouse had ever been built at all, for the Court plays were given in halls designed and constructed long before the drama had taken on high popularity or definite form in England. And Burbage made a playhouse that really served the players. As an actor himself, as one who had observed what the Court entertainments could contribute, he had some sound ideas. The result was the structure we have already seen through Will Shakespeare's eyes as he sat waiting for *Tamburlaine* to begin. It had certain features taken from the morality plays and the inn courtyards. It made provision for the use of stage effects Burbage had seen managed at Court productions. It was better in some ways than our theaters of today—in bringing the audience close to the stage and players, for instance, and in providing for swift changes of scenes through its outer, inner and upper stages. Naturally its capacity exceeded those of the innyards—perhaps quadrupled some of them. Appropriately, Burbage named this player's dream-come-true "The Theatre." For a time, indeed, it was the only one.

The first of true playhouses was a kind of paradise for actors and playwrights alike. It gave them both resources they had never before possessed, and they used it to send the drama in England forward and upward by tremendous leaps. In a short time another playhouse, the Curtain, pushed up not far from the Theatre. In 1587, as we have seen, the Rose, a third one, had risen in the Bankside across the river. By his vision and energy Burbage in ten years had changed the whole character of play producing in England. As time was to prove, he had to some extent changed it throughout the world.

And now we come to the second man who had helped to make London drama what it was when Will Shakespeare first saw it in the Theatre.

4

In the early summer of the year 1587, a young man only a few months older than Will Shakespeare unpacked his clothes and books in a Shoreditch room. He was no stranger to London. Probably he had seen the city half a dozen times before, and had acquaintances there. But now he had the air of one who had come to stay, and his arrival marked a break with his past life.

We don't know what he looked like; but we do know that he could use a sword expertly, that he had a kind of hawk's daring about him, which made him suave with his superiors and often "you-be-hanged-then" with his equals. Over a cup of wine in a tavern he could dispute with brilliance, startling his companions with audacious questions and bursts of disdainful eloquence.

Christopher Marlowe's father was a tradesman, like Will Shakespeare's. He was a shoemaker. That is, he was a merchant who made and sold shoes, and not one who repaired them, although his apprentices probably did that, too. Young Marlowe was more fortunate in his education than Shakespeare. He was born in Canterbury, and there he was able to attend the King's School. From this he was sent to Cambridge University on a scholarship provided by a former archbishop. He was to study there for the ministry.

Long before he had won his Bachelor of Arts degree in 1584, Christopher Marlowe in his own mind had probably said good-by to preaching. In fact, he seems never to have applied himself with much fervor to his studies. Probably he slipped away from the rather grim routine of the university as often as he could, and explored towns and taverns. But there is evidence that he ransacked the university library for books on philosophy and divinity that set forth intricate and even heretical opinions, read history, and pored over maps where seas and cities bore exotic, mouth-filling names. And like Will Shakespeare, he feasted on the rhythm and color of Ovid and Virgil.

In Cambridge he took part in plays aplenty, Latin and probably English. All students were obliged to do so. There, too, he found that he could fashion verse with a roll and ring to it. Probably it was here that he shaped, with his friend Thomas Nashe, most of a tragedy called *Dido,* the story of which the two students found in *The Aeneid.*

At the university Marlowe met the sons of gentlemen and noblemen, and it was possibly through one of these, such as Robert Cecil, son. of Lord Burghley, the Lord Treasurer of England, that he made a contact with officials in the government. He didn't leave Cambridge after taking his B.A. Despite his rather poor record as a scholar, he managed in a very Marlowe-like fashion to stay on, still keeping his scholarship, as a candidate for a Master of Arts—a high distinction in those days. Perhaps the government officials spoke a discreet word at Canterbury, for by this time he seems to have been working for them as an agent. He may even have gone to Rheims, where English youth of "Romish" faith were being prepared at the Catholic Seminary for secret activities in England against their queen. In 1587, when he came up for his Master's degree, there were rumors that he had been there, and meant to return.

Such charges, if proved, would have been sufficient in themselves to deny him his M.A. Apparently the sedate authorities didn't favor Marlowe anyway. He had been absent much, and his one excellence as a student seems to have been brilliance in scholastic disputes. At any rate, the stern dons decided that he was no fit candidate for Master. Then, like a thunderclap, a letter was brought to them from London.

It was from the Queen's Privy Council. Their lordships, the members of that body, touched on the Rheims rumor, and denied that Christopher Marlowe had the intent to go there and remain (they didn't say he had not been there). And they continued:

"Their Lordships request that the rumor thereof be allayed, and that he be furthered in the degree he was to take this next Commencement; because it was not Her Majesty's pleasure that any one employed as he had been in matters touching the benefit of his Country should be defamed by those that are ignorant in the affairs he went about."

The officials stared at each other, and reversed their decision. Christopher Marlowe left Cambridge for London as a Master of Arts.

Marlowe had possibly become acquainted with one or more of the player-companies on earlier visits to the city. If he had not, we can be sure that he managed an introduction of the most favorable kind. He had gentlemen friends, and even noble ones, in the capital. And once introduced, he could dangle himself before the chief man of any troupe in an attractive fashion. He came hot from the university with two degrees. He had acted and written. Perhaps he had a manuscript ready. In any event, he would have presented his case in the best and most confident manner. And soon he put the sheets of *Tamburlaine* into Edward Alleyn's hands.

We have seen what came about as a result; let us consider what it was exactly that Marlowe had done to make this play stand above all others that had gone before it like an oak among hazel scrub.

As we have seen, English plays about great kings had already been written. *Gorboduc* was such a play—a "tragedy" about an ancient British ruler. So was *Cambyses*. Why was *Tamburlaine* so immensely superior to them?

This question leads us first of all to the English audiences of the day. A playwright must please the particular audience he writes for. We shall see later how profoundly this fact affected Shakespeare's plays.

In 1587 Marlowe saw clearly that his audience wanted a certain amount of instruction. Plays from the miracles and moralities down had given information to those who saw them. People expected and valued it. Most of them could read little or not at all, and drama supplied them with "intelligence—" with facts and "features" such as we of today get from newsreels, documentary radio programs, magazines, and books of biography, history, and current problems.

However, as Marlowe saw also, they wanted their information in an exciting and unusual form. They were eager for news of far countries, past or present. They liked astounding events. Indeed, they liked the most extreme violence or horror. They themselves had hard lives; they came in throngs to see actual hangings and beheadings; and they enjoyed watching in their plays such piled-up brutalities and slaughters as would send modern audiences from the theater shuddering.

In *Tamburlaine* Marlowe gave his audience what it wanted. He led them to the East—that mysterious region of which they still thought America was a part and of which they were all talking. He told them the story of a man as ill-born as the lowliest of them who had toppled kingdoms and used sultans for footstools. He brought to the stage the thrill of coronations, the clash of swords, the jingle of treasure, and magnificent orations on the glories of power. His theme and episodes were "naturals" for the crowd he aimed to please.

He accomplished another important thing. He wrote a play without using a Greek or Roman model. To be sure, he scattered references to ancient gods and heroes throughout his drama, but this was ornamental. The general tone of *Tamburlaine* also owes something to the rhetoric of Seneca, who had already influenced Elizabethan writers. His use of murders and ghosts had a decided effect on Kyd, and later on Shakespeare. But Marlowe's job of playwriting was an English job, designed to tell a story to Englishmen, and, incidentally, one that would lift them out of their seats with excitement. Marlowe wasn't worried about how Sophocles or Seneca would have worked. He worked in his own way.

In addition, he made a better play in structure than anyone in England had made. That was not saying too much. English writers had talked of comedies and tragedies, but they had rather vague ideas of how the ancients had constructed either, and were uncertain as to how to proceed themselves. Their characters were weak, and their stories were not built around strong central themes that aroused and held high interest. They usually wandered through a succession of poorly related scenes, which the audience enjoyed, each for itself—and because they had known nothing better.

Tamburlaine was not a triumph of dramatic architecture. For instance, it did not have a story that showed a character changing because of what happened to him, or because of the way in which other characters affected him. Tamburlaine was a conqueror from the start, and kept on being one. His conquests didn't change him as a person. In fact, Marlowe really wrote a kind of pageant about his hero, a succession of vivid scenes. But he did make a great character, he did give a central theme (that of world conquest), and he did contrive his scenes so that each was exciting and so that each kept the audience waiting for the next step in a continuing story. No previous English play had taken one magnificent idea (magnificent at least to the Elizabethans) and pounded it home so that it would work in men's imagination months after they had left the playhouse.

All these accomplishments were important. Yet perhaps the most important accomplishment of all was the new way in which Marlowe used the English language. Most plays up to Elizabeth's time had been written in rhyme. The authors of *Gorboduc,* who were familiar with the unrhymed poetry of the Romans, made a drama in what we now call blank verse. It was a new thing, and considerably talked about, but the verse was heavy and wooden. Each line was a unit in itself ("end-stopped" such are called), and the speeches didn't flow. What succeeding writers did with it in plays like *Cambyses* and *The Misfortunes of Arthur* showed little advance over the bad model from which they worked.

In *Tamburlaine* Marlowe took this cold poetry and put fire into it. He still used the end-stopped line to a large extent, but he made it natural. And occasionally he ran the sense of one line over into the

next, and broke the monotony of the pattern. But chiefly he showed
the beauty and power that could be packed into this unrhymed verse.
He used alliteration and full vowels, sharp consonants and brilliant
pictorial images. Perhaps this is merely saying that he was a great
poet. But in any event his lines startled, jabbed, soared and thundered.

To pull the tripled-headed dog from hell—

that matched in sound the daring and violence of the image it called
up.
        The wondrous architecture of the world—

that gave sweep to the imagination.

And ride in triumph through Persepolis—

that line painted a picture that has lasted more than 360 years, and
still holds its magic. No one, not Shakespeare or Milton, has put more
power and color into blank verse. Ben Jonson named this poetry as
"Marlowe's mighty line," and the phrase fits well.

Marlowe didn't wreck his drama in order to write such verse. He
fitted the resounding poetry deftly into the action. There were more
patches of solid verse than we would like in a drama today, but the
Elizabethan audiences enjoyed those. They savored them as we do
an aria in opera. The actor stood close to them. They could watch his
play of expression and hear every word. They understood the music
of spoken speech. A well-rounded and finely written soliloquy in verse
was sure to win thunderous applause.

Finally, what Marlowe did with his lines was partly an expression
of what he was. The impatient, arrogant, ambitious youth put his
own limitless aspiration into both his play-ideas and the texture of
his poetry. He was to write more plays. All had this spirit of beating
against the very limits of life as if to burst them. Most of his heroes
launched themselves on amazing enterprises, and the leap of their
great spirits put life into their speeches. All in all, Marlowe remade
and recharged English drama. Had he lived longer, he might have
towered beside the few great world writers known to men in all lands.

The work that Marlowe had done was the most glorious and important that Shakespeare found when he came to London. But other writers, too, were already doing much to lift the level of playmaking.

Thomas Kyd, with only a school education, had written *The Spanish Tragedy* about the same time, or a little before, Marlowe wrote *Tamburlaine*. Other university men like Robert Greene and Thomas Nashe had come up to London before or with Marlowe, and were writing better than the playwrights of the fifteen-sixties and -seventies. One of these "university wits," as the group came to be called, was making a special place for himself as a writer for and a director of the choir boys.

But we shall know these men better as we turn again to Will Shakespeare and his first years in London.

IX: PLAYMAKER

THE first months in his Shoreditch lodgings in the winter and spring of 1589 were not easy ones for Will Shakespeare. He was rehearsing and playing by day and sometimes recasting old plays by night. He had been doing such repair work for more than a year. He knew more surely now than he had at first how to make over an outdated or poorly written play. Still, he sometimes found himself weary and disgusted as he bent toward a shortening candle, poring over some dull drama which he was supposed to bring to life.

"Before heaven," he would mutter, "why do I sit mending this offense to the name of writing? With little more labor I could scratch out something of mine own that would do us greater credit!"

We do not know exactly what were these first tasks of the "hired man" of the company. Most of the plays he patched were doubtless undistinguished. They would never have been printed even if it had been the custom of the player-companies to give out their scripts for publication. And it was not. Manuscripts of plays were guarded carefully. No formal copyright existed in that day; once printed, a play was his who published it.

Many *were* printed. Those done by the boy players often came out in book form promptly, perhaps because they were poorly suited to adult companies and were protected to an extent by the sponsorship of the Queen. Others, like *Tamburlaine,* got into print because they were immensely popular. A printer would gladly pay an actor who knew most of the lines of others as well as his own to provide from memory the best text that he could. Or the play might be taken down at the theater itself by the new shorthand that was now being developed. But nobody cared about the less popular dramas which Will had been patching up during his first year and a half with the troupe.

Up to this time he had written nothing of his own. Partly this was because he had been busy with his double tasks, both new to him. Partly it was because he was learning much from the revisions he was making. After all, these faulty scripts had once been used by players. And from Kemp and Bryan he was discovering what virtues they had, and what might be done to make these greater, and to supply others. Then he could see how his tinkering proved up in practice. Such experience tended to make him hold off from attempting a new and wholly original play. When he had digested what he was learning, he would be surer of what he could do.

In a similar fashion, if he had brought a play or two with him from Stratford, he was willing to let those lie untouched for a while. Possibly he had a crude draft of what was later *The Comedy of Errors.* He saw that the longer he waited the better he could recast such pieces.

Meanwhile he was profiting as much from the rehearsals and the actual playing of plays as from his rewriting. He was even learning unsuspected things about his own appearance and talents. He had always fancied himself to be a lively enough fellow, but it was not long after he joined the troupe that it became clear that Kemp had a somewhat different notion about him. The third time the comedian had cast him for an oldish, distinguished part, Will had shown his surprise.

Kemp had given him a quizzical look.

"Is it not a worthy part?" he asked. "A gentleman of the king's housetold?"

"Aye—but 'tis an oldish and solemn fellow—"

"And your fancy runs to this witty rake, perhaps, or the young soldier just back from cutting throats?"

"I could do either, being young, and I hope a fellow of some spirit."

"Aye," chuckled Kemp, "so you think, Will—and I know you are young enough and have a lively way of talking when once engaged. But could you look at yourself, you'd see one that stalks about with an air of meditation and most quiet wisdom. By heaven, I think an owl flew about the house all the night thou wast being born!"

So they had given him parts where dignity was wanted—town officials, fathers, even kings, and swore that he suited them famously. Well, he had smiled wryly to himself, if he fitted into a niche in this temple of acting, so much the better. After all, he was a novice still.

As Will Shakespeare settled into the routine of his London work there were two other activities which tended to postpone the time for attempting something wholly his own.

One was the impact of literary London upon him. There were the books, for instance. He had looked at these wistfully in 1587, fingering a slender purse. By 1589 that purse was heavier. His facility and talent had brought him a better if still humble position in the company as an actor, and special payments for his writing. He had something now to spend at the bookstalls. From Field he could borrow much that he could not buy.

He read verse. The greater poetry of the age was still to appear, but there were collections and individual volumes that he had not seen. There were also books of prose that greatly interested him. Field published Puttenham's *Art of English Poesy* in 1589. Will probably read it in manuscript. Later he quoted from it often in his plays. If he were not already acquainted before leaving Stratford with John Lyly's romance *Euphues,* first published in 1578, he read it now, along with its sequel, *Euphues in England.* And he read a number of the long prose stories written in imitation of Lyly's, particularly Robert Greene's and Thomas Lodge's. One of Greene's romances, *Pandosto,* was later to provide Will with the plot for a play, as we shall see; and Lodge's *Rosalinde* (not published until 1590) would do as much for him.

Quite as important as the books themselves were their authors. Many of them wrote plays, and so were to be seen about the playhouses, or in the taverns where the players dined and talked. There, too, came noblemen interested in writing and the drama—Sir Walter Raleigh, the Earl of Oxford, the young Earl of Southampton, not yet seventeen, and as handsome as a painter's dream of the spirit of chivalric beauty. Such men were often hosts to players and writers, as were lawyers and law students from the Inns of Court and Chancery.

I have said that London was a city of modest size, as we of the twentieth century know cities. It was smaller still as the home of well-educated men of artistic interests. There were only a few thousands of these, and only a few dozen of them were writers. Coming into this circle, Will Shakespeare soon made acquaintances—John Lyly or Christopher Marlowe, perhaps—Thomas Kyd, Thomas Lodge, Thomas Nashe, and many other "wits" who were bombarding the printers and players with their writings. The stimulus Shakespeare would get from these men was to be great.

Take John Lyly, for instance. An Oxford graduate, he had been one of the first of this crop of talented writers to try his fortunes in London. He came of a family of scholars: his grandfather had compiled the Latin Grammar which Will Shakespeare and all schoolboys of the day had studied. More, he had a helpful friend in Lord Burghley. In 1580, perhaps on the fame of *Euphues,* and perhaps with Burghley's help, he became secretary to the latter's son-in-law, the Earl of Oxford. He wrote several plays which were highly successful, and won the post of Assistant Master at St. Paul's Choir School, where he helped to train boy players, and wrote comedies for them.

In the literary world Lyly by 1589 had a fame that was almost fabulous. It had begun with *Euphues*. What was this romance which still had a best-seller brilliance (and a greater influence) after eleven years?

Its style had been the making of it. Lyly had not invented this, but had perfected and temporarily deified it. In general, the sentences were long, deftly planned, with balanced clauses and contrasting metaphors or similies, with alliterations and ingenious plays upon words. To take an example:

Such is the nature of these novices that think to have learning without labor and treasure without travail, either not understanding, or else not remembering, that the finest edge is made with the blunt whetstone and the fairest jewel fashioned with the hard hammer.

This specimen is a relatively short one. Lyly often spun sentences thrice its length, with fearsomely intricate patterns, profusely decorated with references to classic literature and history. Any modern reader who dares to attempt such literature needs courage. However, once used to its mannered phrasing, such a reader can get a certain pleasure from Lyly's work, and can imagine why Elizabethans enjoyed and praised it.

Enjoyed? They reveled in it. It became the fashion in talk as well as in writing. "That beauty in court which could not parley Euphuism," wrote an editor forty years later, "was as little regarded as she which now there speaks not French." To be sure, some sensible persons saw the ridiculous side of the style. Shakespeare later parodied it. But it affected him, too; its impress is on many of his plays. Even today the Lyly touch is enshrined in our word "euphuism," which means an elaborate, "high-flown" way of saying something.

Lyly wrote more plays than romances. When Will Shakespeare arrived in London *The Woman in the Moon, Sapho and Phao,* and *Alexander and Campaspe,* all by the author of *Euphues,* had already appeared on the stage, and the latter two in print. They really started an upward movement in English drama before Marlowe began his greater work. However, Lyly wrote for boys and liked the light and elegant rather than the tragic and powerful note. Therefore he worked in the field of comedy.

Here he had created something different from the clowning and slapstick farce of the moralities, or the early plays based on the classics. He took classical or historical characters—gods and kings, courtiers and artists—and wove glamorous stories about them. The result was an elaborate, fashionable, witty type of entertainment. Servants or other humble persons were brought in to give a contrast to the high-born characters and provide spots of rollicking humor. Lyly could also write graceful lyrics. He used these effectively. In *Alexander and Campaspe* we meet Apelles, the artist; Plato; Alexander; Diogenes, the brusque philosopher. After listening to their polished phrases for a while, and following the love of both Alexander and Apelles for Campaspe, we come to the end of the third act with the servants singing a jovial song:

GRANICHUS (Servant to Plato)
> O for a bowl of fat Canary!
> Rich Palermo! Sparkling sherry!
> Some nectar, else, from Juno's dairy!
> O, these draughts would make us merry!

PSYLLUS (Servant to Apelles)
> O, for a wench! I deal in faces,
> And in other daintier things.
> Tickled am I with her embraces—
> Fine dancing in such fairy rings.

MANES (Servant to Diogenes)
> O for a plump, fat leg of mutton!
> Veal, lamb, capon, pig and coney! [1]
> None is happy but a glutton,
> None an ass who wants but money.

[1] Rabbit. It was used not only for the animal itself, but also as a term of endearment, like the modern "bunny."

CHORUS

> Wines, indeed, and girls are good,
> But brave victuals feast the blood.
> For wenches, wine and lusty cheer
> Jove would leap down to surfeit here!

Sung by boy actors trained to the finest pitch, such a curtain would bring prolonged applause from the ladies and gentlemen of the Court, and give a dash of earthy relief after the patterned speeches of the nobler characters. Lyly's comedy seemed to make the theater a kind of fashionable fairyland, with great ones of antiquity or fable speaking with Euphuistic wit, with the clowns supplying a touch of farce, and the whole wound up in and finished off with the charm of song.

2

Will rose from his table, lit by two tallow candles, when he heard the footsteps on the stairs. He recognized them, and as he opened the door the smiling face of Dick Field loomed out of the dark before him.

"Ha!" cried the young printer. "Wearing your eyes out in double duty, as I've found you doing before!" He sat down on the bed and shook a book at his friend.

"Let those same eyes feast on this," he admonished. "I got it from the printer himself, one who trades wares with me, and owed me something. You will say the writer has outdone himself."

Will took the book.

"*The Faerie Queene*," he read. "Why, it is by the author of *The Shephearde's Calendar*. And a sweet note that same Edmund Spenser has."

"This is another and higher flight than his first, as you will discover," said Field. "Keep it awhile. I shall not have the leisure to look at it soon. Never in our trade was there such a fury of getting out books as in this year of our Lord 1590."

"Why, there were never before so many in England with the schooling to read them, Dick; and more are coming from the schools every year."

"Aye," Field agreed. "Learning multiplies, and every apprentice is eager for a new pamphlet or ballad or book—if he can buy or borrow it. Yes, this passion for knowing has come sweeping in like the plague (but without the sting of death, thank God). Well," he broke off, "what task holds you this night? An old thing to be made new?"

"No," the other replied, "I am on a venture of my own. There is an occasion for some light yet courtly play, and I have promised to fashion it."

"And time you should," said the other. "Have you not mended and acted in plays these more than two years? And written such sonnets as put all others to shame—though you will not let them be passed about?"

"Well, I have been prodding myself to attempt something for this year past," answered the other, "though, despite your good words, I rank not my sonnets with some of Sir Philip Sidney's that I have seen in private copies."

"They soar high," conceded Field, "yet you match them, and will outfly them. But come," he demanded, "what's the story you work with?"

"Why, in brief, one of a certain King of Navarre and his courtiers, who swore to shun women wholly and follow the ways of study, meditation and lofty discourse for three years; yet find love stronger than their vows."

"A pretty tale," assented Field. "And so love wins over all?"

"Why, in a sense, Dick, it does. Yet I think to call the play *Love's Labor's Lost.*"

"And whyfor?"

"Because though the gentlemen end up forsworn, I leave them still waiting for the favor of their ladies."

Field looked at his friend quizzically.

"I know not what to make of you," he sighed. "This last year I have been hearing little but Marlowe, Marlowe. Yet the first thing you set your hand to is a comedy."

Shakespeare smiled.

"'Nay, though I praise it, I can live without it,'" he quoted from *Tamburlaine*. "Why, Dick, I admire Kit the firemaker and thunderer —and sweet singer too—as much as ever, but it was not Marlowe that was wanted. The occasion I spoke of demands something both lively and elegant. And there John Lyly has better shown the way."

"I like not his tortured fashion of writing," protested Field. "This elaborate balancing of phrases and figures like so many juggler's balls —where is the profit? And for the playhouse, why prose? Plays have ever come in verse."

"They have," nodded Shakespeare, "yet perhaps too much. Master Lyly may have shown us a thing there. And his turns of speech are neat—and less tedious in his plays than in his romances. But, Dick, he has a lightness and grace that pleases, and he makes a good song. And he writes prettily of love, which our playmakers have too much neglected. Though in that and other things I aim to better what he has done."

"By putting more iron in it?"

"In a fashion. His stories are light and languid. But mostly his fault lies in thinking too much of the manner of his characters' speech, and in not feeling enough what they are. His men and maids are of wood or painted cloth. Mine, if I can make them, shall be of living flesh. You shall remember them, be they fools or scoffing gallants or witty wantons—or— But you shall soon see. And I have a song or two—"

"Let's hear the song!"

Shakespeare shuffled among the sheets on the table.

"Well, here's a thing you may fancy." He picked up a page and read—

> "When daisies pied and violets blue
> And lady-smocks all silver-white
> And cuckoo-buds of yellow hue
> Do paint the meadows with delight—"[2]

[2] *Love's Labor's Lost*, V. ii. 904–907.

"Ha!" broke in Field. "Stratford in spring, to the life! 'Do paint the meadows with delight!' A fine turn that! Read on!"

"You invite it and shall have it," laughed his friend. "There are four songs of the seasons and once finished with them you shall not escape hearing more unless you flee. Thus *my* labor shall not be lost— having one listener, at least!"

3

So Will was fashioning a play of his own at last. And considering his purpose and his brief experience with the stage, it was a good play. It had, when finished, elegance and wit. Along with these qualities went another of greater importance—notable writing. The writing showed that other creators had influenced the young playwright. Oddly enough (since the theme was one of gaiety rather than power), the imprint of Marlowe was visible. In the opening speech of the king to his nobles, for instance:

> Let fame, that all hunt after in their lives,
> Live registered upon our brazen tombs,
> And then grace us in the disgrace of death;
> When, 'spite of cormorant devouring time,
> The endeavor of this present breath may buy
> That honor which shall bate his scythe's keen edge,
> And make us heirs of all eternity.

Very sonorous and rolling, that: clearly inspired by the "mighty line." In a similar fashion, the influence of John Lyly ran through the play, and especially in the prose scenes between comic characters. But the influence is a curious one to note, for it shows the pupil bettering the master. The Euphuistic touch is in *Love's Labor's Lost,* satirical at times, and livelier and sharper than in Lyly. It shapes more easily to the changing action and moods of the play. In addition, Shakespeare achieved more downright fun than the writer for choir boys.

Partly he did so by shaping comic characters that were more real

than any Lyly had created. There was the ridiculous Don Armado—
a preposterous fellow, yet the more laughable for being believable.
There was the sprightly Moth, a new kind of comic entirely; and there
were Costard and Dull and Jaquenetta. All were persons as well as
laugh provokers. The more serious characters had the same quality of
realness. The jesting Berowne and the sharp-tongued Rosaline—they
were alike, yet how individual! And how naturally they changed from
witty show-offs to man and woman of deeper feeling. Here, in his first
play, Shakespeare had shown the ability to create men and women
of all types as neither Marlowe nor any other writer of that day could
create.

Love's Labor's Lost showed a poet as well as a creator of character.
In this piece, to be seen and heard by a finer audience than went to
the Theatre or the Curtain, Will had cut loose with literary capers. A
number of times he wedged whole sonnets into his dialogue; often he
rhymed in neat patterns. This was suitable for ladies and gentlemen,
many of them learned, and it revealed an easy master of verse and
form.

Finally, he had made the love of men and women more important
and natural in this play than it had ever been made before. Love had
appeared in other plays—Robert Greene had already written of it vividly, and Marlowe had used it effectively in the second part of *Tamburlaine*. Lyly's *Alexander and Campaspe* was essentially a love story. But
the fashion had long been to subordinate love to other desires—that
for power or revenge, for instance. As for Lyly, his love story was a
bird pent in the gilded cage of his mannered writing. In *Love's Labor's
Lost,* love was the proclaimed theme, and dominated and filled the
play. It had an artificial quality, it was not great love, but it was taken
for granted as important and natural. It was also a step toward the
greater love stories that Shakespeare would later write.

In short, the play revealed a strong new writer. A writer of fine
craftsmanship in prose or verse. One who could create characters as
few, if any in England, had done. One who could write gravely or
with gay eloquence, or at the slapstick level—for there is slapstick in

the play that Kemp must have loved, and done famously well.

A great play, then? No. A better play for its purpose than it reads or acts now, a play with fine writing and comedy, but not a great one. Even Shakespeare must have known that it was not well built, for instance. The talk often clogged the action. The plot, apparently the only one Shakespeare ever shaped chiefly by himself, was not distinguished. Nor was it well managed. A few years later Will would have done much better with it. Marlowe, with his well-imagined heroes and clear themes, was still a superior dramatist. His *Tragical History of Doctor Faustus,* which had appeared in 1589, held audiences breathless with the picture of a man deliberately selling his soul for pleasure and power, and moving through fascinating adventures to his horrible final doom.

Marlowe was still the leader in the movement to create new dramatic forms. But Will Shakespeare had joined him, and soon would take over the role of pioneer. He would shake wholly free of the moralities and the imitations of the plays of the ancients (not well understood, as yet, anyway). He would make comedies and tragedies for England that would match those of any age.

4

Let us leave Will Shakespeare at the beginning of this prodigious task. And while My Lord Strange's Men play this witty and berhymed comedy of *Love's Labor's Lost* before the Queen and her ladies and gentlemen (for they were probably the first audience, and certainly heard it later), let us turn back to the playhouse and the actors. Both had helped to teach Shakespeare how to fashion his first original drama.

The playhouse was still the Theatre—Burbage's Theatre. And in this playhouse James Burbage and his sons were all-important men. From a practical point of view, and indirectly from an artistic one, they were important to Will Shakespeare.

We have already met James Burbage of the fifteen-seventies. In 1590 he was older by fourteen years than when he made his dream of a special house for drama come true. He was no longer acting; he helped to manage the Theatre and had a part interest in the Curtain. For the present he is of less importance to us than are his two sons.

There was Cuthbert, who may have acted for a time, but now was serving as his father's business agent. He was a lively, even pugnacious fellow. And there was Richard, only nineteen at this time, but already a player of promise. For him, in years to come, Shakespeare would write many of his greatest roles.

The Burbages seem never to have been meant to lead quiet lives. Long before Will arrived in London they had been in difficulties with the widow of John Braynes, the grocer who had poured his cash and his very grocery shop into the walls and stage of the Theatre.

Braynes had disputed with Burbage over the use of the first moneys that were taken in. He demanded that he should have these until at least a considerable portion of his outlay was repaid. Burbage objected; he wished to pay some outstanding debts first. This dispute was settled, but the partners continued to have trouble. What they took in was not enough to meet expenses and improvements (and doubtless support their two families). They were forced to mortgage the Theatre to a certain John Hide. Then they failed to keep up payments to him, and Hide got title to the property. There was a clause that protected Burbage and Braynes in the use of the playhouse, but the situation was difficult.

When Braynes died in 1586 Hide was desperately eager for his money. Burbage now made him a proposal. Hide would be paid from the gate receipts of the playhouse, but when his debt was discharged he should make over the title of the building to Cuthbert Burbage. Mrs. Braynes promptly made Hide the same proposal, except that the title should come to *her*.

Hide refused both offers.

"No," he said. "You did jointly mortgage it to me and I must assign it back to you jointly."

This suited neither. Finally, in 1589 Hide decided to end the waiting.

"I have forborne my money so long," he declared, "that I can do it no more. They that come first shall have the title of me."

Cuthbert Burbage got to Hide with the money first, and took the title. In possession, he and his father, who in the past had permitted the Widow Braynes to take money at times and to keep some of it, now declared that she must stay clear of the building.

She promptly sued them, claiming her joint rights. This was the state of affairs at the time Will was finishing *Love's Labor's Lost*. Indeed, he may have been at Burbage's house (may even have had a room there) one night in November, 1590, when one Robert Myles, a lawyer acting for the widow, knocked loudly on the door.

Cuthbert Burbage came out. Myles shook a paper at him.

"Master Burbage, I hold here an order from the Court of Chancery, and demand my client's moiety in the playhouse."

"Begone," answered Cuthbert. "Talk nothing to me of moieties."

"It is hers by law and I will have it for her."

At this point James Burbage came to the door. The quarrel waxed hotter, and the Burbages threatened to beat the lawyer off their property.

Myles retired, but came back another night with Mrs. Braynes. But Mrs. Burbage met them and stood them off, while James Burbage thrust his head out the window and called them rascals and knaves.

"I have an order of the court," cried Mrs. Braynes.

"Go, go!" shouted Burbage. "I will obey no such order, and you had best be packing betimes, for if my son come he will thump you hence!"

And about that time Cuthbert did appear, and drove the two off—though he thumped only with words.

Yet it came to blows at last. Myles and his son and a friend appeared at the Theatre and tried to collect money, and young Richard Burbage seized a broomstick and beat Myles. He tweaked the nose of Myles's friend and drove all three away. Just then John Alleyn entered the building (the brother of the noted Edward), for he was acting with the company. Probably Will Shakespeare and others came up, too.

Alleyn asked what the noise was about and Richard Burbage laughed.

"Why, it was Myles," he answered, "the brainless lawyer of the Brayneses. He came for a moiety, but—" and he shook the broom staff, "I have, I think, delivered him a moiety with this."

"He can bring action of assault and battery against you," Alleyn warned him.

James Burbage had joined the group.

"Tush, no!" he exclaimed. "But where Dick hath now beat him and his hinds hence, he and Cuthbert, if they be ruled by me, shall at their next coming provide pistols, charged with powder and hemp-seed, and pepper their legs with the same!"

Thus Will was getting a look at the business side of the theater! But he was also making friends among the actors of the company. George Bryan and Thomas Pope had joined it late in 1588; Augustine Phillips was probably a member already, with John Heminges. About this time or a little later came Christopher Beeston and Henry Condell. All these men were to call Shakespeare their "fellow." They were associated with him in a kind of professional brotherhood. Year after year he and they rehearsed and dined together. They shared, not all equally, in the profits of their work. They walked or rode out into the country that lay almost at their doors. With some of these men, as with Field, Will talked of ideas for plays, or perhaps read scenes from some already begun. With the finishing of his first original play, he took a place of importance among them. He was not only actor and play mender now, but playmaker. Their fortune depended upon his busy pen. Soon he took a part in directing the rehearsals.

It was a little world—this world of the theater—with some resemblances to two worlds we know in our own day—those of the movies and of the radio. The theater into which Shakespeare came was, as we have seen, startlingly different from even that of 1576, when the first true playhouse rose. It was a grown-up theater now, and those who worked in it found grown-up problems. Like the script writers and directors and radio actors of the early nineteen-thirties, the writers and directors and actors of 1590 were experimenting.

Who in America or England in 1920 had heard of a radio announcer? Or a narrator? Who knew that a form called "the documentary" would be developed? Who foresaw the blueprint which a radio program now needs, with its jargon of terms for the use of director, engineer, musicians, sound effects men—"cross-fade," "project," "off mike," "echo chamber," "isolation booth," "segue," "sting," "filter"? Who discussed then if a drama should be narrated or written straight? All these forms and usages came into being as radio developed. Others like them are being developed today.

In 1590, in a similar fashion, the men of the theater were devising forms and techniques. They were using a "chorus," in some plays, to do much of what a radio or movie narrator does for us. They were discovering a special kind of drama which we call the chronicle play (strikingly like some of our motion pictures and radio programs, as we shall see). They were learning how to use music and scenery in new ways. They were experimenting with songs and soliloquies.

Their work was still in that exciting state where a drama was good if it succeeded. They had stopped worrying about the theories and works of the ancients, and were building English plays—plays that would win the crowd. Everything was changing, anything seemed possible. For each year brought a new thing—a kind of story never told before, a kind of character never played, a pattern or scene or acting different from any previously shown. This was Shakespeare's theater as he began his real work—young, dynamic, bursting with adventure and surprise.

X: "CUT IS THE BRANCH"

MEN have written in both prose and poetry of the two young giants who lived a stone's throw from each other on Hog Lane in Shoreditch through the four exciting years that began in 1589. Some have pictured the meteoric Marlowe and the more meditative Shakespeare reading and praising each other's poems, and building at least one drama together.

It is a possible picture. Clearly, Shakespeare saw, read, admired Marlowe's work. The two may have collaborated in the writing of *King Henry VI, I* and *II;* this was long the belief of most scholars, although the latest theory gives the author of *Tamburlaine* little or no part in these plays.

What seems certain is that with only a small group of writers frequenting the few playhouses of London in that day, such men could hardly have escaped meeting. Probably they sat together in one or the other's room, with well-thumbed books and the sheets of unfinished plays or poems about them. Perhaps the hawklike Marlowe, a little patronizing with his M.A. and his fabulous successes, praised the beginner's first play.

"It has a style, Will, and is smoothly wrought," he may have said. "You have a sure touch with words, a nice ear for meter and rhyme."

And as they talked, he may have confided his ambition to write something more enduring and lofty than plays. Both young men knew that drama was not then regarded as true literature.

"By heaven, Will, I hold myself as fit to climb Parnassus as Spenser or even Sidney, and I will yet forge a poem that shall prove it."

And if they sat in his chambers, he may have snatched up some sheets and read from a verse romance which he was composing about the ancient lovers, Hero and Leander. A passage, perhaps, like this—

> It lies not in our power to love, or hate,
> For will in us is overruled by Fate,
> When two are stript long ere the course begin,
> We wish that one shall lose, the other win;
> And one especially do we affect
> Of two gold ingots like in each respect.
> The reason no man know; let it suffice,
> What we behold is censured by our eyes.
> Where both deliberate, the love is slight,
> Who ever loved, that loved not at first sight?

That last famous line was known to Shakespeare; later he quoted it as a kind of salute to its author. And if Will heard it eight or nine years earlier from Marlowe's own lips, he himself may then have confessed to Kit that he too had partly shaped a poem—a story of the love of the goddess Venus for the boy Adonis. Should the time come when he would have leisure to finish it—

But such meetings are only possibilities. It may be they never occurred. Marlowe talked and dined with Sir Walter Raleigh and his friends, where he made much bold talk about the Scriptures, and about faith in general. He smoked a pipe, declaring that "all they that love not tobacco" were fools. He kept up a mysterious contact with the government, frequented taverns between bouts of furious writing, and in 1592 was briefly in danger of his life for his part in swordplay that began at the northern end of the same Hog Lane where both he and Shakespeare then lodged. One William Bradley and he fought there for some minutes, until Marlowe's friend Thomas Watson arrived. He took over, and made an end to Bradley, apparently a quarrelsome fellow. Arrested for murder, the two friends got off, Watson pleading self-defense.

Shakespeare, on the other hand, seems then and later to have had very different habits. Christopher Beeston told his son William, who passed the information on to Aubrey in the late sixteen-hundreds, that the Stratford playmaker was "the more to be admired *quia* he was not a company-keeper; lived in Shoreditch; wouldn't be debauched; and if invited to, writ that he was in pain."

This quaint description etches for us a sober young man busy with several kinds of work, who found little time for frivolity. Shakespeare seems never to have smoked tobacco: he does not mention it once in the whole range of his writings. Again, he treated religion and religious men with unfailing respect. These are important points of difference between him and Marlowe. Perhaps he never had more than a casual acquaintance with the audacious, tavern-haunting creator of *Tamburlaine.*

2

In the year following the appearance of *Love's Labor's Lost,* Shakespeare was busy with a second drama of his own. He got the story for it from a romance, *Diana Enamorada,* written by a Spaniard, Jorge de Montemayor, or from a play based on this. He added to the plot of the original, and *The Two Gentlemen of Verona* came to birth.

In a number of respects it was a distinct advance over his first play.

There was no sign of Lyly or Marlowe influence in it. The plot was a better one for a popular audience of the day. It told a love story, but without the elegant affectation of *Love's Labor's Lost*. Julia, the heroine, who went disguised as a boy to the Court to follow her lover, Proteus, was created with charm, humor, and moving sympathy. The unhappy Proteus, who forgot her to seek the favor of his friend Valentine's Silvia, brought about a situation that gave opportunity for a sharp and four-sided conflict. In two servants, Speed and Launce, Shakespeare again proved delightfully that he had a sure touch for comedy. Also, his writing throughout was smoother and easier than that of *Love's Labor's Lost*.

But in the management of his complicated plot he showed that he still had much to learn about the structure of a play. The beginning was slow and clumsy compared with his later work. The fickle Proteus was not quite believable, and the way in which he was suddenly reformed at the end worked out to be both awkward and unconvincing. Marlowe, moving on from *Faustus* to *The Jew of Malta, The Massacre at Paris,* and the finely planned and written *Edward II,* was still Will's superior in technique.

Indeed, in this final tragic story of a weak and unhappy king, Marlowe showed a deepening sense of character and a growing mastery of playmaking. Here he was no longer riding along on one towering hero tied to one brilliant idea. *Edward II* was no mere pageant of sensational scenes. It showed the interaction between a foolish monarch, his neglected queen, the king's favorites, and his angry nobles. There were at least four major characters, and their effect upon each other built both conflict and the tragic climax. This drama was a promise for Marlowe's future, and for the future of the English stage and its literature.

It was a promise never to be fulfilled. Marlowe was moving fast toward a situation and an event that would put an end to his writing.

He had made enemies. One was the arrogant scholar Gabriel Harvey. Son of a ropemaker, he was a proud and ambitious man, who apparently had clashed with Marlowe at Cambridge.

Another was the playwright and romancer Robert Greene. A man of high talent and prodigious energy, he wrecked himself early by dissipation. Marlowe's successes filled him with envy. He wrote imitations of *Tamburlaine* and *Doctor Faustus,* but they failed to match the originals in art or popularity. Greene took out his spite in biting pamphlets. The final one was written after he had reformed, shortly before his death. It was called *A Groatsworth of Wit Bought with a Million of Repentance.* In this he taunted Marlowe as "a cobbler's elder son," and denounced him as an atheist.

"Wonder not," he wrote, "thou famous gracer of Tragedians, that Greene, who hath said with thee, like the fool in his heart, 'There is no God,' should now give glory unto His greatness. . . . He hath spoken unto me with a voice of thunder, and I have felt He is a God that can punish enemies."

What Greene suggested was clear. Marlowe was not only *his* enemy, but God's as well. The author of *Faustus* had, indeed, been outspoken about religion. He had pointed out inconsistencies in the Scriptures. A government spy later reported him as saying, "He hath read the Atheist lecture to Sir Walter Raleigh and others." Men like Harvey and Greene were helping to spread the word about that he was an unbeliever. Their work would soon make trouble for him.

Greene's deathbed pamphlet, which was edited and published after his death by the printer Henry Chettle, gave a slash at Shakespeare as well as Marlowe. Greene warned his playwright associates—Marlowe, Nashe and Peele—to profit by and avoid his unhappy experiences. And, he added, let them beware of players.

"Base-minded men are all three of you, if by my misery ye be not warned; for unto none of you (like me) sought those burrs to cleave, those puppets (I mean) that spake from our mouths, those antics garnished in our colors. . . . Yes, trust them not. For there is an upstart Crow, beautified with our feathers, that with his *Tiger's heart wrapt in a Player's hide,* supposes he is as well able to bombast out a blank verse as the best of you, and being an absolute *Joannes Factotum,* is in his own conceit the only Shakescene in a country."

Unquestionably Greene refers to Shakespeare in this passage. He is warning his friends against players who seek to become writers, thus turning into rivals likely to do them harm. The phrase "Tiger's heart wrapt in a Player's hide" is adapted from "Tiger's heart wrapt in a woman's hide," in *Henry VI, Part III,* written mostly or wholly by Shakespeare, and probably produced in 1591 or early in 1592. The rest of what Greene wrote in the passage quoted above also applies well to the young actor-writer from Stratford. He was a player, he was known to have revised plays, and Greene had probably heard that he was helping to direct rehearsals. Thus he was a *Joannes Factotum,* or man who did everything. Finally, "Shakescene" is clearly a play on "Shakespeare."

The entire comment, written late in August or early in September of 1592, thus tells us that the varied activities of the young man from Stratford were well known to other writers. Greene was annoyed that a newcomer without university training could so soon take a promising place in his world. The dying man undoubtedly knew that Shakespeare had already written plays of his own, but disdained to speak of the upstart as more than an actor.

Greene's blast apparently brought remonstrances from both Marlowe's and Shakespeare's friends. In any case, Chettle printed in December of the same year a kind of apology for his own part in editing and issuing the pamphlet. His words appeared in *Kind Harts Dream,* another tract. He explained that he had taken Greene's script as he found it, only cutting or moderating some of the more abusive phrasing. As to Marlowe and Shakespeare—

with neither of them that take offence was I acquainted, and with one of them I care not if I never be [This is Marlowe]. The other, whom I did not so much spare as since I wish I had . . . that I did not I am as sorry as if the original fault had been my fault; because myself have seen his demeanor no less civil than he [is] excellent in the quality [profession] he professes. Besides, divers of worship have reported his uprightness of dealing, which argues his honesty and his facetious grace in writing that approves his art.

Chettle's cold words about Marlowe indicate the growing reputation of that writer as an intemperate and blasphemous person. Marlowe knew very clearly, of course, what had been printed and what was being said about him. He was apparently contemptuous of it. Did he not have noble friends—Raleigh, Mr. Thomas Walsingham, and even the Earl of Pembroke? (At this time he was writing for that nobleman's "Servants." Let the jackals snap at his heels. He went ahead with his playwriting. He shaped glowing couplets for *Hero and Leander,* which was lengthening under his impatient hand.

Marlowe shared a room with Thomas Kyd, who also enjoyed the favor of Pembroke. Marlowe jeered at some of Kyd's pious opinions, and ignored his fears as to Harvey, Greene, and others. If trouble came, he could deal with it. Had he not put university dons in their place on occasion, written plays that were the talk of London, dined with noblemen, and slipped out of prison in a day in that affair over the fool Bradley? He, Kit Marlowe, knew his way about. He could manage the yapping pedants and pamphleteers, and any danger they were men enough to contrive.

3

May, 1593. The plague rages in the capital, and Will Shakespeare debates whether to pack and make for Stratford or to wait longer in London. The playhouses have been closed for three months, but he has had work enough to do. He has been finishing that poem about a boy and the Goddess of Love, which he has long had in mind. He could do more with it in idle London than in a crowded house at Stratford. Now, as he pushes aside his breakfast dishes, he is meditating on a trip to Stratford while Field gets on with printing the book. Then there is a knock at his door.

He opens it and sees the face of George Bryan, his fellow actor, strangely pale and grave. There is a youth behind him, a frightened-looking lad, who seems to be a servant.

"What's the matter, George?" Will asks. "You have a long face and a white one."

He gestures his friend into the room, and Bryan beckons the boy, who comes along and closes the door, standing by it. Bryan sits on the bed and speaks three words.

"Marlowe is dead."

"No! You are mad! Of the plague? I heard he had gone to the country, to Walsingham's!"

"Aye, but they brought him back, to appear before the Privy Council. On some matter, they say, touching his talk about religion."

"Then what has happened? Do you tell me that he has gone to the block for a matter of opinion—that Marlowe couldn't find words and influence to work himself out of *that?*"

"Nay, Will; he was arrested, but freed, and to return for further questioning. It was at Deptford—"

"Deptford?"

"Yes—across the river—in an inn there—where this lad serves. And he can tell you fully of the whole affair."

Shakespeare turns to the boy with a questioning glance.

"The way of it was thus, sir," the latter speaks up. "I am serving at the inn there, and my sister is Master Bryan's housekeeper. I came here early the morning—"

"Yes, yes. But about Marlowe. What happened?"

"Why, sir, Master Marlowe, of whom I've heard talk often enough, came to the inn yesterday morning about ten o' the clock, with three others that I will not call gentlemen—"

"Call them what you will. On with it!"

"There was one named Frizer, and another Poley, and another they called Nick, and they were all very secret, sir, and the four of them would have their own room, which my mistress gave them. There they dined, come noon, and after went to walk in the garden, with much talking. And in the same room they supped."

Shakespeare fidgets through this recital, and demands, "And after they supped?"

"Why, sir," says the boy, "there is some wine ordered, and I am to help, and as we come in we see Master Marlowe lying on a bed, and the other three are on a bench before him, gaming. And Master Marlowe is speaking of the bill. 'I came by your invitation,' says he, 'and you shall pay.' And the man Frizer swears he will not. We stand there, for they have no regard for us, so hot are they disputing."

The boy paused and gulped as if shuddering at what he remembered.

"Then Master Marlowe reaches out and snatches a dagger from its sheath on this Frizer's side, and anon he starts up and begins to attack him.

"Then I know not what happens, but there is Master Marlowe on the floor with the dagger driven through his eye, and the three of those rascals looking at him."

"Did Frizer get the dagger from him and stab him?" asks Will.

"Why, if he got it from him, I saw that not," says the boy doggedly, "but stab him I think he did."

George Bryan speaks up.

"Will," he says, "as I make out what happened, the dagger was still in Marlowe's hand. Perhaps he was beating Frizer on the head with the hilt. And the fellow, falling against the others, could not get away, but gave a mighty thrust. And the blade being toward Kit, it was driven into him."

They are silent a moment.

"Well, the manner of it matters not," says Shakespeare. "It is the saddest thing we shall hear for years to come, if we ever hear a sadder. He would have gone far—and high."

"Aye."

Shakespeare spoke softly.

" 'Cut is the branch that might have grown full straight'—"

" 'And burned is Apollo's laurel bough,' " added Bryan. "His words at the end of *Faustus*. I can hear the chorus speaking them. He wrote his own best epitaph."

XI: PLAYER INTO POET

WE shall have to turn back in time a little, for in following Marlowe we have come midway into the year 1593, and left Shakespeare behind. More than nine months had slipped by between the publication of Greene's envious pamphlet and the stabbing at the tavern in Deptford. It was an important nine months in the Shakespeare story.

Sometimes a stream divides and flows in several channels, each branch pushing along on its own course, to merge later with the others. With Will Shakespeare's life, something of the kind had happened. There was a break into three differing activities which continued separately for some years, later to unite again.

One such activity had begun in Stratford—the writing of poetry.

Not the poetry of plays, but songs, lyrics and perhaps some attempts at rhymed narratives. No recognized token of such industry survives. When Will came to London, he continued to compose verse of this sort. He began the story-poem we have imagined him describing to Marlowe—a tale of the Goddess of Love and her passion for the boy Adonis.

Why did Shakespeare make time for poetry during a busy and difficult period of apprenticeship in acting and playwrighting?

First of all, probably because he was at an age when "pure poetry" seems most magical and necessary to a young writer. Even men and women who later show no interest in verse are often passionately devoted to it in their late teens and early twenties. The sheer music of words, the power of separate images and sensuous feelings, the possibility of capturing a fragment of eternity in a phrase or line are never so attractive as in these years. The short lyric, the narrative stanza beckon toward a kind of ecstatic perfection of language which seems as possible to the poet as perfection of physical movement seems to a gifted athlete. Shakespeare felt this strong impulse of the young creator, an impulse at once rapt and joyous.

Again, there were fame and honor. A natural hope of winning these must always have moved him, unconsciously at first, afterwards more consciously. Fame and honor were laudable prizes; a man should seek them. Yet it seemed unlikely that they could be won by the poetry of plays, which was spoken by players and written for mercenary gain. If his own reputation were to grow, it must be by writing that was purely literary. Poems might make William Shakespeare more respected, and even add luster to the family name.

Finally, as he grew in skill and practical experience, and saw books appearing which won positions or noble patrons for their authors, Will must have seen the possibility of indirect or direct profit in poetry. This was a lesser consideration, and scarcely separable at times from the desire for distinction. Yet it was a different thing, as would be shown clearly in his own case.

There had been time for poetry during the busy years with the company from 1587 on. At each summer's end Shakespeare's troupe took a rest. In these vacations, spent at Stratford with his family, Will would have found some hours for working with verse. In the winter there were periods when the rise in plague deaths closed the playhouses. Then, too, the young actor-playwright would have time for his literary projects. Field and others who read his lyrics must have urged him on. By the midyear of 1592 Will had surely made a start with the rhymed story of Venus and Adonis. And about that time began a series of happenings which seemed like a command to push forward with that undertaking.

The first event occurred on June 11, 1592. On that afternoon some of the high-blooded apprentices of whom we have previously heard started a riot at one of the playhouses. The Queen's Privy Council was angry. Abruptly it ordered a closing of all London theaters for three and a half months. Will was away with his troupe at the time, on tour. Probably the Lord Strange's Men heard of the Council's order. At any rate, they continued on the road after their summer recess. They returned to London late in midautumn, doubtless expecting to play there. But the plague had now broken out, and the theaters remained closed up to the last week in December. They reopened briefly then; but the pestilence raged afresh, and late in January the Privy Council again issued an order for their closing. A performance of Marlowe's *Jew of Malta* on February 1 marked the end of all playing.

Will Shakespeare got out his unfinished poem and set to work on it. He may well have expected to have a full month for the boy and the goddess. He had much longer. The plague was to prove the worst visitation London had yet known. The theaters did not open again for more than a year.

2

As he wrote in those sharp February days, building beauty with words as death raged about him, Will must have remembered more than once an event of a late afternoon three and a half years ago, in the autumn of 1589.

It was night, really. The play had been played and the actors were changing for the street in their tiring room on the second floor. The platform below was being swept for the next morning's rehearsal. (There were few continuous runs of single plays in that era; a new bill was usually offered every afternoon.) Will finished changing, and began to descend the stairs at the rear of the building, which led to the backstage lobby below, and the exit to the street. Young Henry Condell was with him.

As they came down they saw a group of men near the door. By the light of the dingy candle-lanterns which hung there, Will made out Kemp and Phillips. Then Condell clutched his arm, arresting their descent. And at that moment the young actor-writer saw clearly a figure he would long remember. It was that of a young man, richly but simply dressed, standing at negligent ease. He looked up, and Will saw a face framed by shoulder-length auburn hair—a face with the chiseled features of an aristocrat and the life and glow of a young god.

"Southampton," whispered Condell.

Kemp had seen the two on the stairs, and beckoned them down.

"My Lord," he said, as they joined the group, "you asked only now who played the king. Here is this same Master Shakespeare I named you. If you admire the way he shakes a scepter, yet the true spear he shakes is a pen. For he rewrote the play you saw, and gave life to it, as he has to others."

Kemp clapped Will on the back and pushed him forward. Southampton's eyes lighted and his face broke into a smile.

"Master Shakespeare," he said, "you send high admiration higher. For I know not if plays are more my delight or the poets that pen them."

In a daze Will felt the clasp of a firm hand and noted the play of color in the manly but sensitive face. He murmured a modest reply. He had heard of Southampton. The boy Earl, ward of Lord Burghley, a student at Cambridge at twelve, a Master of Arts at sixteen—scholar, courtier, athlete—was a name on many lips. And Shakespeare had heard some weeks before that he was coming to Gray's Inn this very autumn for the study of law.

Kemp was speaking again.

"We are dining with his lordship," he declared, "and you shall join us. I'll have no talk of tasks to be done this night. Tush, for the very honor of our quality you shall come, and drink till that wit of yours be kindled, and prove to my lord that there is learning and mettle in our company."

No refusal was possible, nor had Will the desire to make one. Three and a half years later, as he rhymed his tale of boy and goddess on its way, the evening was still etched in clear, high colors on his memory. The grace of the young peer, his masculine beauty, his delight in the company of stage folk—all were still vivid. It seemed as if in him there had been a flowering of all that the age, with its passion for learning, art and elegance, had dreamed that men might become.

That night had marked the beginning of a friendship—the kind of friendship that was becoming possible then between gifted men of humble family and great nobles. Will had written graceful sonnets for the golden youth—we shall learn more of them later. He had supped and conversed with him, through long hours talking of stagecraft and modern and olden poetry. And now he had the encouragement of a more mature Southampton in the project to which he was giving himself. Will had told his new friend of the poem some time before. The story lay in Ovid, and the young Earl had declared a high delight in that poet which matched Will's own, and became a further bond between the two. And he had kindled to the idea of the poem.

"Put speed to your pen, Will," he had cried, "and get it to the printer. I will be godfather to it, and no grudging one. Is your purse long enough to pay for a flight on Pegasus?"

Will had answered that it was. But he knew that if he could write up to his hopes, it would be longer and heavier after he had sent the finished book to the man who, in this tactful manner, was inviting a dedication. Southampton had now come into the control of his estates; he was rich beyond most men's estimation, and as generous as he was wealthy.

With conscious skill and a happy desire to please one he loved and admired, the poet shaped his story to what he felt would be the taste of his patron. The very Goddess of Love sighing in vain for an earthly youth—one indeed much like Southampton himself—that was a fitting situation. And it could be so developed as to arouse the particular delight of a patron who enjoyed both beauty of verse and a novel treatment of love.

Will set the scene amid groves, meadows and flowers. He matched the beauty of goddess and boy with beauty of nature. Here was opportunity for the color and passion that were typical of the Renaissance. Painters had already seized it. Shakespeare himself probably knew a painting by the Venetian artist, Titian, done in 1554, which showed Venus, under a spring sky and on a tree-decked hill, wooing a lovely youth reluctant to be separated from his hunting hounds. Queen Mary of England, Elizabeth's older sister, had presented that picture as a wedding gift to her husband, Philip of Spain (later Philip of the Armada). A copy may have been made and kept in Court, where Shakespeare could have seen it; one can be found in the National Gallery in London today.

At any rate, the poem Shakespeare wrought has much of the spirit of this painting. In both, there is the same lushness of earth and sky. There are the same eager goddess and the same reluctant boy. There is even the same lurking humor aimed deftly at the Queen of Love who has to turn wooer herself.

Shakespeare wrote his poem in a simple six-line stanza which had already been used by Spenser (in his elegy on Sir Philip Sidney) and Lodge (in *Glaucus and Scilla*). He leapt into the story with the directness drama had taught him.

> Even as the sun with purple-colored face
> Had ta'en his last leave of the weeping morn,
> Rose-cheeked Adonis hied him to the chase;
> Hunting he loved, but love he laughed to scorn;
> Sick-thoughted Venus makes amain unto him,
> And like a bold-faced suitor 'gins to woo him.

Thus the first stanza sets up the situation and begins the action. But the rest of the story is not so direct and rapid as the beginning. Rather it is leisurely and ornamental. There is the pouting Adonis being wooed—

> Look! how a bird lies tangled in a net,
> So fastened in her arms Adonis lies;
> Pure shame and awed resistance made him fret,
> Which bred more beauty in his angry eyes.

There is Venus, wondering at his coldness, reminding him of her beauty and charm—

> "Bid me discourse, I will enchant thine ear,
> Or like a fairy trip upon the green,
> Or like a nymph, with long disheveled hair,
> Dance on the sands, and yet no footing seen!"

There is Adonis's horse—a charger—proud, high-mettled, beautiful—

> Look, when a painter would surpass the life,
> In limning out a well-proportioned steed,
> His art with nature's workmanship at strife,
> As if the dead the living should exceed;
> So did this horse excel a common one
> In shape, in courage, color, pace and bone.

And Shakespeare swiftly sketches the noble animal. In like detail he sets forth the embroidered eloquence of Venus, and describes how she swoons when she fears Adonis will reproach her, and then recovers, and how her eyes

> which through the crystal tears gave light,
> Shone like the moon in water seen by night.

And when at length Adonis turns away, and the night passes, and Venus on the following morning listens for the horn that shall tell where he hunts, and hears it at last, the poet describes her running frantically through the woods, then shuddering at the voices of the dogs that have brought the game to bay. She passes them, some torn and bleeding, and one that howls when she speaks to him, and comes at length upon Adonis's body, torn and dappled with "purple tears,"

> No flower was nigh, no grass, herb, leaf or weed,
> But stole his blood and seemed with him to bleed.

So this is the end. She stands and pronounces a kind of curse on all passion that men and women shall know in days to come.

> "Since thou art dead, lo! here I prophesy—
> Sorrow on love hereafter shall attend:
> It shall be waited on with jealousy,
> Find sweet beginning but unsavory end;
> Ne'er settled equally, but high or low
> That all love's pleasure shall not match his woe."

Thus it was a highly-colored poem, wrought in cunning detail like a rich tapestry. Each situation or feeling was embroidered. Each glimpse of grass, of speeding dog or horse, of sunrise or forest tree or forest floor, of woeful goddess or disdainful youth, was woven into one many-toned harmonious picture.

Even today we can admire the intricate splendor of the effect. The ornamental style, the voluptuous pictures—these are less to our taste than they were to that of the Renaissance English reader. Yet we can see the skill and mastery which went into the poem. Its showers of similies and metaphors win our admiration as they won Southampton's. The ease and variety of phrasing are clear to us as they were to him. We can see how surely Shakespeare had already stored away the immense variety of words that from now on was his—a variety so great and so easily used that it never seems heavy, or even at first acquaintance, impressive. We can see how well he had already mastered the harmonies of verse, although his mastery was to grow. No poem in English since Chaucer's time had been so skillfully and musically wrought.

It was an amorous poem—amorous enough for Southampton and his friends to whisper and laugh about—as young men and women of today whisper and laugh about the "bawdiness" of Chaucer, Baudelaire, D. H. Lawrence or James Joyce. Yet compared with other passionate poems of the time it was anything but gross or shocking. There was a kind of delicacy about its franker scenes, along with considerable humor. There was even a strong spiritual note in the poem. Venus is passionate, yes, but she has an ethereal quality, too, as she tells Adonis,

> "Witness this primrose bank whereon I lie;
> These forceless flowers like sturdy trees support me;
> Two strengthless doves will draw me through the sky,
> From morn till night, even where I list to sport me."

And when Adonis finally says farewell to the goddess he does not want, he speaks sharply of the difference between love, which he extolls, and lust, which he denounces—

> "Love comforteth like sunshine after rain,
> But Lust's effect is tempest after sun;
> Love's gentle spring doth always fresh remain,
> Lust's winter comes ere summer half be done.
> Love surfeits not, Lust like a glutton dies:
> Love is all truth, Lust full of forgéd lies."

And finally, after Adonis has died, he melts "like a vapor," and a purple flower, "chequered with white," springs up where he had lain.

Thus the poem is more than a gorgeous and voluptuous picture; it has its overtones of higher beauty. These and the skill and vigor of its lines have helped to give it a lasting distinction.

3

Shakespeare dedicated *Venus and Adonis* to Southampton. His words were smoothly respectful.

TO THE RIGHT HONORABLE HENRY WRIOTHESLEY[1] EARL OF SOUTHAMPTON, AND BARON OF TICHFIELD

RIGHT HONORABLE,

I know not how I shall offend in dedicating my unpolished lines to your lordship, nor how the world will censure me for choosing so strong a prop to support so weak a burden: only, if your honor seem but pleased, I account myself highly praised, and vow to take advantage of all idle hours, till I have honored you with some graver labor. But if the first heir of my invention prove deformed, I shall be sorry it had so noble a godfather, and never after ear so barren a land, for fear it yield me still so bad a harvest. I leave it to your honorable survey, and your honor to your heart's content, which I wish may always answer your own wish and the world's hopeful expectation.

Your honor's in all duty,

WILLIAM SHAKESPEARE

It was an appropriate dedication—the tactful greeting to a great earl from an actor and playwright whose family was not even "gentle." The modesty it showed was usual in such addresses. As a matter of fact, the words were rather confident ones to come from a writer still without a name. Far from showing, as some have suggested, that Shakespeare scarcely knew the Earl and had not asked his permission to offer the book to him, the easy but firm tone of the dedication and the promise of a second poem in the future indicate acquaintance and the assurance of a good reception.

The phrase, "the first heir of my invention," has puzzled some students, but there is no cause for wonder about it. The words do not mean that Shakespeare had written the poem before he left Stratford, or before he had written an original play. They mean merely that this was his first *published* book. An author today may have several unpublished novels on hand, all written before a fourth or fifth that is just getting into print. Yet the latter would unquestionably be his first novel. It was even more so with Shakespeare. He would scarcely count his plays as serious literary efforts, and certainly he would not

[1] Pronounce "Reez-ly."

call them his first writings when they had never made their way to
the bookstalls.

Venus and Adonis, of course, appeared there—early in June. Field,
who had done the printing, placed it in the care of John Harrison at
the latter's shop, The White Greyhound. Harrison was a distinguished
bookseller, or publisher, having been three times warden of the Stationers' Company, and three times chosen its master.

He had an attractive-looking book to sell. It was printed with taste,
and edited carefully, partly by the author himself. Many of Shakespeare's plays were later printed carelessly (doubtless from stolen
copies), and even the great Folio Edition was mostly or wholly edited
by others after his death. *Venus and Adonis* is interesting as an evidence of what we might have got had Shakespeare himself seen all
his dramatic works through the press. The text is clean and correct
throughout. There are no meaningless or jumbled passages. The poem
is a workmanlike job for its day as to both its printing and its editing.
It indicates that Shakespeare wrote carefully and knew how he wanted
his writing spelled and punctuated.

From this and from later publications which he authorized, we get
some idea of what his pronunciation was. Naturally, it was based on
Warwickshire speech. This was broad—that is, it tended to give full
vowels and clear consonant sounds, and to keep certain older pro-
nunciations like "inchaunte," "daunger," "eyther," "joynt," "errour."
Apparently he preferred "ie" to "y." The long vowels appear in
"smoake," "extreame," "loe" (for "lo"), "dooth" (for "doth"), "hee,"
"mee." The sharp consonants come out in words like "lippes," "kisse,"
"didde."

Of course Field had a hand in the editing. He was from Warwickshire, too, but had been printing books in London for fourteen years.
In general, speech was less broad there and spelling simpler. There was
no exact standard as yet for the language as a whole, but printers in the
city tended to feel that their practice was the approved one. Also a
printer had to think about paper. It was far more expensive then than
now (and much better in quality). Lines with words like "kisse,"

"toppes," "smoakie," and so forth often ran over. They took up more paper and made a book more expensive. So for both style and economy Field apparently cut a number of Shakespeare's double consonants and otherwise modified his spelling. "Uppe" and "toppes" and "hilles" became "up," "tops," "hils," for instance. But in other places the longer forms crop out, showing the broader speech and the more elaborate spelling that Shakespeare preferred.

Venus and Adonis was an immediate success. Two years later Thomas Edwards, referring to the accomplishments of English poets, put the Stratford newcomer with Spenser, Daniel and Marlowe. With university students Shakespeare's poem was especially popular. In a Cambridge student play of the time one youth exclaims: "Let this duncified world esteem of Spenser and Chaucer; I'll worship sweet Master Shakespeare, and to honor him will lay his *Venus and Adonis* under my pillow."

Southampton was delighted with both the poem and its reception. We know this from what Shakespeare himself wrote later. Evidently there was a handsome payment as a reward for the dedication. Rowe, when he published the first printed life of the poet and dramatist in 1709, confirmed the Earl's generosity in a rather startling manner. He said, on the authority of Sir William Davenant (who as a boy knew Shakespeare personally), that Southampton "at one time gave him a thousand pounds to enable him to go through with a purchase he had a mind to." That was a fabulous sum—perhaps $70,000 in our money values—and the gift may have grown considerably in being told of. Nor do we know of any purchases Shakespeare made, except possibly to buy in as a part owner of his company, until four years later, when the sum involved was relatively small (£60). But there seems to be no question of the young Lord's generosity to his poet-friend.

In this period Shakespeare may have moved his wife and children to London. John Shakespeare had not prospered in the years since his son had left Stratford. In 1587 he had planned to recover the Asbies, and had brought a suit against John Lambert, son of his brother-in-law

Edmund, in 1589. Edmund had died without restoring the title to this property. However, John Shakespeare dropped the case in 1590, probably because of his status as a recusant. Activity against both Catholics and Puritans increased at this time. Will, meanwhile, had won a position of some dignity and comfort in London. Doubtless he hoped for a still higher income when the theaters opened. He could thus provide a better home for Anne and his three children in the city than they could enjoy in Stratford.

There is one bit of evidence to indicate that he did. The Subsidy Rolls, which fixed the place of residence and the tax to be paid by each citizen, show that in 1595-96, and so far as we know for some time earlier, Shakespeare was living in the Parish of St. Helen's, close to the Theatre. He was assessed £5 on his goods at this residence. This was a rather large sum. Richard Burbage, then a successful actor, was assessed only £3, and his brother Cuthbert, owner of the Theatre, £4. These figures suggest that Will Shakespeare was no longer a mere roomer, but a householder.

If this was the case, his wife, his daughter Susanna, now ten, and the twins Judith and Hamnet, well past eight, may have been with him as he began to win a literary reputation. Later, we know, they were not. But later, too, Shakespeare, though much more prosperous, had lodgings with a London family, where as a roomer or boarder his taxes would not have amounted to £1, let alone £5.

4

After the appearance of *Venus and Adonis*, Shakespeare was still an actor and playwright without a theater, for there was little playing in London during the year 1593. He set about on the "graver labor" which he had promised Southampton to perform for him. It was another narrative poem, and one of a somewhat more serious character than his first.

Some of the soberer critics of the day felt that *Venus and Adonis* was a suggestive and even a lewd performance. They might have added that it lacked a certain depth of feeling. The outstanding feature of the narrative was its rich ornamental beauty. No reader was likely to weep over Adonis's death, or to feel immensely sorry for Venus, although Shakespeare pictured her as suffering prodigiously.

Apparently the poet decided that his new project should be a noble one on which he could write with greater moral conviction. He went to Ovid again for the story of Lucrece, the young Roman wife who was wronged by the princely Tarquin, and killed herself after begging her husband to avenge her. It was thus a poem denouncing the immoral villain and praising the chastity of the heroine. Shakespeare threw himself wholeheartedly into the task of writing it.

For *The Rape of Lucrece* he used a seven-line instead of a six-line stanza, a slightly more difficult form than that he had employed for his first verse-narrative. *Lucrece,* too, is longer in lines by a third than *Venus and Adonis.* To us it is less enjoyable. The story is a painful one. And though it was done with greater vigor and with as great a skill as its predecessor, we miss the rich color and the idyllic beauty of the latter.

Moreover, *Lucrece* drags. As in *Venus and Adonis,* Shakespeare gives in full the thoughts of his characters and their speeches to each other. He never would have let them meditate and talk at such length in a play. And he might have learned from Chaucer at his best to be brief and natural. But not Shakespeare! He poured out stanza on stanza of state of mind or direct speech as if he enjoyed the luxury of being able to do so! It is a great pity. He might have made a natural, direct, lifelike and moving thing of the verse-story. That would have been a revolution as great in its way as the one he was leading in his dramatic writing. But either he perceived no such possibility, or rejected it. Both his stories in verse are ably planned and skillfully written; both, for the modern reader, are overwritten.

Yet the Elizabethan readers praised them. They expected and liked the leisurely style. Perhaps *Lucrece* received even more praise than *Venus and Adonis.* Shakespeare himself seems to have been satisfied with it. His dedication to Southampton was brief and confident. "The warrant I have of your honorable disposition," he wrote (the "warrant" was the "evidence," or, in plain words, the reward he had received), "makes it assured of acceptance." He spoke briefly of his "love" for Southampton as "without end." He signed himself "Your lordship's in all duty."

Thus he was apparently established as a poet with a great patron. Other writers referred to him in flattering terms.

> You that have writ of chaste Lucretia,
> Whose death was witness of her spotless life,

wrote Sir William Harbert. Michael Drayton, also a Warwickshire poet, hailed him as having revived the Roman heroine "to live another age." His name was linked by Richard Carew in an essay on "The Excellencie of the English Tongue" (1595-96) with Chaucer, Surrey, Marlowe, Daniel and Spenser. And there were other like references. *Lucrece* even inspired a rather mysterious poem called *Willoughbie his Avisa,* apparently written by Henry Willoughby, a young Oxford student, which spins the story of an English Lucrece in an Elizabethan setting. Quite possibly Shakespeare himself appears as a character in this curious tale. If so, he is so vaguely sketched that it does not greatly matter.

Perhaps Shakespeare looked forward to composing more narrative poems. Perhaps, on the other hand, there were many forces drawing him back to the theater.

Some of these were practical. He was not of course faced with an either-or choice; he could reasonably hope to write both plays and verse. But in so far as he must make a choice, he must consider that the playhouse promised to provide an income for his family, while patronage was uncertain. A patron might become cold and forgetful; he might suffer a curtailment of income, or even financial disaster. There was the further possibility that Shakespeare may have desired independence, particularly where his patron was also his friend.

There were also artistic considerations. Despite his success with the poems, the young writer may have become a bit weary of his rather ponderous verse-narratives. He may have perceived that his real artistic interest lay in drama, may have suspected also that his chief talent was for writing plays. If the latter were not highly esteemed as literature, perhaps he frankly accepted that fact, and was resolved to be satisfied with the great popular influence they exerted.

At any rate, *Lucrece* was the last of the poems which Shakespeare himself was to publish. With the spring of 1594 the playhouses were about to reopen and they drew him back into their full and astonishing activity. However, before we say farewell to Shakespeare's "pure poetry," we must consider the second of the three activities which he was following in the early fifteen-nineties. None has provoked more wild thoughts or more ferocious debates about him.

XII: THE SONNET MYSTERY

THE group in the Shoreditch tavern leaned eagerly over the table, elbows or hands pressing on the sanded wood. The candles cocked in their pewter sticks threw deep shadows upon the faces. One was reading—

> Leave me, O love, which reachest but to dust,
> And thou, my mind, aspire to higher things;
> Grow rich in that which never taketh rust:
> Whatever fades, but fading pleasure brings—

The young man read well—a good hope for his future as a barrister when he finished his law studies. As he completed the fourteen-line poem, Will Shakespeare, newcome from Stratford, lifted a hand.

"By your leave," he begged, "if you are willing, I must get a quill and some paper, and copy the lines. I would have them by me."

The law student nodded, and Shakespeare called a boy and gave him instructions.

"And now," he said with a smile, "read it again!"

It was in the days before his first original play, before he had met Southampton, that he heard this sonnet of Sir Philip Sidney. (Later he was to write one himself with a somewhat similar theme and accent —Sonnet 146, as it is commonly numbered.) And with the first of these new poems Will was already caught up in the enthusiasm for them. All the lettered men of London were reading and exclaiming over nothing but sonnets, although not one important group had as yet got into print. In a few years many sonnet "cycles" would appear. Books of sonnets would salute the readers of the day like so many noble salvos of artillery. Meanwhile, the fact that they existed only in private form made them the more admired and prized.

Sidney had written 110 of them in the sonnet sequence called *Astrophel and Stella* ("Star-lover and Star"). These sang the beauty and virtue of a known lady—Penelope Devereux, now by marriage Lady Penelope Rich. To print such personal lyrics was considered impossible, although, as we shall see later, "Stella" was perhaps more a peg for the sonnets than a mistress whose favor Sidney desperately sought. He had permitted plenty of written copies of these poems to be made by his friends. Now his heroic death in the Netherlands a few years before (1586) lent these works of his a kind of romantic halo.

The sonnet had not found this sudden rage of popularity because it was a new poetic form in England. It had been glorified by Petrarch more than two hundred years before, and English poets had written it for more than half a century. Perhaps it was an accident that they had not been writing sonnets since Chaucer's time. Chaucer had been to Italy and was familiar with Petrarch in the original Italian. He even translated one of Petrarch's sonnets as a song in his novel in verse *Troilus and Criseyde*. Why not as a sonnet? There is no sure answer to that question.

At any rate, Chaucer wrote no sonnets; and Sir Thomas Wyatt and

Henry Howard, Earl of Surrey, first composed them in English in the fifteen-thirties and -forties—probably Wyatt first, as he was thirteen years the older. Other poets followed where they led, but feebly. It was really French writers like Marot and du Bellay who made the English again aware of sonnet possibilities. Young Edmund Spenser had done rather literal translations of twenty-six of their poems in 1569, when he was only seventeen. Sidney, who knew both Petrarch and his French followers, had started to compose on the new form about 1581. Most English writers of the time were still careless about the use of the word "sonnet," often applying it to any short poem. But Sidney soon made them understand exactly what it was, although he did not live to see how successful he had been.

Undoubtedly Shakespeare had written sonnets before he had met Southampton. But his glorious young friend must have intensified his interest in them. Henry Wriothesley burned with a zeal for lifting the quality of English poetry. Probably he had a full copy of *Astrophel and Stella*. He was related to Sidney, and knew "Stella" herself; several letters from her to him still survive, some written in the middle or later fifteen-nineties, and one penned in 1604.

The sonnets Will Shakespeare wrote during his first and second years in London probably did not follow the form Sidney used. This was essentially the same as Petrarch's. It offered a difficult rhyme problem, for in the first eight lines, or *octave,* only two rhymes were used, and in the last six lines (*sestet*) two was again the usual number. A Petrarchan sonnet had this pattern (each letter representing a rhyme):

> Octave: a b b a a b b a
> Sestet: c d c d c d (or a variant).

Surrey had broken from this difficult pattern in some of his sonnets, making a much easier one:

> abab cdcd efef gg

This was to become the standard form for Elizabethan writers. We still call it the "Elizabethan sonnet." Sidney wrote a few—two of his very best—in this simpler fashion. All that we have of Shakespeare's save one are of the same type. It gives the poet much more freedom than the classical sonnet, and makes for greater naturalness and force.

It was perhaps less than a year after he met Southampton that a situation developed which may have stimulated Shakespeare to write more sonnets. Southampton, as we have seen, was the ward of Burghley. As the boy's official guardian, the Queen's Lord Treasurer had a responsibility for his marriage. He hoped much from the youth, and planned a match for him with his (Burghley's) own granddaughter, Elizabeth Vere, daughter of the Earl of Oxford. The Countess of Southampton, mother of the youth, liked the project. Southampton seems also to have favored it, and to have given some kind of promise.

But he was only sixteen, and was full of activities and dreams in which marriage had no part—hunting and hawking; the practice of arms to fit himself for wars overseas; a delight in books, theaters, plays, and poets. So he kept putting off a final "yes" to the wedding.

Sir Thomas Stanhope, who had a daughter himself, knew that Burghley was annoyed and worried at the delay, and wrote to the statesman explaining that *he* wasn't trying to capture Southampton. In fact, he said, he had talked with the young man's mother (then only thirty-eight, and a lovely widow) concerning the match with Lady Elizabeth.

"You would do well to take hold of it," he advised her, "for I know not where my lord your son could be better bestowed."

"Ah, Sir Thomas," answered the Countess, "you say well. Your thought is mine, and in good faith I have done my best to further it. But I do not find a disposition in my son to be tied as yet."

"Then should you press him to get one," Stanhope said.

"Time may do better there," she replied, "yet no want shall be found in me to help as I can."

She and Burghley summoned the youth's grandfather, Anthony Browne, Lord Montague, to see what he could do, but Montague reported small progress. Burghley was greatly vexed. He felt that the boy was a fool, and set a date—Southampton's seventeenth birthday—when the young lord must commit himself.

By this time the Countess must have been deeply troubled. The

match would ensure her son's future. Moreover, she could not afford
to offend Burghley. Had her son told her something about the poet-
player, Will Shakespeare? Had she seen some of his sonnets? Did she
now send for him to wait on her at Southampton House in Holburn?

"Master Shakespeare, my son lacks a father to show him his best
interest and happiness. He lacks a disposition to wed, and angers my
Lord Burghley, and thereby may mar his future. I have thought of
you in this matter."

"Of me, madam?"

"You might save him from his own folly. He delights in your company and in your verses. And having spoke with you thus, I must
approve his judgment and liking."

"I was never so honored as in hearing you say so, my lady."

"Then I pray you, be my helper. If you approve the marriage, and I
cannot think but you do, plead with him. Do it in the poetry he loves!
What his elders cannot do with chiding, perhaps you, in beauty of
words praising fitness of conduct, might well bring about."

A plea from so fair and exalted an advocate would be difficult for
a young poet-player to resist. Did he hear and heed it? We know that
Southampton never married Elizabeth Vere, but we know also that
17 sonnets by Shakespeare are addressed to a gifted and lovely young
man, urging him to marry. Perhaps 9 more went with them. The 26
stood at the beginning of a volume containing 154 such poems,
ascribed to the playwright when it finally reached the London bookstalls. Let us step forward some years to look at the entire group as it
first appeared. Of all the writings of Shakespeare these poems seem
the most personal. In them many writers have felt that Shakespeare
the man is revealed with startling clarity.

2

One day in June, 1609, Edward Alleyn, the once fabulously popular
actor, now a gentleman and property holder, stopped at a bookstall
in St. Paul's and picked up a little volume. He looked at the title page.
It read:

SHAKE-SPEARES

SONNETS

Neuer before Imprinted.

AT LONDON

By *G. Eld* for *T. T.* and are
to be solde by *Iohn Wright,*
dwelling at Christ Church gate.
1609.

Alleyn had known Shakespeare well, had acted with his company as a kind of "guest artist" in the years from late in 1590 on to 1594. He turned the leaves of the little book and found after the sonnets a lengthy poem entitled "A Lover's Complaint. By William Shakespeare."

" 'Tis but five pence, sir, and a bargain," said the boy who tended the stall.

Alleyn paid the money and took the book with him. It survives today, with "5d" written on the title page.

Alleyn had heard of his friend Shakespeare's sonnets for years. He may have read a number of them in manuscript. For they, like Sidney's, had circulated about in this fashion. One Francis Meres, in his *Palladis Tamia,* a book containing a "Comparative Dis-Course of our English poets," which appeared in September, 1598, had written of them.

"As the soul of Euphorbus was thought to live in Pythagoras," he declared, "so the sweet witty soul of Ovid lives in mellifluous and honey-tongued Shakespeare: witness his *Venus and Adonis,* his *Lucrece,* his sugared Sonnets among his private friends, *et cetera.*"

That was nine years earlier. Many of the sonnets must have been written earlier still, if we allow a year or more for Meres to have become acquainted with them. How and why, after so long a private life, had they suddenly burst into print?

It seems unlikely that Shakespeare had anything to do with the event. The text is faulty in some respects. A few of the 154 sonnets in the volume are poor and would surely have been rejected by him. The series, as we shall see, was not really a unit. Finally, the narrative poem, "A Lover's Complaint," if his at all, is not of the quality that he would have wished to publish at this time, when he had reached his maturity both in skill and in literary judgment.

Nor would he have chosen as a publisher the Thomas Thorpe who was represented by the initials "T.T." Thorpe was an energetic but independent and unscrupulous fellow. It seems certain that he had got hold of the sonnets in some irregular way. The only hint we have of this lies in the rather curious dedication he gave the book:

TO THE ONLIE BEGETTER OF

THESE INSVING SONNETS

Mr. W. H. ALL HAPPINESSE

AND THAT ETERNITIE

PROMISED

BY

OVR EVER-LIVING POET

WISHETH

THE WELL-WISHING

ADVENTVRER IN

SETTING

FORTH.

T. T.

This is possibly a veiled confession that through "Mr. W.H." Thorpe had procured what was supposedly a private copy of the poems. Or it may be nothing but a somewhat quaint but sincere dedication. We shall come back to this little sentence later on.

At any rate, the sonnets came into their public life in the fashion just described. We shall do well to take a look at them and see how they were arranged, and what exactly they were about.

The 154 poems formed three groups—two of them with a distinct character of their own. However, in two of these groups appear sonnets which may have been separate poems, never intended to go with any others. The collection may even have contained some things not written by Shakespeare at all, although this is unlikely.

The arrangement is a rather natural one, as we shall see. It may or may not have been Shakespeare's. Nobody has been able to suggest an order which has been accepted as better. The sonnets as a cycle have the appearance of an unfinished rather than a misarranged work. Had Shakespeare put them to press himself, he would almost surely have taken time to write a few new poems to round out Group Three, and possibly Group Two. The last sonnet for Two is in the form of seven couplets, a different form from any of the others. It is not of very high quality. Group Three seems unfinished in several senses. The last two sonnets are different versions of the same poem, and are clearly inspired by the well-known medicinal springs at Bath. The sonnet that precedes these is not one which would logically close the group. Thus there is evidence that the sonnets were not ready to be published as a book.

The three groups into which they fall are as follows:

1. Twenty-six sonnets, most and probably all to a young man, seventeen of them urging marriage. Perhaps only these seventeen and the final sonnet belong in this group.
2. One hundred and one sonnets, many also to a young man, probably in most cases the same one. He is called by students of Shakespeare "The Friend." These cover a variety of subjects— the beauty of the loved one; the perishable nature of beauty; a

Rival Poet; the writer's suffering during absences from his beloved; his despair over the Friend's coldness or hostility, and over the latter's stealing the love of the poet's mistress; the consolation or happiness which the writer gets from his love; and his pleasure and pride in the belief that his poems will make their subject immortal; and other themes. (The above subjects are not given in their order.)

3. Twenty-seven sonnets mainly to a woman, now known popularly as "The Dark Lady." The title was not given her by Shakespeare, but by the critics.

It should be noted that two of the three groups are written largely or wholly to a man. This was a novel yet an entirely natural thing. Friendship between man and man was then regarded as the highest of relationships. Few women could read or write. The emotional instability of their sex was accepted by many Elizabethans (though not on the whole by Shakespeare). So a man, it was thought, could find more intelligence and dependability in another man. Shakespeare had set out to celebrate a friendship of this higher sort—at least in many of the sonnets.

It is clear enough that if we take these 154 poems as truly autobiographical, they give us dramatic glimpses of Shakespeare's sufferings, joys and meditations over a considerable period of his life—at least three years, and perhaps much more. A young man appears in the last group as well as in the first two; this fact makes a probable connection between all groups.

Some of the sonnets are relatively artificial, as if done as literary exercises. Many, however, have a strongly personal note. Some seem to have been written in anguish. The Friend was clearly of a higher social station than the poet. The latter writes bitterly of his status as a player—

Alas, 'tis true I have gone here and there,
And made myself a motley to the view!

He is stirred deeply when he fears that his friend will forsake him. He despairs over the state of the world, where he finds "art made tongue-tied by authority" (Shakespeare as a player had seen this) and "captive good attending captain ill." And the Dark Lady, who is pictured as anything but beautiful, yet as completely fascinating, drives him to the most vehement self-reproaches and the sharpest agony.

Such feelings have the ring of reality. For a good hundred and fifty years many students of Shakespeare have accepted them as genuine expressions of the poet's acts and sufferings. Such students have been convinced that the Friend, the Rival Poet, the Dark Lady, were all living persons, and could be tracked down and identified. In the process, they have felt, much could be learned about Shakespeare's marriage, his friendships, his attitude toward not a few events of the time. Not a little might even be learned about some of his plays.

The books and magazine articles and speeches and stories and plays that have grown out of such convictions about the *Sonnets* would make a fair-sized library. Blows have been dealt and received which, if made by steel or lead instead of by printer's ink, would have heaped up casualties enough for a small war. And indeed there has been a literary war over the *Sonnets*—the greatest of all time. Let us look into it briefly. The only occasion for it has been the desire to know more about Shakespeare. What has been proved through the long years of literary combat? As a part of Shakespeare's story, the war of the *Sonnets* is worth our attention.

3

From the beginning there have been two groups, each championing a theory about the *Sonnets*. For convenience, let us call them the Believers and the Doubters. Those words describe them well, since one group has been convinced that the *Sonnets* reveal Shakespeare's heart and soul and certain of his acts, and the other rejects completely the idea that the 154 poems reveal much of either. The Believers had among their champions the poet William Wordsworth. In a sonnet on The Sonnet he wrote:

With this key
Shakespeare unlocked his heart.

The Doubters attracted Robert Browning. In an amusing poem called "House," he referred to Wordsworth's assertion and polished it off with the question: "Did Shakespeare? If so, the less Shakespeare he!"

The Believers start out with Thorpe's dedication. Here is a "Mr. W.H." We haven't the slightest reason, they argue, to reject this reference. Clearly it designated a real person, either one who had *procured* the sonnets for Thorpe or one who had "begot" them in the sense of having inspired them. If the latter meaning of the words "onlie begetter" is taken, then clearly Thorpe thinks of W.H. as the Friend. This seems to be his meaning unless he is merely trying to mystify his readers. For he wishes W.H. "that eternitie promised by our ever-living poet." Apparently he refers to the numerous sonnets in which Shakespeare assured his beloved that the poems would make him immortal. Thorpe seems to be saying to W.H.: "I hope you really get what the author says you will!"

Most Believers think W.H. *was* the Friend. Others, however, prefer to think he was merely the person who *got* the sonnets for Thorpe. They disagree on exactly who he was. William Hall, a printer, say some. Sir William Harvey, Southampton's stepfather, say others. Still others suggest a William Hughes. One of the sonnets carries a line, "A man in hue, all hues in his controlling."

It can be seen already that the Believers disagree on meanings and identifications. This disagreement appears when any important point is brought up. The identity of the Friend, for instance. A number of Friends have been suggested. Southampton is the most popular choice. William Herbert, Earl of Pembroke, is the next in popularity. There is quite as much disagreement as to who were the originals of the Rival Poet and the Dark Lady.

But despite these differences among themselves (to which we shall return later), the Believers are unshaken in their conviction that the sonnets reflect Shakespeare's personal emotions and refer to actual people. The sonnets on marriage, they argue, fit into known situations (that is true of both Southampton and Pembroke). So do Shakespeare's references to his humble station in society as an actor. One sonnet (No. 107) refers to an important event, which causes the poet to rejoice (there is argument again as to *what* event, but it was clearly a real one). There are references to other poets' dedicating poems to the Friend (as poets did with both Southampton and Pembroke). There is Shakespeare's absence from his family to provide an opportunity for the Dark Lady to tempt him. Some writers find her running through the plays, too, appearing first as Rosaline in *Love's Labor's Lost* and last as the fascinating and fatal Cleopatra in *Antony and Cleopatra*. One could go on for some time listing more of such "evidence."

There is a specific reference in Sonnet 104 to the length of the acquaintance of Friend and poet.

> Three winters cold
> Have from the forests shook three summers' pride,
> Three beauteous springs to yellow autumn turned
> In process of the seasons have I seen,
> Three April perfumes in three hot Junes burned,
> Since first I saw you fresh, which yet are green.

There are further details which the Believers assemble when they wish to prove some particular point. However, perhaps their chief argument is the accent and vividness of the sonnets themselves.

"These emotions and characters are too real to be imaginary," they declare. "Could a young man be painted with such conviction without a living model? Could a woman of such an unusual personality as the Dark Lady be invented? We can see her very lack of beauty, her wit and grace, can feel the fascination she exercised. Can the sonnets in which Shakespeare expresses his deepest agony and pours out self-reproaches be anything but real? He opens the door to his inner life in these poems."

The Doubters listen to the evidence and the eloquence with a kind of pitying smile. They say:

"Of course something of Shakespeare is revealed in the *Sonnets*. Any writer reveals himself to an extent in anything he writes. And undoubtedly in his remarks about his position as an actor and in the sincerity with which he declares certain beliefs, the *Sonnets* mirror Shakespeare the man. But so do passages in the plays. And as to our taking literally the emotions expressed about either the Friend or the Dark Lady, that is at once unrealistic and insulting to Shakespeare!"

And patiently they go to work to prove that double statement.

They point out, for example, the general nature of the groups of sonnets being written by other poets of the era. These were, argue the Doubters, artificial in character. Take Sidney's sequence. When it was published in 1591, Thomas Nashe wrote of it—

Here you shall find a paper stage strewed with pearl, an artificial heaven to overshadow the fair frame, and crystal walls to encounter your curious eyes, whiles the tragicomedy of love is performed by starlight.

This shows, argue the Doubters, that Nashe and others knew that Sidney had made a group of poems about Stella which were beautiful without being either too serious or too personal. In fact, Sidney could have married Penelope. "I wish him well," wrote her father, the Earl of Essex, not long before his death in 1576, "so well that if God move their hearts I wish he might match with my daughter. I call him *Son*, he is so wise, virtuous and godly."

But the hearts of the two weren't moved. Perhaps, as one theory has it, Sidney fell in love with "Stella" later, when she was already pledged to another. But the more convincing explanation, which tallies with Nashe's description of the sonnets quoted above, is that the lady in the poems was just a literary figure. Sidney's own behavior supports this interpretation. While he was writing *Astrophel and Stella* he was courting his future wife, whom he soon married and with whom he lived happily.

Similarly, the Doubters point out, all other ladies of cycles which appeared in the early fifteen-nineties—Samuel Daniel's *Delia* (1592), Constable's *Diana* (1592), and Drayton's *Idea* (1594) among them— were imaginary creatures. Drayton warns his readers not to hunt for real people in his sequence. Furthermore, the Doubters show, all sonneteers of the time used a common stock of ideas, some invented, some taken from Petrarch, the French poets or the classics. Among such ideas were the promise of immortality to be won for the loved one by the poet, the perishability of earthly beauty, the anguish during absence from the beloved, the misery of the poet when out of favor. The Doubters call attention to the fact that Shakespeare not only uses all these themes, but apparently was influenced by passages in Sidney, Daniel, Drayton, and others.

So, they conclude, the Friend, the Rival Poet, the Dark Lady are not to be taken too personally. They were pegs, just as Stella and Delia were. There may have been a faint basis of reality in them. A young man may have started Shakespeare writing. Doubtless he saw a number of women about the Court and in Shoreditch, and one of them may have been the original of the Dark Lady. But *not* the Dark Lady as she developed in the *Sonnets*.

And that brings them to their second point—that the Believers insult Shakespeare.

"Why," they ask, "are we to believe that the man who created Falstaff, Hamlet, Othello, Viola, Cleopatra, Juliet and other characters who seem more real to us than most of our friends—why are we to believe that he in his sonnets *could* not and *did* not create characters as he did in his plays? Why do Friend and Dark Lady have to be real people? Of course they weren't. As Shakespeare wrote, he developed characteristics for them—invented striking situations. This gave him opportunities for eloquent writing. The feeling? Of course it was Shakespeare's, but only as Juliet's or Hamlet's was."

This is only a part of the very strong case the Doubters make against the *Sonnets* being intimate in the deepest sense. And indirectly they get a considerable amount of support from the Believers—especially when the latter try to prove the existence of real persons who were the Friend, the Dark Lady, the Rival Poet. Let us look at attempts to identify the Friend, for instance.

We have said that Southampton was one candidate. He is in fact the leading one. Much that we know of his relationship to Shakespeare fits in with the belief that the *Sonnets* were written to him. Yet many of the Believers reject him. They go back to Thorpe's dedication, and the initials "W.H." Southampton's were H.W. (Henry Wriothesley).

Those who believe that the Earl of Pembroke was the Friend point out that his initials *were* W.H. (William Herbert). He too was a handsome young man. The Folio Edition of 1623 (after his death) was dedicated to him and his brother, who, say the editors, had "prosecuted both them [the plays] and their author" with "much favor."

But here again we run into difficulties. Pembroke was born in 1580, and would not have been about London until 1596 or 1597 at the earliest. Yet scholars agree pretty well that many of the sonnets were written before that time, in the period from 1590 to 1594. However, since the first mention of them, as we have seen, was in 1598, the Pembroke Believers merely argue for a later date of composition. They made headway for a time, declaring that Shakespeare's many references to his mature age indicated that he was definitely past thirty (which meant that he was writing *after* 1594) and they even produced a candidate for the Dark Lady who was courted by young Pembroke. She was one of the Queen's maids of honor, a Mary Fitton. But it now seems pretty sure that she had light-brown hair and gray eyes (not the coloring of the Dark Lady), nor is there any evidence of Shakespeare's concern with her. It is indeed very improbable that an actor-writer would have more than a fleeting contact with any of the Queen's maids. They were of families far above his social rank. Southampton, Leicester and Sir Walter Raleigh married such women.

Meanwhile, the earlier date of the *Sonnets* has been rather generally accepted. They are full of plays on words and end-stopped lines—characteristics found in the first plays of Shakespeare in abundance, and less in the later ones. Other characteristics seem to place them with his early writing. And if the *Sonnets* are early, then Pembroke's case collapses.

The Believers, who by their quarrels with each other tend to make identification difficult, thus indirectly support the Doubters' argument that the characters of the *Sonnets* are largely fictitious. For if the Believers themselves can't agree on who was the Friend or the Dark Lady, does not this fact throw doubt on the claim that they were actual persons? And so it is with the Rival Poet, who has been identified in turn as Spenser, Marlowe, Daniel, Constable, and others.

A much-commended attempt to fix the date when Shakespeare began to compose his sonnets has, it seems to me, no better title to acceptance than the efforts to find real persons in the *personae* of the poems. This attempt takes the lines quoted above from Sonnet 104 as a basis of procedure, and then assumes that Shakespeare met Southampton just before or after *Venus and Adonis* appeared. As I have indicated, the dedication to this poem and a number of other facts point to an earlier meeting.

In fact, as soon as we seek real proof for any identity or specific date we enter into a maze of bewildering clues, often exciting but usually contradictory, and in the end find ourselves still guessing.

Yet for the Believers this can be said: Shakespeare's Friend and Lady are drawn with much greater sharpness than the characters of other sonneteers. In his sequence, too, we find more references to personal events. The passages of personal emotion are much more convincing in tone. "Just good art," say the extreme Doubters. "The print of actual experience," insist the Believers. The reader must make his own choice.

However, he is not restricted to a choice between the two extremes. A middle course is possible. One can believe, for example, that there *were* originals for these characters, but that Shakespeare developed his story and his feelings beyond the bounds of reality. Such is my own conviction. That Shakespeare wrote the first group of sonnets to Southampton seems certain to me.[1] That many of the later sonnets also were written with the young Earl in mind seems probable. But it also seems probable that Shakespeare invented and exaggerated. Likewise, in my opinion, it is possible that a number of the sonnets were written with other friends in mind, Pembroke perhaps among them, and that some of Group Two may have been written to a woman—Anne Shakespeare, for example. Similarly, the Dark Lady sonnets may have their basis of reality, but probably grew on exaggeration and invention.

The *Sonnets* really remain a mystery. Unless new evidence turns up—letters or records—we shall never have answers to the questions they raise about Shakespeare's private life. And new evidence is not likely to appear. The literary detectives have been long on the job, and have labored prodigiously. Little is likely to have escaped them.

4

But we have the sonnets. Once we step into the sonnet mystery, we tend to forget them somewhat in the concern with clues that might lead to Shakespeare the person. It is time now to go back to the poems themselves.

Indirectly, they tell us not a little about what kind of man Shakespeare was. They show us that he had a rich variety of thought and feeling. As we have seen, these were to an extent the thought and feeling of other sonnet writers of the day. Yet comparing Shakespeare's sonnets with the others, we get a sense of greater sensitivity and depth, and much wider powers of observation. We see a man who loved flowers and makes us see their beauty—marigolds, marjoram, lilies, roses. We see, from his descriptions of riding away from or toward his

---

[1] The "Mr. W.H." in Thorpe's dedication may be Southampton with his initials reversed for politic reasons, or he may be the person who got the sonnets for Thorpe, or he may be someone for whom the real explanation is unknown. The mysterious character may even have been a deliberate invention by the printer, made to whet the readers' curiosity.

Friend on journeys, his feeling for horses. We realize from his frequent mention of the stage and acting that he was now thoroughly a
part of the theater world. We know that he delighted in the play of
sun and clouds, and in the green outdoor world, that he had stood
fascinated gazing at the ocean and its tides, that he was an expert musician and delighted both in music and in watching it being played.

And we get a general sense of his character. He could suffer deeply
(or he could not have described suffering), yet he could rejoice too,
and he had an instinct for ordering his passionate feelings, dark or
bright, and finding a kind of serenity, an adjustment to life based
on understanding as many aspects as possible of each situation he
faced.

Except for the first group of sonnets, he is a more mature Shakespeare than he was in his first plays, or in the two long poems he
wrote. That may be partly because the sonnets invite thought and
direct speculation on life, and because at this time he found them
an easier form in which to express himself. At any rate, this is the
Shakespeare we get.

In the sonnets, too, we find a greater writer than we have yet found.
In *Love's Labor's Lost,* in *The Two Gentlemen of Verona,* in the two
narrative poems, Shakespeare is a skillful and distinguished maker of
verse. Yet the effect is one of amazing competence, especially in the
poems, of skill in phrasing and character building. The poetic quality
of these works is admirable, but it does not stir too deeply either by
its music or by its conviction. In the sonnets it does.

There is a finer music, for instance.

Lines catch us and stop us with their sheer power and beauty. Sometimes they peal forth like the voice of a mighty organ:

> Devouring Time, blunt thou the lion's paws,
> And make the earth devour her own sweet brood.

Again, they have a quieter and more silver sound:

> Clouds and eclipses stain both moon and sun.

Or they carry a rhythm that almost makes the lines dance:

> From you have I been absent in the spring,
> When proud-pied April, dressed in all his trim,
> Hath put a spirit of youth in every thing,
> That heavy Saturn laughed and leaped with him!

Along with the music goes a sharper ability than Shakespeare had shown before to phrase well-known feelings or images. So—

> And summer's green all girded up in sheaves,

or

> Now stand you on the top of happy hours,

or

> And barren rage of death's eternal cold,

or

> Was it the proud full sail of his great verse,
> Bound for the prize of all too precious you?

The combined music and masterful rightness of phrasing in such lines gives them a quality that is unforgettable. They echo in the mind like noble bars of music, or haunt the memory because they put so triumphantly what the reader himself has felt. Where Shakespeare pleased before, he now stirs and summons also.

And along with such triumphs of harmony and image go flashes of personal feeling—brief pictures that are hard to forget.

> Against that time when thou shalt strangely pass
> And scarcely greet me with that sun, thine eye,

brings up an image of two people clearer and more vivid than any camera could catch. And how sharp is this picture of an inner self—

> What wretched errors hath my heart committed,
> Whilst it hath thought itself so blessed never!

But this is the detail of the verse. Some of the sonnets are memorable chiefly for these vivid phrases—even one vivid expression will often give a poem distinction. Some begin with amazing first lines, and end with a rather weak couplet. But of the 154 there are from 20 to 30 that approach perfection as complete poems, and in these we find Shakespeare the master for the first time (assuming them to have been written by 1594). These cover a great variety of thought or feeling. There are sonnets like No. 13 beginning

> Shall I compare thee to a summer's day,

which are notable for their sheer loveliness. There are sonnets like the one in which Shakespeare describes his darker thoughts, beginning,

> When in disgrace with fortune and men's eyes.

There is Sonnet 73, with its marvelous music and haunting tenderness—

> That time of year thou mayst in me behold
> When yellow leaves, or none, or few do hang.

There is No. 90, amazingly sharp and anguished—

> Then hate me when thou wilt; if ever, now;
> Now, while the world is bent my deeds to cross;
> Join with the spite of fortune, make me bow,
> And do not drop in for an after-loss.

Then there is 130, jabbing and jeering at the false sonnetry of other poets, with its excessive praise of their mistresses—

> My mistress' eyes are nothing like the sun;
> Coral is far more red than her lips' red;
> If snow be white, why then her breasts are dun;
> If hairs be wires, black wires grow on her head.

And farther along in the same poem—

> I love to hear her speak, yet well I know
> That music hath a far more pleasing sound;
> I grant I never saw a goddess go,
> My mistress, when she walks, treads on the ground!

And of course, there is Sonnet 66, with its beginning:

> Tired with all these, for restful death I cry,

and the ensuing list of evils which show how keenly Shakespeare was aware of human frailty, cruelty and injustice.

In the sonnets, in fact, Shakespeare shows for the first time the supreme beauty of tone, the incredible sharpness and rightness of phrasing, the power to express feeling and truth that were soon to startle Elizabethan London, and to startle with equal vigor all generations after. He had found from his reading, his growth in craftsmanship, his endless observation of people, something like the full power that he was now ready to use.

Shakespeare's is perhaps the greatest sonnet group the world knows. Petrarch's are more even in quality—dramatic, colorful, smooth and finished. But Shakespeare's rise in peaks to greater heights, and are sharper and more stirring. Whether or not their personal quality was as intimate as some wish to think, it is real and moving enough to remain vivid for each succeeding generation of readers. Every year millions of young men and women discover much of Shakespeare and much of themselves in these varied, exciting, powerful and lovely poems.

XIII: KINGMAKER

IN the late spring of 1594 the theaters were free to open again after almost two years of inactivity. The moment was bright, like sunlight after eclipse or storm. Yet it was a grim moment, too. For as a storm leaves wreckage, so had these years of inaction. The folk of the playhouses looked on a new theater world—a world long abandoned, disorganized, bleakly uncertain, in which few men were sure of the places they had held before.

For the long prohibition on acting had broken most of the great player-companies.

The Admiral's Men had divided in 1591, most of them leaving England for a tour of Europe. When the wanderers returned, the London theaters were closed and there was no reason to reorganize the company.

The Queen's Players and Sussex's Men had struggled desperately to maintain themselves; they were invited to give a few performances at Court and perhaps in the houses of nobles or in hostelries near London; early in 1594 both companies had gone bankrupt.

Pembroke's Players, for a time a flourishing troupe, had taken to the road early in 1593, with the hope of keeping themselves together, but they had not prospered. One Philip Henslowe, father-in-law to the actor Edward Alleyn, wrote the latter from London on September 28 of that year: "As for My Lord Pembroke's [Men] . . . they are all at home, and have been these five or six weeks, for they cannot save their charges with travel, as I hear, and were fain to pawn their apparel."

Of all the troupes, Shakespeare's company, the Lord Strange's Men, had apparently been the most fortunate. They too had taken to the road. But they had been able to persuade Edward Alleyn, left behind when most of his company toured the Continent in 1591, to join them as a guest player. He had acted with them previously on at least one occasion. To be sure, his name was always set down as "Servant to the Right Honorable the Lord High Admiral," but his exact status mattered little. With Alleyn for heroic roles and Kemp for clowning, the Lord Strange's Men had two incomparable leaders. They did well where the Pembroke company had failed.

Sometime in the spring of 1594, Alleyn had left them and gone on to London. This loss did not damp their spirits. The company worked toward the city in May, looking forward to the future with confidence. For reasons soon to be known, the hopes of the troupe hung on Alleyn and on the Philip Henslowe quoted just above. We already know Alleyn. But since we have no acquaintance with Henslowe, and he is to loom large in our story for a time, it will be well to consider this gentleman.

He was a colorless yet important little man. The son of a gamekeeper in Sussex, to the south of London, he was an assistant—a "servant" he was called in a lawsuit—to Mr. Woodward, bailiff to Viscount Montague. Woodward had a considerable fortune. When he died the shrewd Henslowe was on hand to assist his widow, and then to marry her. He took charge of Agnes Woodward's moneys and properties, and in March, 1584, he leased a plot of land in the Bankside (the district on the south side of the Thames, opposite the walled city). Two buildings stood on this plot, and two rose gardens, and some "void ground."

In 1587 Henslowe built a theater on this unused land. Plays were being presented there, as we have seen, when Will Shakespeare first came to London. Henslowe called his playhouse "The Rose," after the gardens lying near it. He made an arrangement with one of his tenants, a London grocer named John Cholmley. Cholmley was to advance certain sums of money, and in return he was finally to receive a half interest in the building. As the grocer Braynes had listened to Burbage's hopes for the Theatre, so Cholmley doubtless listened to Henslowe's prediction that the Rose would be in demand by companies of actors. Could the Theatre and the Curtain serve them all? Furthermore, the Bankside was only a few minutes' row from the very heart of the city—a superior location to Shoreditch, really.

Henslowe was right. The Rose proposed. But alas! grocers seem to have been allergic to playhouses. Apparently Cholmley couldn't keep up his payments. A few years later Henslowe was sole proprietor of the new building, and richer by some pounds of Cholmley coin as well!

In 1590 the Admiral's Men used the Rose, and Henslowe met Edward Alleyn. Alleyn in turn met the former's young stepdaughter, Joan Woodward, and married her. Thus Henslowe acquired a son-in-law fully acquainted with the world of drama. He already had a playhouse. He and Cuthbert Burbage were the first persons neither writers nor actors to become important figures among them. Of the two, Henslowe soon became by far the more powerful. He might be called the first outstanding businessman of the theater. By our standards he was a very little businessman, but by those of his day he was big.

Probably Alleyn rejected the idea of a trip abroad in 1591 in order to stay with his young wife. He was very fond of her. He called her his "mouse" (some modern slang is not so modern). She drew him closer to Henslowe. Alleyn wrote her long letters when he was on the road, and stepfather-in-law Henslowe wrote the answering messages from the Mouse, who, like most women of the time, couldn't read or write. When Alleyn played with Lord Strange's Men in London Henslowe acted as manager for the company, and they used the Rose. Shakespeare's troupe thus became accustomed to both Alleyn and Henslowe, and to the idea of playing in the Bankside. When they could finally return to London for a long stay, they counted on Alleyn as their chief actor and on Henslowe as their man of affairs. Let us keep this situation in mind while we note certain other changes that had taken place in Shakespeare's company.

There were changes of names and patrons. In September, 1593 Lord Strange had become the Earl of Derby, and the players had taken the title of the Earl of Derby's Men. Then, on April 16 in the following year, the Earl died. For a while they called themselves the Countess of Derby's Men, and then, by a stroke of luck, found a new patron in Lord Hunsdon, the Lord Chamberlain. This must have pleased them, for his title and influence were both high. As they took their way to London in May they doubtless congratulated themselves. Now they could reorganize for work in the city, with Henslowe to manage them, with Alleyn as their chief actor, and with Will Shakespeare, wearing new laurels as a poet, to help supply them with plays. But they reckoned without Alleyn and Henslowe.

One night toward the end of May the troupe gathered at James Burbage's house in Shoreditch and heard some astounding news. Shakespeare, James Burbage, Cuthbert, Condell, Phillips, Beeston, Bryan—all listened as Dick Burbage and Kemp told of a visit to Henslowe.

"Sirs, to be brief," said the young actor as Kemp sat by with a scowl "we have been cozened and betrayed. For whereas this morning we thought ourselves My Lord Chamberlain's Men, and looked to have that player who hath the highest repute in London, and a shrewd man of business, for the managing of our affairs, now we have neither, for they have gone over to those that would contend with us for name and fortune."

"Mean you that both Alleyn and Henslowe will none of us?" asked Bryan.

"We mean that the two of them have picked up a dozen starved players and players' boys from the city alleys and brought the Admiral's Men back to life," said Kemp. "And Alleyn will act with them and Henslowe will hold the purse for them."

"And both will abandon our fellowship?" asked Will Shakespeare.

"Nay, that Henslowe doth not say," replied Dick Burbage. "He speaks softly of our all working together. But can there be profit for us in that? These two companies be proud ones, and have been rivals, and how we shall work together I for one cannot perceive. I think one of the two will swallow the other."

"And if this same Henslowe holds the purse strings and plays one against the other, I know which will go down the gullet," declared Burbage. He wrinkled his nose. "There is a strong sea smell about us already!"

The others laughed.

"But for Alleyn and the Marlowe plays he had, we had never dealt with Henslowe," spoke up George Bryan.

"Why, then, do we deal with him now?" asked Shakespeare. "Do we lack a playhouse? What of the Theatre?"

"It needs repair, and cannot be readied for three months," said Cuthbert Burbage. "And these same repairs will put us to no small expense, if we make them."

"Why, then, in time we could have it," said Shakespeare, "and meanwhile use an inn yard. Did you not buy certain plays from My Lord of Pembroke's Men, when they were in straits for money?" he asked Dick Burbage.

The latter nodded.

"A good half dozen," he answered, "and Henslowe has no title in them."

"I have several of my own that need but little work to be ready," Will volunteered. "And as for the players, we have the very king of clowns in Will Kemp, and I will wager that Dick here is ready to step forth and match voice and gesture with Alleyn himself."

"Nay, nay," protested the young actor, but the others murmured hopefully at Shakespeare's remark.

"Yea, yea," Will insisted. "I have a part for you, Dick, that will prove it!"

There was an eager chorus of questions, but Shakespeare smiled and shook his head.

"In good time," he promised. "Yet I will say this—it will vie with *Tamburlaine* and perhaps outdo him, for 'tis an English monster I shall give you. But come, let's make our plans. I think we can easily find the money to mend a playhouse, and what else we need we have!"

2

So Will Shakespeare was in the theater again, with graver responsibilities and a greater share in the rewards to be won. In fact, his would now be a threefold share—first, as a full-fledged player; second, as a part owner or sharer in the company; and third, as a writer.

Actually, Will had never left the theater, although he had not followed the company on its road tours. If the generosity of Southampton and the praise of London writers had encouraged him to dream briefly of a career as a man of letters, he had dreamed cautiously, as we have already seen.

He had never wholly abandoned the writing of plays. Rather he had continued it even while the playhouses were idle, turning to drama at times between the creation of sonnets and narrative poems. We must now pick up the story of this activity. We dropped it in 1591, with *The Two Gentlemen of Verona,* three years before the Chamberlain's Men decided to part with Alleyn and Henslowe.

Even before 1591 Shakespeare had probably been working on certain plays that have already been mentioned—*Henry VI, Part I, Part II,* and *Part III*.

The exact history of these dramas is unknown, and has been the cause of considerable dispute. George Peele was long supposed to have had a hand in them. By almost general agreement among scholars, Marlowe also was regarded as part author of at least two. All the authorities felt that Shakespeare had given the final form to all three, and, as noted in Chapter X, he is now thought to have been mostly if not wholly responsible for the plays. Certainly he was busy with them in the period between 1590 and the summer of 1592.

Of the three dramas, Part II and Part III were printed in 1594 and 1595, respectively. The first was called *The Contention Betwixt the two Famous Houses of Yorke and Lancaster,* and the second *The True Tragedie of Richard Duke of Yorke and the Death of Good King Henry the Sixt*. The *Contention* was not printed until 1623. It may have been written later than the others, although it dealt with earlier events. Naturally, the plays had been acted for some time before they were printed.

Until recently the *Contention* and the *True Tragedie* were thought to have been early but authentic versions of the plays as we now have them. A recent and rather widely accepted theory is that they were not earlier versions at all, but were texts which the printer put together with the aid of one or more actors who had taken parts in the dramas. The differences from the texts we use today are explained as being the mistakes and omissions resulting from the ignorance or bad memories of the men who tried to reproduce the two "histories." Shakespeare is put forward as sole or chief author.

It may be asked why it matters when these plays appeared, or who wrote how much of them. The answer is simple: they mark the beginning of a new type of drama—one as important and exciting to the stage as *Euphues* was to Elizabethan literature. And if Shakespeare was the principal or sole author, he was a pioneer working in a rich but undeveloped field.

Why were these plays new and exciting? A reader today, trying to read them, may stumble about amid ceremonies, marriages, combats, and murders, and lay down the first play half read. But that is no answer. To get one, he will have to work himself inside the mind of an Elizabethan playgoer.

Try it this way: imagine that in this world of the middle nineteen-hundreds there have never been radio sets, newspapers, motion pictures, or historical novels. The only records that exist of the past in America are a few histories, some in bad verse, and most of them dull. In addition, few people can read these histories. Let us assume that *you* cannot. You know about your country chiefly because your parents and grandparents have told you tales about it. From them and from others you have heard of covered wagon days, of the War Between the States, of big financiers and industrialists like Jay Gould and John D. Rockefeller. What you know has thus come to you in unrelated fragments. You have a story about Kit Carson, one about the Lincoln-Douglas debate, one about the Battle of the Wilderness.

Now, there *are* theaters in this twentieth-century world which we have rather thoroughly stripped of other devices for amusement and information. They are simple, but the more important because they afford one of the few kinds of paid entertainment people can enjoy. Suddenly you hear that three plays covering the whole story of the great war between the North and the South are being performed at a playhouse. A friend rushes in to tell you about them.

"Why, it's as if you were right there!" he exclaims. "They show how the war started. You see the plantations and their life—see the northern factory towns. You watch the soldiers gathering—all kinds of quaint uniforms and guns, and flags for the states. There's a scene in the White House with Lincoln. In another, Lee rides in on his white horse. They carry in Stonewall Jackson, shot by one of his own men. Then there's the surrender at Appomattox—you could have heard a man across the aisle from you shift his foot an inch when they played that."

You and dozens of others rush off to the theater.

This imaginary occurrence will give you some idea as to how the Elizabethans greeted the plays about Henry VI. For these plays covered events in English history even more exciting to Shakespeare and those of his time than the California gold rush and the War Between the States are to us. The reign of Henry VI extended from the conquest of France by his father (and its loss after the father's death) down through the greater part of the Wars of the Roses. Those wars had ended just a hundred and five years before *Henry VI, Part I,* was staged. There was scarcely a family in England that hadn't had someone fighting in them. All over the country were places made famous by events in the wars—battles, riots, pageants, marriages, murders. In the forty-four years of the conflict the nobles and princes of the land had hewed each other to pieces with unbelievable enthusiasm and thoroughness. It was chiefly because of the killing off of kings and would-be kings that the Tudor family won the crown in 1485. Henry of Richmond (Henry VII) had by blood about the feeblest title to the crown that could be imagined. Several young Yorkist princes had a far better claim. But Henry had the Lancastrian backing. It was he who faced Richard III in battle and slew him; and by marrying the daughter of Edward IV, he gave his children as good a right to the throne as could be offered. Elizabeth, Shakespeare's queen, was his granddaughter, and the Wars of the Roses had thus made possible her reign.

Now, plays with a background of English history had been written before *Henry VI,* but none had been highly successful. The playwrights had not been equal to producing anything like what Shakespeare (or possibly Shakespeare and Marlowe) could do. Until 1576 there had been no playhouses. Until 1578, when Holinshed's *Chronicles of England, Scotland and Ireland* appeared, there had been no compact and authoritative historical source for such English plays. In addition, up to the late fifteen-eighties, these plays had lacked the popularity they were now to achieve. The young law students and nobles, especially, had been attracted by French, Italian or classical themes. These had seemed more elegant and modish than English stories.

But the defeat of the Armada had turned all Englishmen, even the French- and Italian-speaking dandies, into ardent patriots. They and the folk of the pits both wanted a chance to cheer for England. To see an enactment of her glories, to behold English heroes and hear them speak, this was a delight to them. *Henry VI* let them fill their eyes with English glory, and split their lungs cheering for it. In this it was new.

It was new, too, in the structure of the play it offered. It made no pretense of telling the story of one hero—like *Tamburlaine*. It did not even pretend to make a neat story of any kind. Rather it made a point of *playing history*. This meant that there was *not* one hero, *not* a smooth drama, but rather a series of scenes and stories, like a "documentary" film or radio program today. It is this sticking to the record, sometimes at the expense of "good theater," that won the name for these productions which is most commonly used—"chronicle plays."

The invention of this new type of drama was a shrewd one. Shakespeare and any writers who may have worked with him knew that the Elizabethans wanted to learn something from plays. They knew they were passionately proud of England. Good! These plays would teach them something, and that something would be about their country. Thus two ends would be served. Furthermore, in these dramas the spectators could behold such a company of famous folk and such a succession of events as no earlier plays had ever shown them.

And such proved to be the case. In *Henry VI, Part I,* for instance, the following personages, among others, appeared:

The King, Henry VI

Talbot, the great English leader and hero

Joan of Arc

Richard Plantagenet, later Duke of York

The Duke of Somerset, who quarreled with him

The Dauphin of France

The Duke of Warwick.

This was an exciting group to an English audience in Elizabeth's

time—the great of two nations. And the action of the play was exciting, too. It showed how France, which had been conquered by Henry
V, was gradually lost to the English. It showed how some of the seeds
for the Wars of the Roses were sown. It showed councils, battles, combats, captures, deaths. (There were only six important deaths in Part I,
but Parts II and III did better by *their* audiences—nine apiece!)

What is equally important, these heroic actions were played boldly,
convincingly. The new theaters made this possible. Costumes were
splendid. The multiple stage permitted court scenes, with the inner
stage set up with throne and arras. It permitted scenes before city
walls, where those in the city could appear on the battlements above
(the gallery). Battles could be enacted. The opposing hosts could come
in through the doors on either side, face each other, exchange taunts
and insults, and march off to fight. Then onto the outer stage could
come fleeing soldiers, then perhaps two champions fighting.

Ben Jonson later poked fun at these tremendous actions, which

> with three rusty swords,
And help of some few foot and half-foot words,
Fight over York and Lancaster's long jars,
And in the tiring-house bring wounds to scars.

Doubtless at times the action seemed preposterous to a few of the
more exacting spectators. But most of the audiences accepted the great
illusion and were swept along with it. It was staged with plenty of
dash and some symbolism, like a modern dance-ballet number. And
for gaping thousands, the trumpets really announced the entrance of
kings. For them, too, these armies with banners (only a dozen or so
showing on each side) were real armies. When Richard Plantagenet
and the Duke of Somerset disputed in the Temple Gardens, and Richard picked a white rose as his emblem and Somerset a red one, they
watched breathless. They knew that they were seeing how the two
roses came to have a significance and to give their names to the York
and Lancaster factions, and thus to the great war itself.

To Englishmen flushed with the triumph over the Armada, each of these heroic scenes was like a bugle call stirring the blood. Thomas Nashe wrote of the Talbot episodes: "How would it have joyed brave Talbot (the terror of the French) to think that after he had lain two hundred years in his tomb he should triumph again on the stage, and have his bones new embalmed with the tears of ten thousand spectators at least (at several times), who in the tragedian that represents his person imagine they behold him fresh bleeding!" What was true of Talbot was true also, in various ways, of Richard of York; Warwick; King Henry's queen, Margaret; and of many others. The English theaters were thronged with Englishmen thirsty for these dramatic glimpses into the past of their country, with colored curtains and cloaks, spears and clashing swords, the tingle of battles and the chill of murders.

Shakespeare was still learning from Marlowe when he wrote these plays. Or Marlowe may have contributed certain passages. A dash and arrogance like his appear in many scenes. But the newcomer from Stratford was already revealing qualities which the author of *Tamburlaine* never showed. Marlowe would never have presented the death of Talbot and his son with the restrained tenderness that marks that touching episode. Nor could Marlowe have conceived the character of the unfortunate King Henry—a monarch who is naïve, wholly good by impulse, but unable to strike effectively at his enemies. In Henry, Shakespeare created the first of several noble characters who were betrayed by their own indecision (Richard II, Brutus, Hamlet).

In one scene, the king sits on a hill while his army 'fights. Both his queen and his nobles have told him that they can do better without him. He thinks of the life of a shepherd, and finds it pleasanter than his own.

> Gives not the hawthorne-bush a sweeter shade
> To shepherds looking on their silly sheep,
> Than doth a rich embroidered canopy
> To kings that fear their subjects' treachery?
> O yes, it doth: a thousand-fold it doth!
> And to conclude, the shepherd's homely curds,

His cold thin drink out of his leather bottle,
His wonted sleep under a fresh tree's shade,
. . . Is far beyond a prince's delicates,
His viands sparkling in a golden cup,
His body couchéd in a curious bed,
When care, mistrust, and treason waits on him.

The three parts of *King Henry VI* covered almost fifty years of English history. In them Shakespeare drew or helped to draw the portraits of many celebrated statesmen and warriors of whom all Englishmen had heard. In these plays appear three kings—Charles of France, Henry and young Edward IV, along with princes and queens. These royal persons had been conjured up from the past by the power of dramatic art.

Soon after he had finished his work on this trilogy, Shakespeare had revised a tragedy about a Roman general—*Titus Andronicus*. It was a fearful piece of work—with torture, mutilation and murder running through it. Some people have exclaimed that Shakespeare couldn't possibly have had a hand in such a barbarous play. Of course, he could have, and did. Tragedies were popular and the audience liked plenty of ferocity in them. Shakespeare knew that. He probably left the plot of *Titus* much as he found it, and concentrated on making the piece as playable as possible. In this respect he did a good job. The play shows either that the original was very well constructed or that Shakespeare was improving rapidly as a craftsman. The latter was surely the case. *Titus* was probably finished as early as 1592.

Even before the last play of the *Henry VI* group was presented, the young playwright was looking ahead to a continuation of the story the trilogy had begun. After all, the Wars of the Roses had not ended with King Henry's death. Why not carry them on to their end, to the coming of the Tudors?

Shakespeare may have had a continuation in mind in writing *Henry VI, Part III*. In this play the hunchback brother of Edward IV, Richard, Duke of Gloucester, takes a leading role. It is he who stirs up

Warwick and Edward to win a battle they seem to have lost. It is he who, after Warwick has changed sides and captured Edward, rescues his brother. It is he who stabs another Edward, the young prince who is the hope of the Red Rose, and it is Gloucester who finally kills the boy's father, good, naïve, unhappy Henry VI. And halfway through the play we know what his goal is. When his brother, King Edward, marries a commoner, he looks with greedy eyes at the crown.

> Why, I can smile, and murder whiles I smile,
> And cry "Content" to that which grieves my heart,
> And wet my cheeks with artificial tears,
> And frame my face to all occasions. . . .
> Can I do this, and cannot get a crown?
> Tut! were it further off, I'll pluck it down!

It was the story of this hunchback prince that was the logical successor to *Henry VI*, both in actual history and in drama. For in history the terrific Richard did get the crown. And in drama Shakespeare set forth this story, which he had completed by June of 1594, in *The Tragedy of Richard the Third*.

3

Dick Burbage laid down the sheets of the manuscript and looked at Will as if he had never known him before.

"What's the matter, Dick?" asked his companion.

The two were in the "study" of Shakespeare's little Shoreditch house, and Burbage had been reading the new play.

"Why, it's more than I bargained for," the latter answered. "I ever had faith in your skill with a pen, Will," he continued, "yet I thought not to see you or anyone in England write a play like this."

"Now that Marlowe is gone," the other added.

"Nay, were he alive," Dick persisted.

"It's a Marlowe hero," Shakespeare pointed out.

"Aye, that's true enough," Burbage agreed. "A villain-hero that will outclimb the possible and leave men gasping. And Kit would have given it as loud a thunder as yours, yet this is better than he could do, God rest his soul."

Shakespeare flushed with pleasure.

"Why, thanks for that, Dick. Why better?"

"Because it is as black as Marlowe can paint, and yet not only black. Because it thunders, and yet is not all thunder. This Richard of Gloucester—this fury, this smooth talker, this devil—he's madder than any hero Kit ever painted, yet you make us believe in him. That first scene between Gloucester and Anne—"

"You think it succeeds?"

"Completely. He, the murderer of the lady's husband, lays siege to her love—is cursed, spit upon, denounced, and yet triumphs in the end. There's such opportunity for a player as was never made before."

"Your opportunity, Dick."

"Aye, if I can turn myself like a chameleon from color to color."

"You can. I wrote it for you."

"When he gives her his sword toward the end of the scene—that is the moment," said Burbage. "When he bares his breast and bids her strike. For when she lets the sword fall to the ground, when she cannot strike, every man in the theater will believe the unbelievable!"

So Will had written in *Richard III* the story of this villain—this smooth talker, this furious fighter, this devil in man's shape. And as it was played by the Chamberlain's Men, it swept London. This was a chunk of history indeed! The audiences watched open-mouthed while Gloucester won for wife the widow of Henry's son, whom he had killed; while he disposed of his older brother Clarence; then of the two young sons of Edward IV. And they felt a moral joy when they heard of Henry of Richmond come to slay the monster and free England. Yet perhaps even while they applauded Richard's fall, they admired his infinite daring and courage.

Dick Burbage, mounting this play, rode on it to a fame quite equaling Alleyn's. In the final scene at the Battle of Bosworth Field, Richard is hard pressed. Catesby, his man, begs help of the Duke of Norfolk—

> The king enacts more wonders than a man,
> Daring an opposite to every danger:
> His horse is slain and all on foot he fights,
> Seeking for Richmond in the throat of death.

Then comes Richard himself, shouting—

> A horse! A horse! My kingdom for a horse!

The line caught the fancy of all London, and crowned the play and the actor with immortality.

In fact, Burbage and Richard became entangled in some people's minds. Bishop Corbet told some twenty years later how an old man guiding visitors about the battlefield of Bosworth offered to show them the very spot where the wicked king met his end.

"Here," he said, "calling, 'A horse, a horse,' this same Burbage died!"

The old man had evidently been to London and seen the play and never had forgotten the actor who made it a thing of flame and thunder. In this first great effort of his, Dick Burbage had shown a genius which for twenty years would go hand in hand with Shakespeare's own.

4

As time slid toward 1595, Will Shakespeare was busy with another play which would test that genius. He had gone back in English history to Richard II, son of the Black Prince. This earlier Richard's story was really a prelude to the three plays on the Wars of the Roses. For Richard had been deposed, and his cousin, Henry of Lancaster, had mounted his throne as Henry IV.

This act raised a question concerning the title to the crown. There were rebellions based upon it. But for two reigns (Henry IV and Henry V) the House of Lancaster and its strong kings seemed secure. Then the whole question burst into the flame of the great war under the sixth (and weak) Henry.

Richard II was almost a complete opposite to Richard III. The earlier Richard inherited his crown and had no need to win it by foul means. He was no murderer, and not even a great fighter, like his father. Where Richard of Gloucester had been fiendishly shrewd, bold, and fiercely energetic, Richard Plantagenet was foolishly egotistic, extravagant, indecisive. Some scholars have called him a misplaced poet. That may be hard on those who bear the name.

It was a dangerous thing to write this play. It showed an English king being deposed, murdered. Marlowe's *Edward II* had done that already, but the new drama was more daring, because Marlowe had shown Edward's son taking Edward's throne, while in *Richard II* a new king and a new royal house had been established, and by election. What would the Queen think? What might she do? After all, her title had long been under challenge.

She did nothing at the time, but later she said about the play, "I am Richard, you know." That was after the tragedy had an innocent part in an actual rebellion which brought its author and his company into grave danger. But we are some years away from that.

Burbage apparently played the new Richard as well as the earlier one. Lacking the great height and commanding look of Alleyn, he seems to have been able to project himself into widely different characters where Alleyn could not. He could be the foppish, petulant, haughty, uncertain son of the Black Prince, just as he could give a sense of strength or demoniac power as Talbot or Richard Crookback. And he had opportunities in this play for pathos, shame and agony which he lacked in *Richard III*. When the new Richard's fortunes begin to fade he plunges into the very night of dejection, and exclaims,

> For God's sake, let us sit upon the ground
> And tell sad stories of the death of kings:
> How some have been deposed, some slain in war,
> Some haunted by the ghosts they have deposed,
> Some poisoned by their wives, some sleeping killed;
> All murdered: for within the hollow crown

> That rounds the mortal temples of a king
> Keeps Death his court, and there the antic sits,
> Scoffing his state and grinning at his pomp;
> Allowing him a breath, a little scene,
> To monarchize, be feared, and kill with looks . . .
> [Then] Comes at the last and with a little pin
> Bores through his castle wall, and—farewell king!

Such passages gave Burbage a chance that was rare—for here true drama and the great accent in poetry were fused. Shakespeare had never joined the two so fully before. He wrote other high passages in this play, notably the description of England which is spoken by the dying John of Gaunt—

> This other Eden, demi-paradise,
> This fortress built by Nature for herself
> Against infection and the hand of war,
> This happy breed of men, this little world,
> This precious stone set in a silver sea, . . .
> This blessed plot, this earth, this realm, this England.

In *Richard II,* too, there is a sureness of dramatic clash as well as a sureness and greatness of words. Both in writing and in craftsmanship it was a finer work even than *Richard III.* Here the great poet and the great dramatist were both emerging.

Apparently Burbage and the Chamberlain's Men made the play a success. It was re-acted over a long period of time. But it failed to sweep the town like the story of the Crookback. The foolish king losing his crown and throne and even his life was pathetic, moving, but there was some lack in him for the groundlings and even the galleries. Their shouts were louder and their love greater for the strong, wicked Richard than for the sensitive, foolish, and poetic one.

XIV: TWINS, SHREWS AND FAIRIES

O N the night of December 28, 1594, the students and barristers of Gray's Inn were gathering for the supreme effort of a series of revels which they held during the Christmas holidays. Already they had made festivity for eight days and evenings. They had elected a Lord of Misrule, whom they called "The Prince of Purpoole." They had listened to witty and naughty speeches. Now they were to see a play produced by the Lord Chamberlain's Men, and entertain hundreds of outside guests.

The occasion was a notable one. For three years, because of the plague and the danger of infection, there had been no such activities. The chief guests of the evening were the members of the rival Inner Temple. They had accepted an invitation and had agreed to send a proper ambassador to greet the Prince, who, of course, would preside over the evening's follies.

No college class of today inviting the students of another university could have entered into the preparations for such an event with more care and dash than did the men of Gray's Inn. Both Southampton and the brilliant Francis Bacon—apparently serving as an alumnus—were diligent in the affair, together with the sons of dozens of other families both noble and renowned. But their hopes for a gay and glorious evening were to miscarry.

Apparently too many guests had been invited by the enthusiastic members. The Templars were scheduled to arrive at nine o'clock. Long before that hour the great hall of the Inn was thronged, as the historian of the occasion said, with "a great presence of lords, ladies and worshipful personages that did expect some notable performance." The Templars arrived at the appointed time and wedged themselves into the place somehow, pushing forward their ambassador and his escort of "brave gentlemen." He reached the stage and was received with a speech of mock solemnity, and seated.

By this time, however, there was such confusion and noise that the planned program began to break down. Even on the stage itself there was a "disordered tumult," and finally the Templars became "discontented and displeased," and left the hall. The festivities then got under way again, and at midnight the Lord Chamberlain's Men presented the play—*The Comedy of Errors,* "like to Plautus, his *Menechmus.*" It seems not to have had a very attentive audience—there were still crowding and confusion—but the title was hailed with delight.

"Well named!" cried out one of the crowd. "A play of errors for a night of errors!"

The words were seized on with whoops of jubilation. The historian for the Inn summed up what occurred: "So that night was begun and continued to the end in nothing but confusion and errors, whereupon it was ever afterwards called *The Night of Errors.*"

Thus what may have been, in an earlier form, the first written of all Shakespeare's plays won itself a place in London legend. It was more firmly fixed because of a mock trial held two days later by the Inn members, in which the "Sorceror," or provider of entertainment, was blamed for having "foisted a company of base and common fellows" from Shoreditch to "make up our disorders with a play of errors and confusions." This was all in fun, and the Chamberlain's Men doubtless took no offense. On January 3 they gave another performance —probably the same play—and the Templars were again invited to the Inn. They were "delighted and pleased" by a better-planned reception and performance.

This production of *The Comedy of Errors* reminds us that, along with his more sober work with chronicle plays, Shakespeare was continuing to write the lighter kind of drama which he had begun with *Love's Labor's Lost* and *The Two Gentlemen of Verona*. As we shall see, the play given at Gray's Inn was one of several comedies on which he had been working. These were to give him experience and reputation quite as great as he was earning with his stories of kings.

It has already been suggested (in Chapter VI) that *The Comedy of Errors* may have been written in first draft at or near Stratford in the fifteen-eighties, while Will Shakespeare was teaching at a school. To dramatize Plautus was certainly a natural attempt for a young pedagogue. Of course, such a first version must have had serious faults. Shakespeare, once he was an active player and writer, would have seen them clearly, and would have put the comedy aside for revision. But the play was probably staged as early as 1592, and then, during the long ban on the theaters, revised and streamlined for its presentation two years later. By that time it was a highly competent work as an acting play, although some of its crude rhymes seem to have survived from a period when Shakespeare was a beginner.

As already indicated, the chief source for the *Comedy* was Plautus's *Menaechmi* ("The Twins"). But this Latin comedy had only one set of brothers. Shakespeare added another pair; making twin servants, the Dromios, for the twin masters, the Antipholuses. He also added other characters, and devised other complications for the plot. (The Elizabethans, remember, liked a lot of action.) In fact, the plot was a somewhat dizzy and entangled affair, and Shakespeare might have had great trouble with it in 1591, as *Love's Labor's Lost* and *The Two Gentlemen of Verona* suggest. But now he romped through the difficulties he had created, and tied them up neatly in the end (after most of them had tied up the audience with laughter along the way).

The *Menaechmi,* like most Latin comedies, was a farce. So, to a large extent, is *The Comedy of Errors.* But Shakespeare apparently wanted something more than marvelous slapstick. So he introduced a theme of danger which contrasted with a theme of laughable confusion; and he also developed a love story. These elements make the play something more than mere fun. And they show that Shakespeare was feeling his way toward a type of comedy different from the satirical and farcical Latin models he knew, and different also from the elaborate elegance of Lyly. It would be a comedy mainly about people whom the audience could respect, in which the serious and the ridiculous were set side by side, and by contrast emphasized each other.

2

There were no memorable characters in the *Comedy.* It was a play of absurd complications, and the plot had the right of way. The characters were believable enough to speed the action along, and that was all anybody, including Shakespeare, asked of them. The laughs and surprises came for the most part from the mistakes in identities. They were funny enough in themselves. The play rocked those who saw it with laughter.

The Taming of the Shrew, on the other hand, has memorable characters.

This comedy, which also was ready for the Christmas season of 1594-95, was another revision of an earlier play. It was made over from *The Taming of a Shrew,* which some scholars believe to have been partly Shakespeare's.

Whether or not Shakespeare had much to do with this first *Shrew,* he made great changes in the comedy when he revised it in 1594. He altered scenes, names, the opening of the play, and made considerable changes in the action. He doubled the length of the comedy. But the important thing is that he made use of the idea suggested by the title to create unforgettable situations and characters that are world known today.

Katharina, the girl who all but bit off the heads of young men who tried to woo her, and Petruchio, who not only wooed her but changed her from a scold to a cheerful and obedient wife—these are the heart of the play. They *had* to be strong characters, and Shakespeare made them so. Petruchio especially is a triumphant creation—bold, ingenious, strong willed, with a fury of energy in him. The very task he sets himself means laughter—whether he wins or loses. And each situation is full of it. When he makes love talk to Kate, when he marries her, when he teaches her to value sleep, food, peace—at each turn there is a potential bomb of humor.

And already in *The Comedy of Errors* and in *The Shrew* Shakespeare was developing a kind of instinct for humor which more than all else would make his comedy great. This was it: *to select situations and actions that dealt with feelings shared by many people.*

To apply this to *The Taming of the Shrew*—here was an unpleasant woman. How make her pleasant? That was a challenge to Elizabethan males, for "shrews" and "common scolds" were familiar types. No ordinary citizen who found himself wedded to either could hope for escape in divorce. He had to tame his shrew or be her victim. We have women today (and men, too, of course) who are problems to their mates or friends in a similar fashion.

Again, Petruchio's campaign to change his Kate appeals to feelings that all people have. He becomes very loud, boastful, angry—that's taking the play away from her. What will she do? He keeps her awake at night (who doesn't love sleep enough to know what that means?), starves her, shows her beautiful caps and gowns, only to whisk them away, and at last accuses her violently of trying to oppose him. What will she do in turn?

Each of these situations is an opportunity, and Shakespeare uses

every opportunity with deftness, sure phrasing, keen imagination. He
can make humor of the slightest situation. There is the hungry Kate,
for instance, begging the servant Grumio (who is of course helping
Petruchio with his plot) for food. To emphasize the humor I give
suggestions in parentheses:

> KATH. (*pleading*): I prithee go and get me some repast;
> I care not what, so it be wholesome food.
> GRU. (*deadpan*): What say you to a neat's foot?
> KATH. (*eager*): 'Tis passing good: I prithee let me have it.
> GRU. (*cautious*): I fear it is too choleric a meat. (*new idea*)
> How say you to a fat tripe finely broiled?
> KATH. (*willing*): I like it well: good Grumio, fetch it me.
> GRU. (*hesitant*): I cannot tell: I fear 'tis choleric. (*new offer*)
> What say you to a piece of beef and mustard?
> KATH. (*enthusiastic*): A dish that I do love to feed upon.
> GRU. (*remembering*): Ay, but the mustard is too hot a little.
> KATH. (*hopeful*): Why, then, the beef, and let the mustard rest.
> GRU. (*stubborn*): Nay then, I will not: you shall have the mustard,
> Or else you get no beef of Grumio.
> KATH. (*reckless*): Then both, or one, or any thing thou wilt!
> GRU. (*now he has her*): Why then, the mustard without the beef.
> KATH. (*exploding*): Go, get thee gone, thou false deluding slave,
> (*beats him*)
> That feed'st me with the very name of meat!

A situation understandable to anyone, and a laugh all the world
can join in today as in the fifteen-nineties. Doubtless in the seven years
he had watched men laugh or not laugh at his jests or others', at his
dramatic situations or others', Shakespeare had consciously learned
something of why they laughed. And he had also learned a great deal
unconsciously, had developed instinct as well as knowledge. He would
still write humor that depended on local or timely allusions, but in
the main he picked situations that most men and women anywhere
could understand.

Of course, his comedy was now better for being more competently plotted than it had been, and for being written with more crispness and assurance and speed. *Love's Labor's Lost* had stumbled through poor plotting and long speeches. There was no stumbling in these two new comedies—full of action, suspense and rollicking surprises.

3

The following March the Queen's treasurer made an entry to the effect that he had paid £20 "for two several comedies or interludes showed . . . before her majesty in Christmas time last past." The payment was made "To William Kempe, William Shakespeare, and Richard Burbage, servants to the Lord Chamberlain."

The entry shows clearly who were the chief men in the troupe, and indicates that Shakespeare's position was now unquestioned. This is the first appearance of his name in such records. Always from this time forward the official mentions of him testify to his importance among his associates. This importance had begun with the reorganization of the company, and had grown rapidly during the following eight months.

Chiefly it had grown because of Shakespeare the writer. Aside from his revision of *Titus Andronicus,* he had furnished his fellow players with four plays in this period, all notable successes. The Chamberlain's Men had their older play manuscripts, of course; and they were buying new plays from other writers. But Shakespeare's work was already clearly outstanding. Whether he wrote an Elizabethan documentary on a king that became the talk of the town for its sharp action and stirring poetry, or whether he set the pit roaring with laughter over twins or a shrew, he was equally the master of the crowd and the joy of his fellows. Meanwhile, he was apparently doing his full share as an actor, and probably as a director of his own plays. The acting brought him an additional income, which he had no mind to lose, and the directing enabled him to see his work staged as he wished it to be. But these activities were already becoming less important than his writing, for writing created the plays that fathered all other activities.

By the spring of 1595 Anne Shakespeare and the three children had probably gone back to Stratford. Playhouse London with its rough crowds and elegant patrons would not have suited Mistress Shakespeare. She was thirty-eight now, and turning soberly toward religion. Shoreditch smelled and sounded too much of taverns and buffoonery to please her. It was a poor place for growing children. Country born, she longed for the simplicity and completeness of Stratford. Apparently the family, including Will, was already spending the summers there. Why remain in London for the winter?

Shakespeare himself preferred the country life; or at least he wrote of it with particular enthusiasm. He was never, like Marlowe or Jonson, to praise the city itself. But he wrote with gusto of hunting and falconry, of the dogs and the birds, of the fields, forests, hills and streams. They were already in *Henry VI, Richard II, The Shrew,* and the other plays he had been writing. Thus instinctively, amid the walls and cobblestones and smoky taverns of the city, Shakespeare was carrying about with him images of a greener and sunnier world—the world of Warwickshire.

In the winter of 1594-95 this world was much with him as he wrote a new play. It was a drama different from anything he had yet attempted. It was not farce comedy, though there was much fun in it. It was not a chronicle play, although it presented several rulers and their courts. No, this creation was a thing of a kind all its own—a fantasy. It was mixed together from legend, moonlight, young love, country clowning, and fairy magic. It was called *A Midsummer Night's Dream.*

The framework of the drama was the court of Duke Theseus of Athens, with its preparations for the wedding of Theseus and Hippolyta, Queen of the Amazons. Into this fitted three sets of characters. There were two pairs of lovers, Hermia and Lysander, Helena and Demetrius. (Demetrius had once loved Helena, but now disdained her. He was wooing Hermia, and had her father's support. Hermia, however, preferred Lysander.) There were the Athenian craftsmen, rehearsing the play they hoped to give at the Duke's wedding. And finally there were the fairies, with King Oberon and his Puck, and Queen Titania and her many followers. How all these characters met in a forest near Athens, how the standing quarrel of Oberon and Titania caused complications affecting alike the brash weaver Bottom and the four lovers, and how it was all set to rights in the end—this was the gist of the magic, moonlit and musical extravaganza that Shakespeare made.

In one sense the story was not his. He took Duke Theseus and Hippolyta from Plutarch, Ovid, and Chaucer's *The Knight's Tale* (which also had two young men as rivals in love, and many scenes in the forest). He took the fairy atmosphere partly from Chaucer, too, for in *The Merchant's Tale* Pluto and Proserpina, king and queen of fairydom, quarrel; and partly from Spenser. He may have drawn inspiration from Marlowe's *Dido,* and some from such Lyly comedies as *Sapho and Phao.* But regardless of what he took from such sources (and any Elizabethan writer cheerfully borrowed whatever of plot or character he could lay hands on), Shakespeare made a story completely and wholly his own. The atmosphere, the complicated plot, the triumphant solution, the poetry—all are Shakespeare's, and add up to a play the like of which the world had never known before and has never known since.

The whole was really a fantastic poem, broken occasionally with songs and comic interludes in prose. In a much finer and more literary way, it was to the Elizabethans what a musical comedy is to us. The characters were not important in themselves—they merged into the magic of the whole. And this magic took its strength partly from the ingenuity of the story but much more from the sheer beauty of language that both in speech and song gave atmosphere and seeming reality to this unreal story.

In *Richard II,* as we have seen, Shakespeare had shown that he could marry great drama and great poetry. That play, in spite of being history, had a sustained musical quality higher than anything else he had done. But in *A Midsummer Night's Dream* the poetic level of the play was raised to a height no English writer had ever reached before.

It is a little hard to describe what had happened. In one sense it lay in the texture of the lines; in another it was a sweep of imaginative quality that went through the entire drama.

As to the lines, even there it is hard to measure what was done. Marlowe had written beautiful lines, beautiful passages. He was always a skillful poet, even when not a highly distinguished one. But in the *Dream* Shakespeare made a new kind of beauty. It was never pretentious or thundering, as Marlowe's often was; rather it had a natural and yet highly musical quality. Take the first few lines of the play where Theseus enters with Hippolyta and his attendants, and speaks:

> THESEUS: *Now,* fair Hippolyta, *our* nuptial *hour*
> Draws *on* apace: *four* happy days bring in
> Another *moon;* but *O!* methinks, how *slow*
> This *old moon* wanes; she lingers my desires
> Like to a stepdame or a *dow*ager
> *Long* withering *out* a young man's reven*ue.*

There is nothing tremendously important about this speech. It is casual, giving some information to the audience. Yet the texture of the lines is beautiful. I have underlined the "ow," "o" and "oo" sounds, to show how Shakespeare repeats them. There is a lesser play of "ay" sounds in "apace," "days," "wanes," "stepdame." There is alliteration, too, supporting the rich vowels, and the total effect is one of easy, natural, yet arresting beauty. Such beauty is sustained as the play goes along, now in blank verse, now in rhymed couplets, now in songs, rising in passages to exquisite loveliness. The persistence of beauty is as notable as the high peaks of loveliness that Shakespeare attains.

There is another thing to be said about this poetry. More than ever before Shakespeare was now striking out memorable ways of saying things. Theseus bids Hermia consider if, when she refuses Demetrius, she can accept the life of a priestess—

For aye to be in shady cloister mewed,
To live a barren sister all your life,
Chanting faint hymns to the cold fruitless moon.
Thrice blessed they that master so their blood,
To undergo such maiden pilgrimage;
But earthlier happy is the rose distilled,
Than that which withering on the virgin thorn
Grows, lives, and dies in single blessedness.

All of this passage has phrases that we remember, but the three italicized lines have been remembered so well that they are quoted like the simplest proverbs. "In shady cloister mewed," "the cold, fruitless moon," "single blessedness"—these are Shakespeare language, inventions which those who speak English have used for centuries. Similarly in the *Dream* come lines like (to give only a few)

The course of true love never did run smooth,

and

To do observance to a morn of May,

and

In maiden meditation, fancy-free,

and

The lunatic, the lover, and the poet
Are of imagination all compact.

These were among the first of thousands of phrases in which Shakespeare fused truth and verbal music. Doubtless in 1595 those who saw *A Midsummer Night's Dream* were aware only of its general effect upon them. It was not printed until 1600; they could not single out lines and phrases. But its magic affected them without their fully understanding why.

Most of the scenes of the *Dream* were in the forest near Athens where the lovers met. So far as Shakespeare was concerned, this forest was in Warwickshire. The fairies who appeared there talked of the flowers and creatures that Shakespeare knew at first hand—oxlips, wild violets, woodbine, muskroses, cowslips, enameled snakes, bats, hedgehogs, spiders, newts, snails, bears and boars, doves, owls, and nightingales. These fairies are the fairies that the farm folk about Stratford knew—creatures who played tricks on them or did them good services. And Titania knows the farmland. She describes very accurately the wet summer of the year 1594, which she lays to Oberon's quarrel with her—

> Therefore the winds, piping to us in vain,
> As in revenge, have sucked up from the sea
> Contagious fogs; which falling in the land
> Have every pelting river made so proud
> That they have overborne their continents.
> The ox hath therefore stretched his yoke in vain,
> The plowman lost his sweat, and the green corn
> Hath rotted ere his youth attained a beard . . .
> Therefore the moon, the governess of floods,
> Pale in her anger, washes all the air,
> That rheumatic diseases do abound:
> And thorough this distemperature we see
> The seasons alter: hoary-headed frosts
> Fall in the fresh lap of the crimson rose,
> And on old Hiems' thin and icy crown
> An odorous chaplet of sweet summer buds
> Is as in mockery set.

This passage describes perfectly that dismal summer of 1594, as references in histories and sermons of the day picture it for us. Thus these seventeen lines seem to date the play as done in the fall of that year. Possibly it was produced before the Queen at Greenwich on January 26, 1595, when Elizabeth Vere (whom Southampton had so coyly avoided) married the young Earl of Derby.

There has come down to us a letter of John Lyly to Sir Robert Cecil about this occasion. It was written January 17, and Lyly complained bitterly that he had not been asked to write a play for the wedding.

"Among all the overthwarts of my poor fortunes this is the greatest," he protested. "My wits were not so low but that some invention might have graced if not for content yet for service."

But Lyly's sun was setting and Shakespeare's was ascending. Or was it in this case a moon, since the action was all by night? At any rate, up to that time no play had cast so magic and happy a radiance on the English stage.

4

That stage, whether in the Queen's palace at Greenwich or in the Theatre playhouse (where the *Dream* was shown to the public), was very limited as we know stages. How could it produce a play like *A Midsummer Night's Dream*? In the nineteenth century the piece was considered too difficult for effective presentation. How did Shakespeare's company manage it?

There are several answers. The first is that the very simplicity of the Elizabethan stage had its usefulness. The Theatre, as we shall see later, lacked certain improvements and resources which Shakespeare's company would soon introduce. But it had its inner stage, its outer stage, its second level stages and its trap doors. As a matter of fact, only the first two were needed for *A Midsummer Night's Dream*. It is very simple as to setting and stage properties. For the forest scenes a few bushes, perhaps the actual shrubs mounted on board bases, some branches on the pillars to make them into trees, and rushes on the stage floor for grass supplied everything that was needed when the action was on the outer stage. As a scene was being presented there, the inner stage could be set to indicate a change in locale, if only another part of the forest.

This was very simple, and not too impressive according to our ideas. But the Elizabethan crowds were used to letting their imaginations fill out a suggestion in setting. If a few bushes and branches appeared, of course it was a forest. If curtains and a table and a chair appeared, the spectators filled out the interior of a chamber. In costume they expected more, but they asked little in the way of scenery.

The simple stage with its rapid changes of scene had great advantages. The play unrolled as swiftly and smoothly as a modern film. This was especially important with something like the *Dream;* for the spell, once established, was never broken.

Finally, Elizabethan actors were thoroughly trained to play out this fantasy with deftness and conviction. Many of them were accomplished dancers. All were accustomed to moving about on a stage that put them among the spectators, and to creating and maintaining all kinds of illusions. So they tripped about as elf or fairy, artisan or lover, casting a spell upon the crowd as successful in its way as any cast by Puck or Oberon. The young lovers—both the girls played by artful boy actors—stirred the crowd's curiosity. How would Hermia get Lysander against her father's consent? What chance had Helena, the poor lass, with that disdainful Demetrius? When Puck appeared, the groundlings found a new interest. Here was the hobgoblin all their mothers had told them about, and by Hercules, was he not to the life? When Bottom with his ass's head won the love of Titania, the sailors and apprentices smote each other and roared with laughter. And when even Demetrius was brought to heel by Oberon's magic, that was a thing to see!

It was not a whit less pleasing, that magic, because most of the audience believed in it. Many well-read persons in London of that day were still convinced that in far-off lands lived wild dogs with hands and feet like men, that certain fishes came ashore at night to eat grain in the fields, and that dragons carried on a curious and fearsome existence in Macedonia and elsewhere. According to one Edward Topsell in his *History of Serpents,* these creatures swallowed eggs whole, and then rolled on the ground to break them, ate wild lettuce to help digest apples, and trapped elephants by making a cordon of their knotted tails! Witches and ghosts were grimly real to Elizabethans, fairies were pleasantly so. Shakespeare's audiences believed in springs with magic waters, and not a few spectators had purchased charms to win love or to do their enemies harm. *A Midsummer Night's Dream* thus enacted before them wonders the like of which they believed were occurring somewhere—in Arabia, in China, in Athens, or, on a midsummer's night, even in England itself!

XV: THE LOVERS

IN the spring of 1595 William Shakespeare was thirty-one. Sitting in his Shoreditch lodgings of an early May night, reading some new book that he had picked up from the trestles before St. Paul's or got from Dick Field, he must have reflected with a certain satisfaction upon his past activities in London.

In a swift eight years he had climbed from apprentice-actor and play-patcher to become one of the leading players of his company and the writer who was feeding the Chamberlain's Men with plays on which the troupe's reputation had grown to giant size. No man in the theater world had a position which promised greater prosperity than this young man from Stratford. No, not even Edward Alleyn, who was working with Henslowe at the Rose across the river.

Both these gentlemen heard with amazement the tales of their rivals' success at the Theatre.

"Why, they were like to fail when we brought the Admiral's Men back to life last summer!" exclaimed Henslowe.

"They have what we lack," Alleyn replied.

Henslowe fixed the tall actor with his sharp little eyes.

"What is that?" he asked.

"A new Marlowe."

The face of the older man puckered with annoyance.

"That fellow Shakespeare?" he asked. "Nay, Edward, there are not two Marlowes in one man's time. And as for writers, why, they are to be had by the dozen. Half-starved poets from the universities, eager to sell their pens. Bah!" he sputtered. "We'll have writers. I'll set a pair of them—nay, three, four, if necessary, to do a play!"

(And in the years that followed, he often did!)

"Four are no better than the skill of the best," answered Alleyn. "And I would wager that the best in London writes for those mummers in Shoreditch. We shall work hard and wisely or he will get the bigger crowd!"

For a dramatist in 1595 the crowded pit and galleries offered the final test. Already the time had come when word of a new play by William Shakespeare could send law students of the inns, gentlemen of the Court, and merchants and apprentices of the city off in a great jostling throng to Finsbury Field. They went because Shakespeare gave them superb entertainment. That meant skill. It did not mean that the spectators regarded the plays they saw as notable in a literary sense. As we have seen, what was written for the stage was not rated as true literature. It was less respectable in that sense than radio scripts are today.

Yet looking back through the centuries, we can see that by 1595 Shakespeare had not only tasted commercial success, but had also gone far as a literary artist. Already, for example, though Henslowe would not have admitted it, he had surpassed artistically anything in serious drama done by Marlowe. Both *Richard II* and *Richard III* were superior to *Tamburlaine* or *Faustus* or *Edward II*, if not by a great margin. Of course, only *Richard III* had rivaled Marlowe's "tragedies" in *popularity*. Again, Shakespeare, in his comedies, had done magnificent work in an artistic field that Marlowe had never entered. (Moreover, *The Comedy of Errors* and *The Shrew* were also uproarious commercial successes.) Then there was *A Midsummer Night's Dream*. Marlowe had written nothing to match its blend of humor and magic beauty, although that beauty had owed something to the stimulus of his verse.

Such accomplishments, as we look back on them, pile up an impressive total of superb writing. In variety and quality no other playwright of the age had equaled them, or would. Had Shakespeare died in 1595, he would still be rated as the greatest writer of drama for his era, and the greatest to write in English.

Yet up to that time he had mounted only the lower steps on the stairway of the greatness he would attain. He was now about to climb higher.

2

Two years before Shakespeare was born, in 1562, an English writer named Arthur Brooke had published a romance. He found it, as he was frank to say, in a *novella* by an Italian writer, Bandello. Bandello got the story from an earlier writer, Luigi da Porta, who in turn had borrowed it from a still earlier source—back in the fourteen-hundreds. This is merely to say that the tale was both old and oft-related. The English poet wrote his version in long rhymed couplets. They were heavy, but not without a leisurely charm. He called his poem-story *The Tragical History of Romeus and Juliet*.

The book was mildly popular. There was something poignant and haunting about the story it told. A feud between two great Italian families—love at first sight for the heir of one and the heiress of the other —the two lovers seeking to snatch happiness from the teeth of their quarreling houses—this was a tale with a wide appeal. We read it breathlessly enough today. The English of the fifteen-hundreds found it even more exciting. They, unlike us, knew by word of mouth or personal experience about bitter feuds between great families. And again, they knew the desperation of young love as few modern readers can know it. For in those days matches were usually made by parents, and the lovers who dared to choose for themselves often faced anger, harsh opposition and crushing penalties.

Shakespeare may have read *Romeus and Juliet* before he left Stratford, or soon after he came to London. He may have seen a play in it, may even have started one in 1591 or 1592. If he did, it was only to lay the attempt aside. He was not ready then to write this drama. Meanwhile he had doubtless made the acquaintance of John Florio, the tutor, friend and protégé of Southampton. Later Shakespeare used the translation of Montaigne published by this Englishman of Italian parentage. With the talented Florio he may have talked much about Italy. He may have learned from him, or from traveled Englishmen, or from visitors in London who came from Petrarch's and Boccaccio's land about life in Verona and other cities which he would use as settings for later plays.

When he had at last seen clearly what he would do with the ancient tale of two young Italian lovers, Shakespeare realized that he faced an attempt never made by him or any other writer. He saw that it demanded a warmth and depth and variety of emotion that would challenge all his skill and feeling.

"Dick," he may have asked young Burbage, "can you play a lover of fire as well as one of moonbeams? And make it holy fire that will melt a hard young prentice's heart, or draw tears from a tradesman, or his good wife?"

"What riddle is this?"

"Why, none. But I shall soon try to trap on paper such a love as no player ever poured out. We have been dainty and courtier-like with love, Dick, tied it to kings and wars and made magic of it, but we have never shown the very fiery yet sacred heart of passion. If I can do that it will set all London sighing—and speed a thousand elopements. But you, Dick, must cast the spell of its magic upon men, and you will have only a painted boy to sigh to and plead with."

And while Burbage stared uneasily at his friend, wondering about this new role that was hinted at so strangely, Shakespeare set about working with the story he had found in the rhymed couplets of Arthur Brooke.

3

The play *Romeo and Juliet* followed the old story pretty well. Yet, as Shakespeare had prophesied, it was new.

Partly the newness lay in its attitude toward love. Shakespeare had already written plays with love as a chief element—the clever, courtly love of *Love's Labor's Lost,* the romantic love of *Two Gentlemen of Verona,* the airy, delicate love of *A Midsummer Night's Dream.* But in *Romeo and Juliet* he seemed to ask, "What are lovers?" and by telling his story to give an answer. For in this story we see Romeo of the Montagues falling in love with Juliet of the enemy Capulets, and she with him. We share their rapture, the desperation that comes to them later, their very doom. So, in a sense, the play might be called "The Birth, Life, Death and Immortality of Love." It is all four.

But the newness lay also in the vividness of the characters Shakespeare created in telling this story. Naturally, a play about the very essence of love would have no power over its audiences if the people it told about were vapid and unreal. It would gather strength in proportion to the vividness of its hero and heroine, and of others associated with them.

Shakespeare had already created many lifelike characters. In fact, all his characters had vitality. Some, like Richard Crookback and Petruchio and even the quiet King Henry VI, lingered in the memory. But none except possibly Petruchio had shone with that kind of reality which makes an imaginary character more real to most people than even the real persons they know. In the hero and heroine of *Romeo and Juliet* Shakespeare for the first time created two such per-

sons. Ever afterwards, to think of young lovers has been to think of
Romeo and Juliet. Even a lover today, after three hundred and fifty
years, knows them as well as he knows a brother, a sister, a close friend.
Only his beloved is more real to him, and her, perhaps, he does not
know so clearly.

To understand this (and agree with it) you have only to read Act II,
Scene 2 of the play. As we come into it, the main action has already
begun. We have seen the turbulent hostility between the two princely
houses of the rich Italian city-state, Verona. We have seen the first
meeting of the youth and the girl—neither knowing who the other
was. We have seen how love between them was swift and sure (in
Romeo's case destroying on the instant his calf-love for the captious
Rosaline). We know also, now, that each has learned the other's identity—with a shock, a gasp, it is true, but without any change in feeling. With these things clear, we follow Romeo as he leaps over the
wall of Capulet's orchard (which indeed had fruit trees, but was more
like a large, enclosed garden), seeking Juliet.

Then he sees her.

> It is my lady; O! it is my love:
> O! that she knew she were!

he exclaims, and we share at once his almost reverent excitement. We
are lifted up with him into a mood of rapture, and find even its absurdities glorious—

> Her eyes in heaven
> Would through the airy region stream so bright
> That birds would sing and think it were not night.
> See! how she leans her cheek upon her hand:
> O! that I were a glove upon that hand
> That I might touch that cheek.

Juliet in her window sighs an "Ah, me!" and Romeo stands in a kind
of trance as he looks at her, saying to himself:

> O! speak again, bright angel; for thou art
> As glorious to this night, being o'er my head,

> As is a wingèd messenger of heaven
> Unto the white-upturnéd wondering eyes
> Of mortals that fall back to gaze on him
> When he bestrides the lazy-pacing clouds,
> And sails upon the bosom of the air!

How we see the upturned faces, watch the awesome flight! We are *in* Romeo, we *are* Romeo, caught up by a sureness of warm understanding and a beauty of expression that Shakespeare had never before joined so superbly together. But then Juliet speaks.

> O Romeo, Romeo! Wherefore art thou Romeo?
> Deny thy father, and refuse thy name;
> Or, if thou wilt not, be but sworn my love,
> And I'll no longer be a Capulet . . .
> 'Tis but thy name that is my enemy . . .
> What's in a name? That which we call a rose
> By any other name would smell as sweet—

At once Juliet is as real to us, as much the heart of love, as Romeo. He comes forward now, speaks and shows himself. Juliet feels a natural confusion at having been overheard, but this is banished by her strong sense of the rightness and fullness of her love. And so the exquisite scene advances. The high emotional pitch of it, the perfection of accent, do not flaw or falter. Romeo's candor, Juliet's tender chiding, her instinct to plan for the tomorrow—it is all first love to its most glorious life. Even the final dialogue, with its fumbling absurdities, is perfect.

> Rom. (*Seeing Juliet as she reappears and calls him*):
>   It is my soul that calls upon my name:
>   How silver-sweet sound lovers' tongues by night,
>   Like softest music to attending ears!
> Jul.: Romeo!
> Rom.:   My dear!
> Jul.:   At what o'clock tomorrow
>   Shall I send to thee?

Rom.:   At the hour of nine.
Jul.: I will not fail; 'tis twenty years 'til then.
       I have forgot why I did call thee back.
Rom.: Let me stand here till thou remember it.
Jul.: I shall forget, to have thee still stand there,
       Remembering how I love thy company.
Rom.: And I'll still stay, to have thee still forget,
       Forgetting any other home but this.

No scene like this had ever been written in any language. Perhaps up to this time no writer had felt young love worth exploring in this intimate and vivid way. At any rate, Shakespeare was the first to do it, and none after him has ever done it so well. Perhaps what he wrote here was an echo of his own first love in Stratford; or was it rather the love he had partly missed there, and in his maturity wished that he had known?

In any case, the scene shows us the vividness Shakespeare gave both to Romeo and to Juliet. He gave the same quality to Mercutio, Romeo's friend, whose wit and dash we remember, and whose unhappy death at the hands of the tigerish Tybalt, Juliet's cousin, we mourn. Juliet's nurse (doubtless played by a man—by Pope, perhaps) is another character to remember. Her robust, indiscreet, cunning and talkative personality was really a kind of literary mother to the boastful Sir John Falstaff whom Shakespeare would create a few years later. Finally, the wise Father Laurence is also memorable in a quieter way.

A third element that made *Romeo and Juliet* new—and also great—was its form and quality as a tragedy. Up to the time of its appearance there had really been no true tragedies in English. All the notable dramas that were given the name had either been chronicle plays or had lacked the craftsmanship and writing that might have entitled them to it. Actually *Faustus, Edward II, Richard III* and *Richard II*— two Marlowe and two Shakespeare creations—had been fully tragic in atmosphere, style and ending. With these *Tamburlaine, Part II* might also be grouped. But in such dramas there had been a tendency to follow historical sources too closely; or, as in *Faustus,* the common method of presenting a succession of effective scenes rather than building the story wholly out of character and tragic conflict had exerted too strong an influence. The difference between a tragic panorama and a full tragedy had been slight in all these plays; yet it had existed, and was important.

In *Romeo and Juliet* Shakespeare took the freedom he needed to make a true tragedy. It was, to be sure, a special type, in that it was a tragedy of young lovers, with more gaiety, wit and joy than most tragedies have. But almost from the balcony scene onward the doom of the lovers is foreshadowed. We see them about to be wed. Then, as Romeo comes from the wedding, Juliet's cousin Tybalt challenges him. Romeo refuses to fight and Mercutio scornfully leaps at the enemy in his stead. Romeo tries to part the two, and Mercutio is killed because of his interference. When Tybalt, who has fled, reappears, Romeo attacks and slays him.

The lovers survive this calamity. Juliet realizes that Romeo is the victim of circumstances. She knows, too, that he is more precious to her than a dozen Tybalts. But Romeo is banished from Verona by the Prince. Almost at the moment of the decree, Juliet's parents insist on her immediate marriage to Count Paris, a wealthy young nobleman. To save her from this, Friar Laurence gives her a potion that will cause the appearance of death, writing to Romeo of what he has done. Romeo never receives the letter, and the fatal ending follows as he hears of his lady's death and rushes back to end his life beside her bier. She, awakening from her drugged sleep, refuses to survive him; and dies too.

Here Shakespeare had a clear if complicated story, unencumbered by historical events. He tells it with a moving power. With each somber episode the rapture of the lovers changes and grows darker. Romeo and Juliet also change. From youth and girl they become, step by step, man and woman. The change begins with Juliet waiting for her husband after the wedding. She calls on night to come—

Come, night! Come, Romeo! Come, thou day in night!
For thou wilt lie upon the wings of night
Whiter than new snow on a raven's back.
Come, gentle night; come, loving, black-browed night,
Give me my Romeo: and, when he shall die,
Take him and cut him out in little stars,
And he will make the face of heaven so fine
That all the world will be in love with night,
And pay no worship to the garish sun.

This is already an older and deeper person (though quite as rapturous) than the girl of the first balcony scene. But the news of Tybalt's death ages Juliet with agony, like the agony Romeo himself is suffering as Friar Laurence tries to give him comfort and balance. And when the two have accepted their situation, and Romeo, after visiting Juliet, must make haste to set out for exile in Mantua before daylight comes, it is two graver lovers who watch the sky—

JUL.: Wilt thou be gone? It is not yet near day:
It was the nightingale, and not the lark,
That pierced the fearful hollow of thine ear;
Nightly she sings on yon pomegranate tree:
Believe me, love, it was the nightingale.
ROM.: It was the lark, the herald of the morn,
No nightingale: look, love, what envious streaks
Do lace the severing clouds in yonder east:
Night's candles are burnt out, and jocund day
Stands tiptoe on the misty mountain tops:
I must be gone and live, or stay and die.

And it is a far more mature Juliet who holds the sleeping potion in her hand, and fights down her horrible fears. For a moment it is as if she had heard of golden-haired Charlotte Clopton, and how she had wakened in her tomb at Stratford.

In a similar fashion Romeo, standing in Juliet's tomb before what he thinks is her corpse, has grown to a dignity he never had before.

O my love, my wife!
Death, that hath sucked the honey of thy breath,
Hath had no power yet upon thy beauty. . . .

Shall I believe
That unsubstantial Death is amorous,
And that the lean abhorréd monster keeps
Thee here in dark to be his paramour?
For fear of that I still will stay with thee,
And never from this palace of dim night
Depart again; here, here will I remain
With worms that are thy chambermaids; O here
Will I set up my everlasting rest,
And shake the yoke of inauspicious stars
From this world-wearied flesh.

So the gaiety, humor, rapture, doubt, fear and desperation of growing love are all resolved in this final dark moment. But the course of
their starry passion, though leading to disaster, has deepened and up-
lifted the lovers. Death becomes a kind of testimonial to their faith
in love. If they go out defeated, they are as exalted as victors.

4

The first performance of *Romeo and Juliet* probably was given in
1596. It was of course acted in the Theatre, now a venerable structure
of twenty years' activity. The play fitted the playhouse. For the action
was now in the street, for which the main stage served well; now in
the Capulet ballroom, for which the study would make a fitting back-
drop. Or it might combine the chief acting space below with a second-
level window above, or use the gallery for Juliet's chamber, or the
inner stage (study) for Friar Laurence's cell.

The play went rapidly from scene to scene. The Chorus (much like
a modern radio narrator in function) speaks in a crisp sonnet-prologue
of "the two hours' traffic of our stage." That was doubtless a fairly ex-

act report on the time the performance took—about two-thirds or less of what it would take today. The Elizabethan playhouse permitted this pace, and the play needed it. When, in the nineteenth century, the stage required elaborate scene changes, *Romeo and Juliet* seemed heavy and difficult to give. It only came to life again in the nineteen-twenties, when Jane Cowl and Rollo Peters, using the resources of the modern theater to cut down time between scenes and acts, played it fast again.

How did the Elizabethans like this tragedy of young love?

No description of their enthusiasm for it can be too extreme. It surpassed even *Richard III* in popularity. Law students, noblemen, prentices, merchants, trollops, servingmen—all flocked to the Theatre. The play was the talk of the town and the subject of poems. It was even mentioned in other plays. In one, produced in 1598, *The Scourge of Villainy*, one character asks another:

> Luscus, what's play'd today? Faith, now I know
> I set thy lips abroach, from whence doth flow
> Naught but pure *Juliet and Romeo.*

A printer got hold of a copy somehow, and rushed it into print. At Cambridge University the student-playwrights quoted from it in 1598, and later, in a second play, one of the characters accuses students of imitating the language of the London drama: "We shall have nothing but pure Shakespeare. Mark *Romeo and Juliet!* Oh, monstrous theft!" At Oxford the enthusiasm must have been as great. Later the students of that university, reading a copy of Shakespeare chained to the shelves, wore through the page facing the balcony scene!

Shakespeare was annoyed at the appearance of the "pirated" copy in 1597. He got permission to print *Romeo and Juliet* and *Love's Labor's Lost* (which had also been printed from a defective text) in their correct form. The regular playbooks of the company seem to have been used for this work. In one place, instead of "Enter Peter," the text reads, "Enter Kempe." The publication of two versions of *Romeo and Juliet* within a year gives us a fortunate glimpse of the play in its earlier forms. Later, unfortunately, Shakespeare paid little attention to what the printers did with his plays. He was older, busier perhaps. But we shall speak of his seeming indifference at the time when it was shown.

5

Before leaving *Romeo and Juliet,* let us look at the kind of poetry Shakespeare wrote in it. For just as the tragedy marks a new stage in Shakespeare's growth in the building of serious plays, in the maturity of his outlook, and in his creation of characters, so it shows also his growth as a poet.

Romeo and Juliet draws no sharp dividing line between one kind of poetry and another. Indeed, there is no such line in Shakespeare. But the play does show certain tendencies and accomplishments that are worth understanding.

In Chapter VIII we spoke of what Marlowe had done with blank verse. The best way of tracing Shakespeare's growth is to start with Marlowe. But first let us list certain terms which are used in referring to this kind of poetry, and illustrate them.

End-stopped line. That has been explained. The line is fairly complete in itself. The reader does not have to depend on the previous line or the following one in order to understand it. Example:

See, what a grace was seated on this brow.

Run-over line. This type of line *does* depend upon the line after it. To complete the sense, the reader must go farther. Example:

Takes off the rose
From the fair forehead of an innocent love
And sets a blister there.

Masculine ending. The final syllable of a line which takes an accent and is therefore firm and strong.

Feminine ending. An unaccented syllable, which is also not needed to complete the usual ten, and is therefore light in tonal value.

Examples of both:

> In the name of truth,
>
> Are ye fantastical, or that indeed
>
> Which outwardly ye show? My noble partner
>
> You greet with present grace and great prediction
>
> Of noble having and of royal hope.

Lines 1, 2 and 5 have masculine endings. Lines 3 and 4 have feminine ones.

In several of the quotations above there is a period or question mark in the middle of the line, completing one thought, and leading to another. This is called a *broken line*.

We have already spoken of vowel sounds and alliteration as influencing the tonal quality of lines.

Finally, we should speak of *accent*. In theory, a line of blank verse had five feet of two syllables each, with the accent on the second syllable. Actually, few good lines fall into this exact pattern. Here is one that almost does—

> And say which grain will grow and which will not.

Using the ′ to mark the accented syllable, ˘ to mark an unaccented one, and ˌ to mark a weak stress, you can see that this line is naturally regular, except that the words "say" and "which" do not take accents quite so full as the others. Indeed, some people would argue that there were only three accents in the line—

> And say which grain will grow and which will not,

but the line *can* be spoken naturally with five accents.

That is rare. For most lines tend to have irregularities of accent, often stressing the first syllable—

> Beauty too rich for use, for earth too dear,

and sometimes stressing both syllables in the same foot as "too rich" and "too dear" in the line just above.

Let us keep these irregularities of accent in mind, and go back to Marlowe.

As I pointed out in Chapter VIII, Marlowe used end-stopped lines for the most part, along with masculine endings, and few broken lines. In accent pattern his lines were fairly close to the theoretical blank verse line. (Any skillful and gifted poet, and Marlowe was both, would vary the accent patterns of his lines instinctively.) Marlowe used vowel and consonant sounds skillfully to make musical effects.

In the beginning, Shakespeare followed Marlowe in all these characteristics. There are few run-over lines in the early historical plays, or in *Love's Labor's Lost* or in the other comedies he had written up to 1595. It is surprising how seldom a line is sharply broken. At first Shakespeare did not equal Marlowe in the fine tonal quality of his lines; he began to do so in *Richard II;* and in *A Midsummer Night's Dream,* as we have seen, he wrote with a sheer beauty that not even Marlowe could produce so naturally or sustain so well. In all these plays he had used rhyme to an extent—more than Marlowe had. He used it extensively both in the *Dream* and in *Romeo and Juliet.*

But he had now begun a process which was to continue as the years passed. The general trend was toward greater freedom. These were the particular forms taken:

1. The use of more run-over lines
2. The use of more feminine endings
3. The use of more broken lines
4. Greater variety and irregularity in the use of accent
5. In general, after *Romeo and Juliet,* a decline in the use of rhyme.

These five trends increased in Shakespeare's writing almost year by year. They increased so regularly and steadily that they have been used (and perhaps with too much confidence) to date his plays. Certainly a play with few run-over lines, few feminine endings, few broken lines, and a considerable use of rhyme is an early play. Certainly, too, a play

with many run-over lines, feminine endings and broken lines is a
late play. (The poetry of the later plays was not necessarily *better* than
that of the earlier ones, but it was more flexible.)

Romeo and Juliet is interesting as a study of Shakespeare's progress
in poetry. It is really at the end of his earlier period and at the beginning of his mature, confident work.

The use of rhyme is frequent: there are several sonnets and not a
few rhymed passages. This may mean that the play was begun first
in the early fifteen-nineties, but probably it does not. Rhyme is used
mostly in the earlier part of the drama, when Romeo was a relatively
artificial young man. Shakespeare was mildly satirizing the Euphuistic,
artificial mode of love in these scenes. Once Romeo really falls in
love, rhyme tends to disappear.

In general, Shakespeare was still writing end-stopped lines. He wrote
them exquisitely. For example—

> O! swear not by the moon, the inconstant moon [says Juliet],
> That monthly changes in her circled orb,
> Lest that thy love prove likewise variable.

Other quotations above (such as the passage beginning "O speak again,
bright angel") show how smoothly and with what a fine music Shakespeare could use the more regular type of blank verse. But in *Romeo
and Juliet* he went further than in any other previous play of his in
breaking his lines and running the sense over. As in this dialogue:

> Rom.: What shall I swear by?
> Jul.:   Do not swear at all;
>   Or, if thou wilt, swear by thy gracious self,
>   Which is the god of my idolatry,
>   And I'll believe thee.

There had been a time when Shakespeare, like Marlowe, would have
ended each speech at the end of a line. But now he was making poetry
more natural (though no less poetry), and more varied in its rhythms.
When Juliet wakes in the tomb, shaking off the effects of the sleeping

draught she had taken, and finds Romeo lying dead at her feet, her
words fall into even sharper patterns.

> What's here? A cup closed in my true love's hand?
>
> Poison, I see, hath been his timeless end.
>
> O churl! drunk all, and left no friendly drop
>
> To help me after! I will kiss thy lips;
>
> Haply some poison yet doth hang on them,
>
> To make me die with a restorative.
>
> > *[Kisses him.*
>
> Thy lips are warm!

The accent pattern, it will be seen, is quite jagged and irregular,
with stresses on syllables usually unstressed, with double and even
triple stresses, and with numerous light syllables in other places (where
lines have as few as three accents). Also, there is a tendency to break
the lines. What Juliet feels fits naturally into such patterns, but in
1590 Shakespeare would have kept a smoother verse pattern. More
like this:

> What's here? A cup closed in my true love's hand?
>
> Hath poison been his doom and timeless end?
>
> O churl, to leave no friendly drop for me,
>
> To help deliver me from this woeful earth.
>
> Perhaps some poison hangs still on thy lips,
>
> And if I kiss them I shall get some drops
>
> To make me die with a restorative.
>
> > *[Kisses him.*
>
> The warmth of life is still upon thy lips.

Of course Shakespeare would doubtless have bettered the above,
had he written in end-stopped lines, but however well written, such

lines would lose force and edge.

In all the above quotations there are no feminine endings. In general Shakespeare avoided them. But they come in, especially toward the end of the play—

> Tell me not, friar, that thou hear'st of this,
> Unless thou tell me how I may prevent it,

and

> Lest in this marriage he should be dishonored,
> Because he married me before to Romeo.

There are a number of others. Shakespeare was writing boldly, bending poetry to his dramatic purposes, and making new patterns of sound and accent.

For us it seems fortunate that in *Romeo and Juliet* he was still using chiefly the more even, flowing type of verse. Its smoothness suits the ecstatic nature of young love, and Shakespeare was breaking that smoothness just enough to give emphasis to the extremes of happiness and grief that the play touched in its swift two hours of emotion.

XVI: WILLIAM SHAKESPEARE, GENT.

EARLY in the year 1596, John Shakespeare of Stratford-upon-Avon applied to the College of Heralds for a coat of arms.

It was a renewal of his application of twenty years earlier. Will Shakespeare attended to most of the details. As the older son of the family he was a successful man in London, and could bring influence to bear even at the College, center of social correctness though it was. He could speak smoothly with the beruffed officials and give the desired information with dignity and assurance. His father was an old man now—almost seventy. Without his son's aid he could scarcely have pretended to meet some of the conditions he was supposed to fulfill, such as having "lands and tenements" to the value of £500. He could not even pay the fees demanded by the College. It was both natural

218

nd necessary for Will to manage the whole affair.

However, John Shakespeare felt an immense satisfaction in the
rospect of becoming a gentleman.

"Ill fortune cheated me twenty years ago, Will. I had earned it then.
But now by your help it will come to pass!"

"If you take pleasure in it, Father, I take the more."

"Aye, I take pleasure in it, pleasure enough," the old glover de-
lared. "I can hold my head high in the town again now. And I can
eave this world with a good name."

"Your name ever was good, Father."

Will, like John Shakespeare, looked with satisfaction toward getting
he coat of arms. Probably with even more than his father had. He too
ad cherished the hope of gentility from Stratford days. His work in
he theater had intensified that hope. As a player he was classified in
he statutes of the Queen along with "rogues, vagabonds and sturdy
beggars." The law was plain—"All such ruffians, vagabonds, master-
ess men, common players, and evil-disposed persons" except those
under a "baron of the realm" were subject to arrest and punishment.
True, having a patron, he was safe; yet his calling was slurred by such
anguage, and many people looked down upon it. Like all respectable
actors, Will resented both the slur and the attitude of the public. He
ad written bitterly in Sonnet III:

> O! for my sake do you with Fortune chide,
> The guilty goddess of my harmful deeds,
> That did not better for my life provide
> Than public means, which public manners breeds.
> Thence comes it that my name receives a brand,
> And almost thence my nature is subdued
> To what it works in, like the dyer's hand.

The sonnet may have exaggerated Shakespeare's actual feeling—
for dramatic purposes. Yet from many recorded remarks made in
those days we know that most Elizabethans regarded acting as a not
quite respectable calling. True, players had lordly patrons now, were

educated men, produced dramas written by poets in playhouses that were among the new wonders of the day. Yet they had once been no better than dancers and tumblers, and the old stigma still clung to them. Men like Marlowe and Lyly, who were gentlemen by right of education (and by family, in Lyly's case), could scorn the public's disapproval. Others, like Shakespeare, were forced to endure it.

But a coat of arms would "gentle" Shakespeare—give him a legal equality with many of his acquaintances from the Inns of Court and with fellow playwrights like Nashe and Peele. Southampton could be his friend with less embarrassment. Doubtless, too, Will hoped to lift his profession slightly as he lifted himself. He respected it, and knew that as more actors became gentlemen, acting would be raised somewhat in public opinion. He, like others in the theater, wanted to dissociate players and loose conduct. He would have agreed with what his friend Thomas Heywood wrote not many years later in *An Apology for Actors* (published in 1612):

I could wish that such [actors] as are condemned for their licentiousness might by a general consent be quite excluded our society; for as we are men that stand in the broad eye of the world, so should our manners, gestures and behaviors savor of such government and modesty, to deserve the good thoughts and reports of all men.

Perhaps Shakespeare was the first of all players not born a gentleman to win that title for himself. Certainly he was one of the first. He may have set an example. In his own company alone five of his associates eventually acquired coats of arms—Phillips, Pope, Cowley, Heminges and Richard Burbage. So did actors in other troupes—notably Edward Alleyn, who profited as actor, playhouse owner, and Master of the King's Games of Bears, Bulls, and Dogs; then retired and founded the College of God's Gift at Dulwich in 1619!

Shakespeare could well have felt that he had earned his arms. In the less than two years since he had returned to the theater, he had been a very demon of industry. He had acted, helped direct rehearsals, read the plays of other authors which were submitted to the company. In addition, he had provided five new scripts of his own.[1] True, two of these were old plays which he had rewritten; but for practical purposes they were new. And Shakespeare had more plays under way, or planned. Probably *Romeo and Juliet* was partly done, and the playwright had blocked out a new chronology called *The Life and Death of King John*. A third drama, somewhat like Marlowe's *Jew of Malta*, was taking shape in his imagination, later to be known as *The Merchant of Venice*.

His plays had brought him double money. They had enriched Shakespeare the actor by from £40 to £60 (from $3,000 to $4,500 in our money value). As a "sharer" in the company with the other full-fledged actors he had received a larger sum from them than was usually the case, for all the plays had drawn superbly. Probably he had received a third and smaller income from such money as he had advanced to help repair the Theatre and launch the Chamberlain's Men in London.

So Shakespeare could easily afford the £25 or £30 in fees which he would have to pay to become a gentleman, and he would have money for other expenditures in connection with his new station in life. Already he may have had ideas as to what he would spend and why.

2

If Will was happy at this time in the prospect of becoming a gentleman, he was also pleased with the prospects that had opened up for the Chamberlain's Men. For a time, the future had seemed rather doubtful. Now it looked bright. Let us see what had occurred.

We must go back to the troubles of James Burbage and his sons over the Theatre. So far as the building had been concerned, these had been more or less settled by 1590. But the lease for the land remained a problem.

Crusty old Giles Alleyn, the owner, was responsible for that situation. He had given Burbage a lease until March 25, 1597. Unless it

---

[1] *The Comedy of Errors, The Taming of the Shrew, Richard III, Richard II, A Midsummer Night's Dream.*

was extended before that date, Burbage could not use the Theatre longer, although he had a right to tear down the building and cart it away.

The terms of the lease provided for renewal at the original rent of £14 for a further ten years if Burbage spent £200 improving the "tenements" that went with the property. Burbage had spent the money and tried again and again to get the ten-year extension.

"Nay," Alleyn would tell him, "you have been a bad tenant and owe me rent."

"Which I am ready to pay!"

"I am much troubled in conscience that plays be given here," Alleyn would say then, shifting ground. He was a Puritan. "And the rents are too little for the value the property has, in any case," he would add.

"Which value was given it by none but me and my players!" Burbage would cry indignantly. "But come, come, I understand these niceties of conscience. If more gold cross your palm, conscience will be meek and quiet as a sitting hare. What will content you, then? Come, speak up! If it be in reason, we may yet agree."

"Nay, nay, there is time enough," Alleyn would mutter, and Burbage could get no satisfaction.

However, in this dilemma he suddenly got an idea that seemed more wonderful to him than his original conception of the Theatre, twenty years earlier. It was to build a playhouse within the walled city, in the Liberty of Blackfriars.

That had not seemed to be a possibility in 1576. Perhaps Burbage had then been looking for a plot of empty ground, or for an old building he could tear down. Neither was available. Or perhaps he had merely dismissed Blackfriars as sure to be too expensive for him.

He looked at it now with ample resources available, and with different plans for a playhouse.

"Why, lad," he explained to his son Cuthbert, "what we want is not empty land but a stout building. Such a one as, by knocking down a wall or two, we can make over into a hall. In this hall can a stage be built, and we shall have a theater that will be roofed from the wind and cold of winter. 'Twill bring us a fortune."

"How will you light it?"

"Why, as they light halls for their plays at the Inns of Court, or before Her Majesty. Better things can be done by torch and candle than by murky daylight."

"But what if you find no such hall?" asked the shrewd Cuthbert.

"I have found it already, I think," replied his father with a smile. "The ancient Frater of the monks."

"Ah, that immense barn of a building that was their old dining hall. Yes, it's a strong thing, and large enough."

His father nodded triumphantly.

"I can manage a playhouse there, 65 feet in length and 46 in breadth," he said. "It will answer our purpose well. Think of it, in the heart of the city! There dwell the Queen's Treasurer, and Lord Hunsdon your patron, Lord Cobham, Sir Thomas Cheney and hundreds more. This will be a playhouse for quality."

James Burbage bought the Frater for £600, and began to convert it into a theater. He provided for heating the building with sea-coal fires. He built a stage at one end of the hall. Along the sides and across the other end he erected galleries. Great chandeliers were installed to illuminate the stage.

Will Shakespeare, visiting the building as it rang with saw and hammer, thought he perceived in it a bright professional future to match his new station as gentleman. For the theater would be one for the better born and more prosperous. It would have no pit. Every seat would bring a respectable price—sixpence at least. Only gentlefolk and nobles and prosperous merchants would frequent such a playhouse, and they would make audiences for whom he could write in as noble a vein as he would. He need not think of pleasing apprentices and servingmen. Thus the playhouse taking shape under Burbage's direction seemed to promise a happy future. It would be a true home for the best work he could do.

3

It may occur to you that Will Shakespeare was a bit of a snob. His coat of arms, you will say, meant a little too much to him. He was too much ashamed of his profession. He was too quick to dislike the common folk who crowded the pit and who doubtless had their virtues regardless of their boisterous manners or the exact date of their most recent bath.

If such suspicions have grown on you, they are in one sense just. They tally with facts and probabilities. Shakespeare did yearn for gentility. He was ashamed of being an actor. And while in his own person he never speaks scornfully of the crowd, there are many scenes in the plays which picture it as ignorant, dirty, and easily swayed to violence, while in few passages are the lower classes described with sympathy and respect. From our point of view, we could wish Shakespeare to be somewhat different in all these attitudes.

But his world was not ours, and his attitudes were shaped by his world. It was pointed out early in this book that the medieval age and the modern age had met in the life he knew. In matters social, the medieval still dominated. Shakespeare accepted it. He believed in its layers of authority. He believed in the loyalty of servant to master, of knight to baron, of baron to king. He tended to look upon the higher classes with approval, and to scorn the lowest. Time and again he seems to show his distaste for the dirty, ignorant, changeable, violent crowd of the common people.

On the other hand, Shakespeare was a firm believer in most of the personal virtues that we admire, and he scorned or hated most of the vices we scorn or hate. He had no use for pretentious fops, or for people with pretensions of any kind. None of the characters he paints as admirable speaks discourteously to a humbler person. In several instances (as with Helena in *All's Well That Ends Well*) intelligence and virtue are held up as more important than birth. He believed in rights and liberties under the law. There is evidence that as a person he was friendly with humbler folk, and had their esteem (see Chapters XXI and XXV). In the play *Henry IV, Part II,* which he was soon to write, he approved of a chief justice who dared to imprison a king's son. In *Julius Caesar,* he made liberty a thing of immense value, and tyranny something to be hated and attacked. (Here, of course, he followed the story of Caesar as the Greek biographer Plutarch had told it.) However, the Romans who killed Caesar for freedom's sake were men of family and station, like the great nobles of the English Wars of the Roses. Freedom was *their* right, and perhaps that of all Romans of good family. It was only indirectly of concern to the Roman people, whom Shakespeare paints with kindly contempt.

Of course, in its social rise during the life of father and son, the Shakespeare family had been modern. A tenant farmer's son had become a tradesman. A tradesman's son was now about to become a gentleman. Such changes would have been all but impossible in the fourteen-hundreds, when a man was born into a certain place in society and kept it. The birth of Protestantism as a religion, world trade, new industries, the upsurge of the theater—all had played a lively part in pushing the Shakespeares upward.

But although Will Shakespeare must have known this well enough, and although he was an innovator in his profession, socially he looked toward the past. The society of the future would put greater emphasis on business enterprise and less on military prowess. Wealth would be almost as important as family. Political power would shift from the great nobles to the lesser ones, and to gentry and tradesmen. But Shakespeare shows no love for such a world. He writes of, and seems to admire, a world of lineage and power, the world of great nobles like Leicester, Southampton and Essex. Kings, generals and wealthy gentlemen are his heroes.

Partly he may have accepted this aristocratic universe because he associated with aristocrats, studied how to please and amuse them, and absorbed their attitude toward life. Partly he accepted it because the shape of a more democratic English world had not yet clearly emerged in men's minds. In only a few years it would. And possibly if

Shakespeare had lived into the sixteen-thirties and seen Parliament struggling with the Stuart kings, he would have been drawn to the side of Liberty. He hated injustice, abuse of power, arrogance, pride, cruelty. I myself think that he might have taken his place with Pym and Eliot as a believer in the rights of English citizens. No one can tell. Yet if Shakespeare had lived to take such a position, it would have marked a definite shift in attitude. His writings as we have them indicate that he would have been aware of the abuses of the Stuart kings, but if forced to a choice would have sided with them because he felt it wrong to assault supreme authority.

This attitude of Shakespeare's should be remembered. It affected his everyday life, and it affects his writing. The effect, however, is less than one might believe; Shakespeare after all had a twentieth-century (or even a twenty-fifth century) knowledge of human beings, with a comparable gift of expression. His approval of aristocracy is never marred by a like approval of vice, injustice, tyranny or folly.

4

The bright prospects of the spring of the year 1596 darkened with summer. The first blow was perhaps the greatest that Will Shakespeare ever received. Early in August his only son, now eleven years old, died at Stratford. He was buried on August 11.

If we go by the facts we have, Hamnet Shakespeare is only a name associated with his father's. If we go by what is probable, he becomes much more. A twin, with his sister Judith, he may appear in half a hundred lines about children which Will Shakespeare wrote before and after the boy's death. The poet speaks of a father whose children are nursed "to take a new acquaintance of his mind" (Sonnet 77); as his own often did when he returned to Stratford after being long in London. He speaks of children singing, riding on their father's back. He gives a picture of a child stilled by a tragic story, pausing and weeping; of a father who is a boy again in his son's games, of a boy overawed by his schoolmaster, and many other fragmentary glimpses which seem to be taken from his own experience. In *Titus Andronicus,* the boy Lucius carries a copy of Ovid's *Metamorphoses* about with him—the gift of his mother. And his father says to him

> Thy grandsire loved thee well;
> Many a time he danced thee on his knee,
> Sung thee asleep, his loving breast thy pillow;
> Many a matter hath he told to thee,
> Meet and agreeing with thine infancy.[2]

Here we may well have a glimpse of John Shakespeare and his grandson, as Shakespeare saw them together in the old house on Henley Street.

In *Richard III* the two princes, sons of King Edward IV, may have something of Hamnet in them, but it is perhaps young Arthur in *The Life and Death of King John* who has most of Will Shakespeare's son.

For that play was finished not long after the boy's death. The playwright was probably not in Stratford in August; the Chamberlain's Men were touring Kent. He may have started for Stratford at the end of the summer's work, may even have arrived there without hearing of the tragedy.

If so, it struck the sharper for being discovered abruptly. Hamnet had symbolized the future for which Will Shakespeare was building. Probably he had planned that the boy should attend one of the great universities, inherit the new family wealth, carry on the name. Well-read, clad like a young nobleman, sure of an income, he would be one with whom the poet-playwright could talk of art and learning.

Such dreams were now shattered. There would be no son to continue the immediate family. There were only two girls, neither schooled as Hamnet had been, neither able to perpetuate the Shakespeare name.

Will had probably brought a beginning of *King John* with him to Stratford, intending to work on it in the lull between the summer's tour and the autumn opening of the London playhouses. He may even

---

[2] V. iii. 161–165.

have had a rough draft of the entire play. He was modeling it some-what on a crude older chronicle drama, *The Troublesome Reign of King John*. The character of the boy Arthur was in this play, and Shakespeare had already made him a part of his own more modern version.

John stood far back in English history in comparison with Shake-speare's other kings. His time was almost two hundred years before that of Richard II. The brother of Richard I of England (Coeur de Lion, or the lion-hearted), he is known today chiefly as the signer of the Magna Charta. Shakespeare never mentions that document. He tells the story of John's wars with Philip of France and his dispute with the Pope. Both were complicated by the existence of John's nephew Arthur.

Technically, young Arthur had a better title to the English crown than John. He was the son of Geoffrey, John's older brother. Philip had taken up Arthur's claim, pushed eagerly by his mother Constance. Quite naturally, John disputed it. In the play, as in history, the English king captures the boy. He whispers to Hubert, his jailer, that the young prince must die. "Death. A grave." "He shall not live," the other re-plies.

Later, when Arthur has been taken to England, Hubert comes to carry out a modified but horrible form of his promise. But Arthur, meanwhile, has become well acquainted with him. He senses his keep-er's purpose, then is told it—to burn out his eyes. The boy pleads with his jailer. He reminds him that

> When your head did but ache
> I knit my handkercher about your brows . . .
> And with my hand at midnight held your head,
> And like the watchful minutes to the hour,
> Still and anon cheered up the heavy time,
> Saying, "What lack you?" and "Where lies your grief?"

Was this a memory Shakespeare had of Hamnet? There are other touches which seem taken from the life, and the poignancy of the whole scene may take root from Shakespeare's personal grief. Hubert lacks the heart to carry out his orders. He leaves the boy.

And, pretty child, sleep doubtless and secure.

But Arthur, attempting to escape, leaps from a wall (the second level of the stage) and is killed. He is found by some English nobles, including the Bastard (Sir Philip Faulconbridge, natural son of Richard Coeur de Lion). They think the child has been murdered. As they lift their voices, it seems as if some of Shakespeare's own personal lament had crept into the lines. Cries one—

> This is the very top,
> The height, the crest, or crest unto the crest,
> Of murder's arms: this is the bloodiest shame,
> The wildest savagery, the vilest stroke,
> That ever wall-eyed wrath or staring rage
> Presented to the tears of soft remorse.

The others take up the theme with bitter eloquence. When Hubert appears, several accuse him of murdering the boy. He denies it, and is defended by Faulconbridge. But when the others have left, Hubert's defender tells him—

> If thou didst but consent
> To this most cruel act, do but despair;
> And if thou want'st a cord, the smallest thread
> That ever spider twisted from her womb
> Will serve to strangle thee; a rush will be a beam
> To hang thee on; or would'st thou drown thyself,
> Put but a little water in a spoon,
> And it shall be as all the ocean,
> Enough to stifle such a villain up.

In such tense, jabbing words Shakespeare's own personal sorrow could have had relief.

King John had the faults of dramatized history. The story was not so simple as those of *Richard III* and *Richard II*. Still, the play had power. John himself, neither wholly villain nor wholly hero, was something of an embarrassment to the playwright. But Arthur and Constance were vigorously and sensitively painted, and in Faulconbridge Shakespeare created a vital character—a devil-may-care, blunt-spoken, powerful, scene-shaking fellow who injects humor into the drama (which, in general, Shakespeare had avoided in his previous chronologies) and a fine patriotism. Faulconbridge serves John because John is England, and at the end of the play he speaks words that show Shakespeare's own mounting pride in his native land:

> This England never did, nor never shall,
> Lie at the proud foot of a conqueror,
> But when it first did help to wound itself . . .
> Come the three corners of the world in arms,
> And we shall shock them. Nought shall make us rue
> If England to itself do rest but true.

5

The death of Hamnet Shakespeare was not the only death in the Shakespeare family that year. Harry Shakespeare, the poet's farmer-uncle, must have been ailing before Will left Stratford; he died late in December, his wife soon following him. Probably these events did not touch the poet closely, although they may have saddened him.

Certainly Will was more affected in a practical way by the death of Lord Hunsdon, his company's patron, late in July, and by rumors of opposition to the playhouse which James Burbage was completing in the Liberty of Blackfriars. By the time Shakespeare and others had returned to London in the fall, the householders of that area were wagging indignant heads at the idea of a public theater in their midst. A petition was circulated among them. It was signed by thirty-one persons, including the Dowager Countess of Bedford, the new Lord Hunsdon, and two friends of Shakespeare—Richard Field and John Robinson (later a witness to his will). The Privy Council got the petition in November.

It set forth what Burbage had been doing and hoped to do, and asserted that the proposed playhouse "will grow to be a very great annoyance and trouble . . . both by reason of the great resort and gather together of all manner of vagrant and lewd persons, that under color of resorting to the plays will come thither and work all manner of mischief, and also to the great pestering and filling-up of the same precinct, if it should please God to send any visitation of sickness."

The playhouse would also disturb divine services, the petitioners argued, with drums and trumpets. So they begged the Council to "take order that the same rooms [which Burbage was remodeling] be converted to some other use, and that no playhouse may be used or kept there."

The Privy Council granted the petition. It forbade the use of the Frater for plays.

Had the old Chamberlain lived, he might have prevented such an action. Although his own residence adjoined the Frater, he had been cordial to Burbage's project, and actually helped him with arrangements for the purchase of the building. But his son George felt differently. Undoubtedly Burbage had counted on the Lord Chamberlain's support. Of course, the enterprise was his and not the company's. This explains why George Hunsdon could oppose Burbage's right to use this playhouse and yet remain patron of the troupe; and why Field and Robinson could sign the petition without feeling that they were acting against their friend Shakespeare (although they might have been willing to oppose his wishes in a case involving their neighborhood and hence their families).

Still, the swift collapse of old Burbage's dream must have been a blow to the company. If Alleyn stood his ground, they might lose the Theatre the following April. The Blackfriars' playhouse would have suited them well. Now they must consider other possibilities.

As for Burbage himself, he had sunk his fortune into the new playhouse, and the ban on his using it might as well have been a bullet or a dagger aimed at his heart. He died only a few months after the Council's order, in February, 1597.

To Will Shakespeare and many of his company this event was a kind of signature to an epoch. With the Theatre James Burbage had brought in a new era. That had been twenty years ago, and much had happened in that time. Now the first of all the playhouses might soon be abandoned or pulled down, to disappear with its creator. Was a new age coming in for London drama? At least part of the old was passing.

6

On October 20 John Shakespeare received a grant of arms from the Heralds' College. A shield of gold with a black diagonal band across it; a spear of gold, silver tipped, on the band; above the shield a falcon of silver with outspread wings, grasping a spear; the motto: "Non Sanz Droit"—these made John Shakespeare's badge of gentility, and the badge of his son.

With Hamnet dead, Will Shakespeare may not have rated the title of gentleman as of great moment. Yet it was a ray of light striking through many shadows. If he was indifferent to it at first, he soon changed his attitude.

The launching of *Romeo and Juliet* on a career that would clearly be in all ways successful also brought life and hope to him in these days. On all sides he heard such praise of his skill as no maker of plays had known before. More important, he himself saw and heard the magic of the performance, which seemed to challenge him to match and excel it. The new play now flowing from his pen became a stronger and more living thing.

He had thought at first to take a situation like that in Marlowe's *Jew of Malta* and make it more human and believable. From a tale by the Italian writer Fiorentino in the collection called *Il Pecorone* Shakespeare built up an engaging story of Antonio the prosperous merchant who wanted to help his friend Bassanio capture an heiress, and borrowed money from Shylock, a wealthy Jew, promising to forfeit a pound of his flesh if he failed to repay his loan by a certain date. How Bassanio won the rich and lovely Portia (by a device Shakespeare

found in a Latin tale of the collection called *Gesta Romanorum*—
"Stories of the Romans"); how Antonio failed to repay the money
he had lent Shylock; and how Portia, disguised as a young lawyer,
saved his life—this is a story known the world over. So is the love tale
of Shylock's daughter Jessica and her Christian wooer Lorenzo. This
latter episode and the character of Shylock were the points of resemblance between Marlowe's ferocious story and Shakespeare's more believable and human one.

For Shylock is not a fiend, like Marlowe's Barabas, but a man.under-
standably embittered by contempt, insults and cruelties suffered from
Christians. His determination to have revenge through Antonio is a
natural if regrettable result of his sufferings. While never taking sides
with Shylock, Shakespeare let him present his case. It was a strong
one. In the nineteenth century the actor Sir Henry Irving played
Shylock as a wronged and suffering man. That such an interpretation
was possible shows how justly Shakespeare had set forth the cause of
the Jew.

However, such a portrayal was never Shakespeare's intention. Even
his own sense of justice was probably colored by the prejudice of the
age. To most Englishmen of the fifteen-nineties, a Jew was an infidel
and could rightly be scorned and worsted. A recent case in which a
Dr. Lopez, a Jewish physician to Queen Elizabeth, had been executed
for treason heightened the popular interest in Jews, who were then
rare in England, and set up a special prejudice against them. Today
we have doubts of Lopez's guilt; the Elizabethans had none. They
would not have tolerated a play which justified Shylock. That Shakespeare came near to doing so is an indication of his humane and understanding outlook. Yet doubtless he himself regarded Shylock as a villain, and doubtless Dick Burbage played him as one. The proof of that
lies in the final act. It closes in a burst of singing happiness, *because*
Shylock has been worsted, cruelly fined, and forced to turn Christian!

But as Shakespeare wrote *The Merchant of Venice* he found more
to challenge him than the character of Shylock—the most powerful
character he had yet created. He found the heart-moving picture of

friendship between men which the case of Antonio and Bassanio provided. He found a foil to these rather serious gentlemen in Gratiano, who exclaims with relish—

> Let me play the fool:
> With mirth and laughter let old wrinkles come!
> And let my liver rather heat with wine
> Than my heart cool with mortifying groans!

Launcelot Gobbo, servant to Shylock and later to Bassanio, supplied a new chance for slapstick comedy, which Shakespeare seized with a master's hand. This was Kemp's part. Then, finally, there was Portia—a challenge such as no writer had yet faced. For here was a lady of the Renaissance, as lovely as the loveliest, but as learned as an M.A., as warm of heart as a Juliet, but as wise and able as England's own queen. This type of woman was new. England had such ladies—for example, Lady Pembroke, Sir Philip Sidney's sister. Perhaps Will Shakespeare had met such a paragon. He had tried to create a witty and wellborn woman in *Love's Labor's Lost,* but Rosaline in that comedy was a bit sharp-tongued and superficial. In Portia Shakespeare created a full, complete, shining example of a heroine at once lovely, able and witty. She was the first of a number of such women. For her Shakespeare wrote light, jesting scenes with her maid, Nerissa. For her he wrote the notable plea for mercy which she made at Antonio's trial. And for her he wrote the delightful blend of love and comedy that marks the ending of the play.

It was probably in the creation of the many fine scenes of this drama that Shakespeare was able to put his grief aside. As in *Romeo and Juliet,* here he blended beauty and comedy and tragic action, except that in *The Merchant of Venice* the happier elements came uppermost in the end.

In both *King John* and *The Merchant of Venice* Shakespeare had shown an increasing boldness in the use of verse. The number of feminine endings, run-over lines, broken lines, was increasing. The verse was easy, flexible, yet when the action demanded it, full of eloquence

beauty. While *The Merchant of Venice* lacked a certain force which
omeo and Juliet drew from its poignant story and tragic end, the
le of Portia, Bassanio, and Shylock was the most suave, skillful and
ature that Shakespeare had written.

7

While Shakespeare was writing of merchants, he was managing a
atter of business for himself. This was the purchase of a new home
Stratford.

For some years his own family of four (five when he was with it)
ad either lived in London with him or under the same roof with his
arents at Stratford. But in September, 1594, a fire had swept that
wn, burning on both sides of Henley Street close to the Shakespeare
op and home. A portion of the west end of the building may have
een pulled down by firehooks to save the whole, so that quarters
ere more crowded. After Hamnet's death in the summer of 1596
he house may have had unpleasant associations for Anne Shakespeare.

At any rate, the London playwright and gentleman was now able
o buy a home of his own. And he chose one befitting his new fame
nd station in life. It was nothing less than New Place, the one-time
esidence of Stratford's most noted son, Sir Hugh Clopton. Shakepeare bought it in May, 1597, for a down payment of £60, the total
ost being £120 ($9,000 or more in money values of today).

When Shakespeare bought the property it had not belonged to the
Cloptons for some forty years, and the owner was a William Under-
ill, who had an estate elsewhere and did not live the year around
t Stratford. New Place was in need of repair, but it was still an im-
ressive holding.

It consisted of a plot of land almost 400 feet long and at its greatest
readth, 200 feet. A narrow tongue of the plot, 40 feet wide, faced
n Chapel Street, and the main frontage was on Walker's Lane,
cross which from New Place lay the Guild Chapel. The "great
ouse," a building of brick and timber, had a front of 60, a greatest

depth of 70, and a height of 28 feet. It contained a large hearth and at least 10 rooms. On the grounds were also 2 barns, a barnyard, 2 orchards, and 2 gardens.

Shakespeare had paid a high price for the property—partly because of the fires that had swept Stratford, and made dwellings scarce. Another had occurred in 1595. Still, the playwright had what he wanted. The house was honored in the history of Stratford. To own it was a badge of dignity. With it he acquired space, quiet, and trees and flowers.

He knew that more money would be needed to repair New Place and he was ready to spend this. Soon the work of remodeling began, and it went forward briskly during the following summer. It did not mean much of a drain upon Shakespeare's resources. His plays were bringing him in far more than the money it required. In fact, he was already looking about for suitable farmland near Stratford which he could purchase. As he acquired enough of that, the rents paid by his tenants would support him. In case of need, or at his wish, he could then leave London and the world of the playhouses.

XVII: FALSTAFF AND PRINCE HAL

AS the year 1597 began, Cuthbert Burbage was making a prodigious effort to get a new lease for the Theatre from Giles Alleyn to replace the one that ran out in April.

Alleyn gave him fair enough words.

"We shall agree, Master Burbage, we shall agree," he promised.

"Not if you hold for ten pounds a year more in rent, and only a five-year lease, and you to get the building thereafter," said Cuthbert. "By a thousand devils, I'll tear the house down and cart it to the Bankside before I strike such a compact!"

"Nay, swear not such violent oaths, and talk not of tearing down," protested Alleyn. "The building may stand there safely until we reach an agreement. These terms are not fixed. They can be considered between us, perhaps altered."

"A five-year lease! Why should I haggle for that?"

"It is only that I have much hurt in conscience to see the building used for the giving of plays. I would bring an end to such vanity, as I hope for peace with God. Yet seven years I might consider, or ten—"

Cuthbert came away from such conferences fuming.

"The old hypocrite!" he would exclaim. "May the plague or falling sickness take him!"

Soon he found that the Curtain, nearby, was available; and promptly moved his properties and actors the few hundred yards that separated the two theaters.

"Now let the old fox drive a bargain with me, if he can," he exclaimed. "This will teach him we have less need of him than he of us!"

But Giles Alleyn continued to be stubborn, though he continued also to protest that an agreement could surely be reached. So things stood while the Chamberlain's Men drew crowds to their new playhouse. As a building, it was much like the Theatre, being a copy of that structure, and the players fitted easily into it.

2

Will Shakespeare was writing a new play for them. For some time he had intended to dramatize the deeds of the greatest of England's kings since the Conqueror. At least, that was how he and his fellow Englishmen thought of Henry V, the victor of the great Battle of Agincourt and the conqueror of France. We take a somewhat less enthusiastic view of this monarch today. His conquests, as seen in history, represent a great pouring out of blood and treasure for rather doubtful glory. The French did not wish to be ruled by an English king and did not stay conquered long. Henry merely left a legacy of trouble to his brothers and his infant son. Yet his skill and courage were notable and he had a fine mixture of humor, bluffness, shrewd judgment and heroic energy. The Elizabethans saw these, and were dazzled as if they had looked at the sun.

Shakespeare realized that Henry was too good a subject to use up in a single play. His career had indeed already been dealt with in one drama—a crude and rather boisterous effort of the fifteen-eighties called *The Famous Victories of Henry the Fifth*. This popular but wretched production showed clearly enough that there were two stories to be told about its hero: (1) the story of Henry the Prince (called Prince Hal) and (2) the story of Henry the King.

The *Famous Victories* had been based partly on Holinshed's *Chronicles* and partly on popular legends. The *Chronicles* suggested in one brief passage that the Prince had been a wild and somewhat dissipated young man, who sobered sharply on becoming king. Legend had elaborated this rumor of youthful escapades. The report seems to have had little real foundation. At sixteen Prince Hal was actually a commander on the Welsh border whom his father trusted with considerable responsibilities. But the story of a misbehaving prince who reformed was a much livelier one than that of a responsible young man who merely grew more responsible. So the authors of *Famous Victories* took Prince Hal the rake to their bosoms, and invented companions and adventures for him.

Shakespeare accepted their version and improved upon it. He ended by writing two plays about the engaging but erratic Prince and one about Henry the King. The three were *Henry IV, Part I, Henry IV, Part II,* and *Henry V*. The first two showed Henry as a prince, in England. The third told the story of his conquest of France.

A word about Henry in relationship to other kings, and to Shakespeare's historical plays. As pointed out earlier, Henry was the son of Bolingbroke, the vigorous leader of the revolt against Richard II, crowned at the end of Shakespeare's *Richard II* as Henry IV. In the fifth act of this play, Bolingbroke asks:

> Can no man tell me of my unthrifty son?
> . . . I would to God, my lords, he might be found:
> Inquire at London, 'mongst the taverns there,

For there, they say, he daily doth frequent,
With unrestrainéd loose companions,
Even such, they say, as stand in narrow lanes
And beat our watch and rob our passengers.

If such lines were written in 1594 (Shakespeare may have inserted
them later, after composing the first of the new plays, say in 1597),
the London playgoers had been prepared for the appearance of Prince
Hal on the boards. They would welcome this as a continuation of
history from Richard II's time, as well as for itself. As a matter of
fact, the three plays Shakespeare was now to write would complete
an important gap in his dramatic presentation of English kings. That
done, the actual kings and the plays about them would compare as
follows:

Kings	Plays
Richard II (1377-99)	Richard II (written in 1594)
Henry IV (1399-1413)	Henry IV, Part I (being written in 1597)
	Henry IV, Part II (to be written)
Henry V (1413-22)	Henry V (to be written)
Henry VI (1422-61)	Henry VI, Part I ⎫ written
	Henry VI, Part II ⎬ 1590-93
Edward IV (1461-83)	Henry VI, Part III ⎭
Edward V (1483-83)	Richard III (written 1593-94)
Richard III (1483-85)	

Thus Shakespeare was about to complete a drama cycle of English
kings covering eighty-seven years (*Richard II* begins in the year 1398,
and *Richard III* ends with Bosworth Field, 1485). That is about the
same length of time as from the beginning of our Revolutionary War
to the firing of the first gun in our War Between the States. In *King
John,* of course, Shakespeare dealt with a far earlier period.

When the curtains parted for the first scene of *Henry IV, Part I,*
they took the spectators back to England as it was in 1402, about three
years after Henry's election by Parliament. Those years had not been

peaceful. There had been a revolt for the restoration of Richard, then wars on the Welsh border with the romantic chieftain and magician Owen Glendower. Henry had found himself "shaken and wan with care" in his efforts to control his kingdom.

In the first scene of the drama he received good news. The Earl of Douglas, leading an invasion from Scotland, had been defeated and captured, along with many other noble Scots, by Harry Percy (called Hotspur), son of the Earl of Northumberland. But the King was angry because Percy failed to send his Scottish prisoners to London, and suspected the young leader and his father of disloyalty. The suspicions proved to be just. Both felt that Henry, whom they had helped to crown, had become too aloof and arrogant, and they soon planned to revolt and make the Earl of Mortimer king. By blood he had a better title. (Here was the beginning of the later York-Lancaster feud, for Mortimer's descendants became Dukes of York.)

The play followed this rebellion to its apparent end. In this process it managed to differ startlingly from the other chronological plays that Shakespeare had written.

In the first place, it was not tragic. The ending of the drama was a happy one.

In the second place, it displayed two kinds of comedy, while still keeping its dignity as a play of kings. First, it had its comic aspects in the more serious scenes, for both Hotspur and the Welsh chieftan Glendower were presented with delightful humor. But another source of comedy was broader and more farcical. It lay in the scenes showing the merrymaking Prince and his companions. Such an extraordinary wealth of comic material had never been poured into a chronology. Until *King John,* Shakespeare had always avoided humor in his plays about kings except for the Jack Cade scenes in *Henry VI, Part II,* as if he felt laughter to be out of place. In *John,* however, he created the Bastard (Faulconbridge) and gave him a reckless wit that furnished a certain relief to the darker and more tragic character of the play as a whole.

In *Henry IV, Part I,* the playwright threw aside the last of his doubts about mixing comedy and history. Of course there was comedy in *Famous Victories,* and the very idea of a prince who was an erratic playboy meant that fun would follow. Actually this suited Shakespeare's natural instincts. He saw life as an activity in which laughter and solemnity and tears were blended, and he loved to use these contrasting elements in the same play. We have already seen that his instinct was also to provide certain estimable characters in his comedies, making them part of the general comic situation, but bringing in humbler characters for farce or rollicking humor. Thus the Athenian craftsmen appear in *A Midsummer Night's Dream,* and Launcelot Gobbo in *The Merchant of Venice.*

In *Henry IV, Part I,* these two comic elements were preserved in general, without damaging the play as history. It was a proper enough chronological drama, and yet it was a complete comedy also. This was a new thing in England or any other country.

Supposedly Shakespeare set out to tell the story of a wayward prince growing into a responsible and heroic man. Actually, he depicted a remarkable group of characters which aroused and held the reader's or spectator's interest. These characters were Hotspur, the Prince, and the latter's amazing playfellows—Falstaff, Poins, Bardolf, and the inn hostess, Dame Quickly.

Hotspur, of course, was a great English hero. He was the Harry Percy of the famous Percy-Douglas ballads—"The Hunting of the Cheviot," and such:

> The Percy out of Northumberland,
> An avow to God made he
> That he would hunt in the mountains
> Of Cheviot within days three,
> In the maugre of doughty Douglas,
> And all that e'er with him be.

In the minds of all Shakespeare's contemporaries Percy was a symbol of chivalric daring (how ironic that to be named Percy today should practically brand a boy as a "sissy"!) Shakespeare took this name and symbol and forged a flesh-and-blood hero for them who was exciting and amazing enough to satisfy the most exacting of his listeners.

Shakespeare's Hotspur was built along the lines of the devil-may-care Philip Faulconbridge in *King John*, but was far more vivid and dynamic. He had a perpetual, impatient thirst for glory.

> By heaven, methinks it were an easy leap
> To pluck bright honor from the pale-faced moon!

The more audacious the attempt to be made, the more he liked it. (Something of this quality Shakespeare doubtless found in the ambitious English nobles of his own day—notably Sir Walter Raleigh and the impetuous Robert Devereux, Earl of Essex.) Hotspur had inexhaustible energy, along with great pride, great generosity, and a direct picturesqueness of speech which left laughter or devastation behind it. When his father, his uncle, his father-in-law Mortimer and he met with Glendower, who was ready to help them against the King, Hotspur could not forbear baiting and gibing at the solemn Welshman:

GLEN.: I can call spirits from the vasty deep.
HOT.: Why, so can I, or so can any man;
But will they come when you do call for them?
GLEN.: Why, I can teach you, Cousin, to command
The devil.
HOT.: And I can teach thee, Coz, to shame the devil
By telling truth: tell truth and shame the devil.
If thou have power to raise him, bring him hither,
And I'll be sworn I have power to shame him hence.
Oh, while you live, tell truth and shame the devil.

Glendower was remarkably patient under the raillery of Hotspur, and when he went out for a moment Mortimer remonstrated with the young hero. Percy replied:

I cannot choose: sometimes he angers me
With telling me of the moldwarp and the ant,
Of the dreamer Merlin and his prophecies,
And of a dragon and a finless fish,
A clip-winged griffin, and a molten raven,
A couching lion and a ramping cat,
And such a deal of skimble-skamble stuff
As puts me from my faith. I tell you what—
He held me last night at least nine hours
In reckoning up the several devils' names
That were his lackeys. . . .
                              O he's as tedious
As a tired horse, a railing wife,
Worse than a smoky house.

Percy, in fact, glittered through the play, flashing light and laughter. He had the prodigious courage of an Achilles, the honor of a Roland, the lovable bluffness of a Richard Coeur de Lion, and a wit that made the fabulous in him natural and wholly believable. Shakespeare was never again to paint so delightful a hero.

In fact, he did so well with Percy that he got himself in trouble. For Percy cast Prince Hal, a very engaging and estimable young man, quite into the shade. The Prince was supposed to shine the brighter by worsting so illustrious a champion as Percy. But though Percy was duly slain in battle by the royal Harry, it was the victim and not the victor who filled a golden spot in the playgoer's memory after the play was done.

And yet another character in *Henry IV, Part I* was more vivid for the audiences, and especially for the crowds in the pit, than even Percy. This was the Prince's companion, Sir John Falstaff. This enormous knight was originally called Oldcastle; but Oldcastle was the family name of Lord Cobham, and when protests were made against its use in the theater, Shakespeare agreed to change it. A Sir John Oldcastle had indeed been a friend of Prince Henry, although as a soldier and not as a merrymaker.

I said earlier that Shakespeare improved upon the merry companions and escapades that appeared in *The Famous Victories of Henry the Fifth*. This is understatement. He made an immortal crew with such merry doings as the playhouses of England had never known. Falstaff was the heart and life of the fun. A gentleman by birth, he had become a rascal, a boaster, and a clown. He was aging, and had grown immensely fat with drinking sack (sherry) and eating capon. Nevertheless, he showed an incredible energy for talk and mischief, and a brilliant capacity to squirm out of a scrape. The very sight of this immense, swaggering, bellowing but inspired buffoon, whose every other word was worth a laugh, set the pit to grinning and cheering, while gentlemen in the gallery showed an anticipation of delight that was almost as great.

Many of Falstaff's lines depended upon conditions and happenings of the time. Some of his humor has been lost because of that, and some because of the changes in the language. But the quality of the man still shows clearly enough. There is his part in the first escapade of the play. The Prince's companions planned to rob some travelers. Poins suggested to the King's son a trick by which the two could have a great laugh at Falstaff's expense. The Prince and Poins so arranged matters that Falstaff and three others carried out the robbery. Then the two appeared disguised, attacked Falstaff and his companions with loud shouts, and, although outnumbered, easily frightened them into running off.

When the six met again at the inn, Falstaff made a heroic tale out of his cowardice. He was attacked, he asserted, by an immense number of foemen (who got more and more numerous as he told the story). Then the Prince and Poins revealed what really had happened. The laugh should now have been on Falstaff—a loud one. But he exclaimed—

By the Lord, I knew ye as well as he that made ye. Why, hear you, my masters: Was it for me to kill the heir apparent? Should I turn upon the true prince? Why, thou knowest I am as valiant as Hercules; but beware instinct: the lion will not touch the true prince. Instinct is a great matter. I was a coward on instinct. I shall think the better of myself and thee during my life; I for a valiant lion, and thou for a true prince.

Falstaff went to the wars with the Prince, staking his life in battle against the terrible Percy. But he gave the matter very shrewd attention as the fight was about to begin.

Well, 'tis no matter; honor pricks me on. Yea, but how if honor prick me off when I come on? How then? Can honor set to a leg? No. Or an arm? No. Or take away the grief of a wound? No. Honor hath no skill in surgery then? No. What is honor? A word. What is that word honor? Air. . . . Who hath it? He that died o' Wednesday. Doth he feel it? No. Doth he hear it? No. Is it insensible then? Yea, to the dead. But will it not live with the living? No. Why? Detraction will not suffer it. Therefore I'll none of it. Honor is a mere scutcheon, and so ends my catechism.

This "catechism," given by Pope (who probably took the part) with immense seriousness, and a laugh at every answer, showed Falstaff the philosopher at his best. Doubtless he delighted the groundlings even more when, apparently slain in battle by the Douglas, he lay prone while the Prince killed Percy; then, when the former had left the scene, leaped up and hoisted the body of Hotspur on his own shoulders.

Always at Falstaff's heels came Bardolph, a follower with a face and nose of flaming red. And these two and Poins would have been incomplete without the tavern hostess, Dame Quickly, whose capacity for being deceived and put upon by the fat knight was always worth another laugh. These characters made the play the talk of the town. Falstaff became famous overnight, and was quoted by lords and ladies as a kind of oracle. He has never lost his fame. He lives on with the few great comic characters of history, probably the most buoyant and memorable of them all.

3

The long July evening was drawing to a close, but the new owner of New Place walked slowly between the trim flower beds of his garden, on through the rose arbor and down across the turf of the orchard, then back and down again. In the still twilight he could mark his progress by the changing fragrance of the air.

It was a pleasant stroll. The spicy scent of carnations gave way to the softer breath of roses, and the flower smells to the odor of fresh grass and earth. As he passed through the orchard the dangling branch of a fruit tree brushed lightly against the sleeve of his doublet. He could feel the dew in the darkening air.

His manuscript lay on the table near the arbor where he had been writing. The play was finished, Percy and Prince and Falstaff. He knew what the actors would do with those characters. *Henry IV, Part I* would succeed. And there was good writing in it, too. Some of the verse rang as strong and smooth as any he knew in English, yet it was the salty speech men talked—far more so than he or anyone else had written before. But such writing would bring him neither money nor a poet's name.

Even were it printed fair by Dick Field, like a poem, it would get little regard. Its most eager readers would be some of Henslowe's hireling writers, seeking a tale to adapt. No, lacking the name of art as yet (though there was art aplenty in it), any play he could do served him best when known only to the players that learned their lines.

As these thoughts passed through his mind he looked about—back toward the darkening orchard trees, for he was in the garden now; then in the other direction toward the house. It rose in a proud and massive shadow. Nearer, a pile of building stones loomed up where the masons would need them. Aye, the plays had earned him this, at least. These were Sir Hugh's gardens and orchard and that was his one-time dwelling. When the men had finished restoring the building and the grounds there would be none better in Stratford and none with a nobler past. And he, Will Shakespeare, could walk here on his own turf, among his own flowers, finding his own peace on his own land. Yes, even though Hamnet was gone, he could find peace.

He had turned back toward the orchard, but halted as a light step came toward him.

"Father?"

"Yes, Susanna." The figure of his older daughter came in silhouette out of the dark, a girl's figure becoming a woman's.

"You stay long out of doors, Father. Mother has lit the tapers."

"We will go in soon. I like it among the flowers and the trees. It is good to breathe the air of my own garden."

Susanna hesitated and said shyly:

"It is very different here. All is so much greater and finer."

He smiled at her.

"We are gentlefolk now, and should have a dwelling that accords with our station."

Susanna gave an answering smile, but somewhat doubtfully.

"I think Mother would rather have the cottage at Shottery. She says there is too much to manage here." Then she added: "She says you write plays because you must pay for it."

"Nay, it is all paid for. And it may be we shall yet have the cottage, too, and farmland, besides. Did you practice at your writing today?"

"As much as I had time for."

"I will help you with it tomorrow. I shall be free for such matters now. I am pleased that you wish to have some learning."

"I fear Mother doesn't like it. She says it is an idle thing for a woman."

"It is of little use, indeed, to most women here in Warwickshire."

"But in London many women have learning?"

"Some, Susanna. Like our queen, and not a few of her ladies. And more will have it as time passes."

He paused and added:

"Learning helps a woman little with the management of a house. Yet it can profit her in understanding, in the same way it profits a man. Which may be much or little."

"I have heard you call the writer of a book a learned fool."

"And so is any who makes a poor use of what he knows. But for you—if you marry a man who uses books or loves them, you will be closer to him by the better understanding you have."

"And meanwhile closer to you?"

"Aye, that too."

He felt with a sudden rush of tenderness the eager spirit of this girl-woman, the devotion she would gladly give him. Then he remembered the circle of acts and relationships in which she moved, and sighed.

"Were I more here," he said, "we should do more together."

"Oh, if you were!"

He smiled.

"It may be, with time."

But he did not deceive himself. Susanna was as willing a pupil as Hamnet had been, and perhaps an abler one. But there had been no school for her, and no will to help her except what he had shown. The will and authority of the mother and the town were against her learning and they pressed strongly upon her. He would be much in London.

"Be diligent in your studies, if you find pleasure in them," he said gently at last. "Come, let us go in now."

4

Shakespeare's purchase of New Place brought him back more firmly into the life of Stratford. Aubrey says that he had made yearly visits there from London; doubtless he had managed even more frequent ones. But as a property owner in the town, he felt a greater interest in it and it in him.

In 1596 John and Mary Shakespeare, in association with William, had renewed their effort to recover the Asbies from the Lamberts. Now, in November of 1597, their complaint was heard in Chancery. It dragged on from postponement to postponement. But although nothing was to come of it in the end, it showed the keen interest of all the family in this property.

Shakespeare was also interested in other farmland. Apparently he wished to win an income in this fashion. (The possession of good farmland was as sure a source of revenue as one could find in that era.) The town officials in Stratford heard of this, and one of the former bailiffs, Abraham Sturley, wrote about it to Richard Quyney, a fellow alderman and Shakespeare's old schoolmate, who happened to be in London in January, 1598.

It seems that Quyney's father had heard that "our countryman, Master Shakespeare," was willing to buy some land near Shottery. Probably the playwright had indicated a desire to buy his wife's old home there. Old Adrian Quyney talked with Sturley about this, and suggested that Sturley get Richard Quyney, while in London, to make a different proposal to the writer and player. It was this—that instead of making the Shottery purchase, Shakespeare buy the right to the tithes (or rents) of certain farmlands held by the town of Stratford. This was indeed a purchase that would have carried prestige with it. "By the instructions you can give him thereof, and by the friends he can make therefor, we [that is, Sturley and old Adrian Quyney] think it a fair mark for him to shoot at, and not unpossible to hit. It obtained would advance him indeed, and would do us much good."

This letter shows that Stratford men were likely to visit Shakespeare when in London. It shows too that they recognized the improvement in his fortunes, and had confidence in him. Otherwise they would not have felt that to have him hold town lands "would do us much good." For a tithe holder, after collecting rent from his tenants, paid a smaller rent to the town. It was desirable that he should pay on time. Clearly it was felt that Shakespeare would.

Nothing came of this suggestion at the time, nor of the project to purchase land at Shottery. Some years later Shakespeare made a big purchase of tithes and helped his brother-in-law, Bartholomew Hatha-

vay, to buy his father's old home. Gradually he accumulated the prop-
rty that would give him an ample income. But in 1598 he was not
ble to make a large investment.

However, the respect for his financial standing and the confidence
n his good will which Stratford townsmen already felt is again
hown by a letter Richard Quyney wrote him on October 25, 1598.
t is the only letter to Shakespeare which we have (none survives which
vas written *by* him).

The letter in question was penned in London. With modern Eng-
ish spelling and punctuation, it reads as follows:

Loving Countryman: I am bold of you as of a friend, craving your
aelp with £30 upon Mr. Bushell's and my security, or Mr. Mytton's
with me. Mr. Rosswell is not come to London as yet, and I have espe-
cial cause. You shall friend me much in helping me out of all the
debts I owe in London, I thank God, and much quiet my mind, which
would not be indebted. I am now towards the Court, in hope of
answer for the dispatch of my business. You shall neither lose credit
nor money by me, the Lord willing; and now but persuade yourself
so, as I hope, and you shall not need to fear, but with all hearty thank-
fulness I will hold my time and content your friend; and if we bargain farther you shall be the paymaster yourself. My time bids me has-
ten to an end, and so I commit this [to] your care and hope of your
help. I fear I shall not be back this night from the Court. Haste. The
Lord be with you, and with us all. Amen.

From the Bell in Carter Lane. The 25 October, 1598.
                                    Yours in all kindness
                                        Ryc. Quyney
To my loving good friend
and countryman, Mr. Wm. Shackespere,
dlr. thees [Deliver this—or "these"]

If Quyney had sent this letter, probably it would never have come
into the hands of modern scholars. But he seems to have written it
with the idea of leaving it at Shakespeare's lodgings if the latter was

not there, and going on up the Thames by boat to Richmond, where the Court was sitting. Apparently he found Shakespeare and did not need to leave the letter. He took it back to Stratford with him, and it was found among his papers.

Shakespeare agreed to get the money. Quyney wrote to Sturley about it that very night, for the latter speaks of a letter from Quyney written October 25 "which imported . . . that our countryman, Master William Shakespeare, would procure us money." Apparently this meant that Shakespeare would arrange a loan from someone else, for Sturley adds that he would like the arrangement "as I shall hear when and where and how; and I pray, let not go that occasion if it may sort to any indifferent conditions." (That is, "Don't fail to get the loan if the conditions are at all reasonable.")

Thus the relationship between the chief men of Stratford and the prosperous young player and writer seems to have been one of mutual respect and friendship. Quyney knows and trusts Shakespeare enough to believe that a written note will persuade him to give help. Shakespeare is his "loving countryman." Quyney has confidence in his good will and in his business sense, too; for he will make Shakespeare "paymaster." The man in the city had apparently kept constant acquaintance with his old schoolmates. They knew where he lived, they trusted him, they felt that he would assist them in need.

5

I have already mentioned in Chapter XII a book called *Palladis Tamia,* which appeared in the autumn of 1598 under the name of Francis Meres. This volume, called by its author a "comparative discourse of our English poets," had much to say about the writers of the day. It reproved Peele, Greene and Marlowe for their personal vices, but stoutly praised Sidney, Spenser, Daniel, Drayton and, with notable enthusiasm, William Shakespeare.

Meres's comments on the poems have already been quoted. He

called Shakespeare an English Ovid. But what he had to say of the plays was much more flattering. Again in modern spelling it ran:

As Plautus and Seneca are accounted the best for comedy and tragedy among the Latins, so Shakespeare among the English is the most excellent in both kinds for the stage: for comedy witness his *Gentlemen of Verona,* his *Errors,* his *Love's Labor's Lost,* his *Love's Labor's Won,* his *Midsummer Night's Dream,* and his *Merchant of Venice;* for tragedy, his *Richard II, Richard III, Henry IV, King John, Titus Andronicus* and his *Romeo and Juliet.*

As Epius Stolo said that the Muses would speak with Plautus's tongue if they would speak Latin, so I say that the Muses would speak with Shakespeare's fine-filed phrase if they would speak English.

What Meres says shows pretty clearly that Shakespeare's renown was high. It also tells us much about the plays he had written. The title *Love's Labor's Won* has puzzled scholars. A number of them have thought that it was *All's Well that Ends Well*—a later play. More likely it was *The Taming of the Shrew.* If so, Meres has given a complete list of Shakespeare's plays up to the publication of his book except the three dealing with Henry VI. These he may have thought of as more Marlowe's than Shakespeare's.

Meres had written a tribute that put Shakespeare in a supreme position among the dramatists and poets of the day. This was recognizing a fact; but it is interesting to see that the fact was known and accepted. From this time forward printers often sought to use Shakespeare's name, even for work that was not his. Their efforts were not confined to plays. William Jaggard in 1599 brought out a book of lyrics called *The Passionate Pilgrim,* which he attributed to the now famous writer. He had somehow got hold of two of the "sugared sonnets"; the other eighteen poems are now known or thought to be by other poets. In 1601 Shakespeare seems to have contributed a graceful thing in rhyme, "The Phoenix and the Turtle," to a volume of verse called *Love's Martyr: or Rosalin's complaint,* by an obscure author, Robert Chester.

Such occurrences tend to show the general high regard for the man who only ten years before had been a newcomer in London. In drama, his pre-eminence was clear. However, even in 1598 a challenger had already appeared. In that very year he was to assert himself with a confidence and skill that could not be denied.

XVIII: "RARE BEN JONSON"

AMONG the writers of drama mentioned by Meres was a Benjamin Jonson. In 1598 he was just acquiring a reputation. From that time forward he loomed up larger and larger in Shakespeare's world. In the end he was its master spirit.

Ben Jonson, as he signed himself later, was nine years younger than Will Shakespeare, and his family stood on a slightly lower rung of the social ladder. The latter fact was partly ill-fortune. Jonson's father had been a gentleman, but had died just before Ben was born. Two years later the child's mother had taken a second husband—a master bricklayer. The boy thus became the stepson of a skilled workman. This fact was to annoy and exasperate him later.

The stepfather seems to have been a kindly man. He sent his wife's son to a good private school. Here Ben showed such ability as a pupil that a generous friend had him placed in the famous Westminster School. He was quite as brilliant there, and the patron found some kind of scholarship for him at Cambridge University. However, it wasn't enough to support young Jonson, and soon he was at home again, reluctantly taking up a trowel to aid his stepfather.

But if he was reluctant to take up the trowel, he was far more reluctant to keep hold of it. He simply couldn't stomach bricklaying. So abruptly he left it and set out to see the world. Soon he was serving with the English army in the Low Countries, helping the Dutch against the Spaniards.

A sword suited Ben much better than a trowel. He was fearless, quick, and sturdy. Years later he told the Scottish poet, Drummond, how he got into a hand-to-hand fight with one of the enemy.

"We fought in view of both camps," he declared, "and I slew the fellow and took *opima spolia* from him!"

Picture the audacious Ben laden with the Spaniard's sword, helmet, belt and breastplate—which would be worth enough to get him several books in one of the Dutch cities—striding back to his companions to the clink of this precious hardware and the sound of his comrades' cheers! Ben remembered the moment with relish. He always looked back with a kind of complacent satisfaction upon his life as a man of violence. In the days of his fame he penned some lines "To True Soldiers":

> I love
> Your great profession, which I once did prove;
> And did not shame it with my actions then
> No more than I dare now do with my pen.

But Jonson didn't live by the sword for long. Perhaps he began to hear about the London playhouses. English actors on European tours visited the camps. Some fellow soldiers of Ben's, perhaps the younger sons of gentlemen or noblemen who marveled at his quick mind and prodigious memory, may have sat with him through a play.

Ben would already have read them Latin and English verses of his own making. After the show, over a cup of sack, they may have compared Jonson's verse with that of the drama they had just heard.

"By heavens, Ben, your rhyming makes this doggerel seem like a crow's cawing."

"Aye, yours is both better music and better wit. I'll warrant you could strike off a satiric couplet on the fellow who wrote it that would make the rascal cringe."

"He could, he could! Strike it off now, Ben!"

And Ben, grinning, sipping his sack, at last lifted a hand and improvised:

> Playwright, when first thy limping lines I heard,
> I deemed them by intention made absurd;
> But hearing more, this better thought I had—
> No man could by intention write so bad!

Amid the laughter and bravos that greeted this sally, a hope may have been born. Ben had heard often that money was paid for plays. Why should he not make a trial at writing them? He had read a prodigious amount of Greek, Latin, French, and English tales. In his marvelous memory each was there for him to use, and a number of them had episodes that could be adapted to plays. As for the writing, he seemed born to it. Half his company was laughing over the satiric verses he had made on the Spaniards, the Dutch, the food of the camps, the love adventures of his insuppressible companions. Why not take his way to London when the campaign was finished? He could perhaps start as a player, and write as he found an opportunity.

In any case, when he was twenty years of age Ben had arrived in London. There are legends of his acting for a while. Apparently he made his way without too much trouble, and soon impressed the player-companies with his wit and his amazing knowledge of Greek and Latin. He married, became a father. Early in 1597 he joined the new Pembroke's Men. They had hired a recently constructed play-

house called the Swan, and Ben, like young Will Shakespeare with the
Lord Strange's Men a few years earlier, was preparing to serve as both
actor and writer.

2

Jonson may have met Shakespeare before 1597. In the small literary
circle of London, Shakespeare was already well known when Ben
came to town hoping for a career in the playhouses. The latter, with
his sturdy self-confidence, would quickly have made the acquaintance
of the chief players and writers. He might have been introduced to
the older dramatist by John Florio, who is known to have been Jonson's friend later.

In any case, the two are likely to have been thrown together late in
1596 or early in 1597. In these months Francis Langley, owner of the
Swan, apparently had business with both Jonson and Shakespeare.

The latter, acting for the Chamberlain's Men, may have been looking for a playhouse which his company could use in case the Theatre
should cease to be available after April, 1597. Perhaps Shakespeare
and his fellows actually used the Swan late in the previous year. At
any rate, the playwright was associated in some fashion with Langley,
for on November 29, 1596, the two were named in a lawsuit brought
by a certain William Wayte, who asked that they be bound over to
keep the peace. Wayte also cited two women, Dorothy Soers and
Anne Lee.

Leslie Hotson, the Shakespearean scholar who found this item in
the court records of the time, also discovered that Wayte was only a
front for his uncle, an unscrupulous justice of the peace named
William Gardiner. Almost a month earlier, Langley had asked for
sureties of the peace from both Gardiner and Wayte! Mr. Hotson
shows that the former was as mean and despicable a rascal as ever
presided over a law court, and puts him forward as a far more likely
original for Justice Shallow in *The Merry Wives of Windsor* than
was Sir Thomas Lucy. Certainly Shakespeare seems to have had cause
to be annoyed with the Bankside magistrate. As yet, however, we have

no direct evidence as to how the playwright came to be named in Wayte's plea. Neither do we know who Dorothy Soers and Anne Lee may have been (Mr. Hotson suggests: Shakespeare's landlady and Langley's maid), or why they were listed with Langley and Shakespeare.

The lawsuits, the probable business discussions concerning the Swan, thus link Langley and Shakespeare together during late 1596 and early 1597. Langley and Jonson seem to have had an association at about the same time. For the Pembroke's Men signed a lease for the Swan, which was dated February 21 and was to run for a year. Jonson may have had some part in arranging this. In any case, he was busy that spring helping to write a satiric comedy for his company. Thomas Nashe collaborated with him. The play was called *The Isle of Dogs*, and it was performed on July 21, with Jonson taking a role in it. The next day he borrowed £4 from Philip Henslowe. While acting for the Pembroke's Men he was apparently free to work for other troupes as a writer.

Unfortunately for Jonson, on July 28 the Pembroke's Men, the Swan, and the authors of *The Isle of Dogs* were blasted by an order from the Queen's Privy Council. Elizabeth, declared her ministers, was outraged by this "seditious and slanderous" play. So angry were the Lords of the Council that they ordered all playhouses "plucked down" or at least "defaced" to the point where they would be useless for acting. All playing was forbidden in or within three miles of the city until November 1.

We do not know exactly what the play that caused this devastating order was like. No copy of it survives. It seems to have been a satire on the island of Britain and some of its chief inhabitants.

At any rate, there was a great scurrying about of the Pembroke's Men. Nashe got out of the city. Ben Jonson was not quick enough for that, or else he disdained to flee. He was soon in prison.

Fortunately, things worked out to a less terrible ending than was threatened. No theaters were "plucked down." On October 3rd Jonson and others were released, apparently having pleaded innocence of intent, and offered promises of good behavior for the future. The Rose and the Curtain were permitted to reopen. But the Lord Admiral's Men and the Lord Chamberlain's Men alone were approved as companies which could present plays. Only their theaters could be used. The Swan stood empty, and Lord Pembroke's Men were disbanded.

Jonson must nevertheless have been cheerful over getting out of prison, and doubtless began making plans for new plays. Then came the greatest disaster of his career.

It was a duel. One of the members of the Pembroke's Men and a fellow prisoner of Jonson in the summer was Gabriel Spencer. After his release, this actor had joined the Chamberlain's Men for a time, then quickly shifted to the Admiral's Men. Henslowe apparently thought highly of him. But Spencer and Jonson quarreled, and a duel was arranged in Hoxton Fields. Jonson killed his man.

Henslowe wrote bitterly to Edward Alleyn, then in Sussex, about it:

Now to let you understand news, I will tell you some, but it is for me hard and heavy. Since you were with me, I have lost one of my company, which hurteth me greatly, that is, Gabriel. For he is slain in Hogsdon Fields by the hands of Benjamin Jonson, bricklayer.

The slur on Jonson's former calling and his family shows Henslowe's deep resentment. Meanwhile Jonson had been arrested and indicted. He confessed slaying Spencer, and then took refuge in an English law which offered him a curious kind of protection.

The law was this—that a "clerk" (technically a member of the clergy) could not be executed for murder. Furthermore, any man who could read was a "clerk" and within the protected class. Jonson decided to save his life by reading a verse of Latin, popularly called "the neck verse" because it saved a convicted man's neck if he could read it. The entry concerning the trial reads:

He confesses the indictment, asks for the Book, reads like a clerk, is marked with the letter T, and is delivered according to the statute.

Jonson was branded on his left thumb. "T" stood for Tyburn, the place where he would have been hanged if he had not been able to read Latin!

3

By this time you will picture Ben Jonson as a very peppery and violent fellow, and so in a sense he was. He kept a blunt, forthright way of speaking all through his life; and got into more trouble, as we shall see. Yet Jonson apparently had a warm and friendly disposition under his prickly exterior, and the fame of his high excellence as a scholar was already getting about. People realized that he spoke with authority on matters of literature and the theater. They were willing on that account to pardon a certain arrogance in him.

Indeed, all through these years Ben Jonson had been devouring Greek and Latin texts. He used a sword well, but he was even more skillful with his mind. A remarkable memory helped him out there. It was said later that at the age of forty he could repeat every poem or play he had written, letter perfect. He remembered his classics almost as well.

In sheer knowledge he thus had an advantage over any other playwright of his day, Shakespeare included. For example, he knew Greek comedy and tragedy at first hand where the others were well informed on Latin drama only. But the Greeks were immensely superior as craftsmen, and Jonson began writing plays with a clearer sense of dramatic form than most of his rivals possessed. He was also very willing to borrow from the classics. In his *Discoveries,* little prose essays written many years later, he set down "a goodness of natural wit" and a willingness and ability to work hard at writing and rewriting as two requisites for a good writer. And then he declared:

The third requisite is imitation, to be able to convert the substance or riches of another poet to his own use . . . not to imitate servilely, as Horace saith, and catch at vices for virtue, but to draw forth out of the best and choicest flowers, with the bee, and turn all into honey.

I have pointed out that most Elizabethans "stole" in this manner. But Jonson was probably the greatest thief of them all. From lyrics like "Drink to Me Only with Thine Eyes" to scene after scene in his plays, the originals can be found in Latin or Greek. When he was in his early twenties, Jonson's wonderful memory and his wide reading must thus have been precious aids for filling in what he lacked in direct experience.

But Jonson never stole hastily or clumsily. He considered something he liked in Latin or Greek as merely a starting point.

"To all the observations of the ancients," he declared, "we have our own experience."

He used this. Anything he wrote went through his mind and feeling and came out very English. It was in no way imitative of Horace or Ovid or Aristophanes. It was Ben Jonson. And this was as true in 1597 as it was a dozen years later.

4

The boy was persistent.

"No, Master Heminges," he insisted, "he says you have had the play a week, and he will have an answer, if it is only to get back his manuscript."

John Heminges snorted, and poked about on some shelves in the tiring room of the Curtain.

"Why, then," he said, "he can have the manuscript. Yes, here it is."

"Who is it, Jack?" asked Shakespeare, who, like Heminges himself, was making ready for the morning rehearsal.

"None less than this same Ben Jonson, come with the smell of Tyburn on his thumb," grumbled the other. "And the play—why, it is a strange thing—some good in it—but compared with any comedy of yours—"

"Let me see it. I know Jonson, and have heard good things of him."

Heminges put the manuscript in his hand.

"I tell you it is a poor thing, Will."

"It has a good title, Jack. *Every Man in His Humor.*"

"But I have heard you say that it was a false kind of comedy that took one trait in a man and held it up to ridicule—"

"May be. May be. Yet if one kind of comedy is bad for me, it may be good for another. Besides," with a sigh, "I cannot write all the new plays My Lord Chamberlain's Men enact in London."

And so Shakespeare, according to the story that has come down from several sources, read Ben Jonson's play, and got it accepted by his company.

It was, as Heminges had hinted, a very different type of comedy from any of Shakespeare's own. In these, the humor came from a situation or a meeting of unlike characters, or from the lifelike picture of a character. The laugh was seldom bitter. In *Every Man* Jonson had seized on the idea that in certain persons one quality takes extreme form and dominates the rest. So one man may show unreasonable jealousy; another, boastfulness; another still, quickness to anger; another, the habit of continual worry.

Thus Jonson's characters were really a set of caricatures. This, to his mind, was good; for he believed that a writer of comedy should mercilessly exhibit the faults of men, thus teaching the audience to avoid them. Still, Jonson managed this rather artificial comedy so well that it was both witty and natural. It was up to date, too, with deft references to tobacco and the latest follies in dress and talk. No comedy-satire had ever been so well planned and so vigorously written. A wholly different thing from Shakespeare's *Henry IV, Part I,* it was almost as popular as that successful play.

In 1598, when the Chamberlain's Men produced *Every Man in His Humor,* with Shakespeare acting a chief part (that of Knowell, a worrisome father), a second installment of Falstaff and Company came to the boards. This was *Henry IV, Part II,* which carried the story of Prince Hal on through another rebellion to the death of his father and his coronation as Henry V.

Although some ten years of actual history went by from the death of Percy at the end of the first play to this coronation at the end of the second, the drama made the time seem less than that many months. And it was chiefly a play built around Falstaff and his companions. In addition to Bardolph and Poins, Shakespeare brought in the boastful Pistol. He gave Mistress Quickly a worthy companion in Doll Tearsheet. And finally, he created a set of country clowns, with Justice Shallow as the chief of them.

Both actors and audiences seem to have had an immense amount of fun with these colorful characters. It was said that on the appearance of Falstaff the cracking of nuts in the pit ceased at once, for not a man in the audience wanted to miss a word or gesture of the fat knight. Now it was Falstaff trying to get away from Dame Quickly's inn without paying his bill (and he did, even borrowing something from her as he left), now it was Falstaff and Bardolph examining the recruits Justices Shallow and Silence had called up for them—Mouldy, Shadow, Wart, Feeble, Bullcalf, and so forth. (Recruiting had been going forward in England at the time, and the audience was in the mood for such fun.) Again, it was Falstaff hearing the news that Prince Hal was king, and dreaming tall dreams of the happy days that would now be his.

And then in sudden contrast with these nonsensical episodes, came the newly crowned King passing through the streets of London, and turning cold eyes on his old companion.

> I know thee not, old man: fall to thy prayers;
> How ill white hairs become a fool and jester!
> I have long dreamed of such a kind of man,
> So surfeit-swelled, so old, and so profane;
> But, being awaked, I do despise my dream.

In one of the most devastating speeches in all English literature he bids Falstaff put himself ten miles from the Court, and reform. He shall be pensioned, but banished from the royal presence.

It was a typical Shakespearean touch. Exuberant, roistering comedy suddenly quiets, shrivels into pathos. For be sure, the pit at least sorrowed with the fat knight, and held him to have been treated a bit roughly. On the other hand, Henry V had to emerge as a reformed and righteous king.

The truth probably was that Shakespeare had had about enough of Falstaff. Like Hotspur, "Plump Jack" had been brought in as one of the playboy Prince's companions, and had got somewhat out of hand. What to do with him? He had really, like Percy, stolen the show from the man supposed to be the hero. In an epilogue, Shakespeare hinted that Falstaff would go to France with the new King and "die of a sweat" there. Actually, Sir John never appeared at all in *Henry V*. Shakespeare made an end of him in that play, but he did so off stage. It was apparently farewell forever to Falstaff.

But the playwright reckoned without one of his spectators. Queen Elizabeth, runs a legend that there seems no reason to doubt, had become a Falstaff "fan," like many another highborn person about London. (Poor lonely old lady—she needed laughter in her life now.) She sent word to Shakespeare that he should show Falstaff again— and in love. Apparently she named a date.

As a result, Shakespeare wrote *The Merry Wives of Windsor*. It was done mostly in prose, and its comedy was more farce than that of the two other Falstaff plays—indeed, as writing it was not worthy of them. And in this play, as has been noted already, Shakespeare was supposed to have ridiculed Sir Thomas Lucy in the person of Justice Shallow. But, as I have also noted, the discoveries made by Mr. Leslie Hotson make it possible that William Gardiner rather than Lucy was the target for Shakespeare's wit. The third possibility, of course, is that Shallow was—just Shallow. That is what he had been in *Henry IV, Part II*. Meanwhile, there is argument as to when the play was first given. Some would put it as early as May 24, 1597; others as late as August, 1600! The latter date seems the closer. The play must have followed *Henry IV, Part II*, which was almost surely produced in 1598. The chief reason for taking an earlier date is that the play will thus follow more closely on Shakespeare's legal troubles with Gardiner. But if he wrote without either Gardiner or Lucy in mind (which seems as good an assumption at any), then it is not important to push the date back.

As the great Danish critic Brandes has pointed out, *The Merry Wives of Windsor* is the only play written by Shakespeare which deals with people of his own class. It contains neither royalty nor high nobility. But to draw any conclusion from these facts would be rash. The play was hurriedly written. It is mostly prose. Shakespeare could have done better with it had he had more time. So we can only say that he was quite capable of making a good play about common folk and probably could have made one far superior to *Merry Wives* had he had a desire to experiment with "bourgeois" drama. But Shakespeare had no such desire. His eyes were fixed on heroes whom he considered more important—generals, kings, high nobles and magicians.

5

As the year 1598 ran toward its end, Shakespeare had uneasy moments over his friend Southampton. The young Earl, now in his middle twenties, had got into trouble. After rejecting the young lady who was Lord Burghley's choice for him, and paying for the privilege of doing so, he had won some fame in tournaments and in expeditions abroad. Meanwhile he had paid court to Elizabeth Vernon, cousin of the influential Earl of Essex. There was much gossip about this. The Queen frowned on Southampton's attentions to the lady. She was a royal maid of honor and perhaps because of her own single state, Elizabeth threw a tantrum at talk of marriage for any of her attendants. Southampton was clearly much troubled. Finally he got permission to go on a trip to the Continent, then dashed back early in August and married the lady.

The Queen was furious at this behavior, and ordered the young Earl, who had fled again to France, back to England. He postponed obeying her while friends tried to soften the Queen's heart. His wife was sent to prison, and it was apparent she would soon be a mother. Southampton waited until she was—on November 11—then joined her in the Tower. What would happen to him was uncertain. However, he had the Earl of Essex as a friend and advocate, and Essex now stood high in Elizabeth's favor.

It was in 1598 that another earl began to be seen about London—one almost as handsome and quite as learned as Southampton had been in 1589. This was William Herbert, Earl of Pembroke, the son of Sir Philip Sidney's sister. Later, with his brother Philip, Pembroke would have a close association with the Lord Chamberlain's Men, and presumably with Shakespeare.

But late in 1598 Shakespeare and his associates were less concerned with earls, even if personal friends, than they were about the Theatre. They had a superb assortment of plays—tragedies, chronicles, the romantic comedies of Shakespeare and the one popular satiric comedy of Jonson. Ben was working on a companion piece for them—*Every Man Out of His Humor*. Still, plays were of little use without a playhouse. Did the Chamberlain's Men have one?

For almost twenty months Cuthbert Burbage had been negotiating with Giles Alleyn, but to no point. Meanwhile the Theatre stood unused. It began to be clear that Alleyn would never agree to terms the players could accept. What, then, would become of the building? He had begged them not to tear it down, but having left it there pending negotiations, was it still theirs?

Rumors came that Alleyn did not think so. He was preparing to wreck the playhouse and sell or use the lumber. The Chamberlain's Men rose almost to a man against the idea.

"Why, the whining old hypocrite," said Cuthbert, "is this the return he makes to forbearance on our part? Let him beware. By twenty devils, he shall never pull it down!"

"Can you stop him?"

"Aye, and simply. If any pull it down, we shall do it ourselves!"

"How stands the law?"

"The law! The law! Mark you, by the law the building is ours. But if we wait for the Puritan to wreck it, 'twill be ours no longer. And I know that once *we* have it, he'll need more than hymns and prayers, yes, and more than suits of law, to recover it!"

XIX: SHAKESPEARE OF THE GLOBE

TO a man standing in any Shoreditch lane on that night of December 28, 1598, the locality seemed quiet indeed. Few lights showed in the windows of the scattered houses. The great bulk of the unused Theatre made a silhouette against a sky of cloud and half-hidden stars. The big space beyond that was Finsbury Field lay empty and soundless.

Then the horsemen and carts and wagons came. They rode or drove up, and men tumbled to earth with a pattern of sound that spread and grew. Some got axes and crowbars and bills from the wagons (a bill was a bladed steel hook set on a long handle). Others busied themselves with swords and pistols. One with a horn lantern in hand was

speaking with another in workman's garb, but with an air of authority about him.

"Fall to, Peter Street," said the first. "You know the way of this business. Let the lads get the old barn down as fast and quietly as they can, but let no harm come to the big timbers. We must take the whole frame away, to use again."

"We shall make speed, Master Burbage," the other replied, "and we shall have due care to that which must be kept whole."

He gave orders, the brisk but subdued sound of crowbars against wood, and the careful tapping of hammers and sledges rose above the murmur of talk to break sharply on the dark and silence.

Cuthbert Burbage set down his lantern and walked about among the carts and wagons, looking beyond them toward the Shoreditch cottages.

People had already thrust their heads out of nearby windows, and as the workmen warmed to their assault upon the old playhouse two men came running toward the dim light of the lanterns.

"Forbear, sirs, forbear!" cried one of them.

"Who bids us?".demanded Burbage. He leaped out of the dark, his sword scraping free of its sheath as he spoke. The excited newcomer came to a sudden halt.

"My master, sir, Master Giles Alleyn," he replied stanchly. "It is his property, sir. Ah—" recognizing him—"Master Burbage."

"Even so."

"It is a lawless thing you do, and I pray you call off these men."

"Nay, we have the law; the building is ours," snapped Cuthbert.

"But I have heard my master say that 'tis now his—"

"Says he so? What, then, will he think when we have carted it away?"

Burbage advanced his sword point and the other retreated slightly, but took confidence when he saw that he had a good half dozen companions behind him.

Burbage saw them, too.

"Will!" he shouted. "Dick! John! Lend me some swords' points or ordnance! Here are some that would stay us from our business!"

He stepped forward and brought the flat of his sword down smartly on the cap of a servingman. The fellow squealed.

"Away," shouted Cuthbert, "or I will use the edge on you! We have work here, and it shall be done!"

"If you would but wait until our master returns—" began the first of Alleyn's men.

Dick Burbage, now at his brother's shoulder, spoke up.

"Your master will not come here tonight. He sleeps out of town. Do you think we are here by chance? We know his plans well, and have shaped our own accordingly. And shall carry them out!"

With Cuthbert, he paced before them grimly, his drawn sword catching the dim light as he moved.

"Look ye," said the former to the hesitant group. "We wish no ill to any mother's son of you. But he that lifts a finger to stay us—let him beware. If you like not cold steel between your ribs, or a staff playing a tune on them, stand back!"

A mass of light boards fell from the second story of the building with a dull crash.

"Do you hear that? There will be no stick of the playhouse left here tomorrow noon, and you may tell the old Puritan your master from me to go and look for it. Away, I say!"

Alleyn's men slunk off into the dark, and the crowbars and tapping hammers and falling debris kept up their tattoo on the darkness.

2

The eruption of men and carts on the quiet of Shoreditch had indeed been the result of a careful plan. On Christmas, just three days previous, Cuthbert and Richard Burbage, together with William Shakespeare, John Heminges, Augustine Phillips, Thomas Pope and William Kemp had leased a plot of land in the Bankside near Maiden Lane from a certain Sir Nicholas Brend. They were to have it for thirty-one years, and agreed to pay £14, 10s per annum for it. To this plot of land the timbers of the Theatre were being carried. There a new playhouse, the Globe, would soon rise.

This playhouse was controlled in a fashion never known before. The Theatre, the Curtain, the Rose, the Swan—all had been the private properties of individuals who expected to make money from them. The Globe, in contrast, was jointly owned by a group of seven, six of them actors. The two Burbages at first held five shares, and the others one each. Later there were changes in this distribution. But one thing was fixed—should one of the "housekeepers," as the seven owners were called—wish to dispose of his holding, he must sell it to his partners, or to someone approved by them. Thus with the single exception of Cuthbert Burbage the ownership was controlled by players. As other members of the Chamberlain's Men grew in experience and reputation they might be permitted to become housekeepers.

The joint owners doubtless advanced money for the building of the new playhouse. In return they received "rent." This was clearly defined: it was one-half of all admissions paid for seats in the galleries.

The rest of the money taken in—that is, the other half of what was received for gallery seats and all paid for general admission—went to the other members of the company—the sharers. (General current expenses and the wages of nonsharers would first be paid.) Six of the housekeepers were sharers, too. Accordingly, they received two incomes—one as owners, the other as actors. Such players and apprentices as were not housekeepers could of course hope for a chance to buy an interest in the theater as they rose in their profession.

The new arrangement proved to be a good one. It helped to bind the chief actors to the company, for a man would think well before leaving an organization of which he was part owner. No group of players during this period held together so long as the Chamberlain's Men. Those who were already housekeepers and those who hoped to be both worked together in a spirit of warm friendship. They were truly "fellows."

3

The new playhouse rose proudly under the direction of the master builder, Peter Street. It was to be the most famous and probably the best of the theaters of the day.

It lay only a few hundred feet from the south shore of the Thames, not far from the Rose. Most of its patrons came across the stream by boat or barge. The Globe loomed up, 45 feet high, all told, and covering a space 84 feet in diameter. It looked like a low, roundish castle (of course the actual shape was octagonal), with plastered walls and a little cluster of gabled roofs lifting above the wall at one end.

The Globe rose from ground that had been marshy, but had now been ditched and was fairly well drained. A large open "sewer" ran along one side of it. However, the character of the ground does not seem to have caused the playhouse itself to be unduly damp or uncomfortable. Undoubtedly full provision was made for keeping the ground floor free of water, whether from the land about and beneath it or from rain above.

In its general shape, the Globe was a replica of the Theatre. That is, it was eight-sided, both without and within, and the over-all dimensions were the same. Dr. John C. Adams, in his recent book, *The Globe*

Playhouse,[1] shows convincingly why these facts must be accepted, and gives a wealth of information about the theater, a considerable amount of which I have used in the pages that follow.

There was good reason, already pointed out in the description of the Theatre (Chapter VII), why both playhouses were octagonal rather than round. The former shape enabled the builders to use straight timbers. On the inside, it did away with any need for building an additional frame of boards and lath, and plastering it (as would have been necessary to make the interior round). Also it saved more room for seats. A great deal has been made of Shakespeare's own phrase in *Henry V* when he refers to the theater—

> But pardon, gentles all,
> The flat unraiséd spirits that have dared
> On this unworthy scaffold to bring forth
> So great an object. Can this cockpit hold
> The vasty fields of France? Or may we cram
> Within this wooden *O* the very casques
> That did affright the air at Agincourt?

But "this wooden *O*" should not be taken too literally. The octagonal shape of the theater was in general appearance round. Again, the letter *"O,"* if one must be literal, might be thought of in 1599 as not exactly round, but closer to the shape of the old English ⊕, which was often hexagonal and not circular at all.

As to using the identical shape of the Theatre—that was a matter of using the actual timbers of the older playhouse.

"We shall halve the cost thereby," Cuthbert Burbage had declared. "If the chief timbers are the same, why, Peter Street shall unpeg them in Shoreditch and peg them up again in the Bankside. Age has only seasoned them. And these eight-, twelve- and fifteen-inch beams make up the very heart of our cost. You shall pay as much for them as for all the rest—the lath, light boarding, plaster, thatch and paint. We shall save three hundred pounds."

[1] John Cranford Adams, *The Globe Playhouse,* Harvard University Press, Cambridge, 1943.

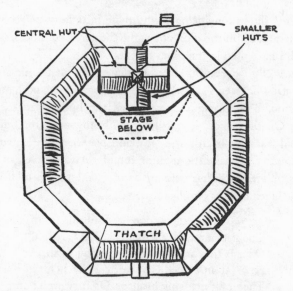

VIEW OF THE GLOBE FROM DIRECTLY ABOVE

It was true, and the cost of the Globe was less than that of other theaters by some such figure.

But while the over-all form of the Theatre was retained, great changes were made in construction within that form. For years Will Shakespeare and his fellows had struggled with difficulties and short-comings in the Theatre and the Curtain. These were remedied in the Globe.

Today we can view buildings from the air. Could an Elizabethan have looked down on the new theater from a helicopter hovering above and a bit to the north of it, he would have seen the octagonal arena as three units:

1. *The roofed-over galleries, occupying a strip along five of the eight sides, and lying somewhat like a gigantic horseshoe with its prongs touching either side of the stage unit.*
2. *The stage unit—a four-story structure occupying the other three sides (the southern end) and most of the space within them.*

3. *The pit—the ground space, open to the sky, which was not filled by the other two units.*

The galleries and pit were simple in structure and function. The former offered seats for spectators, with shelter. The latter provided them with standing space, paved and inclined slightly toward the stage to facilitate drainage and improve visibility, but quite unprotected from the weather.

In contrast, the stage unit was a highly complicated structure. Only recently have its rather remarkable form and resources been clearly understood. Its basement and four levels provided resources which will be startling to most modern readers.

THE BASEMENT

Beneath the Main Stage and the other areas lying to its rear lay a Basement which was a highly important unit for the production of a number of plays.

It was a chamber about 20 feet wide and 40 feet long, and 8 feet from floor to ceiling. To provide this height, the ground had been excavated to a point 3 or 4 feet deeper than the lowest portion of the pit.

The activities of the Basement were chiefly related, directly or indirectly, to trap doors in the stage platforms. A large trap was located in the center of the Main Stage, and in the floor at other points there may have been four smaller traps. A good-sized door was also located in the floor of the Study.

These openings were used for the appearance of fiends or spirits. At other times they represented graves or pits, or clefts in the earth through which unworthy characters sank to "Hell." In several dramas Pluto descended to the underworld through a trap.

In the Basement were machines for hoisting or lowering players through the traps. Here too were stores of fireworks, and materials for making flames, sudden flares of light, or black smoke. The Elizabethans were ingenious in handling such devices. Workmen were at hand when a play required certain effects which they could produce.

The Basement was frequently called "Hell" because of the grisly sounds, the flames and fearful apparitions that issued from it; and because in some plays it was actually designated as that region.

THE FIRST LEVEL

Directly above the front portion of the Basement lay the Main Stage. It rose from 4 to 4½ feet above the lowest portion of the pit, and jutted out into that area. Behind this platform lay the Study, which in the Globe was also important as a playing space. Between its rear wall and the rear wall of the building ran a narrow passage which connected two fairly spacious lobbies, each behind one of the side doors to the Main Stage. In these lobbies actors stood while waiting for their cues. By one of the doors stood the prompter, ready to speak through a wicket designed for him.

At the rear wall of the building, in the hall between the lobbies, were stairs, one flight descending to the basement and another leading upward to the second story.

THE SECOND LEVEL

For some dramas, a considerable part of the action was played on the second level. This contained four stages—the Chamber, directly above the Study; the Tarras; and two Window-stages. All these units will be explained later.

In addition to the stages there were two fair-sized tiring rooms, one behind each Window-stage. There was also space on either side of the Chamber where actors could stand. To the rear were stairs down to the first level, and up to the third.

THE THIRD LEVEL

The space on this story was about equal to that on the second level, and above the Chamber was a Music Gallery, where musicians played behind curtains of thin material which concealed them but did not mute the sound of their playing. The rest of the floor was used for storage.

The front of the Music Gallery, outside the curtains and hence visible to the audience, was sometimes used as a stage. It is known to have represented the keep of a castle, the mainmast of a ship, and a high tower.

THE FOURTH LEVEL

This final story, commonly called the "Heavens," consisted of a cluster of huts with gable roofs, and a small tower. A large hut undoubtedly ran across the building (that is, cross-stage), and there seem to have been a small one in front of this, and another to its rear.

These huts overhung the Main Stage three stories below, and were supported at the front by two sturdy pillars rising from this stage. The floor of the entire superstructure made a ceiling for the outer stage 32 feet below, and for the higher levels. There is evidence that this ceiling was painted blue and covered with stars in the form of the signs of the zodiac. The overhanging "Heavens" made a good sounding board for music and the voices of the actors. It protected the latter from rain.

In the floor of the large central hut (and thus in the ceiling of the stage) was a trap door about 4 by 20 feet in size. Through this, with the aid of machines, stage hands could lower clouds, thrones, chariots, and other objects.

The small hut in front may have housed cannon and supplies of fireworks. In the hut to the rear thunder was probably made by rolling a heavy ball, or "bullet," synchronized with the sound of snare drums and kettle drums in the music loft just below.

The trumpeter stood on a platform, perhaps outside the small front hut.

In the tower above the large central hut hung a bell which was used fairly often in plays. Shakespeare employed it, for instance, in *Macbeth, Othello,* and probably in *Hamlet.*

Thus the stage unit was a place of many rooms, platforms, devices and activities. What improvements over the earlier theaters did it represent?

The basement level was doubtless larger and deeper and in many ways better equipped than the "Hell" of the Theatre, the Curtain, the Rose or the Swan. Experience would have suggested improvements, and the Chamberlain's Men had the intelligence and money to make them. The reputation of the Globe argues that the building marked an advance in stage construction. Probably the traps were greater in size, and the machinery for operating them better designed than was the case with older theaters. Shakespeare used both the Main Stage trap and others most effectively in *Macbeth,* Act IV, Scene 1 (see Chapter XXIII).

On the main level, two highly important improvements had been made.

In the first place, the Main Stage had been enlarged. The sketch on the opposite page shows how this had been accomplished, and the advantages it gained.

In the Theatre the outer stage had been a rectangle 24 feet in width and from 28 to 30 feet deep. Entrance doors had been located at the left- and right-hand rear corners of this platform, in the rear stage wall. Even with rather narrow doors, this arrangement left room in that stage wall for a Study only 15 or 16 feet wide. Furthermore, it meant that actors entering by either of the side doors must advance from the very rear of the stage.

By broadening the rear platform, three improvements were made. First of all, the Study was widened to 23 feet, one foot less than the width of the main stage platform at its front end. The doors were then set in two walls which slanted sideways and forward from the Study. Here there was ample space for them, and they were probably 5 feet in width and 8 or 9 in height—a gain in width at least over the Theatre's doors. Small vehicles could now pass through them, and soldiers two abreast, with spears and standards. At the same time, the entrance points were closer to the front of the stage, and more to the side. The actors came more quickly to their destinations on the platform, and

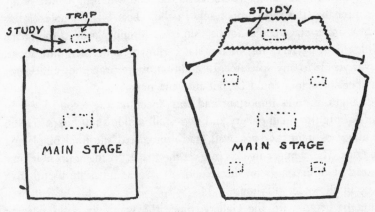

FIRST LEVEL—THE THEATRE   FIRST LEVEL—THE GLOBE

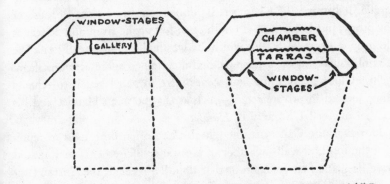

SECOND LEVEL—THE THEATRE   SECOND LEVEL—THE GLOBE

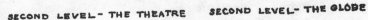

The rough drawings above, intended to emphasize function, are adapted from much more complete and precise diagrams used in *The Globe Playhouse,* by John C. Adams. That book is also the source for the sketch on page 274.

the scenic effect was better.

All these improvements were useful, but the widening of the Study was probably the most important. In the Theatre the whole of this narrow inner stage could not be seen from certain places in the arena. Widened to 23 feet, and of the shape shown in the diagram above, it was visible to any spectator. In addition, more properties and larger numbers of actors could be put into the new Study.

Changes quite as important had been made on the second level. In the Theatre the small gallery and two small windows or boxes, one on each side of it in the back wall, had represented the total of playing facilities. The changes in structure on the first level made possible four instead of three stages on the second, all larger and more useful than those in the older playhouse.

Let us begin with the Gallery. Since the windows could now be moved from the back wall to the side walls, where they were directly above the stage doors on the first level, this unit could be greatly enlarged. It became the Chamber. Its dimensions were close to those of the Study, just beneath it—a width of 23 feet at the front and 20 feet at the rear, a depth of 8 feet, which, as we shall see, was really 11. The Chamber had a door, a window, and a curtained space between them. In the Globe many important scenes were to be played here—chiefly those located in private rooms—such as that between Hamlet and his mother in Act III, Scene 2, of *Hamlet*.

However, the Gallery in the Theatre had often been used to represent the top of a wall—whether of a castle or a city. This may indeed have been the first function of that unit. To meet it, the Tarras (terrace) was developed as a separate playing unit.

In the Globe, it consisted of a narrow stage *in front* of the Chamber. It was from 3 to 4 feet deep and 23 feet wide. The curtains across the Chamber formed its rear wall. When these were drawn back, the Tarras ceased to exist, becoming a part of the larger stage behind it, which thus added the 3-foot overhang to its depth. Yet while the Tarras existed, it gave much more room for actors and action than had the 15-foot wide gallery in the Theatre.

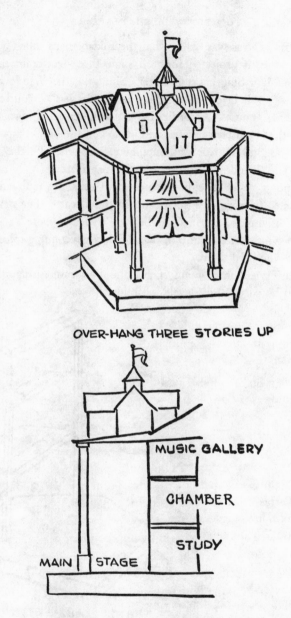

OVER-HANG THREE STORIES UP

MUSIC GALLERY

CHAMBER

STUDY

MAIN STAGE

PROFILE OF GLOBE STAGE

Most of the Tarras was really what the Elizabethans called a "penthouse." That is, it projected forward some three feet from the rear wall of the Main Stage, just below it. Similarly, the Window-stages overhung the wall below them. This overhang was of course usual in Elizabethan houses. Accordingly, playwrights often wrote their plays from the late fifteen-nineties and on so that the Main Stage represented a street, and the rear wall one or more houses, with the Tarras, Chamber, and Window-stages as second-story features.

The Window-stages on either side of the Tarras also represented an important step forward over such units in the Theatre. The new windows, Dr. Adams argues in *The Globe Playhouse,* were 12 instead of 4 feet in width, and about 6 in depth. They gave ample freedom to the players who used them.

Thus there were three main stages and four minor stages in the Globe, distributed on three levels, as follows:

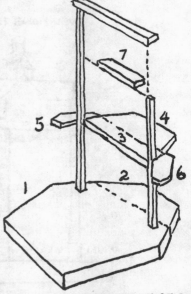

SHAKESPEARE'S SEVEN-STAGE
PLAYHOUSE

FIRST LEVEL

The Main Stage
The Study

SECOND LEVEL

The Chamber
The Tarras
First Window-stage
Second Window-stage

THIRD LEVEL

The Music Gallery Platform

In the past we have tended to think of the Main Stage, of the Study, and of one second-story unit. We should rather think of Shakespeare's stage unit as having seven playing areas, and as being tremendously varied and flexible.

The whole character of Shakespeare's drama is related closely to this multiple playhouse. It made shifts of scenery largely unnecessary, and waits between scenes unheard of. It made the flow of the drama continuous. It enabled what would be a three-hour play for us to be performed in two hours.

The over-all dimensions of the Globe were 84 feet from outside wall to outside wall, and 58 feet on the inside from gallery to gallery. The height to the eaves was 34 feet.

Various calculations have been made of the audiences the new playhouse could hold. Dr. Adams makes an estimate of 2,048. This would permit an intake of from £18 to £20, or perhaps $1,500 in our money values of today.

Now that we have a notion of the resources of the Globe, let us picture its appearance as a palace of pleasure. As we have seen, the stage unit was at the southern end, and the spectators entered from a northerly direction. They came in daylight, and directly from the river, along lanes that took them past houses and gardens. The playhouse would loom up among the smaller structures. Above its door, as they approached, patrons would see a large sign. It showed, says tradition, Hercules supporting the earth on his shoulders. Under the figure ran the motto: *Totus mundus agit histrionem.*

The sign was doubtless in color; so were the huts of the superstructure; the playhouse flag waved at the top of the tower. Once inside, the spectator would find the wooden beams and partitions gleaming in dark paint against the light painted plaster of the wall. The four-storied stage unit was rich with colored curtains, painted pillars and railings, and the deep blue of its ceiling. The tradition of opulence and gilded ornament which the theater keeps today flourished in the Elizabethan playhouses. They in turn probably took their appearance from the coats of arms, the gay cloaks, and the tapestries of the medieval fetes and tournaments.

4

Giles Alleyn had brought suit to get the timbers of the Theatre, now the frame of the Globe. But his case was not a strong one.

In the first place, the Chamberlain's Men had possession of the lumber.

In the second place, they could show that Alleyn had begged Cuthbert Burbage to let the Theatre stand on his property past the date of the lease, in order that the two might reach an agreement. In this fashion he had practically guaranteed Burbage that the building could be removed by the latter if no agreement were made. Since none had been, why should he complain now? Had he deliberately urged that the Theatre be left on his property in order to seize it as a result of the deception? His suit never came to anything.

So, as Peter Street the builder sent the frame of the new playhouse skyward, and the frame became a solid rampart, beam and plaster, the Chamberlain's Men looked toward the day when they would have not only a theater of their own, but the best that England or the world had known.

For Will Shakespeare good news came from the Court. The young Earl of Southampton had been released by the Queen to go with the Earl of Essex to Ireland, there to subdue the Irish rebels. It was not an easy task. The native chieftains in Ireland led their bands out of the bogs for sudden attacks, then vanished. A few months earlier such a sally had resulted in the destruction of Edmund Spenser's castle, with his wife and children. The poet himself had come back to England, and died there in January, 1599.

Essex's enemies had really forced the Irish expedition upon him. He would fail, they believed, and would then have less power with the Queen. But Essex himself expected to succeed. Many Englishmen believed that he would.

As he rode from London late in March the people pressed into the streets, crying, "God bless your lordship!" "God preserve your honor!" Shakespeare may have been among the crowds, swelling the huzzas with his own cheers.

The Globe opened soon after this, and the first play presented there was the story of Henry the King—*The Life of King Henry the Fifth*. It took up the tale almost where *Henry IV, Part II* had left it, and told of the invasion and conquest of France.

Englishmen were ready for a drama depicting this chivalric enterprise, and Shakespeare was in the mood to write one. He used a chorus, or narrator. Before each of the five acts this guide appeared. He sketched in the setting for the action, set the mood of the spectators for what they would see. Shakespeare had never before used a narrator so frequently or intensively, but having decided to employ one in such a fashion, he did so with superb vigor. The five speeches of the chorus keep the audience in the full heroic sweep of the drama, and contain many lines we remember today.

In Henry the Conqueror, Shakespeare did justice both to "the mirror of all Christian kings" and to the English people who made their land a "little body with a mighty heart." Henry's speeches to his army are still models of heroic exhortations. The English captains and common soldiers still hold us with their natural fears and doubts, their bickerings, and their bursts of heroic valor that toppled a kingdom.

If Falstaff did not appear personally in this play, here he made his final bow as Dame Quickly told of his death. And here with Pistol, Nym, Bardolph and the Welshman Fluellen for his characters, Shakespeare fashioned comedy almost as enjoyable as that of the two *Henry IV*'s. In a more elegant fashion the French princess Katharine enriched the lighter side of the play. The short scene, entirely in French, in which she experiments with the English language, made a charming interlude between battles and pageants. It was one of the most delightful spots in the vivid and stirring motion picture of *Henry V* made in the middle nineteen-forties by Laurence Olivier and his associates.

Apparently the play was written as the Irish expedition was getting under way. At least, while the actors made the Globe ring with their heroic lines, Essex was across the sea on the Queen's business. For at the beginning of Act V, describing how London poured out her citizens to welcome back their king from France, the chorus says, in comparison,

> As, by a lower but loving likelihood,
> Were now the general of our gracious empress,
> As in good time he may, from Ireland coming,
> Bringing rebellion broachéd on his sword,
> How many would the peaceful city quit
> To welcome him!

The hope of victory abroad thus gave seasoning to the greatest story of past English glory ever to be told. It made these first months at the Globe unusually happy ones. Probably Ben Jonson's play, *Every Man Out of His Humor,* was shown in the new playhouse. These offerings seemed to promise a glorious future. As a matter of fact, the actuality was to exceed the expectation.

XX: PATRIOTS AND REBELS

EVEN while Shakespeare was painting his picture of the conquer-
ing Henry, he was reading of other conquerors. In particular he
was studying the story of Julius Caesar, which he had doubtless read
in his Plutarch years ago. Caesar and his times were enough in the
playwright's mind while he was writing *Henry V* so that just before
Act V, when the chorus describes the leading London citizens wel-
coming their king, he reaches back to Rome for a comparison—

> The Mayor and all his brethren in best sort,
> Like to the senators of the antique Rome,
> With the plebeians swarming at their heels,
> Go forth and fetch their conquering Caesar in.

Thus already the figure of Caesar, greatest of Roman captains, loomed up in likeness to and contrast with the greatest captain England had known.

Why not? The two made a fascinating comparison. Henry was the hero of clear, practical mind and immense energy, exhorting his followers to triumphs that seemed a succession of furious miracles. Caesar was scholar and philosopher as well as soldier, more the inspired political and military manipulator and less a St. George on horseback. Caesar, again, came from a commonwealth different from Lancastrian England of the fourteen-hundreds. In name, at least, Rome was a republic; and its chief citizens were troubled about, and resentful of, the great powers that Caesar came to hold.

But it was not the mystery of Caesar that Shakespeare was tempted to explore. In his Plutarch he found lives of Julius Caesar; of Marc Antony, Caesar's friend; and of Marcus Brutus, also a friend, but in the end, one of his assassins. Of these, it was Brutus's story that chiefly attracted Shakespeare. Around Brutus he builds his tragedy.

Here is a scholarly patriot, fearful of the great power his friend Caesar wields. Another friend to Brutus, Cassius, points out the danger to Rome that the dictator represents. Brutus is called upon to choose between his friend and his country. And when, choosing his country, he helps kill Caesar, he must carry on the struggle against Caesar's political heirs and also against the small protesting part of his own conscience that makes him question the murder he helped to plan and execute.

Shakespeare's Brutus, like the good but naïve Henry VI and the poetic but impractical Richard II, is something of a bookish hero. But he rises above the weakness of these earlier characters. He is a man of great and stainless reputation, of force in conference, of oratorical power, of military skill. As he appears in the play he is far nobler than Caesar, who is set forth as a fearful yet egotistical tyrant, hoping soon to gild his actual authority with the royal title he has not yet dared to take. But this caricature of the real Caesar (as it undoubtedly is) nevertheless dominates Brutus's story. It is this Caesar who is the occasion of the rebellion and murder that Brutus helps to plan and carry out. It is Caesar, ignoble though he may be, who is the symbol of law and authority. It is in his name that Brutus and his friends are later assailed. It is Caesar who haunts Brutus. To this tragedy in which he is not the hero, Julius Caesar appropriately gives his name.

Few who read these pages are unfamiliar with the great scenes of *Julius Caesar*. Antony's funeral oration, the quarrel between Brutus and Cassius, and Antony's epitaph spoken over Brutus's body, beginning,

> This was the noblest Roman of them all—

so much at least is familiar to most readers, young or older, who will be drawn to read any book about Shakespeare.

But to reread the play in full, especially after having read the lives in Plutarch on which its story was based, is to get a realization of the upward sweep of Shakespeare's genius at this time. Of course other earlier plays by him are in their way as great. *Romeo and Juliet,* for example, and *A Midsummer Night's Dream*. But *Julius Caesar* is a political and oratorical play, with people less young and glamorous, with a scene less the mode and less colorful than Renaissance Italy or legendary Athens. Yet with the first words of the play Shakespeare takes us into Rome and the republic, makes us inhabitants of a city where freedom is immensely prized. With Brutus and Cassius, we care deeply about its loss. We are as Roman in this as we were English when we listened to Hotspur. What Brutus will do about Caesar is as real and exciting as what Henry V would do about France. (To us, indeed, more so.)

That Shakespeare could create such an atmosphere and such interest marked the ripening of various talents we have already noted in him.

There was the talent for sure observation, and for expressing what was observed with just the right detail. That gift enabled him to recreate Rome. His Rome had a dash of London in it here and there, but actually was about as real and true to its time as Plutarch's was. And Plutarch, though a Greek, knew the Roman scene; and could paint it as vividly as any modern correspondent can paint Berlin, Moscow or Nanking.

Again, there was the talent for character creation. Shakespeare, as we know, had always brought the people of his plays to life. But in *Julius Caesar* his genius for making them real seemed to find a new sureness and sharpness. The perplexed Brutus; the indignant, envious Cassius; the vain but hesitant Caesar; the politic but forceful Antony; Brutus's noble wife Portia—all, and other characters of lesser prominence, are so alive and personal that we seem to see them in the flesh, hear their voices, walk their streets and even stand in their houses.

Yet these characters could not have been themselves without the sureness with which they were fitted into the action of the play, and the skill with which they spoke. How easily might a slowness of action or a few flaws of speech have quenched characters and play alike, making them too much Roman history or too much a dull political quarrel. Ben Jonson, four years later, presented a Roman tragedy, *Sejanus,* which had many admirable qualities, yet quietly strangled itself in its own elaborate toga! But no false act or word marred *Julius Caesar.* From the beginning the spectator waited for Caesar's doom, then for Brutus's. As to the speeches, Shakespeare made these both heroic and natural. Perhaps he had won a final mastery of blank verse in creating Hotspur. The poet who could make phrases like "I'll tell you what," and "such a deal of skimble-skamble stuff," part of poetry, could do almost anything. He could put Brutus and Cassius into mere conversation, or charge them with vibrant emotion, or give them the tremendous quality of a great moment.

It is because Cassius can say a line of talk like

> I was born free as Caesar; so were you—

that we know he is natural and real. Then we are moved with him, as Brutus is, when he becomes possessed, and cries:

> When could they say, till now, that talked of Rome,
> That her wide walks encompassed but one man?

Now is it Rome indeed and room enough,
When there is in it but one only man!
Oh, you and I have heard our fathers say,
There was a Brutus once that would have brooked
The eternal devil to keep his state in Rome,
As easily as a king!

It would be easy to go through the play, showing the perfection with which each character is conceived, the sharp reality with which he speaks, the skill with which he is bent to the action. *Julius Caesar* was unique up to now, even for Shakespeare, in the *pre*cision and *in*cision of its people and action. They lifted the playgoers out of London and set them down in a real Rome.

Thomas Platter of Basle crossed the Thames "somewhere about two o'clock" on September 21, 1599, and saw the play "extremely well acted by scarcely more than fifteen players." Probably the Swiss traveler could not understand English well enough to get the full values of the drama. The effect on English listeners was better described by Leonard Digges almost a quarter of a century later—

So have I seen when *Caesar* would appear,
And on the stage at half-sword parley were
Brutus and Cassius—oh, how the audience
Were ravished! With what wonder they went
thence!

Rereading the play, one can imagine—in a scene of electric suspense or thunderclap action—the packed, standing figures motionless in the pit. One can imagine the gentlemen and masked ladies leaning forward in the galleries, rapt; the indolent show-offs reclining on the stage rushes, lifting on their elbows, taut and staring.

There are a dozen moments that might have put such a spell on spectators. The beholders may have hung on the cadences of Antony's funeral oration, relaxing as the roar of the citizens announced its success. They may have listened to the quarrel scene of Brutus and Cassius, scarcely daring to breathe; or may have waited in hushed suspense while Brutus in his tent spoke with the ghost of Caesar. Or they may have followed Antony's words at the play's end—

> All the conspirators save only he
> Did that they did in envy of great Caesar;
> He, only in a general honest thought
> And common good to all, made one of them.
> His life was gentle, and the elements
> So mixed in him that Nature might stand up
> And say to all the world, "This was a man!"

2

"If Evans has a lease on the Blackfriars and can bring the Children of the Chapel to play in it, we may all yet be paupers."

The speaker, a young, harassed-looking man of somewhat untidy dress, flung the words at his companions in the little tavern in the Bankside as if to test their truth.

The others stared at him across the lighted candles.

"Do you think, Master Dekker, that they will draw many from the Globe and the Fortune?" It was the young Earl of Pembroke, quietly but exquisitely attired. "Our older actors have a skill, and those that write for them a talent, that I believe the Children will find it hard to match."

Another and even younger man in the garb of a law student nodded his head.

"Wrens could as easily strive with eagles," he added.

Ben Jonson raised his shaggy head and grinned.

"Nay, Master Francis Beaumont," he said, "what if the boys are not wrens but larks?" He gave a side glance at Shakespeare, sitting at his right. "Our friend Will, here, is a housekeeper and a shareholder and is thereby cemented to the Globe by good gold as fast as the globe on the playhouse sign to Hercules who bears it," he went on. "But I am a free man, and I tell you, Tom Dekker, I would not be sadder if these same boys and their masters paid me a few pounds more a play than do My Lord Chamberlain's **Men**."

"Can you make a good lark's song for them, Ben?" asked Shake-speare.

"Nay, a magpie's, more like," Jonson chuckled. " 'Tis more my style."

"They do sing sweetly, these children," said Pembroke meditatively. "You shall hunt over Europe to find clearer or better-trained voices."

"They dance as well; and let none disparage their acting," said Shakespeare. "For the women's parts, they are as well off as we, who must use boys too. They can all but match our best clowning. No, Ben, if they have Blackfriars, we of the Globe and the Fortune must work the harder."

This talk was on an evening late in 1600, more than a year after the Globe had opened its doors. The men sitting at the inn table, although they may not all have known it, were representatives of changing days in the playhouses. Shakespeare was a symbol of the Chamberlain's Men, now the leading group of actors in London. They were the more clearly superior because they could number him among their members. He was now the outstanding playwright of the time. Their position was the firmer, too, because the second most gifted writer of the day also served them. Ben Jonson had already made his mark.

On the other hand, Dekker was a new writer of plays, and a good one, whose services they did not command. And he was one of a number whose names were just beginning to be heard. Chettle was among them (the man who had printed Greene's attack on Marlowe and Shakespeare). Marston was another. These and half a dozen more were working for Henslowe. He advanced them money. Sometimes, as he had threatened, he made a team of two, three, or four of them, bidding them do a certain play together. Singly or otherwise they combed through the old dramas, looking for ideas. They wrote new pieces. Dekker had just done *The Shoemaker's Holiday*, a comedy with wit and lively songs. Henslowe also had two plays on Robin Hood, written by Chettle and Anthony Munday, which had drawn good crowds. He and Alleyn were working hard to match and excel what Shakespeare's company could do.

Young Francis Beaumont was not yet a playwright. Almost seventeen, he had just left Oxford and come to London to study law at the Inner Temple. But he would leave his studies in a few years and collaborate with John Fletcher, also still unknown, for the enrichment of the theaters. Shakespeare and his fellows would get some of their plays.

Meanwhile Henslowe and Alleyn had erected a new playhouse, the Fortune, to replace the aging Rose. They had engaged Peter Street, builder of the Globe, to put it up for them, and the work had been finished in the early summer of 1600. Clearly Henslowe and Alleyn regarded the Globe as the last word in playhouse design. The Fortune, although square, was otherwise a copy of their rivals' playhouse. The contract for it stated that the new theater was to be in all respects except the shape of the galleries "effected, finished, and done according to the manner and fashion of the said house called the Globe."

Thus at this particular time the Admiral's Men were striving vigorously with Shakespeare's company for the favor of London audiences. For a while they had lost Alleyn (he had retired in 1597); now he was back. He had come at the Queen's own urging. She had missed his stately and distinguished work. But Henslowe was probably even happier to welcome him back than was she. Elizabeth enjoyed Alleyn's acting; Henslowe needed it.

That Henry Evans should now burst into the picture with his boy actors did not make Henslowe's lot easier, or that of the Chamberlain's Men either. Evans was an unexpected rival. Since James Burbage's death, the Blackfriars playhouse had stood idle—except when rented by Richard Burbage, its present owner, for occasional "private performances." Evans had taken it over in September, 1600, for twenty-one years. Then he had won the consent of the Master of Revels and the Queen to present plays there as a "training" for his young actors. Actually, the performances were as professional as any given at the Globe or the Fortune.

Evans was a seasoned producer who had worked under Lyly and the Earl of Oxford. He quickly whipped his company of youngsters into a marvelously skilled troupe. He persuaded Ben Jonson, George Chapman, and others to write for them. Soon it will be possible to note certain effects of his bold invasion of the playhouse world.

3

Meanwhile an event outside that world had cast a shadow on Shakespeare's life. Robert Devereux, Earl of Essex, kinsman and idol of Southampton, had not fared well in Ireland. Both he and the young Southampton had quarreled with other English leaders there. Essex had made no headway against the Irish rebels, and finally treated with their leader, Tyrone, against the Queen's explicit orders. In September, 1600, he deserted his post and rushed to England. Dramatically he broke into Elizabeth's bedchamber and flung himself at her feet.

The old Queen listened graciously enough to her young general. She was sixty-seven now, dyed and painted and bejeweled in the vain effort to hide her years. Essex was thirty-three. The Queen had enjoyed his professions of love and undying devotion. Still, she had never let her loves or likings interfere with her task of governing England, and she must have suspected as Essex pleaded his case that this man almost young enough to be her grandson had bungled his job in Ireland. She told him to report to the Privy Council.

There Essex had plenty of enemies. It was soon apparent that they would not make things easy for him. They questioned him severely about his management of the campaign. Essex for a time was confined to York House and its grounds, watched by the Lord Keeper. Then came the verdict. The Earl was deprived of his offices and ordered to remain in Essex House, his London residence, until further word from the Queen.

There he sulked and brooded. His friends kept themselves discreetly out of the Queen's sight. "My Lord Southampton and Lord Rutland come not to the Court," wrote a friend to Sir Robert Sidney. "The one doth but very seldom; they pass away the time in London merely in going to plays every day."

At the Globe Shakespeare undoubtedly saw Southampton, and heard from him of the impossible task Essex had been asked to accomplish in Ireland. News of this, too, must have seeped through London and beyond it; the people seem to have felt only sympathy for the unhappy Earl.

This was encouraging to Essex's followers, perhaps too encouraging. The situation in England was a strange and uncertain one. Elizabeth was old. How long would she live, and who would succeed her? The whole nation was uneasy about that. Of course, the logical successor was James, King of Scotland, and son of Mary, Queen of Scots. Essex had favored James, who had been torn from his mother and brought up since infancy as a good Presbyterian. But perhaps the people might demand an English king. Essex himself had been compared with Bolingbroke (later Henry IV) a few years earlier, and while he laughed at the comparison, he seems not to have disliked it. And now, as he sat in dejection at Essex House, he may have toyed with the idea that he was destined to be chosen king. His followers may have hoped that he would be.

Yet he was loyal to the Queen, too, and she to him. He fell ill, and she sent eight physicians to him. However, she sent no other and more important tokens of her favor. Early in February, 1601, a monopoly which Essex had held on the sale of sweet wines ran out and was not renewed. This was his chief source of income. Its loss was probably the incident that set him and his close followers to dreaming of power. He *must* have money.

In moments the road to power seemed easy. Essex and his friends would seize the Queen and the unfriendly members of the Privy Council. They would then right their wrongs. They seem to have had no exact plan as to how they would accomplish these ends, or what would follow if they were accomplished.

On Thursday, February 4, some five or six noblemen, including Sir Charles Percy and Lord Monteagle (and perhaps Southampton), came to the Globe Playhouse. They asked what the play would be the following Saturday. Being told (we have no record of what was scheduled), they suggested that Shakespeare's *Richard II* be given instead.

"Why, the piece is so long out of use that we should have small or no company for it," said one of the players who had clustered about the visitors.

"You shall have a company," answered one of the nobles, "for we will come and many with us. And we will get you forty shillings more than your ordinary takings, if you play it."

The players consulted and agreed. It was good business, and they did not understand the purpose behind the offer.

A mob of Essex followers, armed and probably warmed with wine, pressed into the galleries and applauded the old play that showed the deposition of a king. Here in the weak and arbitrary Richard they saw Elizabeth. There in the popular Bolingbroke, seeking justice, was Essex.

They came away from the play bolder and more restless. The following day they filled Essex House, armed and muttering. The place was like a fortress. Government officials led by the Earl of Worcester, and bearing the Queen's warrant, came to ask the meaning of such preparations. Essex spoke vaguely and wildly, saying his life was threatened.

Then he suddenly yielded to the pleas and taunts of his followers, and rushed out. With Southampton, Rutland, Sir Christopher Blount and others, he marched through the streets crying, "To Court! To Court! A plot is laid for my life!"

But only his followers marched behind him. London citizens stared curiously at his straggling company. Soon he found the streets barricaded, with armed men opposing him. He retreated to Essex House. Heralds throughout the city proclaimed him a traitor. That night he and Southampton surrendered and were taken to the Tower.

4

The Chamberlain's Men might well have stood in danger of severe punishment for their special performance of *Richard II*. However, their professions of innocence were accepted. On the evening of February 24, less than three weeks later, they actually played before the Queen.

Already Essex's fate had been determined. For the second time an order for his execution had been issued. The Queen had stopped the first one. This time she may have sat watching the actors and wondering whether or not to save her one-time favorite again. If she did, there was no outward evidence of her hesitation. Essex was beheaded the following day.

The fate of others, including Southampton, hung for a while in the balance. Then some received ruinous fines and some were sent to the block. Southampton, young and popular, was finally spared; but he remained in the Tower, awaiting the Queen's pleasure. He got no word from her during the two more years of life that were hers.

What did it all mean to Shakespeare? Undoubtedly it dismayed him. He saw good friends ruined or imprisoned or beheaded; for a number of the victims had been patrons and acquaintances of long standing. He could scarcely have approved of Essex's timid snatch at power; few Englishmen did. He must also have recognized how poorly it had been planned and put into action.

The failure of the conspiracy may have reminded him of Brutus's more successful attempt in *Julius Caesar*.

More probably it became associated with an intricate play which he was now planning, *Hamlet, Prince of Denmark*. A tragedy on this subject had been written and played a dozen years before. Shakespeare saw that a new and superior drama could be built around the old story. This story involved a king and a hero (his nephew) who wished to strike at him. Shakespeare had seen Essex's distraction, his ashness, his bewilderment. He had seen the cold, impersonal use of royal power. He had seen how fortunes could go up and down, and how courtiers like young Francis Bacon could shift to the wind. Bacon had been a friend and adviser of Essex—an Essex man. At the final trial he denounced his old master.

These and other events and considerations sank into Shakespeare's mind and feeling, to reappear later in his writings for the stage.

5

Meanwhile the life of the playhouses went forward busily. The boy actors opened at Blackfriars and pleased their patrons. Like modern singers with new styles or modern theaters with a new way of doing things, the Children took playgoing London by storm. In this same *Hamlet* which Shakespeare was about to write, he later gave us a fleeting picture of what happened. Rosencrantz and Guildenstern, two former friends of Hamlet, tell the Prince of the arrival of a company of players whom all three of them knew.

HAMLET: Do they hold the same estimation they did when I was in the city? Are they so followed?
ROSENCRANTZ: No, indeed; they are not.
HAMLET: How comes it? Do they grow rusty?

Rosencrantz replies that the actors are as good as ever, but that there is "an aery of children, little eyases" that are now the fashion. They "berattle the common stages" and (he hints) poke fun in their plays at the older actors. Hamlet points out that the boys themselves will grow, with time will want to be adult performers, too; aren't they foolish to ridicule the profession they must hope to follow?

Rosencrantz replies that there has been "much to-do on both sides," with actors and writers taking part.

HAMLET: Is't possible?
GUILDENSTERN: Oh, there has been much throwing about of brains!

HAMLET: Do the boys carry it away?

ROSENCRANTZ: Aye, that they do, my Lord; Hercules and his load, too.[1]

This was really an accurate if very general account of what had been happening in London and would continue to happen for a while. The boys and their writers, on the one hand, and the adult actors and theirs, on the other, began what was known as "the war of the theaters." Authors at first, then actors, were ridiculed in plays. Jonson was very active in this war, with Marston and Dekker, working for Henslowe, as his first opponents. He wrote two plays partly devoted to putting down his enemies. There is some question of his involving Shakespeare. In a student play of the time Kemp says to Burbage:

Oh, that Ben Jonson is a pestilent fellow! He brought up Horace giving the poets a pill; but our fellow Shakespeare hath given him a purge that made him bewray his credit.

A great deal of guessing and studying has been done to discover what this last sentence meant. To date nothing but rather feeble possibilities have been suggested. (We, of course, might miss points that would be clear to the audiences of the time—especially if the dress and features of author and actor were imitated.) Shakespeare's reference to the affair does not show any bitterness.

Indeed, he was probably above that. Ben Jonson, in *Every Man Out of His Humor,* seems to have taken a fling at Shakespeare's coat of arms. He describes a silly one—a boar's (bore's) head and the motto: "Not Without Mustard." This appears to be a fling at Shakespeare's "Not Without Right." But Shakespeare seems to have taken it good-naturedly. The play was produced by his own company, and he may even have had a part in it.

Meanwhile the Children wore out their first burst of popularity. Evans had got into trouble for having seized a gentleman's son and put him in training. He was censured by the Queen's Star Chamber for such practices, and for a time his theater was closed. It was reopened,

[1] A reference to the sign on the Globe Playhouse.

:losed, reopened; and finally, under King James, the troupe got into difficulty after difficulty for ridiculing prominent persons, the King among them. By 1609 the Children ceased to act.

But in the early 1600's they were amazingly good. A German official with the Duke of Stettin-Pomerania heard a boy sing at the Black-friars on September 18, 1602, to the accompaniment of a bass viol. He reported that "unless the nuns at Milan did not excel him, we had not heard his equal in our travels."

Ben Jonson showed his respect and affection for these boy actors by writing an epitaph for one of them. It was Salathiel Pavy, "a child of Queen Elizabeth's Chapel," who seems to have died late in 1601. Master Pavy played the parts of *old* men. But read Jonson's own words—

EPITAPH

Weep with me, all you that read
  This little story:
And know, for whom a tear you shed,
  Death's self is sorry.
'Twas a child that so did thrive
  In grace and feature,
As Heaven and Nature seemed to strive
  Which owned the creature.
Years he numbered scarce thirteen
  When Fates turned cruel,
Yet three filled zodiacs [2] had he been
  The stage's jewel;
And did act, what now we moan,
  Old men so duly,
As sooth, the Parcae [3] thought him one,
  He played so truly.
So, by error, to his fate
  They all consented;

[2] Three years.
[3] The Fates.

But viewing him since (alas, too late!)
    They have repented;
And have sought to give new birth,
    In baths to steep him;
But being so much too good for earth,
    Heaven vows to keep him.

XXI: HIGH COMEDY

TOWARD the end of 1599, after he had brought *Julius Caesar* to
the Globe, Shakespeare had turned again to comedy. Three brilliant plays had poured from his pen—*Much Ado About Nothing, As
You Like It,* and *Twelfth Night* (just being finished in the last days
of 1601).

In earlier chapters I have pointed out that Shakespeare had an
instinct to lift the quality of English comedy as he first knew it in
the late fifteen-eighties.

He had never liked the farce type of comedy that had been favored
by many English writers up to that date. He found it lacking in
variety of character and plot. The characters leaned too much toward
mere absurdity—they were clowns or simpletons or caricatures; the

303

plots suffered from the artificial nature of the people with whom they dealt, and from the wandering, episodic trend inherited from the medieval moralities. As a result, the comedies hit a rather low and mechanical level of interest.

Again, Shakespeare apparently saw little promise, at least for him, in the satiric comedy modeled on the Greek and Roman drama. In this, by taking human weaknesses represented by various characters, and ridiculing them, the dramatist was supposed to show the spectators the dangers and follies of the times, and send them away ready to improve themselves. Shakespeare, of course, tended to draw each of his characters as an individual. He did not greatly like the idea of making one of them represent pride; another, hasty anger; another, folly, and so forth. This remained true even after Ben Jonson showed him that satire could become the basis of admirable comedy.

Shakespeare began to develop his own type of comedy, as I have already shown, by bringing in estimable or noble characters as the chief persons in his lighter plays. This device gave him an opportunity to build a plot that dealt with more than trivial things. As we have also seen, he owed a great deal to Lyly in these respects. His originality lay in the greater depth and realism of his characters, and in the greater vigor and effect of his plots. His comedies now leaned toward farce, now toward fantasy, but were always bursting with color and life. However, the three that he wrote between the summer of 1599 and the end of 1601 represent a particular type which was one of Shakespeare's notable achievements.

As to plot, all three comedies might be called romantic. In each case, the story Shakespeare told dealt with persons of dignity; it was packed with danger and excitement, and in the main it was *not* funny. To be sure, it had a pleasant ending, with an ingenious solution of difficulties, and there were twists of humor along the way.

If the story itself was not a continuous source of humor, what were the sources of it? To simplify, they were:

1. The amusing turns in the plot already mentioned.
2. The wit of the estimable characters.

3. A number of humbler and frequently absurd characters, at whom the spectators could laugh freely (only moderate laughter *at* the the nobler characters was encouraged).

Working with these resources, Shakespeare produced an elegant, happy, swift-moving kind of drama that scholars have named "high comedy." It is "high" because of the social status of the chief characters and because of the superior literary quality at which it aims. The two were related. Noble characters had education, training, and a breadth of experience which humbler ones naturally lacked. And their birth and advantages were supposed by Elizabethans to bring out more fully whatever natural virtue they had (of course it was recognized that in some cases the development took an opposite turn!). In any case persons of high station had a better command of language than their inferiors; and it seemed natural for them to speak in poetry; which, in turn, raised the literary level of the play.

The lower characters, of course, furnished a contrast to the elegance of the higher ones, and gave the cruder, slapstick humor that pleased the groundlings (and the galleries, too). The vigorous plot always included a strong love interest. The danger elements provided melodrama of the better sort. Thus with its wide range of character and talk, this type of comedy presented an unusually full picture of life.

2

Of the three comedies that Shakespeare wrote between the summer of 1599 and the beginning of 1602 the first, *Much Ado About Nothing,* was the most hurriedly composed. Probably it was needed for a particular occasion. At any rate, a great part of it was done in prose (usually a sign of haste with Shakespeare) and the verse does not compare in distinction with that of the other two.

Yet the play stood high in popularity among the playwright's works. Certainly the plot was not responsible for most of the applause and laughter that the comedy always drew from its audiences. The plot presented the story of a noble young man (Claudio) who was tricked into suspecting the girl he intended to marry (Hero). He denounced her at the wedding ceremony and at once found Hero's friend Beatrice and his own friend Benedick enlisted as stanch champions of the accused girl. In the end all turned out well, since this was a comedy, and Hero gladly married the repentant Claudio.

True, the plot produced its sensational moments; but the play lived and still lives chiefly through the character of Beatrice. She was a highly intelligent and charming young lady with a sharp and witty tongue, who was in danger of losing her suitor because of her devastating conversational sallies.

Of course Beatrice did not know at first that Benedick *was* her suitor. She thought him offensively in love with himself, and was bent on puncturing what she regarded as his insufferable complacency. Nor did Benedick for a time have the least inclination to woo Beatrice. His opinion of her was much like hers of him. He himself could perform creditably enough in a caustic battle of wits; and for a time the two traded shrewd and even reckless blows as each tried to put the other down. Then Benedick was persuaded by his friends, who saw the possibility of good sport, that Beatrice was really in love with him, while Beatrice was convinced by hers that Benedick, despite his manner, adored her. Then the fighting ceased; and while the audience was still amused to see the former combatants acting as lovers, the play closed. Probably the hero and heroine fought again after getting married, and enjoyed doing it!

But we began a discussion of Beatrice, and this is to be said in conclusion: she had a sparkle and vitality that has probably never been matched in kind by any woman in fiction or drama. Portia was more lovable, but never flashed and glittered so superbly. And Beatrice for sheer candlepower quite outdid the heroines of the next two plays of Shakespeare, Rosalind in *As You Like It* and Viola in *Twelfth Night*.

This is not to say that I prefer her to them; or that many readers or audiences do. Beatrice glitters and flashes because of her very sharpness. Her capacity to annoy and be elegantly disagreeable is immense. But she has had fewer devotees among scholars and readers than the other two, who are as witty and have more charm and tenderness.

Where did Shakespeare get his model for this heroine? Or for Juliet and Portia, for that matter, who were as marvelous, each in her own fashion?

Millions of scholars and readers have asked this question. For each of these young women has the vividness of complete reality. Readers and spectators alike tend to believe that an original must have existed in each instance—much like the girl who enchanted them in the play. And particularly it has been asserted that Beatrice, Rosalind and Viola show that there must have been actual models for such heroines. A theory which appears in various forms is that Shakespeare fell in love with one woman in London. In loving her he gained the knowledge that made him able to create the others.

The Dark Lady of the *Sonnets* thrusts herself in at this point. Shakespeare, say some imaginative students, loved her over a long period of years. She, it is asserted, is Rosaline in *Love's Labor's Lost,* the Mistress in the *Sonnets,* perhaps a bit of Beatrice, and certainly Cleopatra in *Antony and Cleopatra* (written some years after the period we are now discussing). Yes, all these ladies of plays and poetry are supposed to trace back to one original—a dark, witty, fascinating and not too loyal person.

It is possible. There is little evidence for or against any theory about Shakespeare's women friends.

One small and somewhat spicy clue to his social activities has been found in the diary of a law student of the time, John Manningham. It is dated March 13, 1602, and, modernized in spelling, runs as follows:

Upon a time when Burbage played Richard the Third, there was a citizen grew so far in liking with him that before she went from the play she appointed him to come that night unto her by the name of Richard the Third. Shakespeare overhearing their conclusion, went before, was entertained, and at his game ere Burbage came. Then message being brought that Richard the Third was at the door, Shakespeare caused return to be made that William the Conqueror was before Richard the Third. Shakespeare's name was William.

This morsel of gossip, if based on fact, may have dated back some six or eight years to the first performances of *Richard III*. Or it may have had some kind of foundation in an occurrence around the time Manningham made his entry, when the tragedy may have been replayed. That Shakespeare had some kind of social life in London in these years, and that it included women, is about as sure as that he dined or acted in plays.

But it does not follow that he was passionately in love with a dark or a light lady, or with different ladies successively. It is quite as possible that the women in his plays had no more reality than his own love-and-marriage experience, his knowledge of his growing daughters, and his meetings with women of grace and education in and about the Court.

Even rough Will Kemp knew Mary Fitton; Shakespeare had doubtless chatted with the Queen's maids of honor; and with gentlemen's and noblemen's wives, sisters and mothers. Could he have missed conversing with the Countess of Pembroke, whose sons were his friends and patrons (as we shall see) and whose brother was the famous Sir Philip Sidney? Later, we know, the Countess was Ben Jonson's patroness and friend.

A good guess is that Shakespeare, the master observer, fashioned his Beatrices and Rosalinds and Violas out of what he saw and heard of these women with whom he could talk freely enough on occasion, but could not know as an equal. He marked their wit, beauty, elegance, grace and nobility of mind and heart. He was fascinated, he created.

I say, it is as good a guess as any. And there are some facts which in a very general way seem to favor it.

The first is that Shakespeare's heroines have an immense variety. None closely resembles another (not even Rosaline is much like the Dark Lady, or the latter like Cleopatra). Juliet, Portia, Beatrice, Rosalind, Viola—how sharply personal is each! So are later heroines—Helena, Isabella, Ophelia, Desdemona, Imogen, Miranda.

This gallery of women is too extensive to be nothing but memories of intimate personal acquaintances. Rather they seem so many charming proofs that Shakespeare created mostly from observation and imagination. And that was what we might expect of the greatest maker of characters the world has known. The man who could create Faulconbridge, Percy, Falstaff, Petruchio, Romeo, Mercutio, Shylock and Brutus could be supposed to do about as well with women, for he was clearly a master. Shakespeare may have had a deep interest in more than one woman in London. But we shall get lost if we try to prove it.

Again, if Shakespeare had some great adventure of the heart in London, this did not take his eyes from Stratford. It did not stop him from acquiring land and houses there, as he steadily went on doing. Any personal emotions he had in Shoreditch or the Bankside or elsewhere about the city seem never to have lifted London into a magic city for him. It was Stratford that provided scenic background for his plays, houses and lands for him to buy, a home to which he kept returning.

It could be argued that some frustration in love caused his final return to his native town; but throughout his life Stratford bulks large. If he lived out in London some episode which gave him the key to Woman, it seems never to have shaken his country roots. It is thereby the less a likelihood. Besides, Shakespeare did not need a special key to any group of human beings. He understood them well when he first arrived in London, and his continuing life there merely deepened an already fundamental knowledge.

There is another episode which re-creates for us the rather quiet Shakespeare, cool to habitual drinking and festivity, whom Aubrey described in William Beeston's words.

It is this: about the time he finished his comedies, Shakespeare took lodgings with a wigmaker, Christopher Montjoy, on the corner of Monkwell and Silver streets. This was near Cripplegate, and was a quiet part of walled-in London.

Montjoy was a Frenchman, a Huguenot. He and his wife knew Mrs. Field, the former Madame Vautrollier, for all attended the Huguenot church; and she may have sent the playwright to his new lodgings. The wigmaker seems to have been highly skilled in his trade; and with him lived his wife; his only child, Mary (in her teens); and a young apprentice named Stephen Bellott. A serving girl, Joan, was busy about the house, and seems to have waited on "Master Shakespeare."

Now, Montjoy was worried about a satisfactory husband for his daughter. Stephen Bellott seemed a very good candidate. Montjoy suspected that the charms of Mary had not gone unnoticed by Stephen. Yet the apprentice, a shy fellow, never came to him and never spoke to the girl.

Madame Montjoy had an idea. Their lodger, that grave but pleasant Master Shakespeare! If *he* would speak to Stephen! She herself begged him to do so. He consented. And he proved himself a good matchmaker, for Stephen and Mary joined hands, and late in November, 1604, they were married.

About the Montjoys and the Bellotts we shall hear more later; but Shakespeare's service as matchmaker shows the type of house in which he lodged, and the esteem these industrious, religious people had for him. It suggests a responsible man, probably busy and studious by turns. Doubtless he dined out and spent some evenings with men and women of his liking. This glimpse tells nothing as to that. Its picture is of a rather sober if pleasant Shakespeare, spending enough time at his lodgings to have the confidence and friendship of all intimates of the household.

3

Much Ado About Nothing had more comedy in it than that supplied by the wit of Benedick and Beatrice. It had Dogberry, a constable, and the men who served him.

This was slapstick. All Londoners knew constables and members of the watch. They were the policemen of the fifteen-nineties, and they had a rather hard time of it. Fiery young noblemen often scorned them, apprentices jeered at them, thieves and rascals tricked them. In Dogberry, Shakespeare created a typical London constable—pompous, stupid, wary of getting into trouble by being too vigorous in his office; yet cunning in his animal fashion and likely to turn up—as he did—

with a surprise. His advice to his men was priceless. To one of them he says—

DOGBERRY: You are to bid any man stand, in the Prince's name.
WATCH: How if a' will not stand?
DOGBERRY: Why, then, take no note of him . . . and presently call the rest of the watch together, and thank God you are rid of a knave.

He advises them to make no noise in the streets: "for the watch to babble and talk is most tolerable and not to be endured."

One of the men replies: "We will rather sleep than talk: we know what belongs to a watch."

Then come Dogberry's remarks on thieves.

DOGBERRY: If you meet a thief, you may suspect him, by virtue of your office, to be no true man. And, for such kind of men, the less you meddle or make with them, why, the more is for your honesty.
WATCH: If we know him to be a thief, shall we not lay hands on him?
DOGBERRY: Truly, by your office, you may; but I think they that touch pitch will be defiled. The most peaceable way for you, if you do take a thief, is to let him show himself what he is and steal out of your company.

The immense enjoyment of such dialogue by the Elizabethan audience can be imagined. Every phrase was a hit. Yet in the end Shakespeare more than let Dogberry have his day. It was he and his men who by lucky chance proved Hero innocent.

In *As You Like It* there were also humorous characters of a comparable kind. In fact, there was a larger and more varied group of characters.

Of course, they are less important in one sense than the nobler ones. We quickly fasten our interest on Rosalind. She is the daughter of the true Duke, whom the false one (his younger brother) has driven into exile. This tyrant, Frederick, keeps Rosalind at Court as a companion for his daughter Celia. How Rosalind meets and loves Orlando, then must flee for her life, how she goes disguised as a country boy and Celia as a sister, how they get a cottage in the forest where the true Duke hides, how Orlando arrives there—these are the events we follow.

Rosalind and Celia and others who are wellborn furnish a share of elegant humor in this comedy. But Touchstone, the Court fool, who goes along with the fugitive girls, supplies a great share of it on a lower level (if still courtly); and the country shepherd Corin and the girls Phebe and Audrey provide more. These four make the slapstick of the play, but it is elegant slapstick. Spenser and other Elizabethan poets had written pastorals, imitating the Greek and Latin poems about the loves of shepherds and shepherdesses. So it was natural for such characters to have a certain literary quality about them. Shakespeare made Corin and Phebe and Audrey naïve and laughable, yet they spoke prettily in verse.

Twelfth Night, too, had its outright comic charcaters. They are among Shakespeare's best. The romantic love of Duke Orsino for the Lady Olivia; the love of Viola, disguised as a page, for Orsino; her going as an emissary to plead Orsino's cause with the Lady, who becomes smitten with the "youth"—this is a lively story, and Viola's part in it is a poignant, tenderly humorous one. But Sir Toby Belch; Sir Andrew Aguecheek; Maria, Olivia's maid; and Malvolio, the Lady's steward, are the true comics.

Save for Falstaff and his amazing companions—Shallow, Pistol, Dame Quickly, and so forth—Shakespeare never created so merry a group.

Sir Toby was a high-spirited, wine-loving, song-loving rascal—a kind of smaller Falstaff, who performed more privately—in his niece Olivia's house or garden instead of in a public tavern. Sir Andrew was a pretentious nitwit, somewhat on the Justice Shallow model, but more absurd in his stupidity, cowardice and naïveté. Maria was a shrewd minx, full of wit and strategies. Malvolio was a pompous retainer, "sick of self love," whose egotism made him a logical victim for the wild and somewhat cruel prank which the others played upon him. He is one of the world's great comic characters, not of Falstaff's stature, for he lacked the creative force of Prince Hal's zestful companion, yet a notable contrast to him. For, while the humor of Falstaff lies in his swaggering, gluttonous, impudent, imaginative jollity, the humor of Malvolio lies in his severe, pompous and empty solemnity.

Into both *As You Like It* and *Twelfth Night* comes much talk of love. Love is laughed at and it is praised. There are sweet and romantic descriptions of it. Corin in *As You Like It* says that

> It is to be all made of sighs and tears. . . .
> It is to be all made of faith and service . . .
> It is to be all made of fantasy,
> All made of passion, and all made of wishes;
> All adoration, duty and observance;
> All humbleness, all patience and impatience;
> All purity, all trial, all obeisance.

That is the lover under the spell of love. Viola, disguised as the youth Caesario, and wooing Olivia for her master, Duke Orsino, tells what she would do (were she the Duke) to get Olivia's attention. She would

> Make me a willow cabin at your gate,
> And call upon my soul within the house;
> Write loyal cantons of contemnèd love,
> And sing them loud even in the dead of night;
> Holla your name to the reverberate hills,
> And make the babbling gossip of the air
> Cry out "Olivia!" Oh, you should not rest
> Between the elements of air and earth,
> But you should pity me.

This is romantic dedication to love—rather desperate and fantastic dedication. But it sounds wonderful! When Olivia murmurs, *"You might do much,"* we know that Viola-Caesario has hit close to target center.

Wit, melodrama, farce, romantic love—it was a joyous combination.

Shakespeare seemed happy writing these plays—happiest, perhaps, in *As You Like It,* where he took his audiences to a forest with his mother's name (Arden), and filled it with the trees and brawling brooks, the meadows and pools, the boar and deer of the Warwickshire woodland. Here he let the fugitives live a rude life, but as fine and free as that of the Golden Age. Here he created in Rosalind the sunniest of his heroines. Here he wove four love stories to a happy conclusion.

And yet even in *As You Like It* Shakespeare was beginning to show a disposition to wrestle with more puzzling and serious matters than romantic love. In the play appears a companion of the exiled Duke, Rosalind's father. He is called "the melancholy Jaques," and spends his days in meditation on the disharmonies of the world. He sees a wounded deer, and weeps as the other deer sweep past, ignoring their hurt companion. He swears that the Duke and his retainers

> Are mere usurpers, tyrants, and what's worse,
> To fright the animals and to kill them up
> In their assigned and native dwelling place.

Indeed, the world of serious men seems so awry to him that after meeting Touchstone he comes into the Duke's presence exclaiming:

> A fool, a fool! I met a fool i' the forest,
> A motley fool; a miserable world!
> As I do live by food, I met a fool;
> Who laid him down and basked him in the sun,
> And railed on Lady Fortune in good terms.

He describes how he talked with the fool, who remarked that it was ten o'clock, and in another hour would be eleven;

> And so from hour to hour we ripe and ripe,
> And then from hour to hour we rot and rot.

"Motley's the only wear!" exclaims Jaques, fascinated by the fool who seems to him to hit wisdom as often as folly. He wants a motley coat.

> I must have liberty
> Withal, as large a charter as the wind,
> To blow on whom I please; for so fools have:
> And they that are most galléd with my folly
> They most must laugh. . . .
> Invest me in my motley; give me leave
> To speak my mind, and I will through and through
> Cleanse the foul body of the infected world,
> If they will patiently receive my medicine.

There is much more of Jaques. It is not too clear how wholly Shakespeare was in sympathy with him. But Jaques, questioning the usual way of things, was setting forth the complexity and ills and disappointments of life. So in his speech beginning, "All the world's a stage," he sweeps through the existence of a man in seven stages, beginning with helpless infancy, and ending in the nothingness of the grave.

This and many other speeches are ironic. They echo at times the pleasant pessimism of the French essayist Montaigne, whose works had been translated into English by Southampton's tutor John Florio, and published in 1595, and again in 1600. But Shakespeare seems rather to be questioning than despairing.

True, he had questioned life at moments in earlier plays. In *Richard II,* for instance, and in *King John*. But the questioning had been less direct. Evil and disaster had been seen, lamented, denounced rather than studied. Now, suddenly, the world was far more complex, far more composed of uncertain, contradictory, baffling elements. "I met a fool in the forest!" cried Jaques. It is an exclamation that bids us look at a life of paradoxes. It seems as if, through folly, a man might strike to the truth. Shakespeare wonders. In the midst of his sunniest comedy he stares past the sunshine, like a man looking at the changing forms of a kaleidoscope, who suddenly becomes less interested in their pleasing patterns of color than in a possible clue to the way in which they were produced, and the meaning they may have.

This tendency to brood and question was soon strengthened by the events that sent Essex to the block and put Southampton in the Tower.

4

In *As You Like It* Shakespeare made the only reference to another writer of his time that appears in any of his works.

In fact, he made two references, both to Christopher Marlowe. One he put into the mouth of Phebe, when the poor girl falls in love with the "youth" Ganymede, really Rosalind—

> Dead shepherd, now I find thy saw of might:
> "Who ever loved that loved not at first sight?"

Marlowe, of course, was the author of "The Passionate Shepherd to His Love," one of the most popular lyrics of the era. He was therefore appropriately called "Dead shepherd." The "saw" was a line, quoted in Chapter X of this book, from his poem *Hero and Leander*.

A less direct reference to Marlowe was made by the fool Touchstone, and it referred to the manner of Marlowe's death in the tavern at Deptford. It ran: "When a man's verses cannot be understood, nor a man's good wit seconded with the forward child, Understanding, it strikes a man more dead than a great reckoning in a little room."

These words are better understood if we realize that in 1599 at the command of authorities of the Church of England, Marlowe's translation of Ovid's *Elegies,* just published then, had been burned. This was one of many succeeding abuses heaped upon the memory of the poet who had taught and perhaps worked with Shakespeare. The latter spoke out indirectly but stanchly for his dead friend.

The Touchstone who spoke these lines referring to Marlowe's death was not Will Kemp. The dean of English clowns had parted company with the Chamberlain's Men in the spring of 1600.

When we remember his work as the chief player for Leicester's Men, his great reputation, his long association with the housekeepers and shareholders of the company, this seems surprising. And yet the event must have been in the making for a number of years. With no ill-will toward Kemp, Shakespeare had probably been the chief cause.

The explanation lies in the opposition of two strong characters.

Kemp was a clown of great reputation, but he was a clown of the old school, proud of his ability to jig and improvise, to win laughter with personal expressions and devices that had little to do with any play. In fact, he did not regard the play too seriously. He was Kemp. If he muffed a line, he would bluff his way through.

"I am somewhat hard of study," he was made to say some years later in a play that put him on the stage, "but if they will invent any extemporal merriment, I'll put out the small sack of my wit I have left in venture with them."

In contrast, Shakespeare was a playwright of great reputation. He was also actor and part-time stage director. In the year 1600 he wrote plays out of long knowledge of what he wanted. Each line was important. He resented actors who mis-said what he wrote, perhaps at the expense of both character and scene.

We can imagine the conflict that rose from such a situation. Kemp, growing older, was more than ever unsure of memory; Shakespeare, growing older, was more particular as to accuracy.

"I pray you, Will," we can imagine him saying to Kemp at a morning rehearsal in the empty playhouse, "give more study to your lines. If they are mis-said, the scene fails."

"Tush, tush, lad, I have fathered more lines on the moment than you've labored out in a lifetime by candlelight."

"Be father to fewer of mine, Will. I labor out lines to a purpose."

"And I make the groundlings laugh! Keep that in mind, and scold me not like a shrew!"

There was no reconciling the two points of view. Shakespeare wrote feelingly of the matter in his *Hamlet:* "Let not your clowns speak more than is set down," he admonished in the first Quarto Version of this play (through Hamlet, as he instructed some players). "There be of them, I can tell you, that will laugh themselves to set on some quantity of barren spectators to laugh with them, albeit there is some necessary point in the play then to be observed. Oh, 'tis vile and shows a pitiful ambition in the fool that useth it." Clowns also had their stock jests that they would throw in—worn-out phrases like "your beer is sour" or "Cannot you stay till I eat my porridge?"

Kemp went from the Globe. He left when the playhouse closed for Lent in February, 1600, and danced his way from London to Norwich in less than a month. Every town in England heard of the famous journey. Then the comedian embarked for the Continent to amaze men there. He seemed at the height of his powers.

But in less than two years he was back in London seeking employment with Henslowe. He got two advances from the shrewd money-man of the theater. In November, 1603, he was buried in Southwark, apparently a plague victim. "William Kemp, a man," reads the register. One of his admirers, Richard Braithwaite, wrote an epitaph for him:

> Welcome from Norwich, Kemp! All joy to see
> Thy safe return morriscoed [1] lustily.
> But out, alas! How soon is thy morris done!
> When pipe and tabor, all thy friends, be gone,
> And leave thee now, to dance the second part
> With feeble Nature, not with nimble Art:
> When all thy triumphs, fraught with strains of mirth,
> Shall be caged up within a chest of earth.
> Shall be? They are. Thou hast danced thee out of breath,
> And now must make thy parting dance with Death.

Kemp's last part at the Globe was probably that of Dogberry. A clown with a better memory and a more delicate touch in acting succeeded him—Robert Armin. He played Touchstone in *As You Like It* and Feste in *Twelfth Night,* fools that had subtlety and intelligence and suited Shakespeare's new questioning mood. Shakespeare worked well with Armin; doubtless as a playwright he felt well rid of Kemp. But as a man he must often have missed the robust friend and fun-maker who had been with him on many stages for a full dozen years.

[1] Made by the morris dance. It might read, "Thy safe return danced in so lustily."

XXII: KING'S MAN

AS the year 1603 trembled on the edge of spring, the Queen lay dying at Richmond, nine miles southwest of London. The ministers watching in the sick room were waiting for her to die. The nobles and servants outside were waiting. All England was. Already members of the Privy Council had been in touch with James of Scotland but it would be well if they could seal the promises they had made to him with Elizabeth's own word. They begged her to name her successor.

The Queen could no longer speak. She lifted feeble hands above her head, and made the shape of a crown.

"Your Majesty's Cousin of Scotland?"

Her eyes answered that they had read her gesture well. One who already wore a crown should wear hers.

At eleven o'clock on the morning of March 24 (nine hours after she had died) a group of princes, peers, prelates, knights and gentlemen assembled by the High Cross in Cheapside, with a mass of "common persons" crowding about. Lord Cecil read a proclamation which declared that "the right of succession lieth wholly in James the King of Scots, and he is now justly intitulated with the Crown of England."

"God save King James!" roared prince and tradesman with a common sense of relief.

At his lodgings, or at St. Paul's, talking with friends, Shakespeare must have rejoiced also. He knew that the Queen had done much for England. However, in these last years she had been vain and suspicious and cruel. She had sent Essex to the block and imprisoned Southampton. Now the latter would be free, for he stood high in James's favor.

Like many Englishmen, Shakespeare must nevertheless have felt at the Queen's death the sadness that comes with the ending of an era. For almost forty years he had lived under Elizabeth. What would her passing mean? The question pressed upon him the more sharply because other persons similarly knitted into his past years had recently died. His father, John Shakespeare, had gone a year and a half earlier (September, 1601). His schoolmate and fellow townsman, Richard Quyney, had followed less than a year before.

Meanwhile a young English nobleman, Sir Robert Carey, was riding north bearing the news to the Scottish King. This was a venture of his own. Foreseeing the Queen's death, he had arranged to have a series of fresh horses ready for him at the regular post stations on the way to Scotland. By one of them he was thrown and kicked in the head; but he reached Holyrood Palace in Edinburgh the night of March 26, just after the King had gone to bed. He was taken at once into the bedchamber.

Sir Robert knelt.

"Sire, I greet you as King of England, Scotland, France and Ireland!"

James was immensely pleased. He gave Carey his hand to kiss and promised to make him a Gentleman of the Bedchamber and to tender him other notable offices. He forgot all these promises later, but they sounded sweet to Carey as he knelt before the new King and heard the effect of his golden tidings.

2

James started southward from Edinburgh on April 5, making a slow journey through his new kingdom. He did not enter London, for the plague raged there, but went to nearby Greenwich. By this time the English knew pretty clearly what kind of man was to rule them.

They had drawn no prize. James was now thirty-six, and in his prime, such as it was. But for the offspring of a handsome father (Henry Darnley) and a beautiful mother, he was amazingly unattractive. He stood above middle height (Mary, Queen of Scots, had been a tall woman) but he had an awkward, sprawling way of walking, almost as if his limbs and the body itself moved without relation to each other. His head was ill-shaped and his heavy-lidded eyes protruded unpleasantly. He spoke broad Scots, and his words came in rushes, now with a fit of stuttering, now rapid and confused.

Even more discouraging, James showed quickly that he lacked true common sense and judgment. He was learned, and proud of his book knowledge. But he was clearly impractical—"a wise fool." He didn't understand the English, and showed little desire to know them better. He firmly believed that a king should have absolute power. He was vain, yet indecisive. He could blubber over some departing friend or fly into a childish rage. He was timid, and dreaded the sight of a drawn sword. A Latin saying quickly ran about the Court—*Rex fuit Elizabeth nunc est Regina Jacobus,* which can be translated freely, "We had King Elizabeth; now it's Queen James!"

The King's golden-haired wife, formerly Princess Anne of Denmark, was far better-looking than he. She was also witty and good-humored, but had something of the irresponsibility of a spoiled child. She too believed in absolute royal power. Later she was partly accountable for a greater freedom of talk and manners about the Court than sober Englishmen approved of. Within a few years a good part of the nation had given up hoping for much from King or Queen, but were comforted by the royal children, particularly the charming Princess Elizabeth, and her older brother Henry, the brilliant and high-minded Prince of Wales. This gifted youth clearly looked at King James with realistic eyes. Later he became a great friend of Sir Walter Raleigh, whom James had imprisoned. "No man but my father," he remarked, "would have kept such a bird in a cage!"

But so far as the Lord Chamberlain's Men were concerned, James had one virtue that came close to outweighing all his defects. It was this: he was a passionate patron of the drama. He had shown his fondness for actors and acting in Scotland. He now proved it again in a way most pleasant to Shakespeare and his fellows. Four days after he arrived at Greenwich, James signed letters patent which lifted the Chamberlain's Men into a kind of earthly heaven. He made them the King's Men—his own company!

The document that brought about this change was issued May 19 ("For Lawrence Fletcher and William Shakespeare and others," begins the Latin text in translation), and authorized them to play both "for the recreation of our loving subjects, as for our solace and pleasure when we shall think good to see them." The company could play at the Globe or at convenient places "in any city, university, town or borough whatsoever."

Fletcher's name apparently came first because he had played before the King in Scotland, and was best known to him of any member of the troupe. Shakespeare's place as the second on the list shows his position among his fellows. The others were, in order given, Richard Burbage, Augustine Phillips, John Heminges, Henry Condell, William Slye, Robert Armin and Richard Cowley. These were all shareholders. Lesser players would not have been named.

Ten months later Shakespeare's name headed the company when a grant of red cloth was made to each member, so that all might appear in royal livery. This consisted of scarlet doublet, hose and cloak, with the King's arms embroidered on the sleeve. The costume was probably worn by the King's Men on all public occasions. Somewhat later, the chief members of the company became Grooms of the Royal Chamber. To be a Groom was a distinction; the post also carried certain obligations, as we shall see.

Meanwhile the Admiral's Men became the Prince's Men, with Prince Henry as their patron; and the Earl of Worcester's Players (a new troupe) became Her Majesty's Players. The Children at Blackfriars became the Children of Her Majesty's Revels. Thus the royal family took over the players and playhouses complete.

Shakespeare and his fellows could not now be classed as "rogues and vagabonds." Their entire profession had won high distinction, and a new dignity. When James made his entry into London in March, 1604, they had an honored place in the procession moving from the Tower to Westminster. Before the King rode the great nobles, then came James himself, then the Queen and the first ladies of the kingdom. Heralds followed, then the Queen's and Prince's men in waiting, and then, probably, rode William Shakespeare, clad in his red livery as a Groom of the Royal Chamber, together with his fellow players.

By this time, ten months after James had arrived at Greenwich, the King's Men had played for him many times. They had first been summoned late in 1603. The performance was given on December 2, at Wilton, where James was the guest of the Countess of Pembroke. The next day the players received a royal gift of £30.

It was fabulous! Augustine Phillips must have jingled the gold coins with high jubilation.

"We serve Maecenas! Why, if we got the third part of that from Her Majesty's treasury, we would have been fortunate!"

"No, no," said Dick Burbage, "it is only because we play for the first time at his command."

But he was mistaken. The troupe entertained James on eight occasions in the next three months, and the payments, though not equal to that first one, were most liberal. More than that, the King praised the players, stuttering in his eagerness to do them justice. Financially and artistically, a golden day had begun for them.

3

There had been much verse writing after Elizabeth's death, both to praise her and to honor James. Shakespeare did not join in this activity. He was invited to do so. One scribe sang thus to his fellow bards:

> You Poets all, brave Shakespeare, Jonson, Greene,
> Bestow your time to write for England's Queen!

Henry Chettle, now a fellow playwright, added an appeal to Shakespeare alone:

> Shepherd, remember our Elizabeth,
> And sing her "Rape," done by that Tarquin, Death.

But the playwright wrote nothing about the Queen's passing (unless the vague but beautiful Sonnet 107 refers to it) and nothing in the way of congratulation to James. He would in time honor the King in various dramas; that tribute was still to come.

Shakespeare had his own daily work to do that left small time for writing verses of praise for royalty dead or living. After *Twelfth Night* he seems to have turned to a curious "comedy" which was more tragic than some tragedies—*Troilus and Cressida*. It told the story of two famous lovers against the background of the legendary Trojan War. The play as Shakespeare wrote it seemed to proclaim bitterly the weaknesses of human nature and particularly the faithlessness of women. It contains so much biting irony and harsh denunciation that many scholars have felt that it reflects some violent personal experience of Shakespeare's.

"Consider," they say in effect, "how the great heroes of Homer are portrayed! Agamemnon is a fussy stuffed shirt, Menelaus a stupid ox, Ajax a noisy fool, Ulysses a scheming politician, and Achilles a braggart and a coward. Nor do the women come off better. Helen is a royal strumpet who has caused a needless war. Cressida is the very symbol of falsity. The only good characters are Hector and Troilus, and each in his fashion digs his own grave. Surely this distortion and debasement of a great legend shows that Shakespeare wrote the drama out of the very bitterness of his soul!"

Such comments will not help us to understand Shakespeare. They assume that the whole character of the plays he wrote could be affected by his personal feelings. They encourage us to look for biography in his writings. It is of a piece with the tendency, noted in Chapter XXI, to seek originals for the women of his plays in the Bankside or Shoreditch or Cripplegate.

Actually, everything we know about Shakespeare tends to prove that he did not use his own experiences as the chief sources of any of his plays. In all but one case those plays were built on stories taken from other authors, or on old plays written by others. To be sure, Shakespeare probably expressed his own feelings in many ways as he wrote, but he did so only when they came in naturally. He did not alter characters or twist plots in order to set forth his own opinions. He always followed his source or sources, often in surprising detail, except as he saw opportunities to make better drama by altering the original. In other words, writing plays was a profession with Shakespeare, and he seldom if ever permitted his personal feelings to confuse his task as a dramatist. He wrote good comedy just after Hamnet's death and penned *Twelfth Night* while Southampton lay in the Tower.

And in *Troilus,* as it happens, he followed his usual practice. He found what he thought was a good story. Perhaps it was partly in an old play that has since been lost. We know that the story existed in a number of poems and romances, including Chaucer's brilliant novel in verse, *Troilus and Criseyde.*

Shakespeare took these as his sources. He could not have used Homer for the story, because Homer never told it. The Greek poet mentioned Troilus as one of King Priam's sons, but never even referred to Cressida. The tale of Troilus's love for this lady first appeared in the works of Latin writers of the early Middle Ages. It was retold by later poets right down to Shakespeare's time.

There are two important points to note in connection with this growing medieval story.

The first is that all those who wrote it were pro-Trojan. They praised Hector and Priam and Troilus, and regarded the Greeks as a group of sly, lying, deceitful fellows who had managed to get the upper hand of the nobler Trojans only by trickery. The reason for this pro-Trojan attitude—a contrast to Homer, of course—was that Aeneas, a Trojan, was supposed to have founded Rome; while the English, French and other Europeans looked to Rome as the source of their own culture and even as the first colonizer of their lands.

They were eager to defend the Trojans, indirectly their ancestors. Also, until the Renaissance they had never read Homer. Greek literature, as we have seen, was still known to few even in Shakespeare's time.

The second point concerns Cressida. From the first she had been pictured as fickle. Chaucer shows how she betrayed Troilus, but he doesn't judge her harshly. Later writers did. They told the story of her life after the episode with Troilus was finished, and showed her ending up as what would be called today "a nasty little tramp." In fact, she became the symbol of falseness and immorality.

Now let us go back to the play.

Shakespeare had his story—a pro-Trojan story in so far as the war was concerned, and a story of a thoroughly false woman so far as Cressida was concerned. To be sure, Chapman's translation of *The Iliad* of Homer (the first English one to be made) was now appearing. Shakespeare probably read it; and he or the author of the older play that he used (if there was one) knew *The Iliad* throughout, for *Troilus and Cressida* contains details taken from parts of that poem which Chapman had still to translate. However, there was no story of Troilus and Cressida in the epic, and naturally Shakespeare followed the only accounts that he had. He therefore praised the Trojans and jeered at their enemies the Greeks. And he made Cressida a flirt and a strumpet. To be sure, he did both things with unusual vigor. To this extent he may have written out of a mood of disillusion, for he seems to have penned the play in 1602, when his friends were in the Tower, and all England was on edge waiting for the Queen to die. (The play was entered in the Stationers' Register on February 7, 1603, although not actually published until 1609.) Yet it should be noted that both Shakespeare's attitude and most of the details he uses can be traced to his sources.

I am not going to discuss here another theory to the effect that this play was Shakespeare's contribution to "The War of the Theaters," and that it was here that he gave Ben Jonson a "purge." If this is the case, the text does not prove it.

In fact, so far as can be determined, *Troilus and Cressida* was not produced at all during Shakespeare's lifetime. The 1603 entry describes it "as it is acted by My Lord Chamberlain's Men," but the 1609 edition proclaims the play never to have been publicly presented as a book or an acted drama. Most scholars accept this statement, or think that *Troilus* may have had one or more private productions. As a matter of fact, the strange comedy was unlikely to have appealed to the crowd. It lacked real suspense and was heavy going in many places. The general tone was unpleasant. It had brilliant passages, but Shakespeare himself may have set it aside after it was finished as being unlikely to succeed. Certainly if he had held it up until Jonson's *Sejanus* failed so dismally in 1603, he would have been the surer that so heavy a classical piece was scarcely worth public presentation.

4

On an April afternoon of 1604 London spectators stand or sit at a new Shakespeare play. For more than a year the Globe playhouse had been closed because of the plague. This new piece, *All's Well That Ends Well,* had first been enacted outside the city—before King James himself, so the rumor runs, at Wilton, where he was a guest of the Countess of Pembroke.

It is a comedy, the new piece. The girl Helena, daughter of an esteemed physician, loves young Count Bertram, whose mother is her protector. She forms a mad plot to cure the King of France, suffering from an illness for which her father left a prescription. And now the King appears, completely healed. The girl walks beside him. He bids her look among his gallant young men and make her choice of a husband.

> This youthful parcel
> Of noble bachelors stand at my bestowing.
> . . . Thy frank election make;
> Thou hast power to choose and they none to forsake.

The crowd stirs, leans forward. Here is a new thing—a girl picks the man of her choice by royal command. They see the graceful Helena (a boy, of course, but skilled to imitate a woman's carriage, speech and gestures) walk slowly, almost timidly, in front of the group of courtiers. She begs the King to let her retire. "Make choice!" he cries. And at last she pauses before one youth.

HELENA: I dare not say I take you; but I give
          Me and my service, ever whilst I live,
          Into your guiding power. (*To the King*) This is the
          man.

KING: Why, then, young Bertram, take her. She's thy wife.

BERTRAM: My wife, my liege! I shall beseech your highness
          In such a business give me leave to use
          The help of mine own eyes.

KING: Know'st thou not, Bertram,
          What she has done for me?

BERTRAM: Yes, my good lord;
          But never hope to know why I should marry her.
          . . . She had her breeding at my father's charge.
          A poor physician's daughter my wife! Disdain
          Rather corrupt me ever!

So there the issue is joined, in one of those electrifying scenes Shakespeare knew how to contrive. Bertram is forced to yield. He takes

Helena and a rich dowry given her by the King. He marries her. But rather than stay with her as a husband, he hastens to Italy and a war that is being waged there, sending Helena back to his mother. Bitterly he exclaims:

> War is no strife
> To the dark house and the detested wife!

The audience stirs restlessly as he strides off. Will this amazing girl win him for a true husband? How can she?

Helena, returning home to her friendly mother-in-law, wonders about that herself. Both she and the Countess get letters from Bertram, announcing his determination never to come home while she is there. "Till I have no wife, I have nothing in France." She seems faced with an impossible task. Yet she attempts it. And the two thousand spectators at the Globe find the solution a good one.

Today the character of the gallant girl, despite all obstacles seeking the man of her choice, is still one of the loveliest and bravest of Shakespeare's heroines. She never becomes bitter. Even his insulting letter awakens her pity more than her resentment.

> Poor lord! Is't I
> That chase thee from thy country, and expose
> Those tender limbs of thine to the event
> Of the none-sparing war? And is it I
> That drive thee from the sportive court, where thou
> Wast shot at with fair eyes, to be the mark
> Of smoky muskets? O you leaden messengers
> That ride upon the violent speed of fire,
> Fly with false aim; move the still-piecing [1] air
> That sings with piercing; do not touch my lord!

Yet even while she understands his aversion to her, she has faith that she will overcome it, and sets about doing so. The gentleness, tenderness and bravery that are Helena have charmed men and women alike for all the years since her creation.

[1] The air that always unites, joining its parts together.

In *All's Well That Ends Well* Shakespeare stands forth as something of a democrat. He proclaims in Helena the equality of merit with high birth. The King himself reproves Bertram for his slighting reference to Helena's humble family—

> From lowest place when virtuous things proceed,
> The place is dignified by the doer's deed.

Yet aside from Helena and the defense of merit, the play is not on the level of Shakespeare's best comedies. The verse has the easy grace that was always its author's; seldom more. Rhymed couplets abound. They lack the sparkle of the poet's best. Scholars have suggested that this comedy, like *Troilus,* reflected a somber mood. But again Shakespeare followed another man's story. It was not a wholly pleasant one. Helena had to trick her husband into loving her and living with her. That solution, however, was not Shakespeare's, and he, by the vitality and charm he gave to his heroine, made it more acceptable.

It is of course possible that *All's Well That Ends Well* marks a definite change in Shakespeare's interests and attitudes. He was almost forty now. He may have been losing a natural exuberance that marked his youth and earlier middle age. He had shown in *As You Like It,* in *Hamlet,* in *Troilus,* an interest in the complexities of life, especially the darker ones. It was a natural development in one so sensitive and gifted. Soon he would turn wholly to tragedy, seeking such answers to the Why of human suffering and disaster as art could give. Perhaps this more sober interest impaired the full liveliness that Shakespeare might have brought to Helena's story.

Such cannot be said of the play to which he now turned. It gave opportunity for only a grim kind of humor, and indeed was foredoomed to be the least pleasant "comedy" ever written by him or any other playwright.

He got the story of *Measure for Measure* from the English play *Promos and Cassandra,* published in 1578, and based upon an earlier Italian tale. Shakespeare could recognize elements in it that would please King James, his new Queen, and the Court they were gathering about them.

The scene was laid in Vienna. Here the Duke of the city pretends to leave it for a journey to Poland, and appoints Angelo, a man of high reputation, to rule in his place. The deputy has full power. He decides to clean house while his master is away—especially by punishing severely those who are guilty of immoral conduct. An old law, never enforced under the Duke, provides death as the punishment for adultery.

The plays swings upon this point. Claudio, a young gentleman of supposedly good character, is arrested by Angelo as the man responsible for a child which will soon be borne by his betrothed, Juliet. (Here, before his marriage to Anne Hathaway, might have stood Shakespeare himself.) Angelo condemns Claudio to die; Juliet may live until her son or daughter is brought into the world. Isabella, sister of Claudio, goes before Angelo to plead for her brother's life. She is preparing to become a nun. Her youth, beauty, purity and eloquence have a powerful effect on the Duke's deputy. He is shaken with passion for her. Finally he proposes to spare Claudio if she will become his mistress.

It is a horrible situation. Into it enters the Duke, who had secretly remained in Vienna, and he in his good time sees justice done.

The play has repelled many modern readers. Its shocking aspects, some dealt with humorously, probably appealed to the Court, which showed an increasing interest in the sensational and immoral. The part of the Duke seems to have been written with King James in mind. Early in the play the former says—

> I love the people,
> But do not like to stage me to their eyes.
> Though it do well, I do not relish well
> Their loud applause and Aves vehement.

This was England's new king to the life. James was shy and ill at ease among great crowds of his subjects. Yet he liked to think he was popular.

Again, the Duke disguised himself and studied the way in which Angelo was ruling, and then, having got full evidence, dispensed rewards and punishments in a kind of whirlwind dramatic finish. This was calculated to please James also. He had a high opinion of his own learning, judgment and ingenuity, and a belief that a true king was the best of all persons to act with authority in a difficult situation.

James also enjoyed complex situations that raised points about which he could argue; and *Measure for Measure* provided a number.

How much authority should a deputy have in the absence of the true ruler?

Should laws always be taken at face value, or should they be enforced only as wisdom and a particular situation might indicate?

Were a betrothed couple so close to marriage that the prospect of their having a child should be regarded with tolerance?

Should a sister about to assume holy orders plead for a brother even if he had broken the law?

All these and other questions were raised in *Measure for Measure,* and they were likely to please the King.

But there was more in the play to please him. There was poetry that stabbed with its truth or glittered with its beauty. Isabella's cry against the misuse of authority is as stirring today as when she first uttered it 350 years ago—

> Oh, it is excellent
> To have a giant's strength, but it is tyrannous
> To use it like a giant. . . .
>   Could great men thunder
> As Jove himself does, Jove would ne'er be quiet,
> For every pelting, petty officer
> Would use his heaven for thunder, nothing but thunder!
> Merciful heaven!
> Thou rather with thy sharp and sulphurous bolt
> Splitt'st the unwedgeable and gnarléd oak
> Than the soft myrtle; but man, proud man,
> Dressed in a little brief authority,

>   Most ignorant of what he's most assured,
>   . . . Plays such fantastic tricks before high heaven
>   As make the angels weep; who, with our spleens,
>   Would all themselves laugh mortal!

It is all true, and men with authority today often abuse it as much as Angelo did, or—for Shakespeare was thinking of that, too—any one of a thousand officers in and about James's London.

Of bursts of poetry like that there are a number in *Measure for Measure*, where *All's Well* has few of them. And there are terrific scenes. Perhaps the most touching is that in which Isabella tells Claudio of Angelo's offer. He, after being shocked by it, and assuring his sister he would never let her buy his freedom at such a price, soon weakens. "Death is a fearful thing," he says, begging her to save him. She retorts: "And shamed life a hateful!"

> CLAUDIO: Aye, but to die, and go we know not where;
>   To lie in cold obstruction and to rot;
>   This sensible warm motion to become
>   A kneaded clod; and the delighted spirit
>   To bathe in fiery floods, or to reside
>   In thrilling region of thick-ribbéd ice;
>   To be imprisoned in the viewless winds,
>   And blown with restless violence round about
>   The pendent world . . . 'tis too horrible!
>   . . . Sweet sister, let me live!

In her moral indignation Isabella denounces him as base and cowardly. She has no doubts about right and wrong. She would never sin to free Claudio, although

>   Were it but my life,
>   I'd throw it down for your deliverance
>   As frankly [freely] as a pin!

Clearly in *Measure for Measure* Shakespeare was writing comedy while his instincts drew him toward tragedy. It was a matter of months since he had written *Hamlet*. The first published version of that play

(1603) did not carry the famous soliloquy beginning "To be or no
to be" as we now know it. Perhaps this was recast later, after he ha
penned the passage just quoted above from *Measure for Measure*
There is an earlier speech in this "comedy" in which the Duke, dis
guised as a friar, tries to reconcile Claudio to the idea of death by re
minding him of the worthlessness of life on earth. The Duke exhort
him—

> Reason thus with life:
> If I do lose thee I do lose a thing
> That none but fools would keep. A breath thou art,
> Servile to all the skyey influences,
> That do this habitation, where thou keep'st,
> Hourly afflict. . . .
> 　　　　Thou art not noble,
> For all the accommodations that thou bearest
> Are nursed by baseness. . . .
> 　　　　Thou art not certain;
> For thy complexion shifts to strange effects,
> After the moon. If thou art rich, thou'rt poor;
> For like an ass whose back with ingots bows,
> Thou bearest thy heavy riches but a journey,
> And death unloads thee.

Thus the play presents a kind of debate on the question of whethe
or not life is worth the living. Claudio listens to the supposed fria
and agrees that existence has little value; suddenly seeing a chance t
continue it, he forgets all the arguments he had approved and de
sires to live. Here are the elements, the pros and cons, of Hamlet'
great soliloquy. Of course, Shakespeare may have written the whol
thirty-odd lines of it when he penned the first version of *Hamlet*. Th
fact that the 1603 edition has only some eighteen lines of the soliloquy
many different from the later version, may merely show that the printe
worked from an imperfect manuscript, probably as remembered by
an actor. Yet it seems possible that *Measure for Measure* may hav
helped give the soliloquy its final form. It may have had three stages

a crude beginning in the first *Hamlet* (1601-2), a reworking at more length (and in two passages) in *Measure for Measure,* and a final and superb reworking for *Hamlet* early in 1604. (A new and revised form of the play was published in that year, with the soliloquy much as we know it.)

At any rate, in *Measure for Measure* the playwright was pondering again the value of life and, by implication, its meaning. He was in the mood to face its more sober and even its terrible aspects.

5

The Grooms of the Chamber stood in a corner of the great Banqueting House at Whitehall Palace. Their scarlet livery mingled with the costlier and more individual garments of beruffed and bejeweled noblemen. The Earls of Pembroke and Southampton were there, in charge of the many lords and gentlemen who would serve at this banquet tendered in August, 1604, to the Ambassador Extraordinary from the Court of Spain. He had come to conclude a peace between England and Spain, at war for fifteen years.

"Don John de Velasco," recited Dick Burbage with a twinkle in his eye, "Constable of Castile and Legion, Duke of the City of Fryas, Earl of Haro, Lord of the House of Velasco—"

"Let be, let be!" groaned Augustine Phillips.

"Nay, by your leave," insisted Burbage, "Lord of the House of Velasco, and of the Seven Infants of Lara, Great Chamberlain unto Philip III, King of Spain, Chancellor of State and War, and President of Italy!"

"Bravo, bravo!" cried the young Earl of Pembroke. "A very feat of memory!"

"Nay, my lord," protested Robert Armin, " 'tis but a mouse's portion of what he learns every workday at the Globe!"

"And harder words," added Heminges, "for we master the knottiest tragedies that our Shakespeare can devise—or Ben Jonson."

"Tut, tut—you have all been free from such chores for a good two weeks," said Will himself. "Why protest so loudly? Do you think, my lords," he said, turning to the Earls, "that we shall indeed bid farewell to the Constable soon?"

"After the dinner, and the grand ball, there is no other entertainment," said Southampton. "With fortune, we may part with the Spaniards this week."

A murmur of satisfaction came from the grooms and noblemen. The players had been waiting on the Constable and his attendants at Somerset House for almost two weeks. It had been a pleasing novelty at first, but was a chore now. They gazed around the great Banqueting House and wished that the feast would begin. Although it was full daytime, the servants were lighting the candles now, hundreds of them, each with its glass "chimney," for the Great Hall was "three hundred and thirty and two foot in measure about." As the lights went on, Shakespeare eyed the enormous chamber. The candles lit the ornate ceiling, painted in the semblance of ivy and holly, with hanging ornaments of fruits and vegetables, all spangled with gold. Already, near the entrance, a long table was being laden with vessels of gold and agate and other precious materials. There, too, stood the silver basins in which the King and his guests would wash their hands. The whole place had the appearance of the fabulous, like some Roman or Arabian palace.

Such was the scene in which Shakespeare played a part late that summer as a Groom of the Royal Chamber. The great banquet proved as magnificent an affair as it promised to be. Shakespeare watched his king send a melon to the Constable, and half a dozen oranges on a branch still green.

"Tell him they be fruits o' Spain that ha' been brought to our aine England."

The Constable received the gift, kissed his hand to James, and swore that the gift was more prized as coming from his majesty than it was because it had come from his own country. Then he divided the melon and offered a share to his royal hosts.

And so the great feast went forward, with toasts drunk from golden cups and cups set with diamonds and rubies, and from dragon-shaped cups of crystal. And people shouted: "Peace, peace, peace! God save the King!" For three hours they feasted and drank and spun speeches, and then the great hall was cleared for the dancing—*brandos, plantons, correntas,* and many other dances with French and Italian and Spanish names.

Will Shakespeare watched. If he had lacked knowledge of Court functions before (and he had seen more modest ones for a dozen years), here he learned by doing as well as seeing. Nevertheless, he and the rest of his companions were glad when the Constable finally took ship some days later, and the winds bore him away from England.

6

But royal feasts and ceremonies were a small part of Shakespeare's life in these times. He was busy now with new plays—in *Othello* he he continued the series of tragedies that he had begun with *Hamlet.* We shall consider these in the next chapter. The playwright seems to have been less actor than before—he is not listed as taking a part in Ben Jonson's new comedy *Volpone, or The Fox,* which was produced by the King's Men in 1605. Probably, however, he helped stage this, and acted in some of his own plays. He continued to keep in touch with affairs in Stratford.

There, on July 24, 1605, he bought a part of the lease of Stratford tithes (as Abraham Sturley had suggested he should seven years earlier). The purchase cost him £440—all of $25,000 in money value of today. Shakespeare apparently paid the greater part of it when he bought the "moiety," for the records show that only £20 remained unpaid on January 26 following.

Thus the playwright was a gentleman with a considerable income apart from that he received from the Globe. He may be thought of as using Stratford much as a wealthy man in New York might use a summer home in Maine or New Hampshire. Or as one in Chicago might use a place to the north, on one of the Great Lakes. The difference is that Stratford was not only a part-time home but the home where his family dwelt year-long, and to which he expected finally to retire. But more than that, it was a kind of paying estate. Apparently he made trips thither at least once a year, and sometimes oftener.

The journey took three days each way. Shakespeare usually rode his own horse, stopping at inns along the route. One of his favorites was the Salvation Tavern (later changed to the Crown) at Oxford. It was kept by John Davenant and his wife Jane. They were Puritans, but Davenant was a wide reader and a lover of plays, and his wife was a pleasant, handsome woman. In 1605 several small children were toddling about the place. Robert Davenant, then a two-year-old, told Aubrey years later that "Master Shakespeare had given him a hundred kisses." The Davenants' second son, William, born in 1606, later became a playwright himself.

It seems to have been a pleasant time for the eminent King's Man— the summer days in which he rode through the green heart of England to his birthplace, and the weeks or months he spent in Warwickshire, enjoying the peace of his large house and varied garden.

It must have been a shock to him to learn, in 1605, that the leaders in the Gunpowder Plot, zealous English Roman Catholics, resentful of severe laws which the King was enforcing against those of their faith, had met in Warwickshire and planned there to blow King James and his Parliament sky high. Fortunately for the latter, the plot was discovered and the chief plotters captured.

In Stratford during these summers Shakespeare had made the acquaintance of a young doctor, John Hall, who had settled in the town at some time after 1600. Dr. Hall had studied at Oxford. Later he had continued his training at French and perhaps at other European medical schools. He quickly established himself as a well-schooled and modern-minded physician. He observed carefully, read such new scientific works as he could find, and experimented with new medicines and treatments. He kept notes on his experiences and observations in Latin. From him Shakespeare may have got medical information to use in *All's Well That Ends Well* and possibly even for Hamlet's disturbed mental condition and later Lady Macbeth's. Hall was a Puritan, but had Catholic patients; and of course Shakespeare's father and wife were both Puritans too. In Hall the playwright found a companion with whom he could discuss science, philosophy and probably art as well.

Young Dr. Hall may have known the father before he knew the daughter, but his eyes were turned to Susanna Shakespeare, a girl of religious background like his own, one who could read and write and had both her father's "gentleness" and wit. The two were married on June 5, 1605—"John Hall gentleman and Susanna Shaxpere," runs the entry.

Susanna was twenty-four now, and the doctor thirty-two. The father of the bride must have felt a satisfaction in the marriage. Doubtless he wondered about Judith, his other daughter—less adaptable than Susanna, willful, unlettered. He could hope to have even less influence on her than he had had on Susanna.

These were years of beginnings and endings of life. Shakespeare's sister Joan Hart had borne a young son less than two years before. Late in December, 1607, his young brother Edmund, who had followed him to London and become an actor, possibly at the Globe, died in the city and was buried in St. Saviour's Church, Southwark. For this burial, and a knell of the great bell, the playwright paid 20 shillings, or something like $70 of our money today. The burial entry reads: "1607, December 31, Edmond Shakespeare, a player, in the Church." Earlier that year an infant son of Edmund, described as "base-born," had died. The youngest of Will's brothers had probably led an impetuous and irregular life which had cost the poet some worry.

Mary Arden Shakespeare died the following year, but this was a natural event. She was perhaps in her early seventies, a high age for man or woman of that day. Shakespeare was probably consoled for this expected loss by the granddaughter who was now more than seven months old—little Elizabeth Hall, born February 8, 1608. She was the only grandchild that Shakespeare was to know before his own death. In his will he showed a particular fondness for her.

XXIII: THE PEAKS OF TRAGEDY

WE step back in time six years, and stand in one of the boxes in the lowest gallery of the Globe.

We stand behind ten young gentlemen seated in this private compartment. We see what they see. We hear their talk as they wait for the trumpet call that will announce the start of the afternoon's play.

They are in a pleasant mood. Law students they are; or older friends now practicing at the bar. They have dined well at the Bell or the Mermaid, and drunk enough sack to liven their spirits. Their seats are regarded as among the best in the house, for a man could almost step from the railing at the corner of the box to the main stage; and from here, too, there is as good a view of the pit and galleries as one could wish. The young gentlemen cast their eyes over the crowd,

341

watching the girls with nuts or apples or buns elbowing their way among the apprentices, sailors and tradesmen in the pit, lustily crying their wares. They spy out the few masked women in the galleries and guess at their identity.

The crowd is restless with expectation, for this is a new play. The gentlemen in the box, having looked about enough, are discussing it.

"Was not a piece called by this same title, *Hamlet,* seen in London not ten years past?" asks one.

"Aye, a tale of Denmark," answers another. "A play of revenge, with a squawking ghost."

"Heaven forbid we get that piece reshined, with old faults showing through like stains on an old breastplate."

"Nay, nay," speaks up a fourth somewhat sharply. "This is Shakespeare's."

"Well, well," grumbles the first speaker, "we shall soon see if the name sanctify the effort. Hmm—from the look of your groundlings in the pit, the trumpeter steps forth."

The liveried musician has indeed appeared on the platform of "the Heavens," the colored banneret dangling from his bright trumpet. Our friends in the box cannot see him, for the ceiling of the stage prevents them. However, they hear the notes of his call as these float over the playhouse. They, like others, sit hushed until the silence becomes audible. Then the curtains of the inner stage part, showing the parapet of a castle and, on a painted cloth, a dark sky with stars. A sentry paces there, then comes forward onto the outer stage, his partisan, or long-handled ax, ready in hand. Suddenly he pauses and stands alert, listening.

"Who's there?" asks a voice off stage.

"Nay, answer *me,*" cries the other. "Stand and unfold yourself."

"Long live the king!"

"Bernardo?"

"He."

It is very natural talk, yet with an air of suspense about it.

The second sentry has appeared, and the two stand together, speaking of the night and cold. Then they are joined by two others, also part of the guard. And one of these asks, "What! Has this thing appeared again tonight?"

The audience stirs noticeably. An apparition, it comes out, has been seen. One of the newcomers is Horatio, whom the other has brought along with the hope that the ghost will again appear. Horatio is skeptical about it.

"Tush, tush, 'twill not appear."

And then suddenly it does, an august figure in full armor.

The sentries huddle about Horatio.

"In the same figure, like the King that's dead!"

"Thou art a scholar, speak to it, Horatio!"

"Looks it not like the king? Mark it, Horatio."

And Horatio replies: "Most like; it harrows me with fear and wonder!"

He speaks to the ghost, but it hesitates a moment, then disappears. The men marvel. They sit and talk of the situation in Denmark—a king, Hamlet, recently dead, and his ghost walking. They recall one of his exploits in war and question his reappearance after death.

Suddenly the apparition is before them again, and again Horatio challenges it, begs it eloquently to speak. It listens to him, then once more fades away. The group stands, awed and uncertain. Then Horatio suggests—

> Let us impart what we have seen tonight
> Unto young Hamlet; for, upon my life,
> This spirit, dumb to us, will speak to him.

The others agree, the guardsmen go off the stage. The curtains of the inner recess close. The audience stirs and murmurs.

" 'Tis none of your howling tragedies of Kyd and Marlowe days," speaks up in the box the admirer of Shakespeare.

"No, it is a natural yet haunting thing," admits one of the others. "I felt my hair lifted as by a cold wind."

"Peace, peace," mutters another, as a trumpet blares and the curtains of the inner stage slide back again.

They reveal a throne. From the doors on either side at the rear of the main stage come a king and queen, courtiers, attendants. The two monarchs seat themselves and the king begins to speak.

We learn more particulars of the situation. Hamlet the King has died; his brother Claudius now fills the throne, and Hamlet's former queen sits beside him. And, nearby, clad in black, stands young Hamlet, the dead ruler's son. His uncle chides him for continuing to mourn his father. The queen joins in pleading with her son to assume a more cheerful dress and look, and not to leave the court to take up again his studies at Wittenberg. Hamlet finally agrees, and the others go out. The young man, pale, bearded [1] comes forward and bursts into an anguished cry:

> Oh, that this too, too solid flesh would melt,
> Thaw and resolve itself into a dew;
> Or that the Everlasting had not fixed
> His canon 'gainst self-slaughter! O God! God!
> How weary, stale, flat and unprofitable
> Seem to me all the uses of this world!
> Fie on't! Ah, fie! 'Tis an unweeded garden
> That grows to seed; things rank and gross in nature
> Possess it merely! [wholly]

It is the revulsion of a sensitive young man to events that have appalled him. Less than two months have passed since his father had died, a highly gifted and popular king whom his mother had seemingly idolized! Yet already she has married Claudius. "Let me not think on't! Frailty, thy name is woman." What is more, Claudius is

> My father's brother, but no more like my father
> Than I to Hercules.

---

[1] See II. ii. 599 ff.

> "Who calls me villain, breaks my pate across,
>   Plucks off my beard and blows it in my face?"

The smooth-shaven Hamlet is a modern convention.

Why has she done it? "It is not nor it cannot come to good."

He breaks off as others approach. They are Horatio and his friends, come to tell of what they had seen the night before on the battlements. Now a new Hamlet appears—gracious, eager, witty. He is especially happy to see Horatio, his closest friend, come back from Wittenberg. Then they tell him of the ghost. He is shaken, questions them closely, swears them to silence about what has already happened and what may, and decides to watch with them that very night.

And after a lighter scene in the upper stage dealing with Polonius, the king's counselor, his son Laertes and his daughter Ophelia, Hamlet encounters the ghost, is beckoned by it away from his companions, and is told—

> If thou didst ever thy dear father love . . .
> Revenge his foul and most unnatural murder!

The apparition describes how Claudius poured poison in his ears as he slept in the garden, and by the deed took life, throne and queen. He urges Hamlet to act, and fades with the coming dawn crying

> Adieu, adieu! Hamlet, remember me!

Young Hamlet goes off the stage with his friends, who have found him again. He exclaims:

> The time is out of joint; O cursed spite
> That ever I was born to set it right!

The full situation is now before the audience. A young prince—studious, sensitive, gracious, has been torn with grief over the death of a noble and greatly beloved father, then shocked to revulsion by the hasty marriage of his mother to a dull and brutish uncle. Finally comes the revelation that the uncle is a murderer, whom he, Hamlet, must kill.

Could he act at once, the murder would be avenged, and he himself would become king. But it is clear that he cannot act at once. Already the audience senses that. There may be great practical obstacles—to attack may be dangerous and futile. (Some critics have declared that such difficulties were the chief cause of Hamlet's failure to act.) But there are greater obstacles within him. On these the play turns. And the audience follows this inner struggle, paralleled by outer action, with alert intensity. The spectators sense, as the play goes forward, that such a tragedy has never yet been acted on any stage in England.

2

Why was this so?

Hamlet was indeed the first of five somber dramas that were to tower above anything yet written in English. They tower as high today over anything written since. They are the height of accomplishment by Shakespeare as dramatist and poet. We who follow his story must understand, if we can, the nature of their greatness.

I have already pointed out that tragedy in England as Shakespeare found it in the late fifteen-eighties lacked both a clear artistic purpose and a form. It leaned on the medieval conception drawn from Latin writers and was rather well expressed by the Monk in Chaucer's *Canterbury Tales:*

> By tragedy I mean a kind of story,
> Of him that lived at first in wealth and glory,
> As ancient books remind us frequently,
> And from his height falls into misery,
> And comes upon a wretched end at last.

In other words, to tell the story of the fall of some notable person was the chief aim of the early Elizabethans when they tried to write tragedy.[2] Exactly *how* this story was to be told did not trouble them greatly. They made an attempt to tell it well, to create suspense and contrive some kind of climax. Marlowe, as we have seen, was fairly successful in doing both. But often he told his story in a succession of

---

[2] Some writers of Shakespeare's time tried to present humbler persons as tragic heroes. Their efforts were not artistically successful, but in some ways anticipated the development of realistic tragedy in Ibsen and other nineteenth-century writers.

scenes that lacked any tight dramatic design. In contrast, let us look for a moment at what the Greeks did with tragedy.

They too accepted the idea of a notable hero as being highly important. But the Greek philosopher Aristotle, describing tragedy with the works of the greatest Athenian playwrights in mind, added other important elements.

The characteristics which he notes may be simplified as follows:

1. A Hero, or Protagonist.
2. An action carried out by him.
3. An Antagonist, or tragic force, opposing the Hero.
4. A tragic fault in the Hero.
5. A catastrophe suffered by the Hero, the result of 2, 3 and 4.

These are elements in the *structure* of a tragedy. They can be illustrated by the story of *Antigone,* as told by Sophocles. In Thebes the tyrant Creon has by law forbidden the burial of his nephew Polynices, slain in civil war. Death will be the penalty of any who disobeys his edict. But Creon, whom we may call the Hero, finds that Polynices *has* been buried, and that Creon's niece Antigone, sister of the slain man, interred the body. When he has had it dug up and exposed again, Creon accuses the girl, and seeks to force her acceptance of the law. This is the action. She resists: the law of the gods, she asserts, bade her give burial to a brother. That law was above Creon's. Here appears the Antagonist—the tragic force that opposed Creon partly in Antigone's act and attitude, partly in warnings given to the ruler. He does not heed them—his tragic fault. He demands that Antigone choose between obedience to him and death. She refuses to obey. Finally he confesses his error. He will free Antigone. He will himself bury Polynices. While he is doing this, Antigone hangs herself. Creon's son, her lover, and his wife Eurydice both commit suicide. Creon has now suffered the catastrophe, complete destruction in the loss of all he loved and held dear.

This outline shows the tight chain of cause and effect that was a part of Greek tragedy. As drama such tragedy had architecture. Each element was related in action to the other. The possibilities for suspense were great because (1) the Hero was highly important and (2) the Antagonist, or tragic force, was linked with the most august and holy elements. It was a case of the highest type of human being colliding with heaven itself. This type of tragedy has been called the Tragedy of Fate (the gods, or Fate, being the destructive force).

Greek tragedy was written in verse. Music and dancing had considerable part in it. It was highly unified. That is, there was no change of locality throughout the drama, and the action was practically continuous (only a few hours at most might elapse between one part of it and another). At its best it was a skillfully planned, powerful and beautiful form of art. Aristotle described its effect on the audience as being one of "purgation" through pity and terror. These emotions were aroused by seeing the Hero destroyed. But the beauty of the words and music, the symmetry of the action, and the sense that the calamity was inescapable—these produced a kind of compensating peace in the hearts of the spectators.

I need not go back and make a point-by-point comparison to show how lacking in such careful design and execution were the Elizabethan plays of the late fifteen-eighties. Marlowe's *Tamburlaine* showed weaknesses which were common. Marlowe, as we have seen, worked toward a more effective type of English tragedy. In *Edward II* we get the outlines of it. The King, its hero, is weak. His purpose is neither exciting nor noble—he wants to rule without interference, which means that he will rule badly. However, this purpose is opposed by his nobles, and we get in them an Antagonist. This force is a combination of other men and the social conceptions of justice that they hold. In opposing the King, they are aided by weaknesses in him (the tragic fault). Thus a rough parallel to Greek tragedy can be traced, except that Fate is not the Antagonist. The weakness of the Hero and the strength of his opponents were substituted for Fate.

Scholars later called this type of tragedy, which in a large sense was Shakespeare's as well as Marlowe's, the Tragedy of Will. The name distinguishes it from the Greek Tragedy of Fate. The term is a loose one. More than human wills are concerned. As I have pointed out, the

Antagonist in *Edward II* is not merely his nobles, but the social conception of right that they serve. However, the term "Tragedy of Will" does have a certain justness because in such drama the personality of the Hero and his effect upon his own fortunes are both of tremendous significance.

I have already shown how Shakespeare, following Marlowe, had continued to develop a type of English tragedy. There was a promise of something great in both *Richard III* and *Richard II*. Then there was a sudden fulfillment in *Romeo and Juliet*.

This play had a hero and heroine notable for their station in life, their youth and their high personal promise. It offered an opposing force in the feud between the Capulets and Montagues which was effective and sinister, at times taking on the blind and ruthless power of a malevolent fate. Yet *Romeo and Juliet* remained a kind of special accomplishment because of its fragile, poignant and romantic character. It lacked the terrific and awesome grandeur that Shakespeare's greatest tragedies would achieve.

In *Julius Caesar* there was the promise of something parallel to Greek accomplishment, but certain elements worked against its being fulfilled. The spirit of Caesar hung too constantly over Brutus, lessening his stature. The story was faulty in that its climax centered about Caesar's death. There was nothing in the latter part of the play to equal the assassination scene or Antony's funeral oration. The great quarrel scene between Brutus and Cassius lifted the interest of the spectators and carried them along. But it was not necessary to the plot, and the fact that the audience was glad to have it only emphasized the way in which the action had sagged into a chronicle of military events. Shakespeare had not been able to forge the simple, strong and climactic plot that would have fulfilled the magnificent promise of the first half of the play.

3

We can now come back to *Hamlet* and see how in this drama Shakespeare succeeded in fulfilling the hope of supremely great tragedy, which Marlowe had kindled and which he himself had nursed into an ever-stronger promise.

The key to his success lay in the character of his hero. It was a hero who differed from the Hamlet of the Danish legend, which was the source for both the earlier play and Shakespeare's, as a god might differ from a man.

The Hamlet of the. legend had been princely in blood, ingenious and courageous in action. For the part he had to play in *his* story, these qualities were enough. For the story as Shakespeare wrote it, they were not. Shakespeare's Hamlet is a scholar, poet, and philosopher in addition. He has read widely, talked with men of intellect, asked the meaning of life, and studied how to live it. He can speak wittily or ironically—perhaps the only great hero in all tragedy, by the way, endowed richly with such capacity. Yet he is not a bookish or effeminate prince. He can deal shrewdly with other men, he is a master with the foils, he can act swiftly and boldly in an emergency.

In other words, where the Hamlet of legend had been a hero of the age of chivalry, Shakespeare's Hamlet was a hero of the Renaissance. He was a man of learning and imagination and action fused into one. He was the ideal toward which Sidney, Essex, Southampton and Raleigh had all turned. There was not a gentleman in the Globe galleries who did not recognize the type. "There," thought the self-satisfied ones, "is such a man as I!" "There," thought the more modest, "stands the man I would be!"

The character of Hamlet took on a notable importance because it was popular with the Elizabethans; it took on even greater importance for its part in shaping the play.

Let us go back to Hamlet at the end of the first act. We saw then that one swift sword stroke would have discharged his duty—and, of course, ended the play. We saw that this was not to be. Did the cause lie in any great external obstacles? Some authorities have said so; but Hamlet never mentions such obstacles. Did it lie in his wide learning and philosophic mind? In a sense, yes; but these alone would not have stopped him from acting. It was the impact of startling and horrifying events upon his sensitive and imaginative nature that weakened him. He was already a victim of melancholy before he spoke with his father's spirit. After speaking with it the horrible fact of murder and his duty to avenge it so deepened his sadness and distraction that he was in a pathological state—a state of nervous shock. He could not act as he would have acted if normal. For this reason it is that he hesitates and argues with himself, seeks proof of his uncle's guilt. It is partly because of his abnormal condition that when he has this proof, and an opportunity to act, he makes not even a plan for action. His accidental killing of Polonius puts him in Claudius's power. The king is now convinced that Hamlet is a menace and bends all his energies to destroy him. The events which end the lives of both are not of Hamlet's contriving, although the prince does succeed in dispatching his enemy.

This outline of the action accepts one of a number of explanations of Hamlet. It is the one which I find most convincing.[3] That he was a brilliant, sensitive man in a state of shock explains his hesitations. It explains also his pretense of madness, his rejection of Ophelia, the girl he had loved, his bitter self-reproaches; and the feverish bursts of action in which he found temporary relief. This abnormal state was in many ways a breeder of suffering and disaster. It was a torture to him, postponing his revenge; and it was responsible for Ophelia's madness and death, and directly or indirectly for the deaths of seven other persons (Polonius, Rosencrantz, Guildenstern, Laertes, Claudius, Hamlet's mother and Hamlet himself).

The whole action of the play grows from Hamlet's character and its abnormal state. This may seem to be a weak basis for a strong tragic story. It is not. The expectation of revenge furnishes ample suspense, and intensifies the struggle going on in Hamlet himself. At first this suspense is keyed chiefly to Hamlet's own acts—his pretense of madness, his strangeness toward Ophelia, his plot to "catch the con-

[3] For a much fuller treatment of this and other theories, read pp. 94 ff. of A. C. Bradley's *Shakespearean Tragedy*. Bradley also discusses with force and detail Shakespeare's work as a writer of tragic drama.

science of the king" with a dramatization of the murder the latter had committed. As the king becomes suspicious and then resolved upon Hamlet's destruction, the character of the suspense somewhat alters, but it holds our interest up to the final curtain. Throughout, Shakespeare could follow a single theme leading to a highly dramatic climax. The tension is as great, and the causes for tension as clear, as in any tragedy of Aeschuylus or Sophocles.

To be sure, there are elements of uncertainty all through the play. We are never wholly certain as to what is moving Hamlet. We cannot add and subtract and get an exact sum. But that we should was probably never Shakespeare's intention. His Hamlet was too complex and splendid (if faulty) a hero to be charted fully by any spectator or reader. Shakespeare probably did not wholly understand Hamlet himself. A great character takes charge of an author to a certain extent, and often astounds him.

And in any case the "Gothic" unsureness of Hamlet's image has helped and not hurt the play and the character. Poets, dramatists, critics, philosophers, statesmen—all have found Hamlet worth their study. Millions of individuals have felt a close kinship with him. Even nations have claimed such a relationship—saying, "We are Hamlet. Our weaknesses are his." Men and women are still studying his behavior in the light of modern science. More has been written about him than about any other character in all the range of literature.

4

The saws and hammers rang on the emptiness of the great Banqueting House, but for Dick Burbage and Shakespeare they did not ring loud enough. The two stood at the far end of the 83-foot square room, where a few months before they had served at the banquet for the Spanish Ambassador. They pulled their beards doubtfully.

A bravely clad young gentleman of responsible appearance joined them.

"How do you think it will serve, gentlemen?" he asked.

It was Inigo Jones, architect to the Queen, and at thirty-one already a man of fabulous reputation. He was supervising the erection of a stage in the House.

"Master Jones, I fear it will serve us ill," answered Shakespeare. "Do you mark the faintness of those hammer strokes? They are lost in this too much space. My fellow Burbage here has a lusty voice, and this new play we offer will give him scope enough to use it, yet a voice must have walls to knock against."

"Aye," murmured Burbage, "and the more for a thing like this *Othello*. If those who listen cannot get the words, they lose both beauty and point in one."

Jones shrugged.

"Sirs, it is not my doing. The Queen will have a crowd. I spoke for the great hall of the palace, which is smaller and of better shape, but my voice went unheeded. I am sorry." He smiled and changed the subject. "I hear brave things of this new piece."

"It is an awesome thing," said Burbage.

"A tragedy?"

"Yes, Master Jones—a tale of a Venetian general, a Moor, and such a piteous jealousy as you must see and hear to believe."

"Is it as brave a thing as Master Shakespeare's *Hamlet?*"

"As brave, to my thinking, and as different as—as a night without stars from a night of moonlight."

"Why, Dick," spoke up Shakespeare, "you step into the poet's role. You shall write our next piece yourself."

"I shall first hear him speak this one," smiled Jones, as he moved away. "At least, Master Burbage, you shall have no hammers to rival you!"

On Hallowmas Day, November 1, 1604, less than a week later, the enormous hall was filled, and the King's Men played *Othello, the Moor of Venice.* It was indeed a play different from *Hamlet,* and in its fashion darker. Instead of a hero tangled in too much thinking, Shakespeare had created one who acted from instinct and emotion. Othello, great in battle, great in trustfulness of others, headlong for doing when resolved, is deceived and maneuvered by the malevolent Iago into doubting his wholly innocent wife, Desdemona. Into doubting, and condemning before he hears her. That is the mere backbone of a play which is the most masterly in structure that Shakespeare wrote.

Othello was also a contrast to *Hamlet* in its atmosphere and period. While Hamlet himself was a Renaissance hero, the play was based on a medieval story and was medieval in setting and often in spirit. Its romantic variety of scene, character and episode have made critics call it "Gothic" in structure. *Othello* was a play of Shakespeare's own time, and was direct and simple in spirit and movement in comparison with *Hamlet.*

Yet its basic similarity to *Hamlet* was greater than any differences it showed. Like *Hamlet,* it presented a hero of titanic stature. As in the earlier play, this man was faced with a horrifying situation, leading to a battle that was partly with himself. As in *Hamlet,* the whole action bent toward and was closely related to that situation.

On the night of the production the fears of the players as to the Banqueting House seem to have been justified. In the large square hall their words were blurred, or echoed back to tangle with one another. *Othello* was the last performance given there that season. Later, as we shall see, the Banqueting House was used frequently; probably changes were made to improve its acoustics. Meanwhile the great hall of White-hall Palace was remodeled to serve as a theater. It was about 40 by 90 feet—half the size of the House. Here in the 1604-5 season thirteen plays were given.

Othello was clearly well received at its first performance, in spite of its unfortunate place of presentation. The noble but perverted emotions of the hero, the smooth, cruel yet fascinating villainy of Iago, the poignant innocence of Desdemona were not lost on royal ears. For of the thirteen plays presented that Christmas season, eleven were acted by the King's Men, and eight of them were Shakespeare's.

But the playwright was even then planning a play which by its stature and reverberating excitement must have turned his thoughts from *Othello*. Perhaps his mind was busy with two plays, for it is difficult to tell whether *The Tragedy of Macbeth* or *King Lear* was first to see the stage.

Both so dilate the imagination that they seem like fearsome pronouncements on the life of man. Only the greatest of writers, and he only at the height of his power, could have unleashed the passions that writhe through these dramas like enormous serpents, or control them once they were unleashed.

Shakespeare found the story of Macbeth in Holinshed's *Chronicles of Scotch History,* and that of Lear in the same author's history of British kings, and in Spenser's *The Faerie Queene.* An older play of "King Lier" also existed, and seems to have been published in 1605. Yet each of the two stories grew, under Shakespeare's imagination and skill, into a splendidly yet fearsomely different thing from its original.

Macbeth was a tale of criminal ambition. Like *Hamlet,* it began with the supernatural. But there was no expectation or suspense. The curtain went up on the chanting witches, and the weird scene, ushered in with thunder and played by lightning, was snuffed out in eleven lines, after the promise of a meeting "upon the heath" with Macbeth.

It was a foretaste of the murky, swift and terrible course of the play. *Macbeth* was just half the length of *Hamlet.* It swept along like a swollen river plunging through night. After the first brief scene came a second in which a wounded sergeant told King Duncan of Scotland of great victories just won by Macbeth, the king's captain and cousin. Then came the witches again, and Macbeth, returning from the battle with his fellow captain, Banquo, was hailed by them:

1st WITCH: All hail, Macbeth! Hail to thee, Thane of Glamis!
2nd WITCH: All hail, Macbeth! Hail to thee, Thane of Cawdor!
3rd WITCH: All hail, Macbeth, that shalt be king hereafter!

Challenged by Banquo to prophesy of him, they promised him: "Thou shalt get kings, though thou be none!"

Here was the beginning of the terrible action. Macbeth listened amazed, shaken. He was already Thane of Glamis, but the Thane of Cawdor lived and prospered. And he told the witches,

> To be king
> Stands not within the prospect of belief,
> No more than to be Cawdor.

But as the weird women vanished, envoys appeared announcing that Cawdor had been proclaimed a traitor, and his title awarded Macbeth. What should the great captain think now? Was he bound to become king also? His wife thought that he was; even if he must assist the second prophecy to come true. She goaded him into slaying King Duncan. How this act worked horribly to destroy them both is the story of the play. Again the hero is mighty in stature, again he holds to a terrible purpose while divided against himself.

Macbeth was one of Shakespeare's deepest bows to King James. It dealt with the King's own country. It used the witches, in whom James believed implicitly, to intensify and make more awesome the dramatic story. Belief in the weird and fabulous was common, as we have already seen, and James had many companions in his credulity. (Shakespeare dealt with both ghosts and witches so deftly and impressively that these aspects of *Hamlet* and *Macbeth* offend no spectators today.) Finally in Banquo Shakespeare showed one of James's ancestors, and the first scene in Act IV, in which the witches let Macbeth look into the future, may have shown a spirit dressed to resemble the King.

For this scene both outer and inner stages were used. The witches' caldron bubbled in the aperture of the chief trap of the larger platform, where it could disappear at the appointed moment. The study was a cavern to the rear. Macbeth stood well forward on the main stage. Through the study trap rose successively three apparitions—the armed head, the bloody child (Macduff), the child crowned with the tree in his hand (Malcolm). Behind the inner stage, the rear curtain of which was drawn to show what seemed a further recess in the cavern, would pass the "show of eight kings." Each of these descendants of Banquo would pause briefly as he came into full view, lighted in some ghostly fashion. This scene, with thunder and appropriate music, would play magnificently, delighting alike the King at Whitehall and the apprentices in the pit of the Globe.

Like Hamlet, Othello, and Macbeth, Lear was a hero of great eminence and force, and like them he launched an action which in the end destroyed him. And like *Macbeth,* this fourth tragedy of *King Lear* was abrupt and explosive in contrast with the relative smoothness of the two earlier dramas.

This becomes apparent with the first terrific scene. Here Shakespeare hurls a situation at us that mounts in extravagance from speech to speech. The aged Lear proclaims himself injudicious when he invites his three daughters to bid through public professions of their love for portions of his kingdom. Cordelia, the youngest and his favorite, seems incredibly stubborn as she refuses to enter that contest. The old king is more unbelievable than she as he fails to see the calculated policy of the older sisters, rages at the youngest, and disinherits her. Yet we soon accept as real this violent succession of follies, and watch fascinated the calamities that follow from it.

The pride and imperiousness of Lear become pretexts for Goneril and Regan, soon the joint rulers of his former kingdom, coldly to strip the old man of his followers and his last shreds of self-respect. Along with their cruelty runs the vicious scheming of Edmund against his innocent brother and then his too credulous father. The strength of wickedness becomes a towering thing. Lear cries out against its first impact in his denunciation of Goneril, pleading with Nature to

> Dry up in her the organs of increase,
> And from her derogate body never spring
> A babe to honor her! If she must teem,
> Create her child of spleen, that it may live
> And be a thwart disnatured torment to her!
> Let it stamp wrinkles in her brow of youth,
> . . . Turn all her mother's pains and benefits
> To laughter and contempt, that she may feel

How sharper than a serpent's tooth it is
To have a thankless child!

Then step by step and word by word the full extent of what both
daughters intend is forced upon him, until he cries to the gods above
him for patience.

You see me here, you gods, a poor old man,
As full of grief as age, wretched in both!
If it be you that stirs these daughters' hearts
Against their father, fool me not·so much
To bear it tamely; touch me with noble anger,
And let not women's weapons, water-drops,
Stain my man's cheeks!

But the shock is too great, the force of evil too pitiless and shattering to be borne. Lear in his deep hurt and horror is only a step from
madness. Gloucester, loyally attempting to shelter him, fares worse
than his master; with the approval of the two wicked queens, Regan's
husband Cornwall tears out the faithful duke's eyes. Only the disguised Kent, scorned but still true, and the royal fool are left to attend
mad Lear. Only Edgar, a fugitive from his father, appears to guide
and protect Gloucester. It is a jagged and searing story that seems to
wrench life up by the roots; tender passages of beauty only make
monstrosities more monstrous. In its power and fury the play was
utterly beyond and above anything Shakespeare's audiences had known.
And as we today watch the tragedy move along its shuddering course
to a kind of peace-after-destruction, it has a daring and wildness more
than modern. Its convulsive power, its disorder within fearful order,
its harsh but never wholly articulated meanings make it in the noblest
and most disturbing sense what we call modernistic.

5

These four tragedies are the great ones. *Antony and Cleopatra,* written just after them in 1607, is held by some authorities to be as great.

Certainly it has their sweep. It has a hero worthy of Hamlet or Macbeth in his own different way, and a heroine who is the most fascinating and regal to walk in any of Shakespeare's tragedies. But the play lacks the terrific tension of the other four, and something of their moral grandeur. It is a play about two people weakened and corrupted by love. That they gather a fine dignity in their moments of destruction is at best a compensation. Of *Antony and Cleopatra* itself, and of *Timon of Athens* and *Coriolanus,* tragic dramas written just after it, I shall speak in the next chapter.

What do we find in the four greatest of Shakespeare's plays that tells us why he stands in a supreme place as a writer? What makes Shakespeare Shakespeare?

Part of the answer has already been given. The characters of the four heroes are in themselves creations which have made Shakespeare a living force for men these last three centuries and more. Hamlet, Othello, Macbeth, Lear—we could spare none of them. They have become symbols—Hamlet is the perplexed, sensitive genius; Othello is the great man of action corrupted by jealousy; Macbeth is the fatal victim of ambition; Lear is the too proud man, and too foolish, destroyed by ingratitude.

Not that one can classify any of the four as mere types. They are, above all, memorable individuals. And in their greatness they assert the greatness of the tragedies they dominate.

With them must stand two other unforgettable characters—Iago of *Othello* and Edmund of *Lear.*

Edmund much resembles Richard Crookback of twelve years earlier. He is resolved to advance his fortunes by deceit and treachery. He starts as a seemingly minor character; but from one wicked act to the next swells into such power that in the end he dominates the whole action of the play.

Iago is a far subtler person. He is not passionately ambitious. He professes some ill-will toward Othello, but this is not really important. What excites him is the very danger of the course he steers. It takes masterly contriving to deceive Othello and all the others about him; If Iago is discovered, his life will pay for his attempt. He enjoys this risk. He enjoys manipulating men and women. And so skillful is he that no one suspects him until after he has finished his incredible task.

Characters are one element, and perhaps the most important, in Shakespeare's greatness. But the tragic struggle that is built about each character and the craftsmanship with which it is built are other vital factors. As I have suggested, both of these are in one sense the result of the characters; in another sense they help to shape those characters. Yet characters, tragic struggle, and the art of setting forth that struggle in drama are separate elements. All three blend in the majestic forward sweep of the tragic action, and all are involved in the force and beauty with which that action crashes to an end. With these qualities a fourth can be named—the poetry or prose of Shakespeare's language. In these four dramas it reaches its highest expression, because language always tends to lift with the height and sureness of what must be said.

I have already pointed out that the great tragedies differ sharply from each other. The differences are more than those related to the type of hero and the atmosphere of the play.

Anyone who will read *Hamlet* and then read *Macbeth* will become aware of a contrast in literary quality. *Hamlet* is smooth, polished. It abounds in happy turns of phrase, often we could say pretty turns, such as

> But look, the morn, in russet mantle clad,
> Walks o'er the dew of yon high eastern hill,

or

> The expectancy and rose of the fair state,
> The glass of fashion and the mold of form.

One has the feeling that Shakespeare labored to give this play a high luster of language, and enjoyed his labor. But *Macbeth* seems in contrast to have been written in gusts of intense feeling. It is by comparison brief, jagged, and seemingly contemptuous of finish. *Lear* has a simi-

lar directness and fury, whereas *Othello* is closer to *Hamlet* in giving
an effect of high finish and smoothness. Partly this is due to its superb
structure.

The quality of verse helps to produce these differing effects. *Lear*
and *Macbeth* have more broken lines, more run-over lines, more feminine endings than the earlier plays. By such tests, *Macbeth* was the
last-written of the four; for Shakespeare in general tended to write
with greater technical freedom in each succeeding play.

All the four dramas bring us terrific moments. In Hamlet's soliloquy
we seem to stand on some height of the mind and spirit, looking at
the ills of Now—

> the whips and scorns of time . . .
> The pangs of disprized love, the law's delay,
> The insolence of office, and the spurns
> That patient merit of the unworthy takes,

and even in a confession of its strangeness we seem to get a glimpse of
the Hereafter—

> The undiscovered country from whose bourn
> No traveler returns.

In *Othello* what could be more poignant than the hero's final word
about himself, and his final act?

> I pray you, in your letters,
> When you shall these unlucky deeds relate,
> Speak of me as I am; nothing extenuate,
> Nor set down aught in malice. Then must you speak
> Of one that loved not wisely but too well;
> Of one not easily jealous, but, being wrought,
> Perplexed in the extreme; of one whose hand,
> Like the base Indian, threw a pearl away
> Richer than all his tribe. . . .
> Set you down this;
> And say besides, that in Aleppo once,
> Where a malignant and a turbaned Turk

> Beat a Venetian and traduced the state
> I took by the throat the circumciséd dog,
> And smote him, thus.   *Stabs himself*

In Macbeth the moments following Duncan's murder are among
the most revealing in all the range of literature. Macbeth comes down
from Duncan's chamber where he has slain the king, shaking his
head over his bloodstained hands, and babbling about the two grooms
who lay sleeping by their master—

MACBETH: There's one did laugh in's sleep, and one cried "Murder!"
          That they did wake each other; I stood and heard them;
          But they did say their prayers, and addressed them
          Again to sleep.
LADY MACBETH: There are two lodged together.
MACBETH: One cried "God bless us!" and "Amen" the other;
          As they had seen me with these hangman's hands,
          Listening their fear. I could not say "Amen"
          When they did say "God bless us!"
LADY MACBETH: Consider it not so deeply.
MACBETH: But wherefore could I not pronounce "Amen"?
          I had most need of blessing, and "Amen"
          Stuck in my throat.
LADY MACBETH: These deeds must not be thought
          After these ways; so, it will make us mad.
MACBETH: Methought I heard a voice cry "Sleep no more!
          Macbeth does murder sleep," the innocent sleep,
          Sleep that knits up the raveled sleave of care,
          The death of each day's life, sore labor's bath,
          Balm of hurt minds, great nature's second course,
          Chief nourisher in life's feast—
LADY MACBETH: What do you mean?
MACBETH: Still it cried "Sleep no more!" to all the house:
          "Glamis hath murdered sleep, and therefore Cawdor
          Shall sleep no more, Macbeth shall sleep no more!"

The passage shows not only the effect of a crime upon an imaginative criminal, but the difference between the great-souled Macbeth and

his intense and far more limited wife. He is tremendously affected by his deed, but voices his distraction. She seeks to suppress her feeling, but already is horrified by what has happened as it is described by him. Perhaps no line is such a revelation of bewilderment, the paralyzing impact of an event, and the limitation of a character as her "Consider it not so deeply." Few actresses give it with all its possible overtones.

King Lear has its moments that are as searching and shattering. Lear in the storm shouting in a kind of mad glee at the noise and fury is one—

> Blow, winds, and crack your cheeks! Rage! Blow!
> You cataracts and hurricanoes, spout
> Till you have drenched our steeples, drowned the cocks!
> You sulphurous and thought-executing fires . . .
> Singe my white head! And thou, all-shaking thunder,
> Strike flat the thick rotundity o' the world!
> Crack nature's molds, all germens [seeds] spill at once
> That make ingrateful man!

And even more devastating is his cry as he bends over dead Cordelia—

> No, no—no life!
> Why should a dog, a horse, a rat have life,
> And thou no breath at all? Thou'lt come no more,
> Never, never, never, never, never.

In utterances such as these all four plays rise high and austere above most of what is enduring literature. Yet they are warm and near to us, too, in the human hurt and the sharp personal quality of the stories they tell.

XXIV: PERSONAL OR PROFESSIONAL?

IT was late summer at New Place. Shakespeare sat on a stone bench among his flowers, reading from *Plutarch's Lives*. In the light of the declining August day, a paragraph seemed to strike out from the book and grip his attention.

The next night, he read, *Antonius feasting her, contended to pass her in magnificence and fineness; but she overcame him in both. So that he himself began to scorn the gross service of his house, in respect of Cleopatra's sumptuousness and fineness. And when Cleopatra found Antonius' jests and slents to be but gross, and soldierlike, in plain manner; she gave it him finely, and without fear taunted him throughly.*

Shakespeare paused a moment.

"Antony," he murmured, "and Cleopatra. I wonder if there's a story big enough in that?"

His eyes returned to the book.

Now her beauty (as it is reported) was not so passing, as unmatchable of other women, nor yet such, as upon present view did enamor men with her: but so sweet was her company and conversation, that a man could not possibly but be taken. And besides her beauty, the good grace she had to talk and discourse, her courteous nature that tempered her words and deeds, was a spur that pricked to the quick. Furthermore, besides all these, her voice and words were marvellous pleasant: for her tongue was an instrument of music to divers sports and pastimes, the which she easily turned into any language that pleased her. . . . Antonius was so ravished with the love of Cleopatra, that though his wife Fulvia had great wars, and much ado with Caesar for his affairs, and that the army of the Parthians (the which the King's lieutenants had given to the only leading of Labienus) was now assembled in Mesopotamia ready to invade Syria; yet, as though all this had nothing touched him, he yielded himself to go with Cleopatra unto Alexandria, where he spent and lost in childhood sports (as a man might say) and idle pastimes, the most precious thing a man can spend, as Antiphon saith: and that is, time.

Shakespeare closed the book.

"There," he reflected, "is a woman that men make legends about. If I could bring her to life—" He broke off. "The situation, too, lacks nothing. Here is the world in balance against love. Why, there needs little but to put it into the speech and motions of players."

In some such fashion *Antony and Cleopatra* was born. It must have been during the year 1606, with the last of the four great tragedies under way, that the playwright picked up his Plutarch. The Greek biographer had given him *Julius Caesar*. Perhaps Shakespeare felt that he could find another play between the covers of the book. *Julius Caesar* —hmm—that ended with the death of Brutus, but Antony and young Octavius had lived on, to divide the world between them. And to fight for it in the end. So he had re-read the life of Antony, and found hero, heroine and tragic conflict all spread before him on the printed pages.

2

Shakespeare took them from Plutarch and reassembled them in drama. The first scene reveals the two great forces pulling at Antony. One is Cleopatra, who stands for love and pleasure. Another is the tug of duty that the general feels as one of the rulers of the Roman dominions. His wife Fulvia has died; there is revolt in the territories that Antony controls; there is civil war in Italy itself. Antony knows his duty:

> I must from this enchanting queen break off;
> Ten thousand harms, more than the ills I know,
> My idleness doth hatch.

So he leaves her, makes a peace with Octavius, binds it by marrying Caesar's sister Octavia—beautiful, intelligent, modest. The Romans rejoice—Antony will now leave Cleopatra forever. Enobarbus, one of his captains, knows better.

> Never; he will not.
> Age cannot wither her, nor custom stale
> Her infinite variety; other women cloy
> The appetites they feed, but she makes hungry
> Where most she satisfies.

This is the situation that works out to a tragic end. Antony stays by his new wife for a time; then he is back in Egypt, provoking the full wrath of young Caesar. Caesar seeks him in Egypt. Man against man, Antony is a greater leader and soldier; tied to Cleopatra his courage and skill both wither. Her cowardice and instability infect him. There is one sole redeeming circumstance. Although Antony is brought to his death through his uncontrollable love, that death lifts Cleopatra above the changeable, selfish woman she was. She becomes a person of high dignity—spurning Caesar's mercy. Setting a poisonous asp to her breast, she awaits her death—

> Methinks I hear
> Antony call; I see him rouse himself
> To praise my noble act. . . .
> Husband, I come;
> Now to that name my courage prove my title!
> I am fire and air; my other elements
> I give to baser life.

Here again were great characters, if a not wholly great tragedy. Not wholly great, for the tragic fault is so large in this drama that sympathy with hero and heroine falters. One's feeling is not so much pity and terror as shame. Yet Antony's softness is a part of his nature, just as his high qualities as a statesman and general are. Nor can Cleopatra, being what she is, help but pull down the man she loves. The truth-to-life of the tragedy and its many passages of glowing poetry have redeemed it from the somewhat unsatisfying character of the conflict.

Yet with *Antony and Cleopatra* Shakespeare began to fall off slightly from his highest point of accomplishment. *Coriolanus,* the one remaining tragic drama that was entirely his own, marked a sharper decline. It lacked nothing in good planning or in startling situation. It is written with sustained vigor. But the hero, with his complete scorn of his lowlier fellow citizens, his terrific pride, his needless rages, did not capture Shakespeare's own imagination to the point where he could be made an enduring character. Today few besides scholars read about his unhappy career.

Timon of Athens is better remembered. The rich and generous good fellow who discovers that his friends desert him when he can no longer feast them, who becomes a hermit and denounces mankind as hateful —this figure stands out in literature as one to startle and provoke wonder. Shakespeare gave only a limited amount of help to his making. It was apparently a case of patching up another man's play for the good of the King's Men.

3

Coriolanus was first acted in 1608, seven years after the first performance of Shakespeare's *Hamlet*. Aside from *All's Well* and *Measure
for Measure,* all the dramas of the period were tragedies.[1] All that were
Shakespeare's own were well wrought. It was a period of intense and
superb activity.

The question has been raised as to why the playwright turned to
tragedy for so long a time, never, indeed, coming back to outright
comedy at all.

It has been suggested that these powerful dramas, together with
the rather grim "comedies" of the period, mirror a story of bitterness
and despair lived by Shakespeare the man and cast into dramatic form
by Shakespeare the writer.

We have already considered this suggestion as it applied to *Troilus
and Cressida.* The arguments for it in the case of the tragedies are
similar. There is effort to show that an unsuitable marriage, the imprisonment and execution of friends after Essex's "rebellion," the cor-
rupt Court of King James, and a possible disappointment in love were
all factors in plunging Shakespeare into melancholy, cynicism and
despair. However, such "proof" rests on facts some of which are not
established and some of which are open to various kinds of interpretation. So, as with *Troilus,* the chief evidence that is set forth consists
of passages from the tragedies themselves. The melancholy of Hamlet,
the jealousy of Othello, the towering rage and despair of Lear, the
fears and revulsion of Macbeth—these are supposed to reflect a succession of struggles in the soul of the poet as well as to express the
passions of imaginary heroes. Only out of the most terrifying personal
experiences, it is argued, could Shakespeare have set forth tragic emotion with the poignancy and magnificence that he achieves.

This theory made headway for a time because of the vigor with

[1] Except for the revision made by Shakespeare of another's play, *Pericles, Prince
of Tyre,* to be considered later.

which George Brandes, the great Danish critic, and its most ardent advocate, presented it; and because, too, of its startling and romantic character. Even in recent years the most austere of modern Shakespearean scholars, E. K. Chambers, gave a cautious assent to the idea that the tragedies were written during a period of deep personal disturbance. Out of this crisis, he believed (possibly a nervous breakdown), the playwright emerged into a final period of peace only as the terrific dream exhausted itself.

This entire assumption, whether put boldly, as Brandes put it, or vaguely, as Chambers did, is challenged by similar facts and considerations to those which discredit the personal interpretation of *Troilus*. The theory is also challenged by better explanations as to why Shakespeare wrote tragedy for so long, and by a better explanation of why he stopped writing it.

The stories that Shakespeare used in the seven tragedies of this period and the manner in which he treated them both argue against the idea that he wrote a record of his own personal sufferings into these dramas.

For each of the plays, as we have seen, he had a source. The stories were supplied by other and earlier writers. The tragic hero was known in each case to many intelligent Elizabethan readers because they had read the accounts that Shakespeare used. In the cases of Hamlet and Lear, plays built around the chief characters already existed. Thus in no case did Shakespeare invent a hero or a tragic situation, as one might reasonably expect him to do were these plays deeply expressive of his own sufferings. In each case the evidence indicates that the play had an impersonal origin.

Nor did the poet, so far as can be perceived, alter any of these stories in order to set forth a personal problem or feeling. He did make changes. The endings of both *Hamlet* and *Lear* are happy ones in the original sources—that is, Hamlet is not killed at the time he kills his uncle, and Lear is restored to his throne. In each case Shakespeare rejected such a solution. He made these two heroes tragic victims. Each gained in dignity by the change. Both plays were strengthened. Shakespeare the writer is the only person who appears in such alterations.

Finally, Shakespeare did not add any material to any story which can be recognized as personal. He adds details to sharpen a character and occasionally to intensify an episode. He invents little. Almost all the details of *Hamlet* appear in Belleforest; most of *Macbeth* is in Holinshed; most of *Antony and Cleopatra* is in Plutarch. When the dramatist wanted an additional episode, he did not devise one himself, but turned to a second source. Thus in *King Lear* he seems to have felt the need for more action than the original story supplied, and added the subplot of Gloucester's two sons, the legitimate Edgar and the baseborn Edmund. But he got this grisly episode from Sidney's *Arcadia.*

In general Shakespeare followed his sources with amazing faithfulness. He used many trivial happenings. He used descriptions. The gorgeous picture of Cleopatra and her barge in Act II, Scene 3 of *Antony and Cleopatra* is just a paragraph from Plutarch, set to verse. We have already seen that the character of Cleopatra herself was vividly and fully pictured by the Greek biographer. Shakespeare adds something of intensity and sparkle, but he does not alter the character. No more absurd suggestion was ever advanced than that which puts forward Cleopatra as the stage version of an Englishwoman whom Shakespeare knew and loved. She is pure Plutarch.

Thus the plays themselves give no support to the idea that they were associated with deep personal suffering on the part of their author; rather they discourage such an assumption. They indicate an objective attitude on Shakespeare's part. He finds a succession of stories which seem promising material for plays. He constructs his tragedies from them. The basic tragic emotions and most of the episodes were in these source materials.

Of course this does not mean that no passages in these plays reflected personal experience. Probably a number did. What Shakespeare suffered himself, what he had seen others suffer, what he had heard or read about—all doubtless appear at one time or another and in various forms in the tragedies. But who can say which passages stand for personal experiences, and which for observation or reading? Indeed, who can say that what may seem most personal in quality is not a superb evidence of Shakespeare's genius?

Let us take an example. We can hardly assume that the dramatist had participated in a murder or had associated intimately with men who had. Yet what could seem more fearfully poignant and true than Macbeth's struggles with himself before the murder of Duncan, or his utterances, and those of his wife, just after it? Here is terrific reality that matches any other emotional passage in Shakespeare or elsewhere. Yet we must assume that it is an imagined reality. What, then, of other moving passages?

No, we must remember always that we are dealing with a man of sensitive and soaring imagination, able at will to enter into the feeling of a child, a girl in love, a buffoon, a chivalric conqueror, an outright villain, a mercurial and artful queen. It is safer to assume that in these plays Shakespeare the artist was architect and craftsman. As we shall see later, there are other considerations which press this assumption upon us.

Thus the theory that the great tragedies were written partly or wholly out of personal anguish seems to get little support from a careful examination of the plays themselves. We may justly ask at this point if there is a better explanation of why Shakespeare concerned himself so long and so effectively with the writing of tragedy.

As it happens, there is.

First of all, tragedy was a natural interest for any playwright of the early seventeenth century. It was a natural one for Shakespeare. He had proved this by creating Richard III, Richard II, Romeo, Juliet, Brutus—all genuinely tragic heroes and heroines, before he commenced the series of magnificent portraits that began with Hamlet.

Increasing age was an element in any poet's concern with tragedy. Shakespeare, thirty-seven in 1601, may be said to have reached artistic maturity at about that time. We have seen how in *As You Like It* his attitude toward life had become more questioning and philosophical. Each year brought further reading and experience, which deepened the gravity of his outlook. Men lived faster in Jacobean England than they do now. Accordingly, a theme such as Hamlet's was one likely to attract him. This was not less the case because his chief actor, Dick Burbage, was also at a point where he was ready for roles that would challenge his powers fully. Of course the entire company was ripe in experience and skill.

If increasing maturity drew Shakespeare toward tragedy, the artistic appeal of writing it may have exerted an even stronger attraction. In drama, a play like *Hamlet* or *Othello* was the supreme form of expression, the greatest of challenges to a writer. Here were higher themes than comedy could offer. Here in its nobler *personae,* in its loftier atmosphere, in its philosophic wrestling for a meaning in life, in its more fateful clashes were better opportunities for great poetry. Tragedy seemed to say to Shakespeare: 'If you will climb to the very heights, you must enter my kingdom." And it was indeed in tragedy that he reached the top of his achievement as a writer.

It is well, also, to consider here certain characteristics of Shakespeare's tragedy. What, for example, is its emotional effect upon the spectator? What, again, does Shakespeare seem to say about life through his tragedies, if he has a direct or indirect comment upon it?

As to the emotional effect, it is never in any Shakespearean tragedy an effect of outright despair or utter negation. Rather, each of these dramas is likely to make a reader or spectator feel strongly the grandeur of man, the awesomeness of his talents and powers as these are shown in a Hamlet, an Othello, a Macbeth, a Lear, an Antony. It is true that he feels a great sadness to see such nobility destroyed. Nevertheless, as Bradley has pointed out in his work on Shakespeare's tragedy, there is always a recognition that the hero (and sometimes the heroine) was to an extent self-doomed.

This is as much misfortune, even accident, as fault. In happier circumstances, Hamlet might have acted promptly and triumphantly. Given the merest twist of events, Othello might never have been jealous, Macbeth might never have murdered, Lear might never have disrupted his kingdom. Yet in each story, as it was told, the hero lacked qualities that were needed. He did not quite meet a great emergency. Life had to cast him out as not fully adaptable.

Shakespeare seems to emphasize the inevitability of what happened in each case by showing how, after the tragic action has been completed, life goes on without the hero. Fortinbras comes to rule in Denmark, Cassio takes over Othello's command, the crown of Scotland is figuratively lifted from the head of Macbeth and set on that of Malcolm. Even in *Timon of Athens* we are aware of Alcibiades, the man who believes in himself and in other men, as Timon vents his hate in a final curse on all mankind.

The emotional effect and the tragic structure alike both seem to proclaim the artist at work. He enters greatly and imperiously into each story. And passionately, too. For we must not think of the art that Shakespeare reveals as in any sense an impersonal thing. No man follows aloof and tranquil a theme that cuts to the very core of life. Shakespeare the artist suffered. Each hero was a deep experience that meant strife as well as final mastery. The creator of Hamlet speculated and brooded and knew searing anguish; he plumbed the depths of pity and horror with Lear; he shared the torments of jealousy with Othello and those of crime with Macbeth; he hated and cursed with Timon. The building of tragedies was a searching and savage personal experience, for every sensitivity and feeling and power within him was called upon to lift them into their dark and shining power. The imaginative tension involved was great, the emotion expended was great. The slowing down of Shakespeare's pace of production indicates the complex severity of his tasks. Yet they were exalting as well as exhausting labors, and they could only have been performed with that sure domination of art which alone could give them direction and final, triumphant form.

One last consideration: during this period there were practical reasons for Shakespeare's writing tragedy. These must not be thought of as more than subsidiary to the greater forces of artistic interest and aspiration. Yet they were real and exerted their contributory influence.

Hamlet, in the years following its first presentation, soared to a great popular success. It was "divers times acted by His Highness' Servants in the City of London, as also at the two universities of Cambridge and Oxford, and elsewhere." The captain of a ship off the western coast of Africa records in August, 1607, a performance of the play given by his sailors.

What would such success suggest to a playwright and his fellow actors? The practical logic of the situation would be that Shakespeare should write another tragedy. This was not the chief reason why he did so, but it may well have been a consideration, if a minor one, moving him to write *Othello.* But that drama too was immediately and highly successful, a fact which may well have counted with the writer in essaying *Lear* and *Macbeth.* Shakespeare the actor and theater owner may thus have had an effect upon Shakespeare the writer. For it was a consideration that tragedies were good show business as well as that far higher and more richly satisfying achievement, good art.

4

Thus there is much to persuade us that tragedies were not the result of specific emotional experiences on the part of their author, but rather came to life as supreme artistic accomplishments which called forth and intensified higher passions of their own. Each play had its source in a story Shakespeare found already written. There are no signs of changes or additions made for personal as apart from dramatic causes. On the other hand, there are the highest of creative reasons and there are less important although by no means negligible practical ones why he wrote tragedies rather than other types of drama in the period from 1601 to 1608.

Why did he stop writing them? There is an answer to that question, too, other than the explanation that Shakespeare wore out a deep pessimism or melancholia. He had completed a series of supremely successful dramas that had satisfied in a rich and varied manner a deep artistic need. Probably by 1608 he found no great tragic themes at hand

and had temporarily worked out the tragic vein. Instinctively, he was ready for another type of creative effort. And just at this time a changing situation in the playhouse world helped him to determine what that form of activity would be. The cause for that situation, however, did not lie among the theaters. Let us go beyond them to see its place of birth and something of its development.

XXV: LAST MAGIC

IT was the sixth of January, Twelfth Night, of the year 1605. The almost three hundred "lights of glass" in the great Banqueting House at Whitehall were ablaze, and a multitude of lords and ladies had crowded into the enormous hall to see the Queen's masques.

The place throbbed with excitement. In the murmuring audience were few who had not heard that £3,000 had been paid out by the royal treasurers for this spectacle, the staging of which was in the hands of that magician of architects, Inigo Jones. This was the first formal entertainment given by Queen Anne, and there were few gentlemen or ladies present who did not feel lucky to be there. The Queen herself, with the loveliest of her titled ladies, would appear in the masque. The spectators talked feverishly of what they would see.

"It is called *The Masque of Blackness,* they say, and was writ by Master Jonson the playmaker!"

"They say we shall look on a vast scene by the sea, as like to nature as if Dover Beach lay below."

"There will be a great engine that maketh a simulation of waves, and a boat in the shape of a huge shell that rideth on the water."

So they buzzed. And when, to the strains of music, the curtains that hid the stage parted, their speculations were outdone by reality.

At the edges of the stage stood forests of trees, and beyond them a great ocean, the surface of which moved up and down continuously. In the foreground lay six tritons, or sea-gods, half human, but with blue hair and fishes' tails. And, as Ben Jonson himself later wrote, "Behind these a pair of sea-maids, for song, were as conspicuously seated; between which two great sea-horses, as big as the life, put forth themselves; the one mounting aloft, and writhing his head from the other, which seemed to sink forwards." On their backs rode Oceanus, representing the seas, and Niger, god of the African river of that name.

Behind these, in a great hollow shell floating upon the water, lighted especially with "a chevron of lights," sat twelve black nymphs, daughters of Niger, who was also black. Beside the shell, on the backs of swimming sea monsters, stood twelve torchbearers, one for each of the nymphs. Now to quote Jonson again: "The attire of masquers [nymphs] was alike in all, without difference: the colors azure and silver; but returned on the top with a scroll and antique dressing of feathers, and jewels interlaced with ropes of pearl. And for the front, ear, neck, and wrists, the ornament was of the most choice and orient pearl; best setting off from the black."

This detail gives some idea of the elaborate costuming, which was carried out for every actor. As for the scene, it was all painted in perspective, to seem to slope downward and into great distance—"which decorum made it more conspicuous, and caught the eye afar off with a wandering beauty, to which was added an obscure and cloudy night-piece."

Now, you may be asking, what was this all about?

To which Ben Jonson or Inigo Jones, if able to reply, might ask in turn, "What significance has the setting for any musical comedy of your day?"

For a masque, like our musical comedy, was a great spectacle with a little plot and a pleasant amount of music and dancing. In this particular piece, Niger and his daughters had come afar hunting a fabled land which turned out to be Britannia, or Britain. The nymphs stepped ashore, did a dance, and the masque ended as they sailed away in their enormous lighted seashell, singing.

Just a trifle, you see, as to plot. The entire script for any masque usually consisted of three or four songs and two hundred lines of dialogue in verse. The singing and dancing and the gorgeousness of the spectacle were far more notable than the writing. And yet these rather frivolous spectacles had a deep effect upon the drama of the day, including Shakespeare's. They really launched a new type of play.

It was not that the masque as a dramatic form was new. As we saw in Chapter VIII, masques had been performed in the time of Henry VII, and Elizabeth's Master of Revels prepared some fairly elaborate ones for her. But under James the resources for producing wonders were greater. Inigo Jones was a genius in contriving new and brilliant stage effects. Poet-playwrights like Jonson could outdo the writers of Elizabeth's early reign. Above all, money flowed and splashed where forty years earlier it had merely trickled. The masque began to take on a dazzling glamour. Its wonders were soon on everyone's lips.

It was ideal entertainment for the lazy-minded spectator. There was no need to feel that one was getting educated or improved, as was somewhat the case at *Julius Caesar* or even *Henry V*. Many a courtier, exhausted with Court ceremonies, or feasting and drinking, or flirting, wanted to lean back like a tired businessman of today and enjoy himself. The masque suited him perfectly. A dash of story, some songs, a novel spectacle with rich costumes and scenery and pretty ladies (indeed, the proudest of the Court)—these amazed and delighted him, while not taxing his mind at all.

Nor did he need to feel the least sense of guilt in enjoying this gaudy frivolity. The whole tone of the Court was different now from what it had been under Elizabeth. That queen had loved a good jest, a lively dance, a pretty pageant. But she also liked intelligent talk and a good sermon. While she delighted in Falstaff, so did she in more serious characters. Most important, she insisted on good behavior for both the ladies and gentlemen of her Court. As we have seen, she would send the haughtiest noble to the Tower for what she considered irregular conduct.

James's wife, Anne, had established a different tone for her Court. Drinking became common, even for the women. The talk was immoral, and conduct often matched the talk. Money flowed like the liquor. The whole atmosphere was loose and irresponsible. The empty elaboration of the masque fitted into it. James himself was widely read, and doubtless enjoyed the more serious plays. But he shared the revels and frivolity of the Queen and her companions.

The playwrights were quick to see what was happening. The thirst for getting information and a moral lesson from a play was dying out —at least among the kind of people who filled the boxes and galleries of the playhouses. A lighter, pleasanter type of drama was wanted. Soon the romance and the tragicomedy appeared.

These forms, which often shaded one into the other, had certain features taken over from the masque. They presented some fabulous or legendary setting. They emphasized the marvelous in story and character. Whatever dangers threatened, no likable character got hurt in the end. Music and song were featured, and often pantomimes and dances.

Francis Beaumont and his friend John Fletcher were among the first to introduce these lighter, more romantic plays. Both young men were of excellent family, and knew the ways and talk of the Court. They contrived pretty, fanciful dramas that were more popular than Shakespeare's later tragedies. Shakespeare himself became aware of their work. In 1609 he and his fellows arranged with Beaumont and

Fletcher to write regularly for the King's Men.

But even before this, possibly as early as the summer of 1607, Shakespeare had helped to devise one of the new romantic pieces. It was called *Pericles, Prince of Tyre,* and it was founded on a tale first told in English by Chaucer's friend and fellow poet, John Gower.

There is a bit of mystery about the authorship of *Pericles.*

A certain George Wilkins seems to have written the first draft of it. A man of that name is on record as having penned (or shared in the writing of) two other plays for the King's Men. It has also been discovered that a "George Wilkins, victualer," owned the house in which Stephen Bellott and his wife Mary lived after leaving Mary's father, Christopher Montjoy, the hairdresser, in 1606 (see Chapter XXI). Were the two George Wilkinses the same man? A number of literary detectives think so.

In any case a George Wilkins, whether author and victualer or merely author, brought a play about Pericles to the King's Men. It was not in satisfactory condition. The drama covered a huge span of years. It took its hero and heroine from city to city in the Mediterranean—Tyre, Antioch, Tarsus, Ephesus. It was a typical medieval romance, so long and so tangled in plot that Wilkins got pretty well lost in the confused coils of the difficult story.

However, Shakespeare saw in this sprawling play the fabulous and astounding places and episodes that were then becoming the fashion. He took *Pericles* and recast it. He tidied up some of Wilkins's rhymes (though not all, by any means) and did some fine work in bringing out the beauty and purity of character in Marina, Pericles's daughter. This princess is one of his loveliest and bravest characters. By sheer moral force she puts to shame the wicked creatures into whose power she falls and makes them respect and aid her.

Pericles begins with a rather shocking scene, and brings on the stage a number of wicked and immoral people, although in the end the noble and moral persons are left abundantly happy. The scandalous aspects of the play undoubtedly drew the lively playboys and more daring ladies of the Court to the Globe. A princess in a bawdyhouse! How thrilling!

"Aye, pirates capture her, and sell her, and she's in a rare desperate situation, but gets out of it as rarely."

So the talk went, and six years after its appearance, *Pericles* was still so popular that a playwright wrote in the prologue to a new play:

> And if it prove so happy as to please
> We'll say 'tis fortunate, like *Pericles*.

Shakespeare did not miss the point of what had happened.

He had written and staged *Coriolanus* and *Pericles* at about the same time. *Coriolanus* languished while *Pericles* throve, drew silence where *Pericles* drew praise. Yet the tragedy was much the better play of the two, both as poetry and as drama. The meaning was clear. Tragedy was not good box-office any more. Romance was.

2

It was just about this time that Dick Burbage called a meeting of the housekeepers of the Globe.

"It is this matter of Henry Evans and the lease of the Blackfriars," he explained to the small group—Shakespeare, Heminges, Condell, Slye, and Dick's own brother Cuthbert. "He and his brats can put on no more plays there—or elsewhere, for that matter."

"Sure, they had the favor of heaven to play as long as they did," said Heminges. "Do they think they can mock the King himself? 'I ken the man weel,'" he mimicked, "'he is one o' my thirty-pound knights.'"

Heminges referred to the way in which the boy actors had ridiculed James. The "thirty-pound knights" was a reference to one of the ways in which the King got money—by selling titles.

"Well, they are out of this playhouse and all others," said Burbage, "and good riddance, so far as concerns us. But the point is that Master Evans holds of me a twenty-one year lease on the Blackfriars, and must pay £40 a year for it, and yet he has no use for a playhouse whatsoever."

The handsome actor grinned at his companions as he pointed this out. Shakespeare saw the drift of his remarks.

"This same Blackfriars was once to be a playhouse for our company, as I remember," he smiled.

"Ha!" exclaimed Condell. "We were cheated of that by the residents of the place and the gentlemen of the Queen's Council. But today the obstruction to our using the hall would not be like to stand."

"I have good word that we may play there," said Burbage. "The question is of our profit in doing so. The Globe hath been a cold house for us some of these winters."

The others nodded.

"We shall draw more at the Blackfriars," said Heminges, "and can charge them more. None stand, and 'twill be all gallery admissions."

"And audiences of good quality," added Shakespeare.

Burbage nodded.

"Well," he said, "it is at our pleasure to take the lease up; and if we do, Master Evans himself stands willing to become a housekeeper. With seven of us, 'tis something more than £5 a year that we pay. And if each gets not five times that five each twelvemonth in return, I have no skill at such estimation."

3

That was the beginning of a new era for the King's Men. The seven named above became housekeepers. The company profited by having a heated playhouse for winter days, and one in the very heart of the city.

Four years later a certain Edward Kirkman, who knew the financial problems of the theaters, offered to prove in court that Shakespeare's company "got, and as yet doth, more in one winter in the said great hall [of Blackfriars] by a thousand pounds than they were used to get on the Bankside."

The streets about the playhouse were crowded with coaches, and a few years later the constables and other inhabitants of the Blackfriars district complained to city authorities that "the inhabitants there cannot come to their houses, nor bring in their necessary provisions of beer, wood, coal, or hay, nor the tradesmen or shopkeepers utter their wares, nor the passengers go to the common water stairs without danger of their lives and limbs." This was "every winter day from one or two of the clock till six at night."

Such popularity brought money into the company's till. But it had an effect also upon the future character of English playhouses. As we have seen, most of these had been outdoor affairs—a bit like our modern sports stadia. True, some Court performances had been held indoors, and Evans had used the Blackfriars for eight years. But now the leading troupe of actors, the King's own servants, had moved from the cold stage and dressing rooms of the Globe to a heated, enclosed theater. Here they were to perform for many years. Here men and increasing numbers of women were to get used to the indoor theater, and gradually to demand it. And with indoor production came changes in the shape and lighting and fittings of the stage. Such changes had not yet begun to take place, but when the seven new housekeepers took over the Blackfriars, the way was prepared for them.

The move to the indoor playhouse also had its effects upon Shakespeare. One was financial. His dividends as a housekeeper in two theaters were larger than they had been when he depended on the Globe alone, as the winter intake at the new house was much higher than at the Globe. For the same reason his profits as an actor were greater. But more important was the effect of the new playhouse on Shakespeare's art.

When the company moved to the Blackfriars, it shut out the groundlings and drew gentlefolk as its chief patrons. Lords and ladies from the Court, gentlemen-merchants and shopkeepers and lawyers, and of course the students who had always been playgoers—these were the chief groups that made up Shakespeare's winter audiences. With these, Court influences predominated. Most of the spectators wanted the fabulous, romantic, and not too serious plays that had been pushing tragedy from its once popular position. There was still demand enough for the well-known tragedies. There was demand for comedy, too. But the new thing was the romance or romantic tragicomedy like Shakespeare's *Pericles* or Beaumont and Fletcher's *Philaster*. These plays had a novelty of mood and atmosphere, and used the more popular features of the Court masque—striking stage effects, songs, pantomimes, dances. So the Blackfriars gave a final push to Shakespeare, turning his eyes and imagination wholly toward the new kind of play.

To him it was not as new, perhaps, as it was to others. In his earlier comedies he had often come close to what the Court wanted now. *A Midsummer Night's Dream* had been as fantastic as any of these later pieces. *As You Like It* and *Twelfth Night* had been as romantic. All had brought the audiences lovely songs. It was only necessary to slant the mood away from high-spirited humor and toward a gentle melancholy. In 1609 Shakespeare found this an easy thing to do.

4

Cymbeline, The Winter's Tale, The Tempest—these were the dramas he wrote in the new mode. They were the last he was to write by himself alone. Each had its own strong individuality, yet in certain ways all three were similar.

They were alike in setting. All had a kind of strangeness and unreality about the scene of action. *Cymbeline* brought the spectators to ancient Britain a generation after Caesar's first invasion—an England before England, legendary and remote. *The Winter's Tale* took its audiences to the kingdoms of Sicily and Bohemia, each, except for name, an imaginary land confused both in geography and in time. (Bohemia had a seacoast; and the Sicilians worshiped Apollo, although they seemed in other ways to be a people of the Renaissance!) Finally, *The Tempest* presented an imaginary island, presided over by a master of magic.

Such settings helped to give these plays a kind of dreamlike quality. Another feature strengthened this element. All three dramas made
occasion for songs, music, dances, and two for other decorative action.
Here the influence of the masques appeared.

Cymbeline shows how such items were used. It produced the joyous
song beginning

> Hark! Hark! The lark at heaven's gate sings
> And Phoebus 'gins arise;

and later in the play a dirge was sung at the supposed death of the
heroine, Imogen, with statelier stanzas, yet lovely ones—

> Fear no more the heat o' the sun,
> Nor the furious winter's rages;
> Thou thy worldly task hast done,
> Home art gone and ta'en thy wages.
> Golden lads and girls all must
> As chimney-sweepers, come to dust.

In this drama also Posthumus, the hero, as he lay sleeping in prison,
saw a dream acted out in which his parents and his two brothers cir-
cled about him, and prayed to Jupiter, who descended from heaven on
an eagle amid thunder and lightning and threw a thunderbolt! This
was a feat of stagecraft such as had never before been attempted. It
showed how well designed and skillfully handled was the machinery
of "the Heavens" in the Globe and the Blackfriars.

There was a gayer sort of singing and dancing in *The Winter's Tale,*
most of it as a kind of interlude in Act IV. In *The Tempest* songs and
music and "revels" were scattered throughout the play. "Strange
shapes" went through pantomimes and the sprite Ariel flitted about
on wings. A "banquet" set forth upon a table vanished "with a quaint
device." As we shall see, there was a special reason for the remarkable
stage contrivances of this play.

All three dramas had one more feature in common—a happy ending.
For *The Tempest* this was natural enough, as from the beginning the

lordly Prospero controlled the action, and arranged it at his pleasure
But in the two others the happy ending required the most desperate
ingenuity. Imogen in *Cymbeline* was more in danger than Cordelia in
King Lear ever dreamed of being; Cymbeline himself seemed to have
lost liberty, daughter and kingdom. But Shakespeare resolutely
smoothed each situation out. In *The Winter's Tale* the tragedy was
even more pressing; it actually brought about two deaths and a deal
of unhappiness. But the poet kept working at the situation, and after
a lapse of sixteen years managed to bring it around to a state of joy.

It may justly be asked if these three plays do not suffer as dramas
because of their unreality and (in two cases) the rather forced endings
they achieve. Undoubtedly in a sense they do. *Othello* and *Lear* have
a harsh truth to life which is emphasized by calamity. Their great
characters are greater for this. In height and intensity, they rise above
any figures in the tragicomedies and romances.

Yet the latter bring us a Shakespeare we should be sad to lose. For
some readers these are favorite plays, if not the most admired. The
poet Tennyson died with a copy of Shakespeare in his hands, whispering with difficulty, "I have opened it." The page was turned to the
beginning of *Cymbeline,* best loved by him among all dramas.

What did Shakespeare do in these tragicomedies and romances to
win such tributes for them?

In one sense, the answer is simple. Tragedy is a possible outcome of
human action—perhaps the most impressive that can be imagined.
But comedy with its wholly happy ending is another possibility; and
the outcome in which some tears mingle with joy is a third. Shakespeare had dealt with the first two possibilities for many years. He
was now dealing with the final one. And as he had been a master in
comedy and tragedy, he was a master here as well.

First of all, by the scene and music and shows and dances he created an atmosphere in which suffering was never quite so stark as in
Lear or *Macbeth*. The spectator was in the mood to be sad, but not
wholly to feel the horror and wickedness that were sometimes shown.
Yet such elements were important. The greatness of *Cymbeline* lies

chiefly in the character of Imogen, and we come to know her character mostly through her misfortunes.

First we see her in disfavor with her father because she has married Posthumus, the man she loves. Cymbeline had planned to have her marry Cloten, the stupid son of her stepmother. The king is furious; he sends Posthumus into exile, puts his daughter under guard. It is a gallant girl who can face him, but Imogen does.

We get a glimpse of her devotion to the man she loves as Pisanio, his servant, tells her how the ship that bore his master away left the land.

> For so long
> As he could make me with this eye or ear
> Distinguish him from others, he did keep
> The deck; with glove, or hat, or handkerchief,
> Still waving.

Imogen cries out that she would have watched her husband until he was no bigger than a gnat, then turned away and wept. Her whole thought and feeling are for Posthumus, although she knows that she faces danger in her father's anger, in her stepmother's malice, and in the rude insistence of Cloten on trying to woo her despite her married state.

When an Italian, Iachimo, comes to Britain with a letter from Posthumus, Imogen greets him graciously—

> You are as welcome, worthy sir, as I
> Have words to bid you; and shall find it so
> In all that I can do.

She does not know that her husband has laid a great wager with the Italian upon her virtue—that Iachimo has the letter to give him an opportunity to win Imogen's love. He fails completely to do so. She is wholly and furiously loyal once she sees his purpose. But by a trick Iachimo has himself conveyed in a chest into Imogen's chamber. He emerges there at night, and we see him bending over the princess.

> Cytherea,
> How bravely thou becom'st thy bed! Fresh lily,
> And whiter than the sheets! That I might touch!
> But kiss; one kiss . . .
> 'Tis her breathing that
> Perfumes the chamber thus: the flame o' the taper
> Bows toward her, and would underpeep her lids.

This glimpse of her sleeping, in the reverent words of the man who planned to do her ill, is part of our sense of Imogen. Iachimo steals a bracelet from her wrist, and notes details of the chamber and a mole beneath her breast with which to convince Posthumus that he has been successful.

So, through event by event, she is revealed to us. We see Imogen when she knows that Posthumus believes she has been false to him, when she knows that he has ordered Pisanio (who scorns the command) to kill her. She never ceases to love Posthumus. When he, bitterly repentant of his cruelty, begs Cymbeline that he may die for what he thinks was his crime, Imogen steps forward to take him in her arms.

How complete a proof is Imogen that the derogatory remarks about women that are made in *Troilus* and *Hamlet* and *Antony and Cleopatra* are no personal remarks of Shakespeare! Imogen, of course, stands with Isabella in *Measure for Measure* and Marina in *Pericles* as a passionately pure heroine. She is really no more loyal to her beloved than Julia, Juliet, Rosalind, Viola, Portia, Helena, Desdemona or Cordelia. But because we see her so cruelly and often tried, and because she meets each test so winningly and bravely, she awakens more sympathy and tenderness than perhaps any of the others. However, they stand beside her to remind us that Shakespeare was often the champion of woman, seldom her adversary.

Certainly he was no adversary of Hermione in *The Winter's Tale*. Under the wholly baseless jealousy of her husband, King Leontes, that queen never loses poise or gives ground. She knows she is innocent of his accusation that she was too friendly with his friend Polixenes,

king of Bohemia. And she defends her honor in words of terrible dignity. As she goes to prison she turns to the nobles before whom the
king has accused her—

> Good my lords,
> I am not prone to weeping, as our sex
> Commonly are—the want of which vain dew
> Perchance shall dry your pities, but I have
> That honorable grief lodged here which burns
> Worse than tears drown.

Again at her trial she speaks with the same clear eloquence:

> For life, I prize it
> As I weigh grief, which I would spare. For honor,
> 'Tis a derivative from me to mine
> And only that I stand for.

Hermione does not win the same tender sympathy that Imogen
does; for one thing, she is more self-contained; for another, she drops
out of the story for two acts. *The Winter's Tale* is less the play of one
person than is *Cymbeline*. It suffers on this account. The lack of a
strong central character is a reason for the relatively poor structure
of the play. However, *The Winter's Tale* has its own riches. It creates
four memorable characters where *Cymbeline* has only Imogen to stir
us in a comparable way. Besides Hermione, we cannot forget her lively
but serious champion, Paulina; or the lively but comic Autolycus, a
delicious rascal; or the lovely Perdita. This girl, who seems to be a
shepherdess, is really the child of Hermione and Leontes. Her father
had ordered her taken to a foreign shore and exposed there. A shepherd found her, and reared her as his own. But the royalty in her
shines out. Her beauty and grace attract Florizel, the son of Polixenes
—for it was on the coast of Bohemia that she was found.[1] Some of the
loveliest scenes of the play are those in which we see the prince wooing the shepherd's daughter.

[1] Although Ben Jonson laughed at him for giving Bohemia a seacoast, Shakespeare took it from his source, Robert Greene's *Pandosto*. Greene, a "university
wit," was the more to blame.

In these, too, occur some passages of haunting beauty. Except for two exquisite songs, *Cymbeline* has no supremely fine poetry. *The Winter's Tale* has. In the fourth act of the play Perdita, acting as hostess during a festival at her home, is giving flowers to her guests. She offers some to two older strangers, who are really Polixenes and one of his lords in disguise, come to spy upon Florizel. She says to them—

Here's flowers for you;
Hot lavender, mints, savory, marjoram;
The marigold, that goes to bed wi' the sun,
And with him rises weeping. These are flowers
Of middle summer, and I think they are given
To men of middle age.

She then regrets that she has no spring flowers for Florizel, and exclaims—

O Proserpina!
For the flowers now that frighted thou lett'st fall
From Dis's wagon; daffodils
That come before the swallow dares, and take
The winds of March with beauty; violets dim,
But sweeter than the lids of Juno's eyes
Or Cytherea's breath; pale primroses
That die unmarried, ere they can behold
Bright Phoebus in his strength . . .
bold oxlips and
The crown-imperial, lilies of all kinds,
The flower-de-luce being one.

It is a lovely catalogue (attempted in *Cymbeline,* by the way,[2] but with much less success). No wonder that Florizel replies with perhaps the loveliest compliment ever paid by a youth to his beloved—

What you do
Still betters what is done. When you speak, sweet,
I'd have you do it ever; when you sing,

[2] IV. ii. 218 ff.

I'd have you buy and sell so; so give alms;
Pray so; and for the ordering your affairs
To sing them too. When you do dance, I wish you
A wave of the sea, that you might ever do
Nothing but that; move still, still so,
And own no other function! Each your doing,
So singular in each particular,
Crowns what you are doing in the present deed,
That all your acts are queens.

Such passages (for there are others of fine beauty) give the play its
greatest distinction. And in the same scene is another which offers one
of the few comments by Shakespeare on the art of writing. As Perdita
shows the disguised Polixenes her garden, she speaks slightingly of the
gillyvors (gilliflowers) which are streaked. He asks why she despises
them. She replies that their color pattern is artificial—that art is partly
responsible for it, and nature not entirely. Polixenes answers (the
italics are mine)—

Yet nature is made better by no mean
But nature *makes* that mean: so o'er that art
Which you say *adds* to nature, is an art
That nature *makes*. You see, sweet maid, we marry
A gentler scion to the wildest stock,
And make conceive a bark of baser kind
By bud of nobler race. This is an art
Which does *mend* nature, *change* it, rather, but
The art itself is nature.

These words tell us that far from writing without plan, as some critics
were later to assert he did, Shakespeare considered very deeply how
and why he wrote.

And the story? Yes, it has an importance, too. Fantastic as it is, it
holds us. Hermione was supposed to have died shortly after the birth
of her young daughter. In Perdita we know that something of her
lives on. But when in the final scene Leontes is permitted to view a

new statue of Hermione, and discovers that it is his living queen, we as well as he are joyfully surprised.

5

John Heminges sat quietly with Shakespeare in the latter's London rooms, sipping from a goblet some sack just in from Spain. He had dropped by for a talk chiefly, yet he had some special news.

"The Princess comes soon from school to the Court," he remarked, "and may be wedded within the year."

Shakespeare lifted his brows.

"At sixteen, then; for she is but fifteen now."

"Aye. They say she has all the virtue and gentleness of bearing that her parents often lack." Heminges sighed. "If we could be ruled by the children!"

He was thinking of Elizabeth's older brother, Henry—the Prince of Wales. The latter had continued to show a promise of ability and poise that wakened hope in Englishmen everywhere. He added:

"We shall need a new play when this same Elizabeth is wedded."

The other grinned.

"Speak your reproaches freely, Jack. Say, we need a new play now. Say, this fellow Shakespeare of ours, who once wrote two or three a year, sweats now to deliver one in the same season. For all that is true."

Heminges lifted a hand.

"Nay," he protested. "You have written plays enough if it pleases you to do fewer, or none. Yet," he conceded, "I wait eagerly for the next."

"For that, my thanks." Shakespeare hesitated a moment and then added, "And you shall not wait much longer."

He fumbled among some books and papers on the table and found a pamphlet.

"Have you seen this, or its like?"

Heminges looked at the tract.

"*A Discovery of the Bermudas, Otherwise Called the Isle of Devils,*" he read aloud. "I do seem to recall some such name—and yet—"

"They are islands in the Atlantic; and a year ago Sir George Sommers had his ship driven upon some rocks off one of the shores, and wedged there. He was bound for the Colony of Virginia, in the New World."

"Aye, I remember. And if I heard aright, he got there despite the wreck."

Shakespeare nodded.

"Not a man was hurt. Nine months they stayed in the islands, which were pleasant. Then they adventured in boats they had built, and came to their original destination."

Heminges stared at his friend.

"You find a play in that?"

"Not in these fellows gone to hunt gold or dig the sassafras root in Virginia," answered Shakespeare. "But in the island I have found a play. Look you, Jack, an island! An island in the far mid-ocean, of mild weather and fruits enough. A duke and his infant daughter set adrift in a rotting boat by his jealous brother and others who have robbed him of his dukedom. By mere good fortune, however, a friend stores the craft with food, and also puts into it certain books that were the delight of the unfortunate man. And so, by Providence or what will you—"

"They are tossed up on this selfsame island," Heminges cut in.

"Where else?" asked Shakspeare. "And dwell there for years, the little maid growing to such age as our princess soon will have."

"Why, then, if a young prince comes—" began Heminges.

"Tut, tut," scolded the other, "*must* you be so nimble-witted? Well, in a manner of speaking, it is as you say, but much more must be noted first. How this duke, Prospero, is a master of magic, and gains rule over divers spirits on the island. And how one day, by his divinations, he learns that a ship approaches bearing his wicked brother Antonio and the very King of Naples who had helped the usurper—"

"And will you spin the whole of this tale, spanning some sixteen years, and spread it from Milan to the—the Bermudas?"

Shakespeare smiled.

"No, the time will cover some few hours only, and no place but the sea off the coast of the island, and the isle itself."

"What! Is this some new trial you make?"

"Why, Ben Jonson and some that praise him talk much of action that is continuous and of no change of scene, and I thought to try it. It is no great matter to manage."

"Marvelous! And this duke—this Prospero—does he revenge himself upon his enemies?"

Shakespeare raised his shoulders.

"Revenge? It is not in the grain of him, I think. But you shall soon read for yourself. 'Tis a fairy tale, Jack, yet there is meaning in it. And there is young love, too, along with adventures and magic. Yes, there's enough of love to grace a princess' wedding. The rub is—the play will be done too soon!"

It was done that summer of 1611. Its 2,100 lines made it a light task, relatively—*Hamlet* was almost double its length.

Writing *The Tempest* was a quietly joyous task for William Shakespeare. Now in his forty-eighth year, he was an aging man as age was counted in those days. He had married at eighteen, plunging early into the fuller life of husband and father. He had bent over law records; he had labored as a schoolmaster (who always outlearns those he teaches). For more than twenty years he had known threefold responsibility in the theater: he had written, he had acted, he had directed. He had been a businessman, too—shareholder in at least two playhouses. He had bought green lands, purchased and remodeled a great and ancient house.

All of this together had made an intense, a tiring activity. Shakespeare had loved the building of plays. He had loved the acting and producing of them. Yet at times he had been desperately weary with the pen-pushing, weary with the unending rehearsals, weary with teaching young boys to pronounce words and feelings that were too big for them. *Nay, Thomas, here you must put heart into it—this Viola may be in boy's clothes, but she carries a woman's love. 'Tis a sharp thing, and hurts, and you must speak the hurt.* The triple job had worn into him year by year, bruised some vital thing at his center. The effect was showing. It was true enough, as he reminded Heminges, that he was doing less now—barely a play a year.

Yet the work was not all that had worn and tired him. There was the great pageant of life pushing through London at his door, swirling about shops and palaces. He had watched this for years as it had unfolded itself in a thousand brief dramas—in scenes now gaudy with success, now glowing with romantic love, now jagged with grief or failure. So many jostling, clutching, screaming, stumbling, stricken men!

He had seen Henslowe carefully pulling in his gold—calculating, risking, denying, demanding—often twitching the strings by which he held actors or writers as a puppet master fingers the threads that move his puppets.

He had seen the learned and wily Francis Bacon say and unsay, dodge and duck and praise himself from one position to another.

He had seen brave but rash men like Essex, and brave, imaginative men like Raleigh, climb to dizzy peaks of power, then slide downward to the block or to prison.

He had seen little men with big authority grossly abusing their power.

He had seen fops and spendthrifts and adventurers thronging the streets and lounging on the very stages of the Globe and the Blackfriars.

He had seen innocent men—and women—tricked; he had seen deserving men slighted; loyal men and women cruelly spurned. He had set it all down in sonnet and play—

> And gilded honor shamefully misplaced,
> And maiden virtue rudely strumpeted,
> And right perfection wrongfully disgraced,
> And strength by limping sway disabléd;
> And art made tongue-tied by authority,
> And folly, doctor-like, controlling skill,

> And simple truth miscalled simplicity,
> And captive good attending captain ill.

There it is, much of it, in Sonnet No. 66; and most of what isn't there is in Hamlet's soliloquy—

> For who would bear the whips and scorns of time,
> The oppressor's wrong, the proud man's contumely,
> The pangs of disprized love, the law's delay,
> The insolence of office and the spurns
> That patient merit of the unworthy takes
> When he himself might his quietus make
> With a bare bodkin?

He had written all this ten years ago, or more. In his great series of tragedies, as we have seen, he had played out much of the wrong and dark caught in such lines. He saw the seamy side of life luminously clear. He saw the brighter side, too; he had steadily remembered that. But now the press and scramble and baseness of the Court and city wearied and frayed him more than ever before.

In both *Cymbeline* and *The Winter's Tale,* as in *Hamlet* and *Lear* and *Timon,* he had shown the tawdry side of such life. But in his tragicomedies he had set forth, in contrast, another way of living. In one scene we see Cymbeline's lost sons living a kind of idyllic existence in the wild mountains. Here everything is simple, honest, pure. There are no bad laws, greedy merchants or courtiers, insolent or cruel officials. And in *The Winter's Tale* the life of the shepherds of which Perdita is a part has a like wholesome quality. After the jealousy, violence and cruelty that we have seen at Leontes' Court, it is like a rapturously sweet breath of outer air to one emerging from a tunnel that was hot and dark and long.

In such scenes Shakespeare turned more than ever to nature (for he had turned to it before—particularly in *A Midsummer Night's Dream* and in *As You Like It*). Doubtless the peace of Stratford was in his mind, pulling him toward the sun and the fields. He knew that the green country world was no complete answer. He shows that clearly

enough. Imogen and Perdita both go back to play out their roles at
the spotted Court. Yet the country has been declared, so to speak.
"There it is," Shakespeare seems to say. "Do not forget. It lies within
your reach, with its brightness, its peace, its healing."

In *The Tempest* Shakespeare had a play which gave him a freedom precious above anything he could have sought. Into his hands
had been put an island. He could do with it what he wished. He
could paint its seascapes and landscapes, command its winds and tem-
peratures. He could create its people. In his mood of weariness and disillusion, the possibilities it dangled before him delighted and lifted his
spirit.

He had already the fragments of a story. An old romance from the
Spanish, the record of the shipwrecked Virginia colonists—these were
enough to start the tale of Prospero and Miranda.

Having set the duke and his daughter on the remote island, Shakespeare could create their life and all life in a few striking symbols.
Prospero was the superior man—"in apprehension how like a god."
Shakespeare created his opposite—the beast-man called Caliban, a
"thing" of ignorance and superstition and evil impulses. He created
also other forces—certain "shapes" who required control—the electric
Ariel, swift, happy, heartless—the very spirit of buoyancy. And as
Prospero was wisdom as well as power, so Miranda was the charm and
beauty of sheer innocence.

She has grown to young womanhood on the island without knowing more than its limited landscape, its few inhabitants. When she
sees young Ferdinand, he seems divinely beautiful to her. So do his
shipwrecked companions, when Prospero finally lets them appear.

> O wonder!
> How many goodly creatures are there here!
> How beauteous mankind is! O brave new world
> That has such people in it!

" 'Tis new to thee," Prospero replies with gentle dryness. Yet we see
that there is something in Miranda's vision that Prospero might do

well to recapture, if he could.

It is because Shakespeare in this play made a kind of a world in miniature that *The Tempest* is more than a fairy tale. It has all the lightness and charm of something wholly strange and magical, and yet time and again it starts us following thoughts that go down to the very roots of life. However, these do not make the story heavy. They flash and darken on it, giving it deeper interest, as the changing colors of an iridescent cloth tease the eye. The story is strange enough to hold us. What will Prospero do with his shipwrecked enemies? What luck will Caliban have in plotting against his master with the aid of two tipsy seamen? What is in store for Miranda? We follow the play entranced, charmed meanwhile by Ariel's haunting songs. We remember the free, exuberant spirit, ready

> To fly,
> To swim, to dive into the fire, to ride
> On the curled clouds.

We remember Caliban, the brute-man, at once ridiculous and pitiable, stupid and dangerous. We remember the innocent, joyous Miranda, happy in the newness and brightness of life.

Shakespeare wrote well in this brief, rainbowlike play. The songs are among his most magical. The comic scenes are rich and original. The action is kept to the one locality and covers a time of less than four hours, showing that the dramatic "unities" offered no problem to Shakespeare when he wished to observe them. Finally, the serious verse has a freedom and force that are admirable.

It shows Shakespeare using the broken line, the run-over line, the feminine ending more than ever before. Yet the music is as sweet and easy as that of *Romeo and Juliet*. When Ariel tells Prospero that his enemies are repentant, and that if he could see them his feelings toward them would grow tender—

PROSPERO: Dost thou think so, spirit?
ARIEL: Mine would, sir, were I human.

PROSPERO: And mine shall.
    Hast thou, which art but air, a touch, a feeling
    Of their afflictions, and shall not myself,
    One of their kind, that relish all as sharply,
    Passion as they, be kindlier mov'd than thou art?
    Though with their high wrongs I am struck to the quick,
    Yet with my nobler reason 'gainst my fury
    Do I take part. The rarer action is
    In virtue than in vengeance; they being penitent,
    The sole drift of my purpose doth extend
    Not a frown further. Go release them, Ariel;
    My charms I'll break, their senses I'll restore,
    And they shall be themselves.

Here in thirteen lines are seven feminine endings, five broken lines, and four run-on lines, while the metrical patterns within the lines are richly varied, with extra syllables, inverted accents, and other features besides the breaks. Yet the whole passage has a fine musical ease and clearness, and the freedom of the verse only makes it more enchanting.

    This passage is of course not one of the great ones in the play. For such we must turn to other scenes—like that in which Prospero has caused some "revels" to be enacted for Miranda and Ferdinand, and at their end turns to the latter to reassure him.

                     Be cheerful, sir.
    Our revels now are ended. These our actors,
    As I foretold you, were all spirits, and
    Are melted into air, into thin air;
    And, like the baseless fabric of this vision,
    The cloud-capped towers, the gorgeous palaces,
    The solemn temples, the great globe itself,
    Yea, all which it inherit, shall dissolve
    And, like this insubstantial pageant faded,
    Leave not a rack behind.

But perhaps a more personal quality spoke through Prospero's famous meditation beginning

> Ye elves of hills, brooks, standing lakes and groves;
> And ye, that on the sands with printless foot
> Do chase the ebbing Neptune and do fly him
> When he comes back—

in which he tells of the marvels he has wrought by magic—

> I have bedimmed
> The noontide sun, called forth the mutinous winds,
> And 'twixt the green sea and the azured vault
> Set roaring war. To the dread rattling thunder
> Have I given fire and rifted Jove's stout oak
> With his own bolt. The strong-based promontory
> Have I made shake; and by the spurs plucked up
> The pine and cedar.

But, he continues, he will give up this magic.

> I'll break my staff,
> Bury it certain fathoms in the earth,
> And, deeper than did ever plummet sound,
> I'll drown my book!

Was this a kind of symbolical profession? Was Shakespeare thinking of himself as Prospero, and declaring this to be his last written effort? Was he planning to retire from the stage, like his friend Edward Alleyn? Some have said so. Perhaps he did feel that he would soon cease to write, for a time at least, and this feeling crept into the speech. At any rate, *The Tempest* was the last play he was to do wholly by himself.

XXVI: THE END AND THE BEGINNING

O N the sixteenth of October, 1612, Prince Charles, second son of the King, together with the Earl of Southampton and others, waited at the Whitehall stairs to receive a distinguished guest. It was Frederick, the Count-Elector of the Palatine, a German prince of barely sixteen years, who came as a favored suitor for the Princess Elizabeth's hand.

The visitor, "brown" in complexion, "straight and well-shaped for his growing years," was escorted, with the 150 lords and gentlemen who accompanied him to the great Banqueting House. There the King, the Queen, Prince Henry and the Princess Elizabeth awaited him. He addressed the first three in order, doing it with a grace and confidence that pleased the English spectators.

Then he came to Elizabeth. She, says an eyewitness, "was noted till then not to turn so much as a corner of an eye towards him." Frederick stooped low to take up the hem of her dress and kiss it. "She," runs the account, "most gracefully courtesying lower than accustomed, and with her hand staying him from that humblest reverence, gave him at his rising a fair advantage, which he took, of kissing her."

It was a romantic moment. Frederick, an outstanding Protestant prince, was the popular choice in England for Elizabeth's husband. Both he and the Princess were sixteen. Both were rich in good looks and the promise of high fortune. Shakespeare could not have found a royal couple closer to Ferdinand and Miranda of *The Tempest*. The play had already been performed in the very house where the Prince and Princess had met. It was a natural choice later for one of the many dramas to be given during the festivities of betrothal and marriage.

These were suddenly, shockingly, delayed. Henry, the loved and gifted Prince of Wales, was seized with a fever late in October. On November 1 he was bled by the physicians, and his illness caused all "reveling and plays" planned for that night (All Hallow's Night) to be put off. On the 6th the young Prince died.

To the English it was a calamity. Henry, stanchly Protestant, of the greatest promise in mind and judgment, had seemed a kind of reward to the nation for its having had to endure the odd and outrageous James! "The flower of his house, the glory of his country, and the admiration of all strangers," wrote an English diplomat after hearing of his death. This was a common feeling. Prince Charles, who now became heir to the throne, aroused no like enthusiasm. Perhaps had Henry lived, he might have found the tact and vision to avoid the great Civil War that cost his brother a throne and a head.

But the Count-Elector had come to be married, and the English wanted the marriage as much as he did. On December 27 Frederick and the Princess were betrothed; on February 14, 1613, they were married. Perhaps *The Tempest* was presented in connection with the betrothal, and played again after the marriage. We know that it was performed at least once in connection with these two occasions, as were seven other plays of Shakespeare.

The production in the Banqueting House must have been impressive. The ship on which the first scene was played doubtless tossed about on actual "billows." The "strange shapes" who brought in a banquet for Prospero's enemies were triumphs of the costumer's fancy —with monstrous heads (or perhaps two of them), horns, tails, or what will you. Ariel flew down from "the Heavens" (supported by thin cords or wires) and mounted the air again amid the delighted screams of the Court ladies. The banquet really vanished "by a strange device."

The music was written by a young composer named Robert Johnson, and some of it survives to this day. It was woven through the entire play; there were many references to it in the text. Shakespeare himself must have directed the performance, and possibly he took the part of Prospero. It was the kind of role that tradition says he played, and more than any other it would have delighted and satisfied him.

As for the Princess and her husband, they left England in a cloud of romance and promised glory. Unhappily, both were to end their lives in misfortune and exile. But one of their thirteen children, Sophia, became the mother of George I of England. Young Elizabeth of *The Tempest* is thus the ancestress of all British royalty of the past 230-odd years.

2

In the period from the first performance of *The Tempest* in 1611 to its elaborate production a year and a half later before the royal bride and groom, Shakespeare had apparently divided his time between Stratford and London. Probably he was in Stratford in February, 1612, when his brother Gilbert died. (His brother Richard died about a year later, but it can be assumed that Will was then in London to produce plays for the royal wedding festivities.)

We know that on May 11, 1612, the playwright was in the city. On that day, at the Court of Requests at Westminster, he appeared as a witness and was questioned. The case dealt with a dispute between

Shakespeare's former landlord, Christopher Montjoy, and Stephen Bellott, Montjoy's son-in-law. Stephen was claiming certain goods and moneys which, he said, he had been promised, but never given. William Shakespeare was questioned.

"Do you know Stephen Bellott, the plaintiff in the case; and Christopher Montjoy, the defendant?"

"I do."

"For how long have you had this knowledge and acquaintance with them?"

"As I now remember, for the space of ten years or thereabouts."

"Did you know the complainant when he was a servant of the defendant, and his behavior at that time?"

"Aye; I knew them both; and can say that the plaintiff, Stephen Bellott, behaved himself well and honestly."

"Did the defendant Montjoy in your hearing ever confess to the great profit and commodity he got by the service of the said complainant?"

"To my remembrance, no; but I do believe that the complainant was a good and industrious servant throughout his time of service. I can say no more than that."

So the examination went forward. Almost word for word, though in summary, and not in question and answer, the above testimony stands in the clerk's record. Much more followed. The playwright testified as to Montjoy's apparent satisfaction with Stephen, and as to how Madame Montjoy "did solicit and entreat him" to persuade Bellott to wed Mary; "and accordingly this deponent did move and persuade the complainant thereto." Shakespeare recalled that Montjoy had promised a marriage portion, but couldn't remember just how much it was.

"Was it £50?"

"I cannot say."

"Did the said defendant promise the plaintiff and his wife Mary £200 on his decease?"

"I do not know as to that. The plaintiff Stephen Bellott was dwelling in the house of the defendant at that time, and they had among themselves many conferences about the marriage. But I cannot say more than that."

He had no memory, either, as to what household goods had been promised.

It is not an illuminating glimpse of William Shakespeare. Two hundred and twenty-six years earlier, also in Westminster, the poet Geoffrey Chaucer had been examined by an earlier English court. The record for him was a briefer one, but revealed a number of things —his age, the fact that he had been in France, apparently with the English armies. The name of a town where he had been stationed, or through which he had passed, is given.

These were important items about Chaucer. They were all new, or confirmed other information which had been in doubt. Shakespeare's testimony gives less light on Shakespeare. It tells his age, but we have that from other sources. Only his former place of lodging and his services as a matchmaker add to our knowledge. However, they give us a brief glimpse of him as a friendly lodger.

The testimony suggests one thing more—that this was a matter of relatively little consequence in Shakespeare's life. There is an air of abstraction and haste about his replies as summarized. He couldn't recall the details of what had happened almost ten years earlier. Apparently he didn't consider them important. "And more he cannot depose," while a stock legal phrase, apparently described Shakespeare's mood. His signature approving the clerk's summary is abbreviated and written hastily—"Willm. Shakp."

3

After Princess Elizabeth's marriage in February, 1613, Shakespeare stayed on in London.

He was busy for a time making an arrangement to buy a house near the Blackfriars theater. He made the purchase in March, paying £80 in cash, and letting £60 remain as a mortgage. Apparently Shakespeare got the property as an investment and not as a residence. He rented it at once to John Robinson, who was to appear later in Stratford as a witness to the poet's will. Shakespeare may have had in mind the convenience of such a house to him personally. He may have kept the right to a room which he could use on his frequent trips to London.

In this same month of March, 1613, Shakespeare was also working out an *impresa,* or pictorial device for a shield, to be used by Francis Manners, Earl of Rutland. The dramatist collaborated with his friend Richard Burbage, who excelled as a painter, and who put the playwright's idea into form and color. An entry in the accounts of the Earl of Rutland reads: "Item. 31 Martii [March] 1613 to Mr. Shakespeare in gold about My Lord's *impresa* xlivs. To Richard Burbage for painting and making it, in gold xlivs."

Meanwhile Shakespeare had been drawn back into a certain amount of work for the King's Men. They needed him; for Beaumont and Fletcher, who had begun to write for the company in 1609, were no longer available as a team. Beaumont had stopped writing plays about this time. Fletcher was not well equipped to go on alone. He had depended on Beaumont for plotmaking; Dryden said later that Beaumont was so sound a judge of plays that even Ben Jonson "submitted all his writings to his censure."

It is not clear exactly how Shakespeare acted to assist Fletcher. Three plays have been credited to the two jointly. Of one, *Cardennio,* based on the Spaniard Cervantes' novel *Don Quixote,* no copy exists. Another, *The Two Noble Kinsmen,* tells the story of Palamon and Arcite, as set forth more than two hundred years earlier in Chaucer's *The Knight's Tale.* Shakespeare's part in this is supposed by most authorities to have been small.

He seems to have done much more with the third play, *The Famous History of the Life of Henry VIII.*

In general, it is agreed that Fletcher roughed out this drama and that Shakespeare revised it by editing, by rewriting some scenes, and by adding a few new ones.

This opinion prevails because the structure of the piece is poor.

"Who would make a poor plot," ask the scholars, "Fletcher or Shakespeare? The answer *must* be the former. He was known for his lack of ability as a playmaker. In contrast, Shakespeare was a master craftsman. What happened is clear. Shakespeare saw that the drama was badly planned, but would have to be rewritten if its faults of structure were to be corrected. He didn't try to correct them. He worked on the characters and on the verse."

This is a logical argument. But others, chiefly E. I. Fripp, contend stoutly that the play was mostly Shakespeare's. The chief characters, says Fripp—Cardinal Wolsey, Queen Katharine (of Aragon) and others, are too fine and strong for Fletcher to have created. Structure? Bah, exclaims Fripp! Shakespeare had got structure out of his system doing *The Tempest*. He designed *Henry VIII* as a kind of pageant, attempting no real plot, and concentrating on the separate scenes.

You may accept the theory you like best. As to the play, it has great dramatic moments. When Katharine kneels before Henry, suspecting that he means to divorce her, and makes her plea—

> Sir, I desire you do me right and justice
> And to bestow your pity on me,

when she pleads her innocence and dignity, fences with Wolsey, accuses the Cardinal of enmity to her, and finally walks majestically from the court, no spectator can sit unstirred. Nor can any fail to be moved when Wolsey is at last cast off by the King, and bursts into bitter self-reproaches, beginning,

> Farewell! A long farewell, to all my greatness.

It is a moving soliloquy, ending with the strong simile

> And when he falls, he falls like Lucifer,
> Never to hope again.

If Fletcher wrote that, he wrote beyond his previous best. If Shakespeare wrote it, he wrote well. Apparently the play was thought of at the time as mostly Shakespeare's, as we shall see later. But in the early summer of 1613, the important thing was not the authorship but the production of the play for the first time at the Globe, on June 29.

It was a balmy afternoon, full of sunshine. The new play, possibly called *All Is True,* with a subtitle about Henry VIII, was to be sumptuously produced. There was special matting for the stage, the knights and even the guards were elaborately costumed. The flashing arms and the painted curtains gave a rich pageant quality to the show. Well along in the first act, at the entrance of King Henry, cannon were shot off.

Nobody noted this at the time except as a part of the spectacle. Unfortunately, some of the wadding from the artillery had caught fire, and lodged in the thatch of the playhouse roof. A few saw some smoke, but thought it hung in the air after the discharge of the cannon. Meanwhile the thatch was ignited, and the flame ran about underneath the surface until finally it burst into a full-blown blaze.

The spectators rose shouting, and rushed for the doors. A few days later a balladmaker told of their pell-mell rush.

> Out run the knights, out run the lords,
> And there was great ado;
> Some lost their hats, and some their swords,
> Then out run Burbage, too.
> The reprobates, though drunk on Monday,
> Prayed for the fool and Henry Conday. [Condell]
> *O sorrow, pitiful sorrow, and yet all this is true.*

Shakespeare ran out as well as Burbage. The playhouse books and perhaps other valuables seem to have been saved. No lives were lost.

"Only one man had his breeches set on fire," wrote Sir Henry Wotton, a statesman of the time, to a friend, "that would perhaps have broiled him, if he had not, by the benefit of a provident wit, put it out with a bottle of ale!"

But no one could put out the flames that wreathed the walls of the theater. In an hour the Globe had burned down to its foundations. To Shakespeare and others, watching, much more was burning than the wood and fabric of a playhouse. Hours of rehearsal for the afternoon's play, great moments of laughter or despair, the loveliness of Viola or Imogen, the flight of Ariel, the sheer beauty of great poetry masterfully rendered—such memories seemed to go up with the flames. Shakespeare, turning a few days later toward Stratford, carried with him the image of a few charred timbers rising from a bed of ashes. With the Globe gone, there seemed to be less in London to hold him, or to call him back.

4

Homeward bound, at the Crown Inn at Oxford, Shakespeare sat with his old friends John and Jane Davenant. He had dined; and after a long day in the saddle he was pleasantly tired, and spoke longingly of getting to Stratford, and staying there.

"You will not be so often in London?" asked Davenant.

"It is my great hope."

"But you are accustomed to the town and the Court, Master Shakespeare," spoke up the innkeeper's wife. "What will you do year-long in a little place like Stratford?"

"I shall rest, mistress," the writer-actor smiled.

"And then?" asked Davenant.

The smile deepened.

"Why, then, rest again." The twinkle faded in the deep eyes, and Shakespeare spoke simply. "I am tired, and I think not well. My son John Hall shall watch how I do, and give me such medicines as fit my condition. He has as great a skill as any physician in England. When I am no longer weary to the bone, and ill, perhaps I shall think of London again."

"You've had enough of it for a time, I warrant," agreed Davenant. "Myself—I hold little with much that goes on there." He hesitated, then asked, "Will you write plays in Stratford?"

"While I rest?"

"Nay, then. But will you perchance cast an eye on those already writ, to make a full book of them? They are fine stories, and as good verse as a man can read."

"And they are all the property of my company, good friend John, who would not have them printed for others to steal."

"In time they would agree."

"Aye, so Jack Heminges tells me. But if they should, what shall it profit me? Plays bring no man esteem as a poet, despite what my good friend Ben Jonson may think, and the printer takes the money. Nay—for now I'll have no printing of plays. Let men that like them hear them. When they draw the crowds no more, and I am rested, then will be time enough to think of printing."

So he sought rest in Stratford. It was not a return to a strange place, which might disappoint him. He had gone to its fields and streams and woods often and often before, and found a kind of restorative in them. Nor did he lack old friends there, or kinfolk, or new friends.

Anne, almost sixty years of age, probably supplied little but a sense that things were going on as they had gone. But Susanna was there, with her widely read and inquiring husband. Judith was at New Place —impetuous, willful, still unmarried. Shakespeare liked her animation and dash, if he wondered a little now as to what would become of her. She was long past the usual marrying age—almost twenty-eight.

There were many old friends—Hamnet Sadler, after whom Shakespeare's son had probably been named; Philip Rogers, the apothecary; Henry Walker; Julius Shaw, later to be a witness for the first draft of Shakespeare's will. These were all merchants, but of the new generation that read and wrote. In Stratford, too, the town schoolmaster was an old acquaintance, and an amusing one—Alexander Aspinall. He was a diligent, peppery, long-winded fellow, whom Shakespeare probably pictured for us as Holofernes in *Love's Labor's Lost*. Then there were various folk of better station—Thomas and John Combe, Thomas Reynolds, Anthony and John Nash. All were gentlemen, well read and appreciative of the talent and energy of their townsman who had towered so high in the playhouse world.

Doubtless Shakespeare had acquaintances also among the nobles and gentlefolk who owned estates in the neighborhood. Sir Henry Rainsford and his Lady, for instance. She was the original for the heroine of Michael Drayton's sonnet-sequence *Idea*. Drayton, long a casual friend of Shakespeare, came often to Clifford Chambers, the Rainsford estate, which lay just outside Stratford. The Rainsfords and many of the other families of distinction were patients of Shakespeare's son-in-law, Dr. Hall.

When the poet-player arrived from London that July of 1613, he found this same son-in-law highly indignant at a slander against his wife Susanna. A young man named John Lane had been talking about her, accusing her of misconduct with a certain Rafe Smith. It seems to have been a malicious bit of gossip, utterly without foundation.

Mrs. Hall sued Lane for slander in the Ecclesiastical Court of the diocese, and the case was called for July 15. The slanderer failed to appear. Various witnesses testified for Mrs. Hall, and she was declared free of blame. On July 27 young Lane was excommunicated by the Bishop.

Any self-respecting woman might have acted as Susanna did. Her father, had he been in Stratford when the slander was first known, might have urged her so to act. The only other course was contemptuous indifference.

That neither Dr. Hall nor Susanna seems to have considered ignoring the slander was in harmony with their religion. Both were Puritanical in their faith. Neither seems to have been extreme. Hall had Roman Catholic and Church of England patients, and was apparently on the friendliest terms with them. Susanna was later remembered as "witty above her sex," and sympathetic with all her neighbors. Yet in both husband and wife these amiable qualities went along with a high sense of conduct; and not to challenge such an act as young Lane's would have been unthinkable. His talk, as the Halls saw it, was not only hurtful to them, but an affront to decency and a danger to the entire community.

This episode reminds us that living in Stratford meant to Shakespeare living among Puritans. Anne Shakespeare also was one, and so were many of his friends. In 1614 the town records show that a Puritan preacher was staying at New Place. How did this religious atmosphere suit the actor and writer, retiring with the hope of rest and quiet?

The logical answer is that it suited him to this extent—he must have expected to find it. His father had been a nonconformist. Doubtless some of his brothers had been also. His wife had shown Puritanical leanings.

Shakespeare himself had been subjected to very different influences from those which had moved the rest of his family. In London, Puritan and player had clashed. Southampton's family background had been Roman Catholic. The Court and those close to it naturally gave full allegiance to the Church of England. Probably Shakespeare did.

We can only guess at this. His writings show a deep concern for moral values, a wide knowledge of the Bible, a respect for earnest men of religion. Some of his characters gibe at Puritans; others denounce churchmen who abuse their high offices. One would gather that Shakespeare was little interested in creed, and much concerned with spiritual values. Unlike Jonson and others, he never takes sides in the religious quarrels of the times. One can imagine him saying: "Is there not something higher and better than this perpetual argument over the letter of a faith; have not Christians worthier things to do than to persecute each other for manifestations of belief?"

One would feel that Shakespeare had Catholic friends, Church of England friends, and friends among the Puritans. He would have respected the high and responsible outlook of intelligent leaders in the latter group. Men like his son-in-law were widely read in literature, wrote Latin poetry, and showed little, if any, of the fanaticism that other Puritans later brought to the American colonies. Shakespeare had no quarrel with John Hall and his kind.

Probably the two men had interesting talks with the preacher who was Shakespeare's guest in the spring of 1614. We have evidence that the visitor was not extreme in one respect. The reason that he appears in the Stratford records is that the corporation sent him "one quart of sack and one quart of claret wine." It cost less than a shilling (the two quarts) and doubtless Dr. Hall and Susanna and Anne and Will Shakespeare himself had a taste of it, along with the preacher.[1]

Shakespeare had other guests at New Place, and probably few of them were divines. The house was large—later Queen Henrietta, the wife of King Charles I, used it as her headquarters when she stopped briefly in Stratford with an entourage. But Shakespeare could well afford to maintain it, even without revenue from writing and acting.

He was really a wealthy man now. He owned other houses than New Place, as we have seen—several in Stratford and one in London. From the Stratford tithes and nearby farm lands he drew a considerable income. He may still have drawn an income as a housekeeper from both the Blackfriars and the Globe, or may have sold his interest in one or both of the playhouses. It has been estimated that these two sources alone were worth £80 a year; the tithes brought £38, other income from lands, houses and loans at least £12 more. That is £130 a year, or between $8,000 and $10,000 in our money values.

Of course this was a retirement income. When working in London as an actor and writer, Shakespeare got his shareholder's money, his payments for plays written, benefits for successful plays (one performance was called "The Poet's Day" and the author got all the receipts after expenses had been met), special payments for performances at Court, and wages from the King as a King's Man and, separately, as a Groom of the Chamber. Joseph Quincy Adams has estimated that Shakespeare's yearly income at the height of his activity was about £386. This would amount to three times what he got after retiring from London.

But even in 1614, enjoying the lower of these two incomes, Shakespeare was a man of property and influence. Doubtless he would have been asked to serve Stratford as an official had it been practicable for

[1] Puritans frowned on drinking to excess, but they and most other Englishmen of the time, clergymen included, drank moderately of ale and wine. In that day no moral principle except moderation was involved.

him to do so. That he never did argues either that he was expected to
return to London, or that he was not well. The latter seems the better
explanation of the two, although we have only straws of evidence to
go on.

In July, 1614, Shakespeare's friend John Combe died, leaving the
playwright a memorial legacy of £5. William and Thomas Combe,
John's sons, fell heir to their father's estates. Soon they proposed to en-
close certain of their lands, which, the Stratford council feared, might
have a disastrous effect on some of the village farms, including those
from which Shakespeare and others received an income.

Few citizens thought that the Combes would go through with the
project. One who did was Thomas Greene, Shakespeare's cousin. He
was then clerk of the council, and began a vigorous fight to stop the
enclosure. He and other officials at once appealed to Shakespeare, apparently thinking his support would be valuable and that he might
have influence in London.

The Combes were just as eager to have Shakespeare on their side.
They offered him a guarantee against any financial loss resulting from
the enclosures. On October 28, 1614, Shakespeare accepted their offer,
and signed articles protecting him. There is some reason to believe
that he got protection for his kinsman Greene also.

Thomas Greene went on with the fight—a more heroic figure in
this affair than his gifted cousin. He rode to London on November 12,
1614, to lay the case of the town before the Privy Council. In a few
days Shakespeare also came to the city in company with his son-in-law,
John Hall.

Greene at once went to see him. He wrote in his diary for November 17, "My cousin Shakespeare coming yesterday to town, I went to
see him how h did." This statement suggests, along with the presence
of Dr. Hall, that Shakespeare was unwell, and that his son-in-law had
accompanied him to London (apparently because the poet had private
business there) to make sure that in an emergency he could be on hand
to help his father. Of course, this is not a necessary reading of Greene's
remark. "To see him how he did" might have indicated a social visit

purely. Yet both having been recently in Stratford, Greene would have known very well how his cousin did unless the latter had been unwell.

In any case, Greene talked over the enclosure situation with Shakespeare and Dr. Hall, and recorded that they doubted if anything would be done by the Combes. But Greene did not accept this bit of wishful thinking, and he and the council continued to prepare for a fight. In the end, they won out. They got a partial victory in 1615 when Sir Edward Coke, Lord Chief Justice of England, ordered that "no enclosure shall be made within the parish of Stratford, for that it is against the laws of the realm, neither by Mr. Combe nor any other, until they show cause at open assizes to the Justice of the Assize." Three years later, after Shakespeare's death, the matter was settled completely in favor of Stratford.

5

Except for the one visit to London mentioned above, there is no evidence of Shakespeare's presence there after July, 1613. No new plays by him appeared in the following years. There is no sign of any further collaboration with Fletcher or others. There are no records which show him to have been in London on legal or Court business. Apparently he was residing in Stratford permanently. He may have planned to do some writing there; he seems never to have done so. He may have been tired; he may still have been unwell. In January, 1616, he made a will—not necessarily a sign of ill-health, but a possible one. Then suddenly his daughter Judith stormed into the quiet of his days.

She got married. At thirty-one years of age she joined her future to that of Thomas Quyney, aged twenty-six.

This young man was the son of Shakespeare's schoolmate Richard Quyney, twice bailiff of Stratford, and a successful merchant. Thomas's grandfather will be remembered as a fellow alderman of John Shakespeare. The groom himself wrote a beautiful hand; one of his signatures is as clean as an illustration in a writing manual, and has a triple cushion of scrollwork beneath. He also had some knowledge of French.

Still, he was a young man, and, as it proved later, not a very responsible one. Shakespeare may have been doubtful of the marriage. He was made less favorable toward it when Quyney failed to make a promised settlement of land on his wife, and to get a special license necessary in the eyes of the church for marriages performed between the twenty-eighth of January and the sixth of April.[2] As a result, the couple were twice cited to appear at Worcester and were finally excommunicated on March 12.

But the marriage had meanwhile taken place—on February 10. The Stratford vicar and his assistant were liberal, and performed it. Doubtless it was celebrated heartily by the two families and their friends.

There is only one possible reference to the festivities. This was made by the Reverend John Ward, vicar at Stratford some forty-six years later—1662-1681. According to him, "Shakespeare, Drayton and Ben Jonson had a merry meeting and, it seems, drank too hard, for Shakespeare died of a fever there contracted."

This may refer to an after-wedding meeting. It may have been unconnected with the wedding, taking place some weeks later. It may represent mere rumor. Drayton was apparently as moderate in his habits as Shakespeare seems to have been; Jonson drank freely, but some authorities argue that his being in Stratford was highly improbable. In any case, the little thumbnail flash of the three poets in a "merry meeting" is what we have. There is no evidence as to *why* Drayton and Jonson were in Stratford, but there is none that they were not. Certainly Shakespeare fell ill not long after Judith's wedding.

The illness has been diagnosed by some as chronic Bright's disease, by others as typhoid fever. The former would best account for a long period of illness, and Shakespeare's inactivity for two and a half years; the latter would be a natural illness in Stratford, where conditions existed for the spread of typhoid.

We know that Shakespeare was seriously ill on March 25, for on

[2] The Anglican church was of course the only accepted religious institution in England. Puritans and others would have to accept its control over births, marriages, and similar matters.

that day he sent for his lawyer, Francis Collins, to revise the will he had prepared two months earlier. Apparently he was anxious to make quickly the changes he had in mind. For instead of letting Collins draw up a new will, as would have been logical because of the number of changes, Shakespeare merely had the lawyer rewrite the first sheet and insert in the rest of the document such changes as he dictated.

The chief alterations related to Judith. She had been a spinster in January; now she was married. Shakespeare bequeathed her altogether £300—a good sum; but he changed the item giving her his plate, which he now gave to little Elizabeth Hall, his granddaughter. This may have indicated some displeasure with Judith, as the plate would have been useful to her. However, after a bequest to his sister Joan, and gifts to friends, including Richard Burbage, John Heminges, and Henry Condell, Shakespeare gave the remainder of what he had to "my daughter Susanna Hall."

It was a far larger portion than he had given Judith. We do not know its exact value. Shakespeare may have sold his housekeeper's share in the Globe at the time of the fire. (The playhouse was soon rebuilt, with tiled roofs!) That share was worth between £200 and £300. He may also have disposed of his interest in the Blackfriars, which was even more valuable. If he had taken such action in the case of either or both playhouses, Susanna would have inherited the money he received, or the properties he had purchased with it. She became the holder of all his investments and lands and houses, less anything that might have been sold (a very unlikely possibility) to provide Judith with her inheritance. Evidently Shakespeare felt that the Halls were best fitted to carry on the family tradition, and purposely gave them the means to do so.

Anne Shakespeare was mentioned only once in the will. Her name appears in an insert added on March 25. This reads: "Item, I give unto my wife my second-best bed, with the furniture." (That is, the mattress, pillows, coverings and hangings used with it.)

This item has caused a deal of disputation.

"Proof complete of the contempt in which Shakespeare held his aged wife!" gloat those who wish to believe the marriage a failure.

"Proof of Shakespeare's deep consideration for his wife!" retort their opponents.

A great deal can be said on both sides. Certainly many men of the time took occasion to mention their wives in their wills with high praise and words of endearment. Some such references might have been expected were there a close bond between Anne and William Shakespeare. On the other hand, it can be well understood that at the age of sixty the wife may have been a chronic invalid. She could not read or write. Her daughter Susanna later showed the highest devotion to her. Possibly the care of her mother had been a matter which Shakespeare and his daughter had discussed in detail. The item about the bed may have been designed to give the ailing woman a personal satisfaction. It would have been the one she used; the "best bed" would have been reserved for guests. This explanation of the bequest portrays Shakespeare as having little active feeling for his wife, but a concern for *her* feeling. Evidently she had kept a strong sense of her bond to him. Seven years later, just before her death in 1623, she "did earnestly desire to be laid in the same tomb" with the poet. For this wish the parish clerk at Stratford in 1693 is the authority. His statement seems to represent a local tradition.

But to return to Shakespeare and the will—after the changes were completed, Shakespeare signed it. He signed it three times. The signature at the end, on the third sheet is firm: "By me William Shakspeare." That on the first sheet is less certain; the signature on the second one is shaky, as if he were able to write only with difficulty. Yet he lived on for almost a month. On April 23, possibly the exact day of his birth fifty-two years earlier, he passed away. For two days the body lay in state at New Place. On Thursday, April 25, it was buried in the Stratford church, within the chancel rail and almost in front of the altar. Here, in a wooden coffin, the poet was lowered into a grave over which a flagstone making part of the church floor was laid. On this slab were engraved four lines which, according to tradition, Shakespeare wrote himself:

Good friend, for Jesus' sake forbear
To dig the dust encloséd here;
Blest be the man that spares these stones,
And curst be he that moves my bones.

The command has been obeyed. Several times a plea to open the grave has been made—once in order that the playwright might have a niche in Westminster Abbey with other famous poets of his land. But the simple quatrain on the stone slab has proved to be an effective warder. Shakespeare still sleeps beneath the floor of the Stratford church, and probably will until Doomsday.

6

The burial in the church before the altar was Stratford's tribute to Shakespeare as a citizen and landowner. Within several years a monument in stone was prepared, to be placed on the wall to the left of the church as one faces the altar. We do not know who ordered and paid for this. It may have been Dr. Hall. It may have been he and certain of Shakespeare's friends in London and Stratford, acting together. It may have been wholly the project of friends, without aid from members of the family.

The probability is that Shakespeare's London associates had the chief part in creating the monument. It was designed and executed in London by Garret and Nicholas Johnson (originally "Janssen"), two Flemings who were eminent as sculptors and designers of tombs. They had prepared a costly monument for John Combe (possibly through Shakespeare's recommendation to the heirs). They had executed a more elaborate one for the Earl of Rutland, in Leicestershire. Their workshop was in Southwark, near the Globe. All this suggests that London friends had a part in the work. So does the figure of Shakespeare as it appears in the monument. It shows the upper half of the body, with the poet, pen in hand, looking up as he pauses in his writing. This was probably not the form of representation that Susanna, Dr. Hall, or Anne Shakespeare would have chosen. They would have preferred to forget the playwright and remember the country gentleman.

Even more important is the inscription beneath the sculptured figure. There are two lines of Latin verse, then six of English.

With the Latin in translation, the whole reads as follows:

In judgment a Nestor, in genius a Socrates, in art a Virgil,
The earth covers him, the people mourn him, Olympus has him.

Stay, Passenger, why goest thou by so fast?
Read, if thou canst, whom envious death hath placed
Within this monument—Shakespeare, with whom
Quick Nature died, whose name doth deck this tomb
Far more than cost, sith all that he hath writ
Leaves living Art but page to serve his wit.

Obiit Anno Domini 1616
Aetatis 53 die 23 Aprilis

Here is a pretty full recognition of Shakespeare's significance as a great artist; it was not likely to have originated in Stratford. It is the first recognition of that sort to be made after Shakespeare's death. There had been praise to a similar effect during his life, but such praise may be mistaken, or wear out. Praise after death has more promise of lasting. For when a writer dies, he begins to be seen in perspective. The erection of the monument was a kind of promise for the future.

It was soon more than matched by a different but far more valuable kind of memorial. In 1623 two of Shakespeare's "fellows," John Heminges and Henry Condell, brought out an edition of the poet's plays.

Exactly what this meant can best be understood by taking account of what had been published previously. As we have seen, from time to time a number of Shakespeare's plays had been printed. They had appeared in little books called quartos—a term which referred to the size of the book page. To produce such a page, the standard large sheet of paper used by the printers was folded twice. This made four smaller sheets, or, counting both sides, eight pages all told. The actual size of the quartos varied somewhat. The standard may be thought of as 6 by 8 inches.

Altogether, nineteen plays had been printed in quarto form, including one brought out in 1622. Heminges and Condell now republished all these except *Pericles, Prince of Tyre,* and added eighteen dramas that had never been issued before. Even if they had done no more than make these new dramas available, they would deserve our deepest gratitude. Had the plays not been printed in 1623, many of the eighteen might have been lost forever, or have come down to us in poorer versions than those we have.

However, there are two more reasons for our being grateful to Heminges and Condell.

The first is that they not only added to the number of Shakespeare's plays that we have received, but also gave us those plays in a fairly authentic form. We have only to read the poorer quartos to see what mutilated texts might have come down to us had not these two friends of the playwright collected the plays for printing.

The second reason for gratitude is that Heminges and Condell were close friends of Shakespeare; and, by publishing his works so soon after his death, showed clearly which ones his friends and fellow actors regarded as mostly or wholly his. Any drama not included by them in their collection lacks one important title to be regarded as Shakespeare's. Its authenticity must be more fully established than if it had been approved for that book.

The collection of 1623 was printed on large pages, the greatest known size for any single copy now in existence being 8¾ by 13¾ inches. This page was more than twice the size of that used in the quartos, and was called "folio." The standard printing sheet was folded only once, making two sheets, or, counting both sides of each sheet, four pages. Since the 1623 printing was the first to be made of such a book, it is known as the First Folio. The volume contained 908 pages. It was quite a financial undertaking for Heminges and Condell. As we shall see, they were eager for a good sale.

Doubtless the two friends did their utmost to provide a good text for every play they printed. Some of the quartos had been set from promptbooks or other good manuscripts; in such cases the Folio was set from them. Heminges and Condell had the use of whatever books the King's Men possessed. They may have gone to Stratford, and Dr. Hall may have given or lent them such manuscripts as Shakespeare himself had kept. The player-editors believed, as we shall see, that they had made great efforts to get the best possible texts; certainly they show a deep desire to do their best for their dead friend and fellow worker. However, they were not well suited to the task of editing Shakespeare. The final texts show many omissions, repetitions, sense-less readings, and printer's errors which Heminges and Condell failed to catch. Sometimes it seems as if they must have turned the job over to the printers and forgotten it. They were of course unused to literary work, and they were getting old.

What plays did these friends regard as wholly Shakespeare's, or enough his to be included in their collection? *Pericles,* as we have seen, they excluded; apparently they thought it more Wilkins than Shake-speare. They included *Henry VIII,* all three parts of *Henry VI,* and *Titus Andronicus.* They did not include a number of plays which had already been published, or would later be published, as Shakespeare's. They omitted a number which some scholars would later put forward as his. Such dramas include *The Two Noble Kinsmen, The History of Cardennio, Edward III, Sir Thomas More, A Yorkshire Tragedy, Sir John Oldcastle, Locrine, Thomas Lord Cromwell, The London Prodigal, The Puritan Widow,* and *The Troublesome Reign of King John* (not to be confused with Shakespeare's own play on John).

Of these eleven works, sometimes called the "Shakespeare Apocry-pha," the Stratford dramatist is thought by most authorities to have had some hand only in the first two. They find the barest touch of him in *The Two Noble Kinsmen;* as to *Cardennio,* no copy of it exists. A number of scholars believe that Shakespeare wrote one or more passages for *Sir Thomas More,* and perhaps for *Edward III.*

Shakespeare's possible contributions to the former of these two plays have a particular interest for scholars and readers. The play exists in manuscript. It was revised considerably, and there are passages in a number of hands, one of which, some experts believe, is Shakespeare's own. The additions made in this script are indeed not unworthy of him, and perhaps (the evidence is dangerously doubtful) offer us samples of his handwriting.

Pericles is generally accepted as enough Shakespeare's to be put with his genuine works.

The Folio gives us more than the plays: it gives us personal information about Shakespeare. The dedication, for instance, tells us that the two brothers, William Herbert, Earl of Pembroke, and Philip Herbert, Earl of Montgomery, had been friends and patrons of Shakespeare. These were the sons of Sir Philip Sidney's sister Mary. "Since your Lordships," write Heminges and Condell, "have been pleased to think these trifles something heretofore, and have prosecuted both them and their Author living with so much favor, we hope that (they outliving him, and he not having the fate, common with some, to be executor to his own writings) you will use the like indulgence toward them [that] you have done unto their parent. . . . For so much were your Lordships' likings of the several parts, when they were acted . . . the volume asked to be yours."

As for their own labors, "we have but collected them, and done an office to the dead . . . without ambition either of self-profit, or fame; only to keep the memory of so worthy a Friend and Fellow alive as was our SHAKESPEARE."

Here is a glimpse of the enthusiasm of two earls for Shakespeare's work, and of their friendship and favor toward him.

Heminges and Condell refer slightingly to the plays here, because such was the fashion. In an address "To the great variety of readers," they speak with wholly different accents. In this essay we see Shakespeare as they saw him, and the picture is startling.

After a direct appeal to the public to "buy" ("whatever you do, buy!"), they tell how they came to issue the Folio, and what it means to them. Every sentence of this long paragraph is precious. If only they had written several more!

"It had been a thing, we confess, worthy to have been wished, that the Author himself had lived to have set forth, and overseen his own writings; but since it hath been ordained otherwise, and he by death departed from that right, we pray you do not envy his friends the office of their care and pain to have collected and published them—"

So runs part of the first sentence; it is worth breaking here. It is almost a statement that Shakespeare had agreed to prepare the plays for printing—one can imagine that the subject had been discussed. Heminges and Condell do not say so definitely, yet they talk all around such an assertion.

"And so to have published them," they go on, "as where (before) you were abused with divers stolen and surreptitious copies, maimed, and deformed by the frauds and stealths of injurious impostors, that exposed them—even those are now offered to your view cured, and perfect of their limbs; and all the rest, absolute in their numbers, as he conceived them."

Here is a clear statement of the authentic quality of the Folio plays. Heminges and Condell had made a conscious effort to give a true text; and no one had so good an opportunity as they. They go on now, in the same sentence, for I have again broken it, to speak of Shakespeare himself—

"Who, as he was a happy imitator of Nature, was a most gentle [noble] expresser of it. His mind and hand went together; and what he thought he uttered with that easiness that we have scarce received from him a blot in his papers."

There is a flash of Shakespeare the writer—natural, sure in conception and execution.

"But," the two go on, "it is not our province, who only gather his works, and give them you, to praise him. It is yours that read him. And there we hope, to your divers capacities, you will find enough, both to draw, and hold you; for his wit can no more lie hid, than it could be lost. Read him, therefore; and again, and again! And if then you do not like him, surely you are in some manifest danger, not to understand him. And so we leave you to other of his friends, whom, if you need, can be your guides. If you need them not, you can lead yourselves, and others. And such readers we wish him."

This is a touching tribute. Heminges and Condell were the sole survivors of the old Chamberlain's Men who had built the Globe. (Dick Burbage had died in 1619.) They would naturally have appreciated Shakespeare the playmaker (and, so far as the record shows, neither acted in any plays but Shakespeare's after his death!). But here we find them with a keen sense of the literary value of the plays. Their conviction was even stronger than Shakespeare's own. Probably he knew that his work was more than good. Yet a mixture of fatalism, indifference, modesty, and practical considerations seems to have kept him silent with respect to his plays, or to any literary work. In his will he makes no mention of either books or manuscripts. But Heminges and Condell were up in arms ready to fight battles for his immortal fame. No greater tribute could be offered by any friends.

Or is that the case? For perhaps in the same volume there is a greater one.

Several writers had contributed commendatory verses for this occasion which were set as a preface to the plays. They were by Leonard Digges, "I.M.," Hugh Holland, and Ben Jonson. It is Jonson's tribute that may be thought of as even greater than that of Heminges and Condell.

For Jonson was Shakespeare's sole rival during the latter's best years of writing. He penned delightful comedy, stately tragedy. Many of his songs live today. Doubtless Shakespeare's popularity and success annoyed him at times. It is untrue that he was jealous of Shakespeare in any mean way. He spoke out his opinions frankly, and frankness has been confused with malice.

Jonson himself later said that he "loved the man and do honor his memory (on this side idolatry) as much as any." It is a true statement. Jonson as a craftsman was moving in a different direction from Shakespeare. He admired order, sought to achieve it. He told Drummond, the Scottish poet, that "Shakespeare wanted art." He said, when the players told him that Shakespeare never blotted a line—"Would he had blotted a thousand!" He felt that Shakespeare "flowed with that facility, that sometimes it was necessary he should be stopped." There was meat in all these criticisms, but we need not stop here to extract it. The fact is that, holding as he did conceptions of art which were different from Shakespeare's, Jonson in his commendatory verses gave as fine a judgment of Shakespeare as any man has made before or since.

His "To the Memory of My Beloved, the Author Mr. William Shakespeare" shows by its very title the warmth of Jonson's feeling. But there is more than feeling in the lines that follow. There is great critical judgment. He begins by declaring that Shakespeare's writings are such

> As neither man, nor muse, can praise too much.
> 'Tis true, and all men's suffrage.

Then after a few lines not so directly on the subject, he bursts into a eulogy:

> Soul of the age!
> The applause, delight, the wonder of our stage!
> My Shakespeare, rise! I will not lodge thee by
> Chaucer, or Spenser, or bid Beaumont lie
> A little further, to make thee a room:
> Thou art a monument without a tomb,
> And art alive still while thy book doth live,
> And we have wits to read and praise to give!

That is a ringing declaration. Note the exactness of the adjectives, the boldness and sharpness of the imagery. Yet Jonson goes on to make

THE END AND THE BEGINNING

precise comparisons with authors past and present. Were he making
judgment for the years (and he was) he would tell, he says:

> how far thou didst our Lyly outshine,
> Or sporting Kyd, or Marlowe's mighty line.
> And though thou hadst small Latin and less Greek,
> From thence to honor thee, I would not seek
> For names; but call forth thundering Aeschylus,
> Euripides, and Sophocles to us;
> Pacuvius, Accius, him of Cordova dead,
> To life again, to hear thy buskin [3] tread,
> And shake a stage; or when thy socks were on,
> Leave thee alone for the comparison
> Of all that insolent Greece or haughty Rome
> Sent forth, or since did from their ashes come.
> Triumph, my Britain, thou hast one to show
> To whom all scenes of Europe homage owe.
> He was not of an age, but for all time!

There is much more in the same vein. And finally there comes what
is a supreme tribute from Jonson. After speaking of Shakespeare's
naturalness, he adds:

> Yet must I not give nature all; thy art,
> My gentle Shakespeare, must enjoy a part.
> For though the poet's matter nature be,
> His art doth give the fashion; and, that he
> Who casts to write a living line must sweat
> (Such as thine are) and strike the second heat
> Upon the Muses' anvil; turn the same
> (And himself with it) that he thinks to frame,
> Or, for the laurel, he may gain a scorn,
> For a good poet's made, as well as born.
> And such wert thou!

[3] The buskin, or boot, was worn by the tragic actors of Greece; the socks when
comedy was done.

So Jonson, the greatest critic of the day, writing without envy or idolatry, gave his greater friend and rival such an appraisal as no writer since him has equaled in the same space. Probably his ringing words made thousands of Englishmen of the day realize what a man had moved and created among them.

7

Ben Jonson also had a word to say about an engraved portrait of Shakespeare which appeared in the Folio. He wrote:

TO THE READER

> This Figure, that thou here seest put,
> It was for gentle Shakespeare cut;
> Wherein the Graver had a strife
> With Nature to outdo the life.

There were more lines to a similar effect. The engraving, done by a young Fleming, Martin Droeshout, is a bit wooden, and shows Shakespeare with an ample, baldish forehead, quiet eyes, and a scant mustache and beard.

It is one of the two likenesses that authorities approve without much dispute among themselves. The other is the bust on the monument, which shows an older Shakespeare who had lost more hair and gained more beard. It has been believed by many that the sculptors used a death mask for this image. Some scholars even feel that the effects of the final fever can be noted in the puffiness of the cheeks. This image was painted. It showed Shakespeare with auburn hair and hazel eyes.

"The Flower Portrait," an oil painting now in the Stratford Memorial Museum, has been held by some Shakespearean scholars to be a better likeness than either the engraving or the bust. Its admirers believed for a time that it was painted by Martin Droeshout, uncle to the Droeshout who illustrated the First Folio. The picture shows a man strikingly similar in age and features to the subject of the engraving, with the same coloring as that of the bust on the Stratford monument. In the upper left-hand corner is an inscription, "Willm Shakespeare 1609." The champions of this portrait suggest that the younger Droeshout used it as a model for his effort "to outdo the life."

But the picture has been vigorously challenged. Highly competent skeptics have attacked it as lacking a known origin and an early history. They argue that the inscription is not printed in the correct style for the supposed time of painting. In their opinion the Folio engraving was not made from the portrait, but the portrait from an improved form of the engraving! This view has been accepted pretty widely by leading specialists.

The engraving and the Stratford monument bust are both authentic to this extent: they were accepted as likenesses by Shakespeare's friends and, in the case of the bust, presumably by his family. Both friends and relatives may have been too easily satisfied; or they may not have been satisfied, but merely resigned to accepting a poor job as the best that could be had.

On the other hand, no other representations can be verified even to such an extent. There are many candidates. Perhaps the chief one is the "Chandos" portrait, so called from the Duke of Buckingham and Chandos, who owned it for a time. This rather Latin-looking Shakespeare has a highly respectable pedigree—by legend! It is said to have been painted by Richard Burbage, who gave it to the actor Joseph Taylor, who gave it to Sir William D'Avenant, son of John and Jane Davenant of the Crown in Oxford. Unfortunately no part of this rather romantic story can be proved.

Nothing can be proved, either, with respect to the "Grafton" portrait, which is undoubtedly the most satisfying of all likenesses made during Shakespeare's own time. It shows a youth of twenty-four, and bears the year 1588 in the right-hand corner to match the age in the left. The face is both firm and poetic—an ideal young Shakespeare. "Yet," sighs J. Dover Wilson after praising it, "there is no real evidence, and I do not ask the reader to believe in it. . . . All I suggest is that he may find it useful in trying to frame his own image of Shakespeare." [4]

For the "Ely Palace Portrait," discovered in a broker's shop in 1845, there is not even a legend. It has never been proved a fraud, but has never been shown to be genuine. The "Hampton Court Portrait" also has no pedigree other than the fact that a king, William IV, bought it as a likeness of Shakespeare and hung it in a palace. The "Ashbourne Portrait," picturing a fair-haired Englishman dressed in black, is popular with many who find it a more acceptable Shakespeare than that shown by the bust or the engraving. The list could be long continued. None of the dozens of paintings that have been put forward have more than their own charms and some strong wishful thinking to support them.

Shakespeare's portrait reminds us of another type of "copy"—the descendants he urged the young Friend in the *Sonnets* to produce. We have seen that Shakespeare's son died, that both his daughters were married, that in 1616 Susanna had one daughter already eight years old. She had no other children. Elizabeth Hall became Elizabeth Nash, and on her husband's death married Sir John Barnard. She died in 1670, without issue.

Judith had three boys—Shakespeare, Thomas and Richard. None lived to marry. Judith herself outlasted them, outlasted Susanna (who died in 1649) and finally passed away at the age of 77, the oldest of the Shakespeares.

So the direct line died out. Through Shakespeare's sister Joan, however, a number of descendants of John and Mary Arden Shakespeare

[4] *The Essential Shakespeare,* by J. Dover Wilson. Cambridge, England, The University Press, 1932, p. 9.

lived on to perpetuate the same blood that the poet had, both in England and in America.

So much for the flesh-and-blood descendants and kin of Shakespeare. What of his writings? Their history in detail belongs to another kind of book than this, yet a word about the creations that were the chief purpose and meaning of our hero's life seems a kind of necessary ending for this record.

During the seventeenth and eighteenth centuries his fame grew; Voltaire knew him in France and Goethe in Germany; while in England even men like Pope and Dr. Samuel Johnson, each with an outlook sharply different from Shakespeare's, worked to give him a higher standing. But with the nineteenth century came a new and greater enthusiasm, and a growing sense of what the dramatist and poet had accomplished. The discovery of many new facts about him, the more expert editing of his works, the fuller understanding of his times and the playhouses in which he toiled, such accomplishments have helped to show him in full dimension. Finally, a thorough study of Shakespeare's poetry and his dramatic craftsmanship as contributions to art has rounded out our sense of his importance.

Shakespeare has often been called the greatest of writers. In telling his story in these pages I have tried to explain the nature and the height of his genius. The sense of what he did can be sharpened by a brief comparison with what others accomplished before him, or have done since.

In mere variety of creation Shakespeare undoubtedly stands alone.

There are his songs. We have forty of these, most of them in the plays, a few in volumes of verse. Were he known for nothing else, the best of them—there are at least a dozen exquisite ones—would make him a great lyric poet. In sheer song he ranks with Burns and Heine.

There are the sonnets. Petrarch's chief title to fame lies in his fourteen-line tributes to an idealized Laura; and Petrarch's fame is great.

Shakespeare in a very different way created a body of like poetry as great or greater.

There are the comedies. Aristophanes, Terence, Ben Jonson, Molière —such writers have living names today because of the humor they brought to the stage. Shakespeare brought as much in wit, in contrived farce, in delightful nonsense; in the sharpness and depth and sympathy with which he created characters he surpasses all of them.

There are the tragicomedies. They fill a small area in which Shakespeare is supreme. The high point is *The Tempest,* with its blended enchantment and humor, and its allegorical passages that seem to flash glimpses into the meaning of the larger life beyond the faery island. Perhaps *A Midsummer Night's Dream,* more fantasy than comedy, belongs with it.

There are the tragedies—a lordly group of them. Some readers may prefer the more severely sculptured dramas of Aeschylus, Sophocles, Euripides. A few may prefer the finely wrought modern plays of Ibsen. But none will question Shakespeare's position among the few very great writers of tragedy; while many will hold that his towering heroes, his mighty yet deeply human themes, and his superb poetry lift him above all comparison.

So in his range, in the reach of his genius, he stands alone. In each of many fields he is great. And in this fact lies a partial explanation of his varied excellence. His songs gain in quality because the man who wrote them was also a writer of delightful comedy and moving tragedy. His sonnets are fuller, deeper, sweeter for the same reason. And, in turn, his comedy and tragedy both gain in life and beauty because they were made by a singer.

As to the texture of poetry, as to the insight into life, as to the ability to create men and women of make-believe who are more real than the folk about us—this I have dwelt upon enough in other pages. In the end Shakespeare's gallery of heroines, rascals, villains, heroes, demigods proclaim his supreme achievement. Puck, Bottom, Faulconbridge, Juliet, Mercutio, Romeo, Shylock, Portia, Falstaff, Brutus, Rosalind, Touchstone, Beatrice, Dogberry, Viola, Malvolio—how long the list is already before we come even to *Hamlet*. It could well be thrice as long. No other writer has left a like group of characters. They are so rich, so varied in quality, that they become symbols we use in talking of life. A thousand of their phrases are daily on our lips, reminding us that we live out our days in a companionship with Shakespeare.

BOOKS ABOUT SHAKESPEARE

The fifteen titles listed below represent a personal choice, based on usefulness, interest and originality. Some of the volumes selected have only one or two of these qualities; a few, all three. Because new discoveries have made many older works of reputation no longer accurate in important respects, only one title earlier than 1914 has been included.

Adams, John Cranford, *The Globe Playhouse,* Harvard Press, Cambridge, 1943.

The most recent book on the playhouse used by Shakespeare and his company from 1599 onward. Clear, accurate, and comprehensive, this volume clarifies many questions under dispute and modifies or makes untenable a number of previously-held beliefs.

Adams, Joseph Quincy, *A Life of William Shakespeare,* Houghton Mifflin, Boston and New York, 1923.

A biography which touches all phases of Shakespeare's life, although attempting little in the way of critical evaluation. Still the most readable and useful book for the general reader.

Baker, George Pierce, *The Development of Shakespeare as a Dramatist,* Macmillan, New York, 1914.

A stimulating and highly valuable work about Shakespeare as a craftsman. However, in some technical matters, such as playhouse construction, it is now misleading.

Bradley, A. C., *Shakespearean Tragedy,* Macmillan, London, 1905.

Still the outstanding work in this field, which, however, involves much opinion and conjecture.

Brandes, Georg, *William Shakespeare,* Macmillan, London, 1924.

A colorful, vigorous, and enjoyable life by one of the world's great critics. However, it presents a personal view of the dramatist which is open to challenge at many points.

Brown, Ivor J. C., and Fearon, George, *This Shakespeare Industry,* Harper, New York, 1939.

An amusing and instructive account of the activities that have developed as a result of Shakespeare's world reputation. It contains a useful survey of the many disputes about authorship.

Chambers, E. K., *The Elizabethan Stage,* Clarendon Press, Oxford, 1923. 4 vols.

The standard work on the playhouses and player companies of Shakespeare's day. Comprehensive and valuable, although at some points dated by more recent publications.

Chambers, E. K., *William Shakespeare: A Study of Facts and Problems,* Clarendon Press, Oxford, 1930. 2 vols.

Highly valuable for its admirable summary of our factual knowledge about Shakespeare, and for the texts of original documents, or quotations from these, which it contains.

Craig, Hardin, *An Interpretation of Shakespeare,* Dryden Press, New York, 1948.

A scholarly, readable, and stimulating interpretation of Shakespeare's writings.

Fripp, Edgar I., *Shakespeare, Man and Artist,* Oxford Press, London, 1938. 2 vols.

A work characterized by personal bias, and rambling as to organization, but valuable because of the author's wide knowledge, particularly of the Stratford aspects of Shakespeare's life.

Harrison, G. B., *The Elizabethan Journals,* Macmillan, New York, 1939.

An imaginary diary, although based entirely on fact, which gives a highly valuable picture of Shakespeare's times.

Smart, John Semple, *Shakespeare: Truth and Tradition,* Longmans, New York, 1928.

A biographical essay, finely conceived and written, which corrects many misconceptions about Shakespeare, and adds greatly to our positive sense of his art and personality.

Spencer, Hazleton, *The Art and Life of William Shakespeare,* Harcourt, Brace, New York, 1940.

An independent, interesting, comprehensive and scholarly survey of Shakespeare, with a good bibliography and a valuable account of stage productions of the plays from the seventeenth century to the present day.

Van Doren, Mark, *Shakespeare,* Holt, New York, 1939.

An appreciation of the plays and poems which is often both original and stimulating.

Wilson, J. Dover, *The Essential Shakespeare: A Biographical Adventure,* Cambridge Press, Cambridge, 1932.

A vital and imaginative effort to give a sense of Shakespeare as person and artist.

Wilson, J. Dover, *The Fortunes of Falstaff,* Cambridge Press, Cambridge, 1932.

A vigorous interpretation of the greatest of Shakespeare's comic characters, which will modify or revise many traditional ideas about Falstaff.

THE IMPOSTORS

A POSTSCRIPT

THE IMPOSTORS

A POSTSCRIPT

WHILE *To Meet Will Shakespeare* was being planned and written, I was frequently asked a question by those who heard of the book. "What are you going to say about Bacon?" it ran. Or, in varied form: "What about the Earl of Oxford? Is it true that he was the real Shakespeare?"

I was startled by the persistence with which this type of question recurred. It was put by perhaps every third person who discussed the projected volume with me. One was a nationally known radio commentator. Another headed the information service of an English-speaking nation. Still others were writers. Together they were convincing proof of a widespread and persistent doubt that William Shakespeare wrote the works standing under his name.

Accordingly, it seemed desirable to add a brief section to this book dealing with the question of Shakespearean authorship. I cannot go into that question exhaustively. The arguments for "real Shakespeares" as set forth in magazine articles, tracts and volumes would make a mountain of material. To discuss them fully would require a long book, and *To Meet Will Shakespeare* is already long. Yet this is possible: to outline the authorship controversy, to show the nature of the proof that exists for and against the reality of Shakespeare as a writer, and to examine in detail the case of one candidate put forward to supplant him. Most readers may then be able to make a judgment for themselves. Those still in doubt will be in a better position to continue a study of the question.

2

The thesis of any man or woman who argues that Shakespeare did not write Shakespeare can be put in a single sentence. "The works called William Shakespeare's," it runs, "were not written by anyone bearing that name, but by another person (or persons) who used that name because he (or they) did not wish to admit, or could not, the authorship of the plays and poems."

That is a fairly simple statement. It is essentially the same whether advanced by the advocates of Bacon, Oxford, or any other candidate.

Two considerations which affect this assertion, but do not involve direct proof for or against it, should first be noted.

One concerns the time at which the non-Shakespearean theory of authorship was put forward. It first appeared in Herbert Lawrence's *The Life and Adventures of Common Sense,* in 1769.[1] Nobody took the suggestion seriously; and it was not until 1848 that a true beginning of the authorship controversy was made. J. C. Hart, in his *Romance of Yachting,* repeated the assertion that Sir Francis Bacon had written the plays and poems called Shakespeare's. The concealed authorship theory now came alive. It gained wide popularity first in the United States, then later in England and on the Continent. However, not until the early nineteen-hundreds were a number of "Shakespeares" first put in nomination.

Naturally, the lateness of these challenges to Shakespeare's authorship does not prove them unsound. Still, it casts a certain suspicion upon them. If Shakespeare were not Shakespeare, why was his own age ignorant of the fact, or the succeeding age? After a time gap of from 200 to 300 years, can men today be sure of matters unknown to those of a remote period?

The other preliminary consideration relates to the number of claimants put forward as the "real" author or authors. Altogether, more than a dozen have been suggested. We may list six of these, as follows:

1. Francis Bacon, Lord Verulam, Viscount St. Albans (1561-1626), philosopher, essayist, statesman. First suggested in 1769, and supported by such writers as Ignatius Donnelly, Delia Bacon, Sir Edward Durning Lawrence, and Mrs. E. W. Gallup.

[1] The supporters of Bacon assert that his authorship was hinted at from 1597 onward. See *Baconia,* January, 1935, Bertrand G. Theobald. Of course, since any hints that may have been offered were never recognized either by the public or by scholars, for all practical purposes they did not exist.

2. Roger Manners, fifteenth Earl of Rutland (1576-1612), descendant of Richard Plantagenet, father of Edward IV. First nominated in 1907, and supported by Professor Celestin Demblon, Lewis F. Bostlemann, and others.

3. William Stanley, sixth Earl of Derby (1561-1642), a peer also of royal blood, first proposed in 1919 by Professor Abel Lefranc, and approved by R. M. Lucas and others.

4. Edward de Vere, seventeenth Earl of Oxford (1550-1604), Great Chamberlain of England, poet, patron of writers and actors. First proposed in 1920 by J. Thomas Looney, and supported by Percy Allen, B. R. Ward, B. M. Ward, Dr. Gerald Rendall and Eva Lee Clark.

5. Sir Edward Dyer (1543-1607), first proposed by Alden Brooks in 1943.

6. Authorship by a group of writers. Originally suggested by Delia Bacon in 1857, and revived in 1931 by Gilbert Slater. Among those suggested for such groups are Marlowe, Oxford, Bacon, Raleigh, Lord Paget, Lord Buckhurst, and the Countess of Pembroke.

There are additional candidates. One is "Anne Whately," and we shall glance at her case later. Perhaps the most baffling anti-Shakespearean campaign was waged by Sir George Greenwood, a British Member of Parliament, who refused to name any "real" author, but merely argued that Shakespeare himself was not satisfactory, and that the problem of authorship needed further study.

By the professions of their own apologists, all but one of the above candidacies are false ones. Unless we accept the group theory, or Greenwood's, we can have only one author. If it is Bacon, it is not Rutland, Derby, or Oxford. If it is Oxford, it is none of the other five. The mere number of claimants may well raise the question: "If there are six cases to be made for various authors, and five cannot be accepted, is any of them sound?"

The variety in age among the candidates also promotes skepticism. Did Sir Edward Dyer write no plays until he was 46 (if we accept the dating of the dramas as from 1590 on)? Could Oxford, dying nine years before Shakespeare's last work was produced, really have penned the nine tragedies and tragicomedies none of which was presented until after he was in the grave? Did Rutland write chronicle plays at the age of 14? Did Derby live on for 28 years after his last play was first enacted?

The champions of each candidate naturally have answers to such questions. We shall consider some of these. Meanwhile, the very number of proposed "Shakespeares," as much as the lateness of their appearance on the literary scene, provokes skepticism and requires some kind of convincing explanation.

However, there are more explicit obligations which the challengers must meet. Four in particular should be listed:

1. *The challengers must show that William Shakespeare lacked the necessary qualities for writing his own works.* For if it cannot be shown beyond reasonable question that the supposed author was incapable of this task, the greatest of reasons for discovering another author disappears. Most supporters of "concealed authors" tacitly or openly admit that they have no case until the "Stratford" Shakespeare is fully discredited.

2. *The challengers must offer a theory of authorship which satisfactorily explains away the many appearances of plays and poems under Shakespeare's name.* This obligation is as clear as 1. We have work after work printed as Shakespeare's. Unless there is proof that this credit was falsely given, it is strong evidence for the orthodox view of authorship.

3. *They must also explain away a long series of statements and acts which confirm Shakespeare's authorship of his own works.* We shall see later what these acts and statements are. They comprise even stronger proof of Shakespeare's identity as a writer than the appearance of his name on a succession of title pages.

4. *Finally, each group of challengers must show positive as well as negative proof that their candidate was the author.* This is axiomatic. Even if great doubt can be cast upon Shakespeare's authorship, some kind of positive evidence, in fact, stronger positive evidence, is needed to establish the case of any substitute, especially when we have so many candidates.

3

Let us first look at the charge that Shakespeare lacked qualifications for writing his own works. A great cloud of allegations has been tossed up by those who have tried to prove this assertion. It will be necessary to strip these of the persuasive eloquençe in which they are usually dressed, and examine them as a series of brief statements. Here are the greater number of the "proofs" of Shakespeare's incapacity as an author:

1. His parents were ignorant, unlettered persons.
2. We have no evidence that Shakespeare ever attended school.
3. According to Aubrey, he left school early—a proof of scanty education (this somewhat impairs the force of 2).
4. His signatures show that he wrote with difficulty and probably read with as much.
5. According to Ben Jonson, he had "small Latin and less Greek," but the works of Shakespeare show a man of wide and accurate classical learning.
6. He was the son of a butcher and apprenticed to a butcher—further evidence of lowly station and accomplishments.
7. The deer-stealing episode and the holding of horses at the playhouse door are evidences of his irresponsible and humble character.
8. He lacked the knowledge of law that the plays and poems reveal.
9. As a tradesman's son, William Shakespeare of Stratford must be presumed to have been ignorant of chivalric sports; but the author of the Shakespearean works knew the terms and usages of all the noble pastimes—falconry, the chase, tourneys, and dueling.
10. The "Stratford Shakespeare" lacked opportunity as a youth to know good speech and manners, and to get an inbred familiarity (shown in the plays and poems of Shakespeare) with court usages.
11. From 1596 to 1604, a period during which many important Shakespearean plays appeared, Shakespeare the actor and man of affairs was too busy with practical matters to have written these dramas. The purchase and repair of New Place, several lawsuits,

the acquisition of other properties, and a certain amount of trading in local produce would have left inadequate time for writing after his work as a player was completed.

12. We have facts about Shakespeare as actor and man of affairs. Were he also Shakespeare the writer, would we not have evidences of literary activity in letters written to or by him, in his will, or in references to him by his contemporaries?

Those who have read the foregoing chapters of this book will recognize at once that many of these statements are doubtful or untrue.

In Chapters I-IV the "gentle" character of the Arden family and the highly responsible position of John Shakespeare have been indicated, together with his probable ability to read and write.

His son's schooling, as also brought out, is well indicated by such evidence as we possess. It may be pointed out here that Richard Quyney, like Will Shakespeare the son of a merchant and town officer, cannot be shown to have attended the King's Free School, either, since no records for the school exist. But the presumption is that the two as boys received similar educations, and Quyney wrote easily in Latin and English.

The argument that Shakespeare's signatures indicate a poorly educated person ignores the wretched handwriting of many famous men, including Napoleon and Horace Greeley. Also, it takes no account of the apparently routine and hasty character of three signatures, nor of the fact that the remaining three seem to have been written when the playwright was ill.

The "butcher boy" and deer-stealing and horse-holding legends have been dealt with in earlier chapters. Even if all true, they prove nothing as to Shakespeare's ability. Ben Jonson worked as a bricklayer and served as a common soldier, and yet became both playwright and notable scholar.

Knowledge of law and chivalric sports, as we have seen, could have been acquired by Shakespeare either through actual service in an office and at a manor house, or by observation and reading.

The idea that the few business and legal activities of Shakespeare during the period of 1596-1604 would have prevented his writing is nothing short of preposterous. There is no evidence that the sum of such activities would have taken more than a few weeks' time. It could easily have been handled on summer visits to Stratford and by letter.

As to evidences of his literary life in the form of letters, we are simply unfortunate in having none. But we lack them for a host of other authors of his day. It would have been fortunate had Shakespeare mentioned books and papers in his will, but it is understandable why he did not. After specific bequests, all his property went to Susanna, and she and her husband were the only members of the immediate family likely to have been interested in "literary remains." Dr. Hall may have had personal instructions from Shakespeare about them.

Finally, as to the entire question of training and experience, we can profitably ask what was the endowment of other dramatists. We know that Jonson was the stepson of a bricklayer, and never had a university education. Other writers of the day had modest origins. Marlowe was the son of a shoemaker, Kyd of a scrivener, Chettle of a dyer. Furthermore, Kyd, Chettle and Munday, in addition to Jonson, were not university men. Yet all these playwrights, and others of humble birth and limited education like Dekker and Rowley, became playwrights, and some devised dramas about kings and statesmen which no one found lacking in a knowledge of courtly life.

All these facts being considered, we can scarcely conclude that Shakespeare lacked either opportunity or capacity for becoming a great writer. The evidence rather indicates that his family, his education, his environment and his experience were favorable to his becoming the author of the works that bear his name. When it is remembered that the burden of proof is upon those who challenge him, the plea that we must look for another author because he lacked the capacity to become one must be rejected as lacking wholly the support that would entitle it to serious consideration.

4

In the Elizabethan and Jacobean eras, Shakespeare's name appeared frequently as an author. Of 19 quarto editions of the plays, 15 bore his name on the title pages. *Venus and Adonis* and *The Rape of Lucrece* both contained dedications signed by him. The *Sonnets,* published in

1609, were "Shake-speare's." The Folio Edition of 1623 credited him with 36 plays.

To such evidence the testimony of Francis Meres should be added. It will be remembered that in 1598 he listed 12 plays, 2 narrative poems, and the sonnets as the works of William Shakespeare.

The total of such pronouncements is impressive. What proof has been produced to cancel them?

Two types of "proof" have been attempted. One rests upon the assumption that the social or political eminence of the true author made it impossible for him to acknowledge the Shakespearean writings. Therefore, runs the explanation, this person used the "ignorant player" as a mask. Carefully hidden during Bacon's, Oxford's, Rutland's or another's lifetime, the secret playwright and poet went to his grave unrecognized. Only hundreds of years after his death was he at length revealed by the ingenuity and diligence of his present advocates.

The evidence offered in support of such argument is always indirect and circumstantial. The case really depends upon the assertion that Shakespeare was incapable of authorship, and on a consequent willingness on the part of the reading public to accept a bold conjecture and a few facts that seem to confirm it. We have seen that Shakespeare's alleged incapacity has not been proved and is not even plausible. Nevertheless, let us look more closely at the suggestion that a real author might have hidden his identity because to acknowledge plays and poems would have been damaging to his reputation and career.

It is true that plays lacked standing as literature, and that highly placed persons might wish to avoid acknowledging responsibility for them. Still, they did not always do so. Take, for example, Thomas Sackville. With Thomas Norton he was coauthor of *Gorboduc*. At the time he helped to write this drama, Sackville was a nobleman and a Member of Parliament. Norton was a young lawyer not of noble blood. Sackville could easily have let his collaborator take full credit for their joint composition. He chose instead to claim his share. Nor did the act seem to injure his reputation. He was soon made a baron, and later still Earl of Dorset!

Naturally it does not follow that every nobleman would wish to acknowledge the authorship of plays. Bacon or Oxford might have felt differently from Sackville, although Oxford let enough be known about his skill at playmaking so that Francis Meres in 1598 named him as one of the "best for comedy." As I shall show later, that was probably a bow to rank rather than to artistic skill, but it indicates that Oxford did not object to being known as a playwright.

As a matter of fact, were a nobleman writing Shakespeare's plays, it is difficult to see how he could have concealed his identity. At any one time from 1590 to 1613 (the time span of the Shakespearean dramas) there were never a dozen notable dramatists writing. The actors in all London seldom if ever numbered more than sixty in those years. The nobles keenly interested in plays were a mere handful. In this small world it would have been difficult for a peer to have written thirty-odd comedies and tragedies without the fact being well known. If well known, we should expect to find a number of allusions to it. Again, it would have been still more difficult if not wholly impossible for a player who was not a genius to act the part of one. Could the kind of Shakespeare the iconoclasts picture have deceived his fellow actors? Could he have imposed upon other writers like Jonson, Marlowe, Beaumont, Chettle, Chapman? Could he have collaborated with such men, as Shakespeare is supposed to have done? Could he have made last-minute revisions, or coached actors (a tradition as to Shakespeare's work which was explicit in the late sixteen-hundreds)? Could he have done these things for twenty-odd years? The whole story begins to shake and buckle as soon as it is closely examined.

Some iconoclasts recognized the difficulty of this type of story, and soon a second and different one appeared. The real author, it was asserted, used a "mask" for reasons of national security.

I shall discuss this theory later, in examining the positive case of the one claimant to Shakespeare's work whom I shall consider in detail. Its soundness can then be weighed fully. In my opinion, it is no stronger than the first explanation.

Yet as to either of them, a further question must be raised. Why was Shakespeare's name appended to the signed dedications of *Venus and Adonis* and *Lucrece*? These poems appeared in print before any plays credited to Shakespeare. Why was an "ignorant player" set up as the author of these when a fictitious name would have done as well? And in any case, was there cause to conceal the authorship of poems?

Clearly not for reasons of national security. For social reasons, then? The record tells us that this was not the case. Wyatt and Surrey were both men of rank and family. So was Sir Philip Sidney. So was Edward de Vere, Earl of Oxford, for whom twenty-four poems were published under his name or initials. James I of Scotland did not disdain the reputation of poet. A poem survives signed by Queen Elizabeth, and we have a number from her cousin Mary of Scotland, and from Mary's son James (James VI of Scotland and James I of England).

It is true that the noble or royal poet did not take his poems to a printer. But he showed them to his friends, who "took copies," and the lyrics were published. In the case of Sidney, *Astrophel and Stella* appeared after his death. The fact to be noted is that such poems *were* published, and were properly credited.

Thus, if the "real author" of Shakespeare's poems were noble, and hid his authorship, he was unique among all the noble writers we know. He may have been unique. But the very natural way in which Shakespeare's two verse narratives appeared, with a fellow townsman as the printer, with their wholly natural dedications, and with large dashes of Warwickshire spelling, casts a sharp suspicion on a plea that they were anyone's but Shakespeare's. So, too, does their reception. Had the name of the author been merely a mask, we might expect some knowledge of the fact, and some recognizable reference to it.

5

Let us now look at certain statements, acts, and circumstances which show us that Shakespeare was an author.

A number of these are trivial. Greene's "Shakescene" comment and Chettle's apology to Shakespeare in 1592 tell us very little about him, but they do not tally with the possibility that he could have been lending his name to someone else. Greene says that the player from Stratford was a man of all work. We get a picture of a literary beginner trying his wings, perhaps chiefly by recasting the plays of others. Chettle's comment indicates, however, that Shakespeare had done something all his own, or that his touch was recognized. For he speaks of the young man's "facetious grace in writing, that approves his art." Both pictures are fleeting, but both show us an author.

Rowe, the first formal biographer of the playwright, adds two details in his references to Southampton's gift of £1,000, and to the Stratford writer's part in getting *Every Man in His Humor* accepted by the Chamberlain's Men. For both these items we have only Rowe's authority, but neither has been disproved. Both picture a writer.

We may pass over the many voices lifted in praise of *Venus and Adonis* and *Lucrece* in the years just following their appearance. They comprise a body of evidence that Shakespeare was known as a writer. We may do no more than note the enthusiasm shown by university students in their plays from 1597 to 1601, in one of which Burbage and Kemp speak of Shakespeare as a dramatist. To the students the playwright was more than a shadow. "O sweet Master Shakespeare! I'll have his picture in my study at the court!" exclaims one. This sounds like a reference to a flesh-and-blood man. And again, when Francis Meres speaks of the author's "sugared sonnets among his private friends," we seem to get a personal touch, as if Meres had known some of these friends or had been one himself.

The monument erected in the Stratford church soon after Shakespeare's death represents an act which proclaims William of Stratford an author. As pointed out in Chapter XXVI, the very pose of the figure is emphatic. The verses reflect high confidence in Shakespeare's genius as a writer. Were the men responsible for this tribute completely deceived as to who Shakespeare was, and as to his abilities? That seems impossible. Were they in league with the "real Shakespeare" to perpetuate a fraud? That is quite as fantastic.

An attempt has been made in recent years to show that the bust now in Stratford was wholly changed when it was repaired in the eighteenth century. Fortunately the records tell us that the chief care of those in charge of the work was to see that the original was in no way altered. The repairs seem to have been trivial.

Like the monument, the Folio of 1623 gives us ample evidence that Shakespeare was both actor and playwright. The testimony of Heminges and Condell, of Jonson, of Digges, has been rehearsed in

Chapter XXVI. It covered many points.

The very date of the Folio confirms the orthodox position as to authorship. It was brought out just seven years after Shakespeare's death, and must have been in preparation several years earlier. Had Oxford or Dyer written the plays, the date should have been earlier, for they died in 1604 and 1607, respectively. Had Bacon or Derby been the author, it should have been later, for Bacon lived on until 1626 and Derby until 1642.

But let us come back to Ben Jonson. His verses on Shakespeare's picture and his glowing tribute to Shakespeare the writer are notable in themselves. Jonson knew Shakespeare well. The latter is "my beloved," "my Shakespeare," "my gentle Shakespeare." He is identified with Stratford by the phrase, "sweet swan of Avon."

The only answer that has been made to this and the other testimony of the Folio has been that the entire publication, as respects authorship of the plays, was a gigantic pretense. "Jonson," says the Oxfordite Percy Allen darkly, "was writing under orders he dared not disobey." The reader must form his own judgment as to whether or not, twenty-two years after Oxford's death, this is a reasonable assertion.

However, we still have other testimony which indicates whether or not Jonson's comment was a pretense. In the winter of 1618-19 he visited Scotland and spent the Christmas season of several weeks with the Scottish writer William Drummond, at the latter's home near Edinburgh. Drummond made a record of Jonson's conversations.

In this record stands Jonson's remark that "Shakespeare wanted art." There, too, appears his gibe at the "seacoast of Bohemia" in *The Winter's Tale.* Clearly he spoke of the prominent King's Man as a fellow writer, somewhat lacking in dramatic skill and precise information. Would such remarks apply either to Oxford or to Bacon? (Remember that, according to Allen, Jonson knew the "true" identity of Shakespeare.) Again, the author of *Volpone* showered Drummond with spicy gossip about Donne, Marston, Sidney, Drayton, Daniel and others, and even professed to know about Queen Elizabeth's sex life! If he had such a morsel as the knowledge that Shakespeare was a mere "front," would he have withheld it?

We have other and later comments from Jonson. In his *Timber, or*

Discoveries, published in 1642, and written in the sixteen-thirties, he has a note entitled *De Shakespeare Nostrat*—"concerning our Shakespeare." Here occurs the comment quoted in Chapter XXVI concerning the writing habits of his dead friend, and his loving him and honoring him "on this side idolatry, as much as any." Jonson goes on:

He was (indeed) honest, and of an open and free nature; had an excellent phantasy, brave notions, and gentle expressions; wherein he flowed with that facility, that sometimes it was necessary he should be stopped: *Sufflaminandus erat,* as Augustus said of Haterius. His wit was in his own power; would the rule of it had been so, too. Many times he fell into those things could not escape laughter: as when he said in the person of Caesar, one speaking to him, "Caesar, thou dost me wrong." He replied, "Caesar did never wrong but with just cause," and such like, which were ridiculous [Shakespeare apparently corrected this passage]. But he redeemed his vices with his virtues. There was ever more in him to be praised than to be pardoned.

This note deals with a social equal and a fellow writer. It all but shows us Shakespeare in his shirt sleeves, writing. It is about as conclusive evidence as one could ask that Jonson was not commenting upon a name used to mask someone else, but upon the actual man with the pen.

Finally, we cannot ignore the way in which the plays fit into the life of Shakespeare the man from Stratford. In *Love's Labor's Lost,* in *A Midsummer Night's Dream,* in *As You Like It* we have country scenes that are all true Warwickshire. The actor's calling of the author is suggested by many references to the stage and acting. That calling is revealed again in the *Sonnets,* where it is a matter for awkwardness and shame. In the *Sonnets* again we find the author riding long distances on horseback, clearly alone. This was a known experience for Shakespeare as he journeyed from London to Stratford and back; but it was an unlikely one for any of the pretenders. Oxford would always have had attendants.

Many other passages in the plays and poems fit into what we know of Shakespeare's personal life. He shows a detailed knowledge of glove-making, his father's occupation. He shows, just after his son's death, a deep interest in young Prince Arthur. He reveals, just as he was super-intending the repair of New Place, a concern with architecture. Dozens of further parallels have been pointed out.

This immense array of acts, comments, and parallels needs more than fantastic conjectures and whispers of planned deception to convince a realistic reader that they should be set aside. They are so numerous, varied, and interconfirmed that they stand above the froth of adverse comment like a great rock of reality.

6

I stated at the beginning of this Postscript that I would examine in detail the case for one candidate whose supporters have put him forward as the real author of the Shakespearean plays and poems. The time has come to consider such a case.

Francis Bacon was the first person to be proposed as a substitute for William Shakespeare, and in my opinion he is the most gifted of all those suggested. However, his position is far weaker now than it was fifty years ago. His natural bent for science, law, and statecraft, the improbability that he could have found time for writing a great body of plays and poems while discharging his heavy duties to the government and writing the books known to be his, the great differences in his prose style and Shakepeare's—such considerations have worked against him. The attempt to prove that he left cipher messages in the plays revealing his authorship has collapsed under deserved ridicule. Finally, the most active candidate today is unquestionably Edward de Vere, Earl of Oxford, whose supporters must now be regarded as both more numerous and more ingenious than the Baconians. Accordingly, I shall consider the case for him.

When J. Thomas Looney, a retired schoolmaster, set forth the case for Oxford in 1920, his first assumption was that William Shakespeare could not have been the author of such works as are attributed to him. In support of this belief Looney put forward most of the arguments and assertions about Shakespeare's family, education, and experience that have already been dealt with in section 3 of this Postscript. I shall not refer to these again except as they require special attention as part of other evidence.

Looney passed from his first contention to a proposal that, since William Shakespeare cannot be accepted as the author of the plays and poems, we should study these works carefully, and deduce from them the chief characteristics of the person who wrote them. He himself found that these characteristics were a marked familiarity with classical literature, a considerable expert acquaintance with law, a knowledge of aristocratic sports, and a full acquaintance with noble society and speech, and with Court procedures. He therefore concluded that the writer he sought was an aristocrat. Casting his eye over the noblemen of Elizabeth's time he found Edward de Vere. In his opinion the Earl was exactly the kind of person who might have written *As You Like It, Henry V,* and *Hamlet.* Finally, he studied Oxford's life for evidence to support his strong but still tentative belief.

I myself am inclined to distrust any personal portrait of an unknown author built up from a study of his works, however searching. Many writers have traits in common, and these may spring from a variety of causes. Moreover, a creative artist often pours out in verse or drama ideas and feelings which he as a person does not reveal. Writing can express a hidden as well as a visible man. However, let us consider the traits Looney found in the works of Shakespeare as characteristic of the man who wrote them.

In section 3 I have already pointed out that a knowledge of law, aristocratic sports, and the ways of royal and noble persons do not necessarily indicate noble birth. I have shown there and in the early chapters of this book that William Shakespeare of Stratford could have acquired such knowledge. Let us bear this in mind, and then let us ask if we should not add further characteristics to Mr. Looney's list as given above. I suggest adding the following qualities as clearly attributable to the author of the Shakespearean plays and poems:

1. A keen sense of humor, including wit, high good spirits, and an ability to laugh at himself.
2. A knowledge of the middle and lower classes as well as of the higher. This knowledge is apparently gained from the "inside."

3. A knowledge of small-town and country ways, including non-aristocratic sports and trades and customs.

4. An instinct for adjusting to life rather than for fighting it and rebelling against it.

Most reasonable persons with a full knowledge of Shakespeare's writings will, I am sure, agree that these four traits were apparent in whoever wrote them. Looney includes none of them.

Having added to the characteristics of the "real author," let us consider how they fit the Earl of Oxford.

From what we know of him I should say that Edward de Vere was a man of fuller classical knowledge than the plays and poems of Shakespeare show, a man with less legal interest (there is almost no evidence of such interest in Oxford's poems or letters), and a man with a more special knowledge of "chivalric" sports, particularly those related to forms of combat. Any careful reader of Oxford's life, about which our knowledge is not too great, will, I think, find ample evidence to support what I say. I shall not go into these questions, however, as I think it at least arguable that Oxford matches fairly well in these particular traits the man we find suggested in the Shakespearean works. Certainly the Earl had a full knowledge of courtly speech and courtly procedure.

In all other respects I feel that the evidence indicates that he was a very different person from the author of the Shakespeare plays and poems.

Aside from Meres's reference to him as "best for comedy," there is no indication that he had a sense of humor. And with respect to that reference we learn from Puttenham that any comedies written by Oxford were unknown to readers of the day. They are unknown to us. There is only the faintest trace of humor in the poems generally conceded to be the Earl's. In a considerable number of letters, there is none whatever. We have knowledge of many things done by Oxford. A few are gracious. But most of them paint for us a picture of an egotistical, pettish, rash, violent and arrogant man.

There is Oxford killing an undercook with a fencing sword at the age of seventeen. Burghley seems to have had difficulty in presenting this as a case of self-defense. There is Oxford dashing off to Brussels without the permission of the Queen. There is Oxford confessing in his early twenties to debts of £6,000 (about $450,000 in our money values). Later, abroad, we find a young man demanding more money of his father-in-law, and reproaching him for paying creditors. "If I cannot pay them as I would, yet as I can I will, but *preferring my own necessity to theirs*" (Italics mine). The traveler returns to suspect and quarrel with his wife, apparently without just cause. For years he refuses to see or communicate with her. He engages in a famous quarrel with Sir Philip Sidney. He refuses to dance at the Queen's request before several foreign ambassadors. He writes constantly and solemnly of his place and honor. Apparently he annoyed and disgusted other courtiers. One of them, Gilbert Talbot, son of the Earl of Shrewsbury, in telling of Oxford's rivalry with others for the Queen's favor, remarked: "If it were not for his fickle head he would pass any of them shortly."

Such items are the typical ones we have about Oxford, aside from the report that he was interested in letters and the drama, and was a generous patron. Never is there a sign of Oxford's laughing at his difficulties. From what we know of him it seems impossible that he could have created the comic characters of Shakespeare with their wit, variety and abounding good spirits.

There can be little likelihood of this self-centered, arrogant man knowing and understanding the middle classes, studying the small towns and their ways and trades and pastimes. As a youth, Edward de Vere lacked opportunity for observing men outside a narrow circle. A noble ward, he lived with Burghley in the latter's enclosed estate near London. His daily regimen of study and exercise was severe. At the university and at Gray's Inn he was freer; but he was always a peer, always attended, always faced with the obligations of an aristocrat. Evidently he practiced dancing and various forms of combat, for soon he was highly proficient in both. If in the country, he hawked or hunted. In short, his very position limited sharply his opportunities for a broad life, and his inclinations were apparently in the direction of such pleasures as he shared with others of his own class. It is difficult to imagine his finding time or desire for an acquaintance with glovemaking, the sports of village boys and their elders, the ways of the farm and village housewife.

Finally, Oxford lacks completely the philosophical poise that we find in Shakespeare. If there is any one characteristic that is ever present in the latter, it is the knowledge that man must eventually adjust to even the most tragiç situations. Shakespeare knew that the adjustment must be both inward and outward. We see this deep recognition in both sonnets and plays, time and time again.

But Oxford's life is a continuing record of a failure to adjust. He could not adjust himself to his income. He could not adjust to restrictions upon his traveling. He could not adjust to a faithful and patient wife. He could not adjust to his religion; he turned Roman Catholic, then soon turned violently upon the Catholics.

One could cite further episodes and comments from the somewhat meager record of Edward de Vere to show his dissatisfactions, his lack of consideration for others, his bursts of petulance and anger. A kind of sub-Byronic note sounds in some of his poems, such as these lines which apparently refer to his domestic difficulties:

> Fain would I sing, but fury makes me fret,
> And rage hath sworn to seek revenge of wrong;
> My mazéd mind in malice so is set
> As Death shall daunt my deadly dolors long;
> Patience perforce is such a pinching pain
> As die I will, or suffer wrong again.

This is an artificial, whipped-up kind of emotion, not the sublimation of pain which we find in the *Sonnets* when Shakespeare laments. Oxford in his attitude toward life was a ranter and a self-absorbed egoist, a little man in a big place. Philosophically, he and Shakespeare had little in common.

If the characters of the two are so unlike, what remains?

There is the allegation that Oxford wrote or helped to write the plays of Shakespeare as part of a service done for the national security.

This suggestion was advanced some years after the Vere case was first presented, apparently as the result of a discovery that in 1586 the Earl was granted a yearly pension of £1,000, which seems to have been paid in the beginning at least from a special secret service fund. Gilbert Slater in his book *Seven Shakespeares* (1931) built up a daring theory on the fact of this pension. The only credible explanation for it, he argued, was that Oxford was paid to render a notable service. This, he suggested, was the organization of a group of authors who would use the drama as an instrument of propaganda. Their plays would promote patriotic feeling and defend the Queen against her domestic and foreign enemies. The activity, to be effective, must be secret. Accordingly, the Earl went into a kind of semiretirement from public affairs. Slater believed that he cooperated with six other writers, and that one important result was the body of work known as Shakespeare's. Regular Oxfordites are not inclined to share the credit so freely with possible collaborators.

I myself have no particular theory as to why the Earl of Oxford received a pension of £1,000 for some twenty years; for it was continued to the time of his death, a year after the accession of James. B. M. Ward, himself an Oxfordite, suggests in his competent life of the Earl that the pension was granted with the understanding that he should maintain a troupe, with authors, to produce plays for the Court. This is a possible explanation. So is another to the effect that in some unknown fashion Oxford was helping to safeguard the Queen. He had already furnished information about the dangerous activities of certain English Roman Catholics in the pay of Spain. However, these explanations are conjectures, like Mr. Slater's. I cite them only to show that his suggestion is by no means the only conceivable one. Indeed, I feel certain that if a scholar one day digs from Elizabethan records the true reason for the pension, it will *not* be that Edward de Vere was paid to organize propaganda in the form of plays.

Why should such a task have been assigned?

To be sure, both the Queen and the Privy Council recognized the value of having the support of the nation. They sought it. They issued proclamations, instructed preachers what to preach, and summoned parliaments to vote aid. Such measures were successful. No special payments were made to have them carried out.

Now, the player-companies were under the control of lords who in turn were subservient to the Queen. The Privy Council regulated both their number and their right to perform. In a feudal sense the actors and theater owners were thus Elizabeth's creatures. They, along with their many writers, would have leaped at a word to render her a patriotic service. The Queen or the Council would have shaken with laughter at the idea of paying anyone to organize them for an obligation they owed.

But let us assume the extreme of improbability, and say that Oxford was paid to create, intensify and sustain patriotic feeling through drama. Let us assume further that the Shakespearean plays were a chief result of his efforts. Do these indicate that he earned his pension?

If we take the dramas performed between the years 1590 and 1604, inclusive (the Earl died in the latter year), we find that they fall into two groups. Nine of them are based on English history and are patriotic in feeling. Seventeen, including the comedies, the two Roman plays *Titus* and *Julius Caesar,* and the three tragedies *Romeo and Juliet, Hamlet,* and *Othello,* are of a miscellaneous character but cannot possibly be regarded as patriotic or as dealing with the national crises that marked the last dozen years of Elizabeth's reign.

Thus if Oxford, with or without collaborators, were using the drama for propaganda, and employing the name of Shakespeare as a "mask," he was carrying out his commission in a strange manner. Even the historical plays should not have been more than fillers in a truly aggressive campaign, which, one would expect, would strike sharply at domestic traitors and the Spanish danger. If Elizabeth were paying £1,000 a year for propaganda against active enemies, she would have been outraged at this feeble effort. Invariably she demanded full value for her money.

One of the ways in which Looney sought to build up his case for Oxford was by calling attention to the latter's poems. In fact, he issued a volume of them containing no fewer than 48 lyrics, although experts had never previously credited Oxford with more than 24.

How was the number doubled? Looney achieved his feat by appropriating for Edward de Vere poems previously supposed to have been the work of other poets. For example, he took all the songs in John Lyly's plays—13 of them. He argued that "Lyly has shown himself in some of his work to have been noticeably deficient in lyrical capacity" [just how, I for one am not aware]. He then pointed out that Oxford, a poet, was Lyly's patron. Then the leap came. "It is not an unreasonable assumption . . . that they [the poems] were a contribution made by Oxford to Lyly's dramas"!

Emboldened by this achievement, Looney added 11 more poems which hitherto had been assigned to Sir Walter Raleigh, Marlowe, Queen Elizabeth, and others. In one collection they had been signed "Ignoto." Therefore they must be Oxford's!

The reader can make his own judgment upon such literary gymnastics. They might well raise the question of whether or not the poems signed by Oxford were really his. Perhaps Lyly or another was the true author!

However, assuming them to be genuine, let us consider the argument of the Oxfordite Percy Allen that there are striking parallels between passages in these lyrics and certain passages in Shakespeare's works, and that a presumption is thus created that the Earl wrote the latter.

Allen finds in Oxford's "Desire" the lines

> The lively lark stretched forth his wing,
> The messenger of morning bright,

and compares it with Romeo's words,

> It was the lark, the herald of the morn,

concluding that the similarity is evidence tending to show that one man wrote both quotations. Then Chaucer was Shakespeare, too, for he tells us that

> The bisy larke, the messager of day,
> Saluëth in hir song the morwe gray,

and Spenser is as much the "real poet," for he announces that

> The merry lark her matins sings aloft

in the gray before dawn.

In a similar fashion, other alleged parallels prove nothing except that a certain literary convention was commonly used, or that a certain type of sentiment was popular at a given time. Many Elizabethan writers give us passages that can be paralleled rather strikingly by lines in the *Sonnets*.

Again, Allen finds evidence that Oxford wrote the Shakespearean works by taking certain situations in the plays and finding these repeated in his candidate's actual life. Thus he "identifies" Oxford as Romeo, Juliet as Anne Cecil, and Rosaline as Queen Elizabeth! Of course any young courtier of the time, in love, would have served for Romeo as well or better than the Earl, who apparently showed no great passion for his wife. As to the Queen, how fortunate for Oxford that she lacked Allen's sharp eye! Rosaline was rather hastily abandoned by Romeo, with some uncomplimentary remarks. Elizabeth would not have been pleased had she thought herself portrayed in this young woman.

One could explode "argument" after "argument" based on comparisons between passages of verse, or on "identifications." Such so-called evidence is altogether too vague, subjective and doubtful to be of value.

As for Oxford's poetry, this final word should be said: the poems that are by common consent authentic bear less resemblance to Shakespeare's verse than many passages in such poets as Sidney, Drayton, Marlowe, Jonson, Dekker, Heywood, or Daniel. Oxford's best lyrics are good, but Looney himself concedes their inferiority. They were written by a young Vere, he says; Shakespeare's writing shows the mature work of the same man. The obvious answer is that had Oxford really been Shakespeare he would have shown somewhere in his 24 poems a startling richness and promise, such as Keats, Shelley, Milton, and Tennyson all showed in their early work.

Let us now look at what might be called the general thesis of the Oxford supporters. This explains their candidate's life and the alleged Shakespearean authorship by adapting the life to the plays and poems.

It requires much adaptation. The dating of Shakespeare's plays and verse can hardly begin before 1590, when William Shakespeare was 26 years of age. Oxford was then 40. Why had he not already poured out a distinguished body of work, perhaps his best? The Oxfordite answer is that he had. Some of the works had been written, but not revealed. The biographer, B. M. Ward, believes that the Earl sought publicity for his early lyrics, nursing the astounding hope that Elizabeth would make him poet laureate. This would have been an unprecedented and even shocking act (since no peer had hitherto regarded it as good form to publish his poems) but Oxford, Ward feels, thought he could persuade the Queen to it. Failing, he resolved "never again to allow his name to appear in print."

No evidence for this amazing suggestion exists, but Vere's supporters accept it with aggressive faith. It explains completely, they assert, the absence of all verse and dramas after the fifteen-seventies bearing their hero's name. According to them, this very lack of signed writings is strong presumptive evidence of their main thesis. Oxford, they argue, was praised by high authorities as a poet and playwright; well, then, what became of his work? Clearly, it is what we know as Shakespeare's! It began appearing in the early fifteen-nineties, just as the Earl withdrew from active public life. Similarly, some of it appeared for years following his death in 1604.

From 1575 to 1590 is a span of 15 years; from 1604 to 1613 is a span of 9. The first period should have been Oxford's best as a writer. If he were then writing the works of Shakespeare, why were the first of them held back for perhaps ten or twelve years? Similarly, if he wrote the great tragedies during the fifteen-nineties and early sixteen-hundreds, why were they held back?

Of course, a fresh series of assumptions is the answer to such questions, but they hardly satisfy a host of reasonable doubts. I wish to offer a far more convincing explanation, which will relieve Oxfordites of all further need to speculate, and the reader from all obligation to puzzle and wonder.

I suggest simply that Oxford was a young peer who wrote a number of fairly good poems in his early and middle twenties, and then ceased to write, as many young men with the impulse to authorship did then, and still do today. The mature Edward de Vere, like Southampton and other peers, satisfied his cultural interests by becoming a patron. There are only 24 of his poems surviving because this was the bulk of all the creative writing he ever did!

The known facts bear out this theory much more fully than they do the theory that Oxford was Shakespeare. One of the first assumptions of the Earl's supporters is that his high genius as a writer was widely acknowledged. The chief authorities cited are Gabriel Harvey, Francis Meres, George Puttenham, and William Webbe. I suggest that their comments *do not show Oxford's eminence as a writer at all*. I suggest that they show instead that Oxford was highly regarded *only among such noblemen as were then writing.*

Let us consider Webbe's statement. He wrote in 1586, and what he said was that *among titled authors* "the Right Honorable Earl of Oxford may challenge to himself the title of the most excellent among the rest." With Sidney dead that very year, what writers of rank were there? Puttenham, three years later, spoke of "another crew of courtly makers, noblemen and gentlemen, who have written excellently well, as it would appear, *if their doings could be found out and made public with the rest,* of which number is first that noble gentleman, Edward Earl of Oxford."

Thus we see that Oxford is extolled only as a poet among the courtiers. Puttenham did not even know his work.

What Gabriel Harvey had to say confirms even more explicitly the limited rating given the Earl by Webbe and Puttenham. Harvey addressed Oxford at Cambridge University, in the presence of the Queen, as one of a number of courtiers whom he praised in Latin verse. He began by prophesying that the peer would prove to be a "native-born Achilles." This remark was doubtless based on the young man's success in tournaments.

He then referred to Oxford's poetry, saying: "I have seen many Latin verses of thine, yea, even more English verses exist; thou hast drunk deeply not only of the Muses of France and Italy, but thou hast also learned the manners of divers men, and the arts of foreign lands." This is the remark quoted to prove that Oxford was an eminent poet.

But Harvey had more to say. He went on:

"O thou hero deserving of renown, throw aside the insignificant pen, cast away bloodless books, and writings that serve no useful end; now must the sword be put to play, now is a time for thee to sharpen the spear and employ great engines of war."

This address defines Oxford's place in English letters. He was a poet, but not one of importance. His forte was fighting. Let him turn to his real work, and spend no further time on relatively frivolous pastimes!

We still have Meres. He wrote in 1598. He had read Webbe and Puttenham, and heard rumors of Oxford's having written some pieces for Court entertainments. The Earl was widely known as a generous patron. Meres might profit in the future from his good will. Graciously he listed the nobleman as among the "best for comedy." It is a casual mention, and not specific like his extended praise of Shakespeare.

A further bit of evidence should be noted. During the fifteen-eighties and fifteen-nineties a number of writers dedicated books to Oxford, among them the poets George Gascoigne and Thomas Churchyard. In these dedications Oxford's *interest* in the arts was always emphasized. In none was he referred to as a writer. Added to the Webbe, Puttenham and Harvey comments, this series of omissions helps to define Edward de Vere as a gifted young amateur who quite naturally stopped writing as he grew older, perhaps before he was thirty.

A sensational but curious argument has been made by the Oxfordites concerning two pictures alleged to represent Shakespeare—the so-called "Ashbourne" and "Hampton Court" portraits. "X-ray and infra-red photography," declares a recent supporter of Edward de Vere, "reveal that beneath both of these pre-1616 portraits are the likenesses of the Seventeenth Earl of Oxford." He then asks triumphantly, "What words can explain away this newly discovered scientific evidence?" [2]

I am puzzled by the inference which the writer seems to draw from the photographs he mentions, granting that they show what he informs us. In the first place, the only representations of Shakespeare that have a title to authenticity are the Droeshout engraving and the Stratford bust, with the "Flower Portrait" as a third picture with disputed claims. So we seem to be dealing with two paintings which are not known to be paintings of the dramatist at all. How, then, can they have any significance for us?

Again, since to paint on a used canvas was relatively common in the seventeenth century, even if two representations of Oxford were painted out and two likenesses of William Shakespeare were painted in, would the act necessarily have any great significance? And if it had any, would the meaning rather not favor the person whose portrait remained? In other words, why should a friend of Oxford wish to obliterate his likeness? In the seventeenth century the X-ray and infra-red photography were unknown. Even the art of removing an

[2] Letter by Glendon Allvine, New York *Herald Tribune*, June 29, 1947.

outer coat of paint to reveal what originally lay beneath it had not been developed. Therefore to paint out Oxford was supposedly to obliterate him for all time! Or is it being suggested that the painter foresaw the development of modern science and the most technical types of photography?

One final Oxfordite adventure, and I will close. When Looney proposed Oxford as the author of the Shakespearean works in 1920, he deplored the efforts of the Baconians to establish their case by cipher. It was an unfortunate episode, he said.

But Looney was of course unable to control all his followers. One of them, George Frisbee, has devoted the better part of a book to arguing that Oxford's authorship of the plays and poems is established by code.[3] For example, Mr. Frisbee finds that by picking out certain letters in the dedication of the *Sonnets* he receives the message: "E. Devere." Unfortunately, the Baconians found proof in this very page that *their* man was the author of the ensuing poems. I myself, venturing into this agitated millpond of ciphery, discovered that "B. Ionson" was clearly planted in this curious message devised by Thomas Thorpe in 1609. Oh, yes—one can get *his* name with even greater ease!

Frisbee is an obscure Oxfordite, but Percy Allen is one of the leaders. Yet he too has succumbed to the fascination of secret codes. He found himself much interested in the fifteenth stanza of *Lucrece*. It runs as follows:

> But she, that never coped with stranger eyes,
> Could pick no meaning from their parling looks,
> Nor read the subtle-shining secrecies
> Writ in the glassy margents of such books.
> She touched no unknown baits, nor feared no hooks;
> Nor could she moralize his wanton sight,
> More than his eyes were opened to the light.

If the reader will read the first letter of each line from the top down, he will get the following: BCN WS NM, which Allen interprets as "BaCon, W. Sh., NaMe." The fact that Bacon pops up, and not Oxford, doesn't bother him at all. "It is probable," he suggests, "that

[3] George Frisbee, *Edward de Vere: A Great Elizabethan,* Palmer, London, 1931.

Bacon and Oxford wrote in collaboration."

Now, I was not impressed with this message, and decided that I could find another in the same poem with a very different meaning. Sure enough, I did. Stanza 35 of *Lucrece* reads as follows:

> Shameful it is; aye, if the fact be known:
> Hateful it is; there is no hate in loving;
> I'll beg her love, but she is not her own;
> The worst is but denial and reproving.
> My will is strong, past reason's weak removing.
> Who fears a sentence, or an old man's saw,
> Shall by a painted cloth be kept in awe.

If the reader will follow the same process, he will find SH ITM WS. Clearly this settles the matter. It means: SH—Shakespeare; ITM—Is The Man; W.S.—William Shakespeare. It is really a neater message than that of stanza 15.

We could travel on into other wonderlands—into Alden Brooks's plea for Sir Edward Dyer, who, he suggests, used the astute business-man Shakespeare as a kind of minor partner. Dyer, according to Brooks, wrote where grace or eloquence or beauty was required; Shakespeare supplied slapstick comedy. We could review the Derby and Rutland cases, but they are comparable with Oxford's. (It seems at times as if the iconoclasts were really unconscious literary and social snobs—why this passionate search for an author of royal blood? According to the record, princes are the least likely material for great authors.) I could entertain you with Alfred Dodd's *The Marriage of Elizabeth Tudor,* in which he argues that after a secret wedding with Leicester, the Queen bore two amazing brothers, Bacon and Essex! Mr. Dodd spices this romance with a dash of ciphery.

My favorite volume in this library of conjecture is one by William Ross, a Fellow of the Royal Institute of British Architects, which he entitles *The Story of Anne Whately and William Shaxpere.* It is a work of imagination. Anne Whately, it seems, was a nun residing near Stratford. Attracted to the handsome youth, William Shaxpere, who came soliciting business for his father, she began writing sonnets to him. This led to a romance, and got Anne's name on a marriage license. But the marriage never took place; for she, older than the young man, was satisfied to see him marry Anne Hathaway, who had a prior and more tangible claim upon him. Anne Hathaway Shaxpere became the dark lady of the *Sonnets*. How Anne Whately wrote all of these, and the plays and the other poems also, the reader can discover for himself, if he can procure a copy of this remarkable book.

I had thought at first that Mr. Ross might have written this romance as a kind of public service. I dared to wonder if his Anne Whately were not the impostor to end all impostures. I imagined Mr. Ross saying: "You see, here is a woman Shakespeare, and to create her I have made as preposterous a tale as man can concoct. But once you accept the premises, the case for her works out as well as that for Bacon or Oxford. Shall we accept all of them for the nonsense that they are?"

But I fear that I gave Mr. Ross a keener sense of humor than he possesses. I think he believes in his lady Shakespeare. And I shall not be the one to say that she is the least deserving of impostors. If one enters into a region where fantasy and romance take charge of literature, shall one not walk with boldness and give his faith to the all-but-impossible?

7

What conclusions must logically be drawn from a comparison between the case for William Shakespeare as the author of the plays and poems standing under his name, and those for other candidates?

One all-important fact stands out clearly. The Shakespeare case is supported by many facts and specific comments. The evidence for it is direct, and it is great both in volume and in variety. In contrast, all other cases are "if" cases. *If* Shakespeare can be shown too ignorant and too lacking in experience to have been a notable author, *if* the testimony of title pages, literary critics of his own day, fellow writers, fellow actors, the Stratford monument, the First Folio can justly be set aside, then only can we consider as a possible candidate Bacon, Oxford, Derby, Rutland, or any other. The argument for Shakespeare may well rest on this single impressive consideration. As we have seen, all the evidence that has been put forward to show that he could not have been the author of his works fails to prove him incapable, while in opposition to the facts supporting his position we have little more than daring conjectures.

But even if we go beyond the conclusive contrast between his case and all others (as I think we cannot in logic) we find further weaknesses in the cases of all impostors. The late date at which other candidates were all put forward has never been satisfactorily justified. Their number still remains a highly suspicious circumstance. And finally, except for discredited cipher arguments, we have nothing but ingenious theories, any of which can be challenged at numerous points. Not one clear statement from a seventeenth-century writer or other person in a position to know says "Oxford (or Bacon or Derby or Rutland) wrote the works supposed to be William Shakespeare's." As John Semple Smart has pointed out, after rejecting Shakespeare because the proof for his authorship is supposedly insufficient, the advocates of other authors put forward candidates about whom, as playwrights and poets, far less is known.

For those who still have doubts at this point, the only remedy is further investigation. In the course of that, if attempted, they should read Smart's *Shakespeare: Truth and Tradition,* J. M. Robertson's *The Baconian Heresy: A Confutation,* the appendix in Sidney Lee's well-known life of the playwright, and *This Shakespeare Industry,* by Ivor Brown and George Fearon. The last-named book gives an amusing and useful summary of the entire controversy over authorship, without drawing specific conclusions.

However, the final source for all who desire earnestly to find the truth must be the many works on the period in which Shakespeare lived, his own writings, and the lives and dramas and poems of other writers of his day. A study of these has satisfied every eminent scholar who has devoted his life to acquiring a knowledge and understanding of the greatest of poets. It will satisfy, as it has in the past, the great majority of intelligent readers. They will find that increasing knowledge only confirms for them the reality of William Shakespeare as actor, playhouse owner, gentleman, and most gifted of writers.

INDEX